THE GUN DIGEST® BOOK OF COMBAT HANDGUNNERY

5th Edition

Massad Ayoob

Published by

krause
publications

700 E. State Street • Iola, WI 54990-0001
Telephone: 715/445-2214
Web: www.krause.com

Please call or write for our free catalog of publications.
Our toll-free number to place an order or obtain a free catalog is 800-258-0929
or please use our regular business telephone 715-445-2214.

Library of Congress Catalog Number: 2002105091

ISBN: 0-87349-485-7

Printed in the United States of America

About The Author

At this writing, Massad Ayoob is completing his 30th year as a police firearms and deadly force instructor, and his 28th as a sworn police officer. That time frame encompasses 20 years as director of Lethal Force Institute, 15 as chair of the firearms committee for the American Society of Law Enforcement Trainers, 11 as a senior research associate for the Center for Advancement of Applied Ethics at Carnegie-Mellon University, 14 years as a police department prosecutor, and two years as co-vice chair of the forensic evidence committee of the National Association of Criminal Defense Lawyers. He has spent more than a decade as a trustee of the Second Amendment Foundation. Ayoob has served for many years as handgun editor of *GUNS* magazine, law enforcement editor of *AMERICAN HANDGUNNER*, and associate editor of *COMBAT HANDGUNS, GUNS & WEAPONS FOR LAW ENFORCEMENT,* and *GUN WEEK*.

In 1995, Ayoob won the first National Tactical Advocate award and in 1998 he was voted Outstanding American Handgunner of the Year. He has also won the Roy Rogers Award for advocacy of responsible firearms use, and the James Madison Award for advocacy of Second Amendment rights of private citizens.

The author of nearly 3,000 published articles on weapons, law enforcement, martial arts, self-defense, and crime prevention; he is also the author of numerous books in the field. The best known is *In the Gravest Extreme: the Role of the Firearm in Personal Defense,* which is widely considered to be the authoritative text on judicious use of lethal force by private citizens for self-protection. Others include *Fundamentals of Modern Police Impact Weapons, Hit the White Part, The Truth About Self Protection, StressFire, StressFire II, StressFire III,* and *Ayoob Files: The Book.* He has also written several book-length annual editions of *The Complete Book of Handguns.*

The winner of numerous state championships and two national champion titles, and holder of three national records in combat handgun shooting, Ayoob passed these skills on to his two daughters. At age 19, Cat Ayoob won High Woman at the demanding National Tactical Invitational, and at age 13, Justine Ayoob and her father earned national champion parent/child team honors at the first National Junior Handgun Championships.

Dedication

In large part, this book is about survival. If you think about it, family is the strongest motivation to survive.

My father, Massad George Ayoob, a gunfight survivor, taught me the gun and the knife at an early age. The time came when this knowledge kept me alive. My mother, Mary Elizabeth Ayoob, hated guns and never fired one, but she understood why my dad and I went shooting and carried guns, and she approved. I always appreciated that. My older sister Elizabeth taught me a lot about life. Her Stevens .22 rifle was the first gun I ever fired. I was 4 at the time. Had she not died too young, I think she would have done much good for many.

My wife for more than 30 years, Dorothy Hodgman Ayoob, tolerated my police career and made my writing and teaching careers possible. Our daughters, Cat and Justine, were our *raisons d'etre*. Both have made their parents enormously proud.

It is to these six people, my first nuclear family now gone from this earth and my second nuclear family for whom I pray for long life, that this book is dedicated.

Massad Ayoob
September 2002

Acknowledgments

A whole lot of folks have contributed to the pool of knowledge this book shares with you. I see my job as being a conduit of information to you, the reader. Those who provided me this information include, but are certainly not limited to, the following.

In terms of handguns, thanks go to such master gunsmiths and designers as George Sheldon, Armand Swenson, D.R. Middlebrooks, Rick Devoid, Wayne Novak, two generations of Irv Stones, Bill Wilson, Les Baer, Nolan Santy, the Clark gunsmithing family (The late, great Jim Sr., Jim Jr., and Kay Clark-Miculek), Lou Ciamillo, and Larry and Ken Kelly. Much knowledge of Smith & Wesson has been gleaned from the great Archie Dubia at the S&W Armorer's School, Tom Campbell, and Tom Gordon and the crew at the S&W Performance Center. Ron Power put me up at his house in Missouri for days as he showed me the intricacies of the S&W revolver mechanism. Al DeJohn contributed Colt revolver knowledge when he was head of the Colt Custom Shop. Such masters of the Python as Reeves Jungkind, Jerry Moran, and the late Fred Sadowski also helped create this book. Bill Ruger, Sr. was a valued friend who taught me much about gun design, and I learned a lot about Bill's brainchildren from Chris Peters, the former head of the Ruger Armorer's School, who is now out on his own. Much insight into the inner workings of the Beretta came from Jim Horan and Ernie Langdon.

In my firearms training career, I was fortunate enough to have as mentors men like Lt. Frank McGee, the legendary NYPD master instructor; Bill Jordan, who needs no introduction; world champion and master instructor Ray Chapman; and Charlie Smith, the great FBI firearms instructor who founded the Smith & Wesson Academy. I learned much about the tactical use of firearms over the years from Jeff Cooper, Clint Smith, Chuck Taylor, Pat Dalager, John Shaw, Mike Plaxco, George Harris, John Peterson, John Meyer, Tom McTernan and John Cerar, and LAPD firearms training experts Dick Newell, Lou Salseda, John Helms, and Larry Mudgett. Bob Cappelli, Sebastian Ulrich and the late Louis Seman of the Illinois State Police gave me much insight into the use of the semi-automatic pistol in police service when their agency became the first to adopt one. Jeff Chudwin, chief of the Olympia Fields, Ill., Police Department has always been a great source of tactical knowledge, as has his colleague Al Kulovitz. Richard Davis, the inventor of and world's leading authority on soft body armor has been a steady source of information as have his colleagues Ed Bachner and Dr. Aaron Westrick. Jim Cirillo and Bill Allard of the NYPD Stakeout Squad were unstinting in sharing the knowledge acquired in their unit's many gunfights, as were members of LAPD's Special Investigations Section. Chuck Higbie, the founding commander of LAPD's Officer-Involved Shooting Investigation Team taught me valuable lessons, as did Lt. Cmdr. Vern Geberth of the Bronx Homicide Task Force, the author of the definitive text *Practical Homicide Investigation.* I learned a great deal about death investigation and the nature of gunshot and knife wounds from such great medical examiners and pathologists as Dr. Joe Davis, Dr. Charles Wetli, Dr. Valerie Rao, Dr. Charles Petty, Dr. Werner Spitz, Dr. Vincent DiMaio Sr., and Dr. Vincent DiMaio Jr. Jim Lindell of Kansas City was my mentor in learning handgun retention and disarming, eventually becoming an instructor and then a trainer of other instructors in that discipline. Lon Anderson and Terry Smith taught me to teach the PR-24 baton at the international level, and taught me things that kept others and me from being hurt on the street.

I also learned a great many things from officer survival gurus Bob Lindsey, Jefferson Parish, of the Los Angeles County Sheriff's Department, and Rich Wemmer, of the LAPD.

Understanding the psycho-emotional impact of having to use deadly force is a gift I owe primarily to Dr. Walter Gorski in my early days, and Dr. Alexis Artwohl in later years. Many thanks to the psychiatrists and psychologists, such as Dr. Anthony Semone in Pennsylvania and Dr. Richard Mack in Los Angeles to whom I've referred post-shooting trauma sufferers. My friend and colleague Col. David Grossman, author of the brilliant study "On Killing," is an inspiring teacher who not only gave me much insight in person, but was kind enough to write the foreword for one of my recent books.

There is an ethical component to this. I extend thanks to Professor Preston Covey, head of the Center for Advancement of Applied Ethics at Carnegie-Mellon University where I've been a senior consultant for 12 years. Preston also served with me and many fine men and women for several years on the ethics committee of the American Society of Law Enforcement Trainers (ASLET).

We who write about guns would be handicapped without our contacts at the gun factories. Sometimes I've been able to go directly to the CEO: Bill Ruger, Sr. and later Bill Jr. at Sturm, Ruger, Thanos Polyzos at Para-Ordnance, Sandy Chisholm at North American Arms, and the Seecamp family at the firm that bears their name. More commonly, we work with patient press liaisons such as Cathy Williams at Beretta, Chris Edwards at Glock, Dwight Van Brunt at Kimber, Laura Burgess at SIG, Vicki Lawrence at Springfield Armory, and Ken Jorgensen and Peg Cowell at Smith & Wesson. My thanks to all, and to their predecessors.

A word of appreciation is due to my chief of police, Russ Lary. He's the kind of commander whose men would follow him through the gates of Hell, and knowing Russ, he'd probably find some way to get the warrant. Thanks also to Earl Sweeney, director of the New Hampshire Police Standards and Training Academy and probably the most awesome walking repository of police-related case law I have ever met.

Finally, a public acknowledgement to the members of ASLET's firearms training committee: Bill Usilton, Harvey Hedden, Dave Spaulding, Steve Smith, John Meyer, Grace Matthews, Vince O'Neil, Rich Grassi, Clive Shepard, Eddie Parham, and especially Sgt. Brian Stover of Los Angeles County Sheriff's Department, the hard-working vice chair of the committee. As chair for the last 15 years, it has been one of my life's great pleasures to work with this band of dedicated professionals.

Massad Ayoob
September 2002

Table of Contents

CHAPTER ONE

The Defensive Combat Handgun: An Overview

It is an honor to have been asked to write this edition of *The Complete Book of Combat Handgunnery.* Whomever steps into this authorship has several big pairs of shoes to fill.

It has been my privilege to know all the authors of the previous editions. They're all fine men, and I've learned a lot from all of them.

This topic has been, literally, a life-long study for me. I grew up around guns, in part because my father was an armed citizen who survived a murder attempt because he knew how and when to use a handgun. He had learned that from his father. My grandfather, the first of our family to come to this country, hadn't been on these shores long when he had to shoot an armed robber. I grew up with a gun the way kids today grow up with seat belts and smoke detectors. It was simply one more common-sense safety measure in a sometimes-dangerous world.

The day came when what I had learned from my forebears, in terms of having defensive weapons and learning skill at arms, saved my life, too, and the lives of others I was responsible for protecting. I passed the skill on to my daughters. My eldest got her license to carry concealed when she was 18. A year or so later, the Smith & Wesson 9mm in her waistband saved her from two would-be rapists. She represented the fourth straight generation of my family in the United States to be saved from violent criminals by a lawfully possessed firearm.

There is such a thing as paying back. It's sort of like courtesy of the road. You can't adequately thank the person who helped you and gave you what you needed, so you thank them by helping the next person in that situation and giving *them* what *they* need.

Life takes us down unexpected paths. If, during my somewhat rebellious teen years, you had asked me what I was least likely to become, I would probably have answered, "Cop or teacher." Before long, I had become both. Pausing for a 25-month breather in the early 1980s, I've been a police officer since 1972, and have been teaching about guns during that entire time. My first article in a gun magazine was published in 1971.

There have been a lot of books and thousands of articles under the dam since then, and enough training to fill seven single-spaced résumé pages. Competitive shooting has been good to me; I've earned several state championships, a couple of regional wins, two national champion titles, and three national records. Only a couple of state championships still stand today. I've spent 15 years as chair of the firearms com-

mittee for the American Society of Law Enforcement Trainers, a few of those also as a member of their ethics committee, and a couple of years as co-vice chair of the forensic evidence committee for the National Association of Criminal Defense Lawyers. As an expert witness for the courts for more than 20 years, I've learned that reality and ethics often have little to do with why a justifiable homicide in self-defense has been brought to court as a wrongful death suit, or a murder or manslaughter charge, but I am very proud of the small part I played in getting a lot of wrongfully-accused people acquitted.

We live in interesting times for armed citizens. On the one hand, our rights to protect our loved ones and ourselves are constantly attacked by people, often rich and powerful and articulate, who just don't have the first clue. On the other, so many states have passed "shall issue" concealed carry laws that more law-abiding citizens can carry hidden handguns in public today than at virtually any time in the last century. The exhaustive research of professional criminological and legal scholars has proven beyond a shadow of a doubt that the more who carry legal firearms, the fewer crimes of violence will occur. Professor John Lott was correct when he titled his scholarly and unimpeachable study of the subject *More Guns, Less Crime.*

Researching these things, studying how they happen, and how to prevail and survive if they happen to you, has become my life's work. I founded the Lethal Force Institute in 1981, and it has been a labor of love ever since. The on-scene management of violent criminal threat is a life study, and a multi-dimensional one that goes far beyond the gun itself. We cannot cover them all in one book. No one can. Even a library of books would not be a complete study, because criminal behavior, patterns of violent encounter and criminal tactics, and the laws that encompass these things and more, are all dynamic and fluid and subject to change. It is the classic example of "As soon as we get all the answers, some SOB changes the questions." Working full-time as a teacher and researcher in the field, and part time as a cop and expert witness, fate has put me at a good vantage point to see changes coming early.

The purpose of this book is to transmit a working knowledge of the current state-of-the-art of defensive handgun technology and its corollary topics, of how to effectively use them and how to find out how better to use them and more importantly, *when* to use them. Every effort will be made to explain where certain recommendations and trends came from.

Our guns, ammunition, and holsters are better than ever. So are state-of-the-art techniques that have been developed from modern and "post-modern" studies of what happens to the human mind and body under life-threatening stress. Better than ever also is our understanding of courtroom dynamics as they apply today in the often terrifying aftermath of the justified use of deadly force.

These skills are needed today. Since September 11, 2001, many experts believe they will be needed more than ever. The continued ability to choose to develop these skills, and exercise them if we must, is constantly under attack. It will be a long, hard fight, perhaps a never-ending one, but in the last analysis, that is the nature of the human experience.

I hope you find this book useful. If something seems new and radical compared to older "doctrine," try it yourself before you decide. I can promise you that there is nothing recommended in this book that has not been proven where it counts.

Thank you for taking the time to read this…and thank you especially for caring enough about the people who count on you to invest the time in the first place. Good luck. Stay safe.

Massad Ayoob
Concord, NH, USA
2002

CHAPTER TWO

ENDURING CLASSICS

The Single-Action Autos

The Model 1911

Roald Amundsen reached the South Pole behind a team of 17 Huskies. The most popular song of the year was "Alexander's Ragtime Band," by Irving Berlin. Ty Cobb was the dominant baseball star. Marie Curie won the Nobel Prize for chemistry. Milk was 17 cents a gallon, two bits would get you 10 pounds of potatoes and three pennies change, and 18 cents bought a pound of round steak. Louis Chevrolet and W.C. Durant introduced the former's automobile. Born in that year were Lucille Ball, Mahalia Jackson, Vincent Price, Ronald Reagan, Tennessee Williams, and the Colt Government Model .45 caliber "automatic pistol."

The year, of course, was 1911. The prices (including that of the Colt) have multiplied. The Chevrolet is vastly changed. The people, for the most part, have passed into

Gen. William Keys, USMC (ret.) has revitalized Colt's commitment to the 1911 since he became CEO of the company.

history. Only the 1911 pistol remains with us largely unchanged, and still going strong.

Today, if the covers of gun magazines are any indication, the 1911 is the most popular handgun design of its time. A scan through the catalogue pages of *Gun Digest* shows it is also the most influential. It seems that every year brings at least another 1911 "clone" to the marketplace.

Little has changed in the pistol's core design, but many subtle evolutions have taken place. The first wave came after WWI, when the American military began a study of how small arms had performed in the most recent conflict. The study was rather leisurely, it appears, as the list of complaints wasn't announced until about 1923. About half of the doughboys thought the trigger of the 1911 was too long. Many said the grip tang bit their hands. Most found the front sight post and rear notch so tiny as to be useless. It was also noted that when soldiers missed with it, they generally hit low.

About 1927, answers to these concerns were implemented, creating the 1911-A1 model. The grip tang was lengthened to prevent bite to the web of the hand. The trigger was shortened dramatically, and the frame at the rear of the trigger guard was niched out on both sides to further enhance finger reach. Believing that the low hits were a function of the pistol "pointing low" as opposed to the operators jerking their triggers, the designers gave the A1 an arched mainspring housing that sort of levered the muzzle upward and made the gun "point higher." Finally, a slightly

The 1911 is a classic that remains in service. This officer wears his Kimber stainless .45 to work today.

The 1911's ergonomics are timeless. The author used this 1991-A1 Colt tuned by Mark Morris to place 2nd Master in the 2001 New England Regional IDPA Championships.

Para-Ordnance pioneered the high capacity 1911. The author used this one frequently at the National Tactical Invitational, where its extra firepower (14 rounds total) came in handy.

better and more visible set of fixed sights was mounted to the pistol.

Gun companies and steel foundries were also making advances in metallurgy. It is generally accepted today that early 1911s are made of much softer steel than the 1911-A1 and later commercial Colts. This is why pistolsmiths have historically recommended against tuning early guns for accuracy. They felt the soft steel would not "hold" the fine tolerances required in precision accurizing, a process that became popular among target shooters in the 1930s and has remained a cottage industry within the gunsmithing business ever since.

The 1950s brought the epoch of Jeff Cooper who, writing in *Guns & Ammo* magazine, almost single-handedly re-popularized the 1911. Its one-third firepower advantage over the revolver, eight shots to six, plus its rapid reloading was but one advantage. The short, easy trigger pull – particularly when the gun had been worked on – delivered better hit potential under stress than the long, heavy pull of a double-action revolver. Though it appeared large, the Colt auto was flat in profile and easy to conceal, particularly inside the waistband.

The resurgence of the 1911's popularity had begun. By the 1970s, copycat makers were coming out of the woodwork. Through the 1980s, it at last occurred to makers to furnish the guns at the factory with the accoutrements that were keeping a host of custom pistolsmiths in business. These included wide grip safeties to cushion recoil, with a recurve to guide the hand into position and speed the draw, and a "speed bump" at the bottom edge to guarantee depression of the grip safety even with a sloppy hold. This part was also available "cut high" to allow the hand to get even higher on the grip. A low bore axis had always been one reason the pistol felt so good in the hand and was easily controlled in rapid fire by someone who knew the right techniques. Now, even the folks at the Colt factory began relieving the lower rear of the trigger guard, in hopes that the hand could ride still higher for even better performance. Now too, at last, 1911s were coming out of the factories with heavy-duty fixed sights that offered big, highly visible sight pictures.

There were also high-capacity versions, first with metal frames and then with polymer. Once, it had been standard procedure to send your Colt to a gunsmith to have it "throated" to feed hollowpoints and semi-wadcutters; now, Colt and Springfield Armory and Kimber and many more were producing the guns "factory throated."

By the dawn of the 21st century, the 1911 still ruled, though Colt did not. Kimber had become the single largest producers of 1911 pistols, offering a variety of sizes and formats. Springfield Armory was close behind in sales and equal in quality. Customized target pistols still ruled the bull's-eye firing lines, as they had for decades, but now competitors were showing up and winning with factory match 1911s from Les Baer and Rock River. Since the International Practical Shooting Confederation was founded at the Columbia Conference in 1976, the 1911 had ruled that arena, but now the winning gun in IPSC was

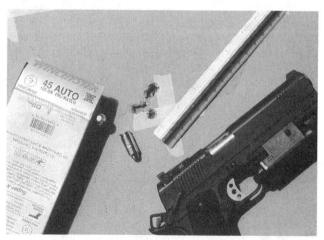

1911s are capable of awesome accuracy. Springfield Armory TRP Tactical Operator pistol, mounting M3 Illuminator flashlight, put five rounds of Winchester .45 Match into this 1-inch group, hand held with bench rest at 25 yards.

Four top-quality manufacturers and styles of modern 1911s, all .45s. From top: Compact Colt Lightweight CCO. Service Kimber Custom II. Hi-Cap Para-Ordnance P14.45. Tactical Springfield TRP with extended dust cover and M3 light.

Colt collectors will spot the WWII-vintage ejection port and sights on "retro" Colt 1911A1, reintroduced in 2001.

The P-35

"Porgy & Bess" opens in New York, and Steinbeck's "Tortilla Flat" is published. The hot dance is the Rhumba. Milk is up to 23 cents for half a gallon (delivered, of course). Boulder Dam, Alcoholics Anonymous, and the Social Security Act all come into being. It is the birth year for Woody Allen, Elvis Presley, Sandy Coufax, and the Browning Hi-Power pistol. It is 1935.

The P-35 was the last design of John Browning, who also created the Colt 1911. Many would also consider the Hi-Power his best. Known in some quarters as the GP or *grand puissance,* the pistol may owe more of its ingenuity to Didionne Souave than to Browning. In any case, it was the first successful high-capacity 9mm semiautomatic, and for more than a quarter of a century was the definitive one. It remains today the standard-issue service pistol of Great Britain and numerous other countries.

For most of its epoch, the P-35 was distinguished by a tiny, mushy-feeling thumb safety and by sights that were not the right size or shape for fast acquisition. In the 1980s Browning fixed that at last with its Mark II and later Mark III series pistols, which reached their high point in the Practical model. Good, big sights…a gun at last throated at the Browning factory to feed hollowpoints…big, positively operating ambidextrous thumb safety…legions of Browning fans were in heaven. That the guns by now were being manufactured for Browning in Portugal instead of at the Fabrique Nationale plant in Belgium mattered only to the most rigid purists.

Like the Colt 1911, the P-35 is slim, easy to conceal, and comfortable to carry. The 13+1 magazine capacity seemed to be its big selling point. But if people bought it for firepower, they kept it because it had a more endearing quality: It simply felt exquisitely *natural* in the human hand.

Before people used the word "ergonomics," John Browning clearly understood the concept. No pistol is as user-friendly. Col. Cooper, who has been called "The High Priest of the 1911," once wrote that no pistol had ever fit his hand better than the Browning. What a shame, he added, that it was not offered in a caliber of consequence.

Produced for the most part in 9mm Parabellum and occasionally in caliber .30 Luger, the Browning got a boost in popularity stateside during the 1990s when it was introduced in .40 S&W. The bigger caliber feels rather like a 1911 slide

less often the old Colt than a high-capacity variant like the STI or the Para-Ordnance.

Over the years, the 1911 has been produced in a myriad of calibers. The .38 Super 1911s and hot 9mm variants win open class IPSC matches in the third millennium, and fancy inside, ordinary outside 1911s in caliber .40 S&W rule Limited class in that game. The 9mm 1911 is seen as the winning gun in the Enhanced Service Pistol class of the relatively new International Defensive Pistol Association contests, but the .45 caliber 1911 is much more popular, known in IDPA circles as a Custom Defense Pistol. However, in IDPA, even more shooters use Glocks or double-action autos, making the Stock Service Pistol category even more populous than the 1911 categories. The overwhelming majority of 1911s in serious use today are .45 caliber. No one has yet made a more "shootable" pistol in that power range.

Thus, with timeless continuity, the 1911 has outgrown the Colt brand with which it was once synonymous.

on a P-35 frame, but it shoots well. There were early reports of problems, but the factory quickly squared these away. The 9mm Browning has always been a rather fragile gun when shot with heavy loads. I've seen baskets of broken Browning frames in English military stockpiles and in Venezuelan armories. The hammering of NATO ammo, hotter than +P+ as produced by England's Radway Green and Venezuela's CAVIM arsenals, was the culprit. Fed the hot loads only sparingly, and kept on a practice diet of low-pressure standard American ball ammo, the 9mm Browning will last and last. The massive slide of the .40 caliber version, along with its strong recoil spring, is apparently enough to keep the guns in that caliber from breaking epidemically.

The Browning's mechanism does not lend itself to trigger tuning in the manner of the 1911, that is one reason it has never been popular with target shooters. For most of its history, its magazines would not fall free unless the pistol was deprived of one of its trademark features, the magazine disconnector safety. The latter, when in place, renders a chambered round unshootable if the magazine has been removed. In the 1990s, Browning came up with a magazine with a spring on the back that positively ejected it from the pistol.

The timeless styling of the Browning made it a classic, but make no mistake: Its easy "carryability," and especially its feel in the hand, have made it an enduringly popular defense gun. From petite female to large male, every hand that closes over a Browning Hi-Power seems to feel a perfect fit. One caveat: Though it will hold 13+1, serious users like the SAS discovered that it wasn't very reliable unless the magazine was loaded one round down from full capacity. Just something to think about.

Classic Double-action Autos

Some gun enthusiasts would argue whether the words "classic" and "DA auto" belong in the same sentence. Can there be such a thing as a "classic" Mustang? Only to the young, and to fans of the genre. Ditto the DA auto.

Surely, in terms of firearms design history, there were at least a couple of classics. The Walther designs of the 1920s and 1930s are a case in point. There is no question that the P-38 dramatically influenced duty auto designs of the future, though no serious gun professional ever made that pistol his trademark if he could get something else. European soldiers and police dumped them at the first opportu-

nity for improved designs by HK, SIG-Sauer, and latter-day Walther engineers. South African police, who stuck with the P-38 for decades, told the author they hated them and couldn't wait to swap up to the Z88, the licensed clone of the Beretta 92 made in that country.

The Walther PP and PPK have timeless *popularity* that comes from small size and ease of concealed carry, splendid workmanship in the mechanical sense, and a *cachet* more attributable to the fictional James Bond than to genuine gun experts who shot a lot, though the great Charles "Skeeter" Skelton was a notable exception who actually carried the PP and PPK in .380. By today's standards, the ancient Walther pocket gun is a poor choice. If it is not carried on safe, a round in the chamber can discharge if the gun is dropped. If it is carried on safe, the release lever is extremely awkward and difficult to disengage. The slide tends to slice the hand of most shooters in firing. Walther .380s often won't work with hollow-points, and though inherently accurate thanks to their fixed-barrel design, often require a gunsmith's attention to the sights to make the guns shoot where they are aimed. There are not only better .380s now, but smaller and lighter 9mm Parabellums!

In the historical design and "influence on gun history" sense, one could call the Smith & Wesson Model 39 a classic. But it, too, was a flawed design, and it would take Smith & Wesson almost three decades to really make it work. The S&W autoloader was, by then, a redesigned entity and a part of the new wave, rather than a true classic like the 1911 or the Hi-Power.

S&W Service Revolvers

In 1899, President William McKinley signed the treaty that ended the Spanish-American War, the first of the Hague Accords were drafted, and Jim Jeffries was the heavyweight-boxing champion of the world. Born in that year were Humphrey Bogart, Gloria Swanson, James Cagney, Fred Astaire, and the Smith & Wesson Hand Ejector .38 revolver that would become known as the Military & Police model.

The Smith & Wesson double-action was the "Peacemaker" of the 20th century. As the M&P's name implied, it was the defining police service revolver for most of that century, with many thousands of them still carried on the streets today. S&W revolvers fought with American troops in both world wars, Korea, and Vietnam. There are doubtless still some in armed services inventories to this day.

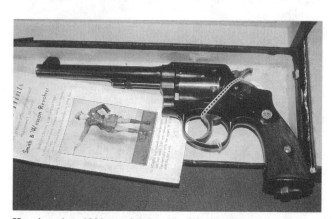

Here is a circa 1930s production 6-inch S&W M&P with factory lanyard loop and instruction guide.

Markings show that this pre-WWII S&W M&P was worked over by Cogswell & Harrison of England.

S&W's Military & Police Target model .38 Special predated the K-38 Masterpiece series.

One of the first of many small modifications to the design was a front locking lug that, many believed, made the Smith & Wesson a stronger double-action revolver than its archrival, the Colt. While the Colt had a better single-action cocking stroke and trigger pull for bull's-eye target shooting, the S&W had a smoother, cleaner double-action trigger stroke for serious fast shooting. It was largely because of this that, by the end of WWII, S&W was the market leader in the revolver field. It remains there to this day, though at this writing Ruger exceeds S&W in total firearms production.

The most popular by far was the .38 frame, now known as the K-frame. One thing that makes a classic handgun is perfect feel. The average adult male hand fits the K-frame perfectly. Larger hands can easily adapt. Smaller hands adapt less easily. In 1954, Border Patrol weapons master Bill Jordan convinced Smith & Wesson to beef up the Military & Police .38 and produce a gun of that size in .357 Magnum. This was done, and another classic was born: S&W's .357 Combat Magnum, a staple of the company's product line to this day.

The same mechanism was adapted to a .44/.45 frame gun, known today as the N-frame. In 1917, S&W engineers created half-moon clips to adapt rimless .45 auto cartridges to revolver cylinders, to fill the Army's need for more handguns during WWI. This concept lives today in S&W's Model 625 .45 ACP revolver, a gun all the more practical

At left: Jordan, living legend to handgunners, matter-of-factly completes what men who should know call the fastest draw of any living man.

Inset: Massad Ayoob discusses the .41 Magnum load with Bill Jordan, who helped develop it. Jordan proved as fast with his smile as a gun.

The author at 25 with Bill Jordan. Bill is demonstrating the S&W .41 Magnum he helped bring into existence.

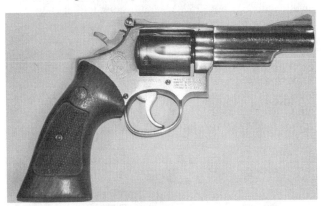

In the 1970s, the S&W Model 66 became a modern classic.

S&W created clips for .45 ACP cartridge, and the 1917 revolver was born. The series reaches its zenith in the Model 625 revolver, this one was tuned by Al Greco and is wearing Hogue grips.

Tapered barrel (upper right) was standard configuration of S&W M&P until the late 1950s. Never discontinued, it was overshadowed by the more popular heavy barrel configuration, below.

America's most popular service revolver before WWII, the Colt Official Police .38 Special was subsequently pushed into second place by the S&W. This Colt wears a Pachmayr grip adapter, a common accessory.

State-of-the-art equipment at the end of the police revolver era: A Colt Python with Hogue grips in Bianchi B-27 holster, with speedloaders in a Safariland quick-release carrier.

since more recent full-moon clips allow the fastest possible six-shot reload. The first of the classic N-frames was the exquisitely crafted .44 Special Triple Lock. 1935 saw the next giant step, the first .357 Magnum revolver. That gun lives today as the practical, eight-shot Model 627 from the Smith & Wesson performance center. The N-frame was also the original home of the mighty .44 Magnum cartridge in the legendary "Dirty Harry" gun, the Model 29.

In the 1970s, it became the habit of police to train extensively with the hot .357 Magnum ammunition they were carrying on duty, with the particularly high-pressure 125-grain/1,450 fps load being their duty cartridge of choice. This was too much for the .38 frame guns, which began exhibiting a variety of jamming and breakdown problems. S&W upscaled to a .41 frame gun, which they dubbed the L-frame. This turned out to be a much sturdier .357 Magnum, the most practical version of which is probably the seven-shot Model 686-Plus.

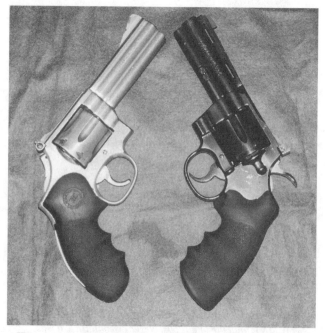

Here are two classic .357 Magnum service revolvers. Left, S&W 686; right, Colt Python. Both of these wear Hogue grips.

There were some growing pains, including L-frames that broke or choked. S&W got that fixed. By the time they were done with it, the L-frame was utterly reliable and deadly accurate…but by that time, police departments were trading to auto pistols *en masse,* sounding the death knell for what many believed was the best police service revolver ever made.

Colt Service Revolvers

Colt's service revolvers, like S&W's, trace their lineage to the 1890s. The Colt was the dominant police gun until the beginning of WWII, with S&W pulling ahead of their archrival in the post-war years and achieving near-total dominance in that market by 1970. Thereafter, Smith service revolvers were challenged more by Ruger than Colt.

The early Army Special and its heirs, the fixed-sight Official Police and the Trooper, were slightly larger and heavier than their K-frame counterparts. While the medium-build S&W was constructed on a true .38 frame, the Colts were actually built on .41 frames. Tests in the 1950s indicated that the Colts were stronger and better suited for hot loads like the .38-44, which S&W only recommended in their .45-frame guns.

Some gunsmiths felt the Colt would stay accurate longer, because its design included a second hand (cylinder hand, that is), which snapped up to lock the cylinder in place as the hammer began to fall. Others said it was less sturdy, because the primary hand seemed to wear sooner than the S&W's. Certainly, there was little argument on trigger pull. Virtually all authorities agreed that the Colt had the crisper trigger pull in single-action and the S&W, the smoother stroke in double-action.

In 1955, Colt introduced what would be their ultimate classic in this vein, the Python. Originally intended to be a heavy barrel .38 Special target revolver, it was chambered for .357 Magnum almost as an afterthought, and that changed everything. The full-length underlug and ventilated rib gave not only a distinctive look, but a solid up-front hang

S&W's Centennial Airweight is a classic snub. This original sample from the 1950s has a grip safety, a feature absent on the modern incarnation.

S&W Model 640-1 is the J-frame Centennial rendered in .357 Magnum. These Pachmayr Compac grips help to cushion the substantial recoil.

that made the gun seem to kick less with Magnum loads. At the time, the best factory craftsmen assembled the premium-price Python with extra attention lovingly added to the action work. Though he chose to carry a Smith & Wesson as a duty gun, NYPD Inspector Paul B. Weston, an authority of the period, dubbed the Python's action "a friction free environment." Few challenged the Python's claim as "the Rolls-Royce of revolvers."

The underpaid cop of the time carried one as a status symbol if he could afford it. Three state police agencies issued them. A few went out to selected members of the Georgia State Patrol, and more than that were issued to the Florida Highway Patrol, while the Colorado State Patrol issued a 4-inch Python to every trooper. Today, no department issues this fine old double-action revolver. All three of the above named SP's have gone to .40 caliber autos: Glocks in Georgia, Berettas in Florida, and S&Ws in Colorado.

The Classic Snubbies

Up through the middle of the Roaring Twenties, if you wanted a snub-nose .38 you were stuck with a short .38 caliber cartridge, too, the anemic little round that one company called .38 Smith & Wesson and the other called .38 Colt New Police, in their Terrier and Banker's Special revolvers, respectively. (As late as the early 1970s, the Boston Police Department still had a few Banker's Specials issued to detectives. By then, the gun was a true collector's item.)

Then, in 1927, Colt took 2 inches off the barrel of their smaller frame Police Positive Special revolver and called the result the Detective Special. The rest, as they say, is history. A six-shot .38 Special small enough for the trouser or coat pocket, and easy to carry in a shoulder holster, was an instant success. "Detective Special" became a generic term, like "kleenex" or "frigidaire," for any snub-nose .38.

Late in 1949, Smith & Wesson entered the small frame .38 Special market with their Chief Special, so called because it was introduced at an annual conference of the International Association of Chiefs of Police. It only held five shots, but was distinctly smaller than the Colt. Immediately, it became a best seller among both cops and armed citizens.

After *that* little ace trumping, Colt was quick to respond. Both firms had built ultra-light revolvers for the USAF's

The shrouded hammer makes S&W Bodyguard snag-free while retaining single-action capability. This is the stainless version in .357 Magnum.

Colt's .38 Detective Special is absolutely a modern classic. This sample is the popular 1972 style.

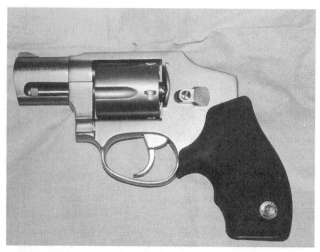

Taurus CIA (Carry It Anywhere) effectively copies the established styling of the S&W Centennial series. It's available in .38 Special and .357 Magnum.

Aircrewman project, and Colt was first to market with the Cobra, a Detective Special with a lightweight alloy frame. The alloy in question was Duralumin, aluminum laced with titanium, Alcoa #6 or equivalent. The company also came up with a bolt-on device aptly called a "hammer shroud." It covered the hammer on both sides to keep it from snagging in a pocket or coat lining. Paul Weston had correctly described the Colt hammer spur as being shaped like a fish-hook. The Shroud covered the hammer, left the tip exposed to allow single-action thumb-cocking if necessary.

S&W threw a two-fisted *riposte*. Their aluminum-frame snubby, being smaller, was also a tad lighter. A Detective Special weighed 21 ounces, and a Cobra, 15.5 ounces. S&W's Airweight revolver in the Chief Special was listed as a feathery 12.5 ounces compared to 19 ounces in all-steel configuration. Also introduced (first in Airweight, in fact) was their Bodyguard model with built-in hammer shroud. Sleeker than the shrouded Colt, it was also more pleasant to shoot; the rear flange of the screw-on Colt shroud had a ten-

Shown with his firm's CIA, Taurus CEO Bob Morrison is proud that his firm's snub-nose .38s are among the most popular.

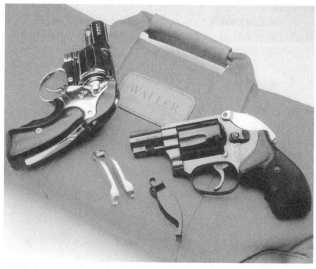

Colt hammer shrouds for D-frame guns (left) and a new variation for J-frame S&W's (right) are available through W.W. Waller & Son.

Bob Schwartz at Waller offers a hammer shroud for the S&W Chief Special that turns it into the Bodyguard configuration.

dency to bite the web of the hand. However, the S&W was more difficult to clean in the area of the shrouded hammer, which proved to be a dust-collector with both brands.

Next came a true "once and future" classic, the Centennial. Smith & Wesson took the configuration of the old New Departure Safety Hammerless top-break and grafted it onto the .38 Special Chief, creating what had to be the sleekest revolver of the genre. It even had the antique gun's signature "lemon squeezer" grip safety, the only solid-frame S&W ever so equipped. Ironically, because few shooters had yet mastered the double-action shooting concept and most felt they needed the crutch of cocking the hammer to hit anything, sales of the Centennial were mediocre and the gun was discontinued. As soon as it became unavailable, the Centennial became a much sought after "in-gun" among the cognoscenti. It was reintroduced, *sans* grip safety, and has been a best-seller ever since.

By the end of the 20th Century, the classic .38 snub had evolved further. The Colt had been given a heavy barrel treatment in 1972. Even before then, serious shooters tended to prefer the Colt over the Smith in a small snubby. The sixth shot had been the least of its advantages. Most found that with its bigger sights and longer action throw – the one comparison between Colt and Smith in which the Colt would likely be voted to have the better DA pull – the littlest Colt would outshoot the littlest Smith. Now an ounce and a half heavier, with a lot more weight up front, it kicked even less than the S&W and tended to shoot like a 4-inch service revolver. In the latter 1990s, the action was updated and stainless versions were produced, including a splendid .357 Magnum version called the Magnum Carry. The gun then went out of production, though at this writing, was high on the list of "old favorites" to be reintroduced by Colt under the new management regime of retired Marine Corps General Bill Keys.

The baby S&W, meanwhile, had been in stainless and Airweight, and even lighter AirLite Ti (titanium) and SC (scandium) models. Calibers included .22, .32 Magnum, .38 Special, 9mm, and .357 Magnum. A "LadySmith" version had also been marketed successfully. The firm had made larger versions in .44 Special.

During that period Taurus had come up from a cheap alternative to a genuinely respected player in the quality handgun market. Their Model 85, resembling a Chief Special, was particularly accurate and smooth, dramatically underselling the S&W and becoming the firm's best seller. The new millennium saw the CIA (Carry It Anywhere)

Classic combat revolvers are far from obsolete. These StressFire Instructor candidates at Lethal Force Institute learn to shoot and teach the wheelgun.

hammerless clone of the S&W Centennial. The first to produce a "Total Titanium" snubby, Taurus made their small revolvers primarily in .38 Special and .357, with larger snubbies available in .44 Special, .45 Colt, and even .41 Magnum.

Rossi also sold a lot of snub-nose revolvers. So did Charter Arms in its various incarnations from the 1960s to the 21st Century. Charter's most memorable revolver was the Bulldog, a five-shot .44 Special comparable in frame size to a Detective Special.

Beyond Classic

Each of the combat handguns described above remains in wide use today in many sectors of armed citizenry, and/or security professionals, and/or police and military circles. Some consider them still the best that ever existed; others put them in second rank to the guns of today. Certainly, those classic revolvers remain in the front rank for those who prefer that style, but in autoloaders, there are many more modern choices. Who is right about what's best today? Let's examine "the new wave" of combat autoloaders, and see for ourselves.

Purchasing Used Handguns

Buying a used handgun isn't as fraught with peril as buying a used car. It's a smaller, simpler mechanism. If it has been well cared for, you'll be able to tell.

Buy from people you can trust. It's a sad commentary on human nature that so many people will deal with a lemon product by simply selling it to someone else. Most reputable gun dealers will stand behind the guns in their second-hand showcases. They may not be able to give you free repairs, but if something goes drastically wrong with it, someone who makes his living from the goodwill

of the gun-buying community will take it back in trade and apply what you paid for it to something else you like better.

Some gun shops have a shooting range attached. With a used gun, you can normally pay a reasonable rental fee, take the gun right out to the range, and give it a try. If you don't like it, you paid a fair price to try a gun. If you do buy it, most such dealers will knock the gun rental off the price, though it's not fair to ask them to knock the range fee off, too.

Though pitted and ugly with its badly worn finish, this S&W Model 15 was clean inside and tight. It would shoot 1-inch groups at 25 yards with match ammo.

Universal Examination Points

As a general rule, a gun in pristine condition outside has *probably* been well cared for internally. This is not written in stone, however. Accompanying this segment are photos of a vintage Smith & Wesson Model 15 Combat Masterpiece .38 Special. It was found for sale among several others in a North Dakota gun shop in 1998, bearing a price tag of $130. Externally, what blue hadn't been worn off had been pitted. It looked as if someone had left it out in a field for the last couple of years. However, when the

Checking the bore without bore light. A white card or paper is held at the breechface and a flashlight is shined on the white surface, lighting up the bore so the interior can be easily seen from the muzzle end.

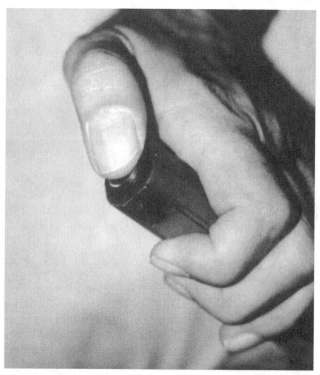

The thumb rotates against the muzzle of an empty 1911 with the slide closed to check for sloppy fit.

buyer examined it, he found the bore to be perfect, and the action so smooth and in such perfect tune it felt as if it had just left Smith & Wesson's Performance Center. He cheerfully paid the asking price, took it home, and discovered that it would group a cylinder of Federal Match .38 wadcutters into an inch at 25 yards.

It can go the other way, too. One fellow left the gun shop chuckling that he'd bought a fancy, premium brand .30/06 rifle, without a scratch on it, for at least $300 less than what it was worth. Then he got it to the range, and discovered it was less accurate than a Super-Squirter. Only then did he check the bore, to discover it rusted to destruction. The previous owner had apparently burned up some old, corrosive WWII surplus ammo in the expensive rifle and neglected the necessary immediate cleaning chores. The gun needed an expensive re-barreling job.

Before you do anything else, triple check to make sure the handgun is unloaded. I have seen people work a firearm's action at a gun show and freeze in horror as a live round ejected from the chamber. Don't let your natural fire-

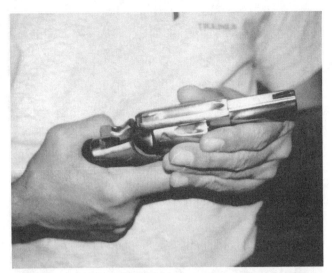

Testing a revolver's timing. With the free hand thumb applying some pressure to cylinder as taking a radial pulse, the trigger finger starts a double-action stroke…

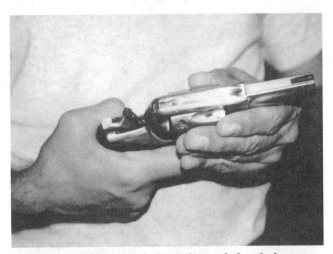

…and the cylinder has locked up tight even before the hammer falls, showing that this Ruger Service-Six is perfectly timed, at least for this particular chamber.

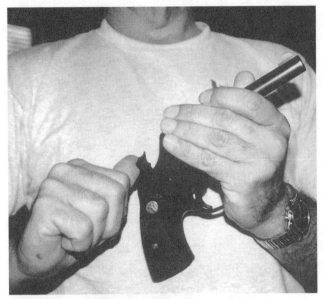

Testing for "push-off" with cocked Colt Official Police. Hammer stayed back, passing test.

arms safety habits grow lax because the environment is a shop or show instead of a range.

Have a small flashlight with you, and perhaps a white business card or 3x5 card. (The Bore-Lite made for the purpose is, of course, ideal.) With the action open, get the card down by the breech and shine the flashlight on it, then look down the barrel; this should give optimum illumination.

If the bore is dirty, see about cleaning it then and there. The carbon could be masking rust or pitting. What you want to see is mirror brightness on the lands, and clean, even grooves in the rifling.

Watch for a dark shadow, particularly one that is dough-nut shaped, encircling the entire bore. This tells you there has been a bulge in the barrel. Typical cause: someone fired a bad load that had insufficient powder, and the bullet lodged in the barrel, and the next shot blew it out. The bulge created by that dangerous over-pressure experience will almost certainly ruin the gun's accuracy. Pass on it.

Try the action. If everything doesn't feel reasonably smooth and work properly, something is *very* wrong with

the action, and unless home gunsmithing is your hobby, you probably want to pass on it.

Now, let's branch into what you need to know about function and safety checks for revolver versus auto.

Checking the Used Revolver

Double check that the gun is unloaded, and keep the muzzle pointed in a safe direction. Check the bore and action as described above.

If it has both double- and single-action functions, cock the hammer. Keeping fingers away from the trigger, push forward on the cocked hammer with your thumb. If it snaps forward, you've experienced "push-off." This means either that the gun has had a sloppy "action job" done on it, or was poorly assembled at the factory, or has experienced a lot of wear. Since most experts believe a combat revolver should be double-action only anyway, and a good plan is to have the single-action cocking notch removed after you've bought it, this may not matter to you. Keep in mind, how-

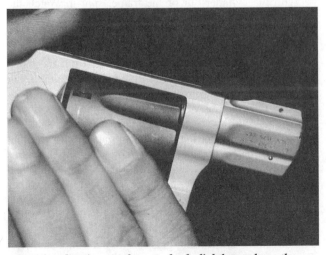

Drawing the trigger or hammer back slightly to release the cylinder locking bolt, slowly rotate the cylinder to analyze barrel/cylinder clearance.

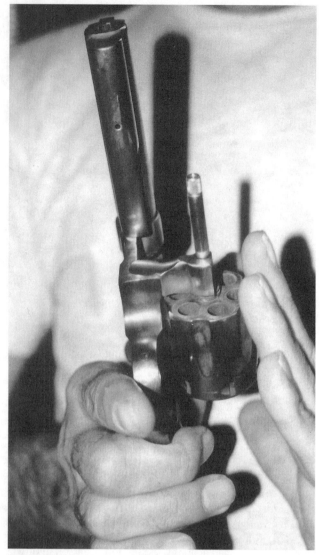

The cylinder of S&W 686 is opened, then spun. Watch the ejector rod. If it wobbles, it's out of line and may need replacement.

The author drops a pencil, eraser-end first, down barrel of cocked and empty S&W 4506. Note hammer is back, and decocking lever up...

... when the decocking lever on the left side is depressed the pencil stays in place. This shows that the decocking mechanism is working properly.

ever, that it's an early warning sign that something else might be wrong with the gun.

With the cylinder out of the frame, spin it. Watch the ejector rod. If it remains straight, it's in alignment. If it wobbles like the wheels of the Toonerville Trolley, it's not, and there's a fairly expensive repair job in its immediate future.

Close the cylinder. Looking at the gun from the front, push leftward on the cylinder as if you were opening it, but without releasing the cylinder latch. Watch the interface between the crane or yoke, the part on which the cylinder swings out, with the rest of the frame. If it stays tight, the gun is in good shape. If there's a big gap, it tells you that some bozo has been abusing the gun by whipping the cylinder out of the frame like Humphrey Bogart. This will have a negative effect on cylinder alignment and will mean another pricey repair job. A big gap in this spot always means, "don't buy it."

With the cylinder still closed and the muzzle still in a safe direction, take a firing grasp with your dominant hand. Cup the gun under the trigger guard with your support hand, and with the thumb of that hand, apply light pressure to the cylinder. Use about the same pressure you'd use to take your pulse at the wrist. This will effectively duplicate the cylinder drag of cartridge case heads against the frame at the rear of the cylinder window if the gun was loaded.

Now, slowly, roll the trigger back until the hammer falls. Hold the trigger back. With the thumb, wiggle the cylinder. If it is locked in place, then at least on that chamber, you have the solid lockup you want. If, however, this movement causes the cylinder to only now "tick" into place, it means that particular chamber would not have been in alignment with the bore when an actual shot was fired. Armorers call this effect a DCU, which stands for "doesn't carry up." You want to repeat this check for every chamber in the gun.

When the revolver's chambers don't lock into line with the bore, the gun is said to be "out of time." The bullets will go into the forcing cone at an angle. This degrades accuracy, and causes lead shavings to spit out to the sides, endangering adjacent shooters on the firing line. As it gets worse, the firing pin will hit the primer so far off center the gun may misfire. With powerful loads, it will quickly lead to a split forcing cone. It definitely needs to be fixed. (When you get an estimate, if the armorer or gunsmith says you need a new ratchet, get a second opinion. Maybe five out of six times, all the gun needs is to have a new cylinder hand stoned to fit. Replacing an extractor is at least four times as expensive.)

Do all that again, and this time, once each chamber locks into place, wiggle the cylinder. If there's a lot of slop and play, there's a good chance that perfect chamber/bore alignment will be a chancy thing, and accuracy will suffer. This is generally a sign of bad workmanship in a cheaply made gun, and excessive wear in one of the big-name brands.

Push the cylinder back and forth; front to back and vice versa. A lot of slop means excessive headspace. Particularly with a big-bore or a Magnum, it may be a sign that the gun has been shot so much it's approaching the end of its useful life. A good gunsmith can fix this with some cylinder shims, however.

Get some light on the other side of the gun, so you can look through the gap between barrel and cylinder. Hold the

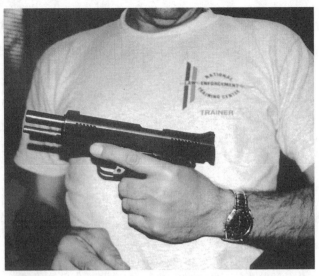

In a test that will make you cringe, unloaded pistol begins at slidelock with finger on slide release lever…

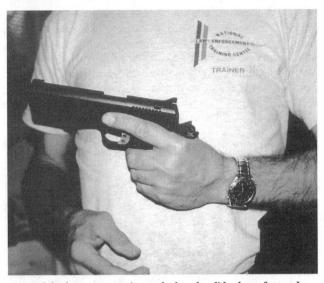

…and the hammer remains cocked as the slide slams forward. This shows Kimber Custom .45's sear mechanism to be in good working order. However…

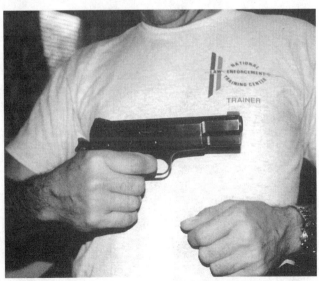

With magazine removed, hammer cocked, and safety off, the trigger is pulled on an empty Browning Hi-Power. Hammer does not move, demonstrating that magazine disconnector safety is functioning as designed.

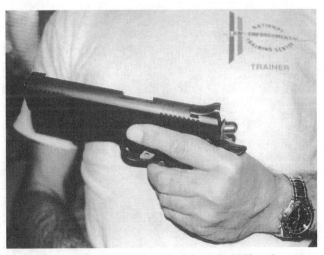

… if the hammer had "followed" slide to the half-cock position as replicated here, gun would need repairs before being worthy of purchase.

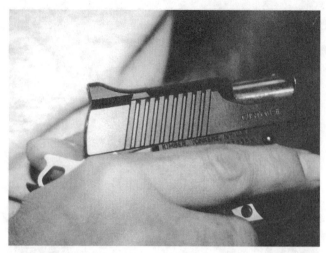

A less abusive test for hammer-follow on an auto is to hold it as shown and repeatedly flick the hammer back with the free hand thumb.

hammer back with your thumb until the bolt drops, and then rotate the cylinder, watching the gap. If you examine enough guns, you will find some that actually touch the forcing cone of the barrel. This is unacceptable; the cylinder will bind, the trigger pull will become uneven, hard, and "grating" as your finger works to force the cylinder past the

Check to see if magazines insert and drop out cleanly. This HK USP40 Compact passes the test.

bind point, and eventually the gun will lock up and stop working. On the other end of the spectrum, you may see a barrel/cylinder gap so wide that you could probably spit through it without touching metal. You can expect poor accuracy and nasty side-spit from such a gun. Reject it unless the seller is willing to pay for the repairs to bring it up to spec.

If the cylinder comes closer to the barrel on some chambers than others, the front of the cylinder is probably not machined true. Most experts would pass by such a revolver.

Autoloaders

With any autoloader, double check that it is empty and keep the muzzle in a safe direction. Try the action a few times. When you rack the slide, everything should feel smooth. The slide should go all the way into battery – that is, all the way forward – without any sticking points that require an extra nudge. If the gun binds when it's empty, you *know* it's going to bind when the mechanism has to do the extra work of picking up and chambering cartridges. If the gun is clean and is binding, pass it by.

Make sure magazines go in and out cleanly. Some guns (1911, for example) are designed for the magazines to fall completely away when the release button is pressed. If the test gun won't do this with new magazines that you know are in good shape, there could be some serious warpage in the grip-frame or, more probably, something wrong with the magazine release mechanism.

Some guns (early Glocks, most Browning Hi-Powers, any pistol with a butt-heel magazine release) can't be expected to drop their magazines free. However, the magazine should still run cleanly in and out of the passageway in the grip frame.

You want to check the sear mechanism with a hammer-fired pistol to make sure there won't be "hammer follow." The test itself is abusive, and you want to make sure it's OK

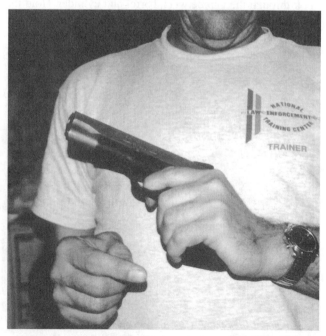

Checking the manual safety/sear engagement on a 1911. First, cock the empty gun, put the manual safety in the "on safe" position, and pull the trigger firmly as shown...

with the current owner before you do it. Insert the empty magazine and lock the slide back. Making sure nothing is contacting the trigger, press the slide release lever and let the gun slam closed. Watch the hammer. If the hammer follows to the half-cock position or the at-rest position, the sear isn't working right. Either it has been dropped and knocked out of alignment, or more probably, someone did a kitchen table trigger job on it, and the sear is down to a perilously weak razor's edge. Soon, it will start doing the same with live rounds, which will keep you from firing subsequent shots until you've manually cocked the hammer. Soon after *that*, if the malady goes untreated, you will attempt to fire one shot and this pistol will go "full automatic."

Because the mechanism was designed to be cushioned by the cartridge that the slide strips off the magazine during the firing cycle, it batters the extractor (and, on 1911-type guns, the sear) to perform this test. However, it's the best way to see if the sear is working on a duty type gun. (Most target pistols have finely ground sears and won't pass this test, which is yet another reason you don't want a light-triggered target pistol for combat shooting.) If this test is unacceptable to the gun's owner, try the following. Hold the gun in the firing hand, cock it, and with the thumb of the support hand push the hammer all the way back past full cock and then release. If when it comes forward it slips by the full cock position and keeps going, the gun is going to need some serious repair.

If the pistol has a grip safety, cock the hammer of the empty gun, hold it in such a way that there is no pressure on the grip safety, and press the trigger back. If the hammer falls, the grip safety is not working.

If the gun has a hammer-drop feature (i.e., decocking lever), cock the hammer and drop a #2 pencil or a flat-head Bic Stik pen down the bore, with the tip of the writing instrument pointing toward the muzzle. With the fingers clear of the trigger, activate the decocking lever. If the pencil or pen just quivers when the hammer falls, the decocking mechanism is in good working order. However, if the pen or pencil flies from the barrel, that means it was hit by the firing pin. You're holding a dangerously broken gun, one that would have fired the round in the chamber if you had tried to decock it while loaded.

Now, to test the firing pin, we'll use the Bic Stik or the #2 pencil again. This time, we'll pull the trigger. If the writing implement is launched clear of the barrel, you have a healthy firing pin strike. If it isn't, either the firing pin is broken or the firing pin spring is worn out.

Caution: In both of the last two tests, wear safety glasses and have a clear "line of fire" with no one in the way! That sharp-tipped pen or pencil will come flying out of the barrel with enough force to cause a cut or nasty eye damage! Also in both of these tests, you'll need an empty magazine in place if the pistol has a magazine disconnector safety.

To make sure that the magazine disconnector safety is operating, remove the magazine from the empty pistol, point it in a safe direction, and pull the trigger. If the hammer falls, the disconnector device either is not working or has been disconnected.

A sloppily fitted auto pistol is not likely to deliver much in the way of accuracy. Bring the slide forward on the empty gun, put the tip of a finger in the muzzle, and wiggle it around. If it's tight, it bodes well for accuracy. If it slops around a lot, the opposite can be expected. With the slide still forward, bring a thumb to the back of the barrel where it is exposed at the ejection port, and press downward. If it gives a lot, that tells you that the rear lockup isn't as solid as you'll need for really good accuracy. In either of these measurements, it's hard to explain how much play is too much. Try this test with some guns of known accuracy, and you'll quickly develop a "feel" for what is and is not what you're looking for with that particular make and model.

Summary

Well-selected "pre-owned" handguns are an excellent value. Firearms are the ultimate "durable goods." How many people do you know who drive their grandfather's car or keep the family food supply in their grandmother's ice box? Probably not too many. But if you start asking, you'll be amazed how many people you know still cherish their grandparents' firearms.

It's no trick at all to find a perfectly functional combat handgun, revolver or auto, on the second-hand shelf at half the price of a new one. That leaves you more money for ammo, training, skill-building…and enjoying the life and the people you bought that gun to protect.

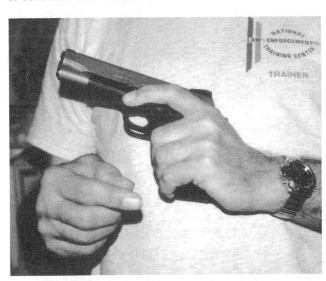

…now, remove finger from trigger guard…

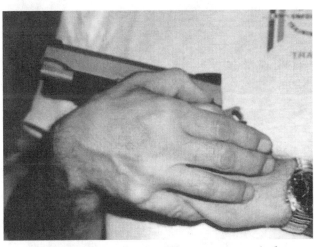

… and release the thumb safety. If hammer stays motionless as shown, that portion of the mechanism is in good working order. If hammer falls at this point, gun is DANGEROUSLY damaged!

CHAPTER THREE

MODERN PARADIGMS

The Glock

Gaston Glock had made a fortune producing assorted polymer items at his factory in Austria. His reputation was such that more than one firearms company soon approached him to make a polymer pistol frame. Being (a) a manufacturer, (b) a businessman, (c) a designer, and (d) smarter than hell, it occurred to him that he could design his own gun to manufacture. He set his design team to work, giving them a clean sheet of paper.

In the early 1980s, there was little new under the sun in the form of handguns. The most high-tech auto pistols were largely refinements of older designs. For example: take the 1950 Beretta service pistol, add on a 1930s vintage Walther-type hammer-drop safety and a 1908 vintage Luger magazine release, and you had the "new" Beretta. But what came off the Glock drawing board was something new indeed.

It looked like something out of Star Trek. It was sleek, with a raked back grip angle that could be compared to a Luger or a Ruger only in the angle, not in the shape. It was square at front and back. It had no hammer, inside or out; the pistol was striker fired. The polymer frame, plus a design created from the ground up for economy of manufacture, ensured under-bidding of the competition. The other makers' guns carried 14 to 16 rounds of 9mm Parabellum, but this one

carried 18. The trigger pull was very controllable, and consistent from first shot to last. More importantly, the thing worked with utter reliability and survived torture tests.

It wasn't the first "plastic gun." Heckler and Koch had pioneered that more than a decade before, with plastic framed P9S and VP70Z lines, only to be met with poor sales. No one predicted success, figuring that the Austrian army's adoption of the pistol was merely a sign of chauvenism.

It is doubtful that any greater underestimation was ever made in the world of the handgun.

The Glock's entry into the American handgun marketplace was nothing less than stunning. The American branch of the firm, Glock USA, was established in Smyrna, GA. A couple of guys who knew the marketplace were on board: Bob Gates, late of Smith & Wesson, and Carl Walter.

In the Glock light-weight, compactness, controllability and power come together in the author's favorite of the breed, the .45 caliber Glock 30. This one holds the short 9-round magazine designed for maximum concealment.

Author appreciates "shootability" of Glocks. He used this G17 to win High Senior and 2nd Master at 1999 New England Regional IDPA Championships, placing just behind national champ Tom Yost.

A number of signs in the marketing heavens were in alignment, and this confluence of the stars would make Glock the biggest success story in firearms in the latter half of the 20th century.

American police chiefs still clung tenaciously to their service revolvers. Unique among police equipment, the revolver had not changed materially since the turn of the century. Uniforms were better, the cars had modernized along with the rest of America, communications were state of the art, and even handcuffs had improved and been streamlined. But if you went to a police museum, you would find that only two things had gone basically unchanged since the dawn of the 20th century: the police whistle, and the police service revolver.

Patrolmen's unions and well-versed police instructors were clamoring for autoloaders. For years, the chiefs had put off these requests with stock answers. "Automatics jam." "Our guys won't remember to take the safeties off when they draw to fire in self-defense." "They're too complicated." "Automatics cock themselves and go off too easily after the first shot."

Meanwhile, instructors were chanting the old military mantra, "Keep it simple, stupid." Any auto adopted by most of them would have to be simple, indeed.

Enter the Glock.

It endured torture tests for thousands of rounds. Buried in sand and mud and frozen in ice, it was plucked out, shaken off, and fired. It worked. Sand and mud and ice chips flew along with the spent casings, but the guns worked. One adventuresome police squad deliberately dropped a loaded Glock from a helicopter at an altitude of 300 feet. The gun did not go off. When it was retrieved, though one sight was chipped, it fired perfectly.

Safety? There was no manual safety per se. All safeties were internal and passive. "Point gun, pull trigger," just like the revolver. When BATF declared the Glock pistol to be double-action only in design, the argument about cocked guns being dangerous went out the window, too.

The first pistol was the Glock 17, so called because it was Gaston Glock's 17th specific design. It became the flagship of

a fast-expanding fleet. Though Glock would later describe it as "full size," it was actually smaller than a Model 1911 or a Beretta 92, more comparable in overall length to a Colt Lightweight Commander, and it weighed even less.

Next came the even smaller Glock 19 with its 4-inch barrel. The 16-shot 9mm was roughly the overall dimensions and weight of a Colt Detective Special with 2-inch barrel that held only six rounds of .38 Special. At the other end of the size spectrum, Glock introduced a target model in the late 1980s, the 17L with 6-inch barrel. This gun had a light 3.5-pound trigger pull, a pound and a half lighter than the standard gun. Other trigger options were also made available. New York State Police said they'd adopt the gun, but only if Glock made it with a heavier trigger. Thus was born the New York Trigger, which brought the pull weight up to roughly 8 pounds. NYSP adopted the Glock 17 so equipped, and their troopers carry it to this day.

1990 was a pivotal year for Glock. They announced their big-frame model, the Glock 20 in 10mm, the caliber

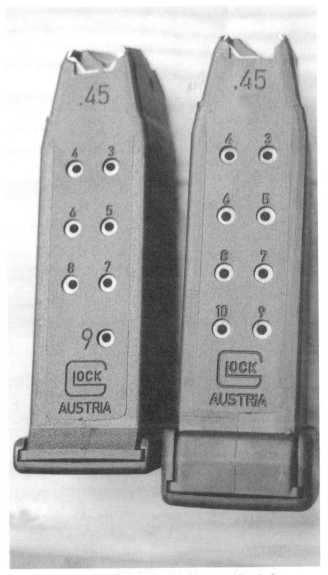

Different magazines add to the Glock's versatility. Left, a short-bottom nine round magazine for maximum concealment; right, 10-round mag with little finger placement support. Both are for the Glock 30 .45 auto.

The Glock 17 holds 18 rounds of 9mm Parabellum in a pre-ban magazine. This specimen has Glock's oversize slide release and Heinie sights.

expected to sweep law enforcement after the FBI's recent announcement of adopting the S&W Model 1076 in that caliber. The gun was quickly adapted to .45 ACP. In January of that same year at the SHOT Show in Las Vegas, Smith & Wesson and Winchester jointly announced the development of the .40 S&W cartridge. Gaston Glock returned home with ammo samples and very quickly the standard Glock was reinforced to handle the more powerful cartridge with its faster slide velocity. Within the year, the South Carolina Law Enforcement Division had adopted the full size Glock 22 in that caliber and proven it on the street, and others were ordering the compact Glock 23.

In 1993, after a gunman with a 9mm murdered a young NYC cop while he was reloading his mandated six-shot revolver, the Patrolman's Benevolent Association at last prevailed over management and NYPD reluctantly went to the auto. All new recruits would have to purchase a 9mm instead of a .38, and in-service officers could buy one if they wanted. NYPD had always required their personnel to buy their own guns. Three double-action-only 16-shooters were authorized: the SIG P226 DAO, the S&W Model 5946, and the Glock 19. The Glock was by far the lightest and most compact for off duty and plainclothes carry, and by far the least expensive; it became first choice by such an overwhelming margin that many observers around the country thought NYPD had standardized on the Glock.

In the mid-1990s, the company found another huge success with their baby Glocks. The size of snubby .38s with twice the firepower and more controllability, the babies shot as well as the big ones. They were dubbed G26 in 9mm and G27 in .40 caliber. Slightly larger compacts were offered in 10mm Auto and .45 Auto, the Glocks 29 and 30 respectively. When a groundswell of popularity emerged in police circles for the powerful and accurate .357 SIG cartridge, Glock offered that chambering through the line as Model 31 (full size), Model 32 (compact) and Model 33 (subcompact).

The company didn't stop there. Integral recoil reduction ports were offered, creating a factory compensated gun in either compact or full size. These kept the same model numbers as the base guns, but with the suffix "C". The firm also introduced the "Tactical/Practical" series. Midway in length between full size and long-slide, they were exactly the length of the old Colt Government Model. This suited the .40 caliber G35 well for the Production class in IPSC shooting (where that caliber barely "made major"), and the 9mm G34 perfectly for Stock Service Pistol class in IDPA, where Dave Sevigny has used one to win repeated national championships. A number of departments from Nashua, NH to Kerrville, TX have made the Glock 35 the standard issue duty pistol, usually with a retrofit of a New York trigger.

By the turn of the 21st century, the Glock pistol dominated the American law enforcement market to the tune of roughly 65 percent.

Modifying the Glock

The pistol comes from the factory with what the company calls a "standard" trigger, which uses an S-shaped spring to connect the trigger to the unique cruciform sear plate. (The "Tactical/Practical" comes with a 3.5-pound trigger, like the long-slide 9mm 17L and .40 G24 models.) Supposedly delivering 5 pounds of pull, the standard trigger generally weighs out to about 5.5 pounds. Most civilian shooters leave it as is, as do many police departments including Washington, D.C. Metro, the Illinois State Police, and the FBI.

Many, including this writer, have followed the lead of the NYSP and gone with the original weight New York Trigger, now known as the NY-1. The intention of this design was to mitigate accidental discharges caused by human error. There is some three-eighths of an inch of travel from when the Glock trigger is at rest and ready to when it reaches its rearmost point and discharges the pistol. On the standard set-up, it feels like a Mauser military rifle trigger with a long, light take-up and then about a tenth of an inch of firm resistance before the shot is fired. When human beings are in danger, their inborn survival mechanism triggers a number of physiological changes, one of which is vasoconstriction. That is, blood flow is shunted away from the extremities and into the body's core and the major muscle groups. This is why frightened Caucasians are seen to turn ghostly pale, and it is why frightened people become clumsy and lose tactile sensation in their fingers under stress. In such a situation, it is feared that if the finger has erroneously strayed to the trigger prematurely, the shooter won't be able to feel it taking up trigger slack until too late.

The advantage of the NY-1 trigger is that it offers a very firm resistance to the trigger finger from the very beginning of the pull, a resistance so strong it probably *will* be palpable to the shooter even in a vasoconstricted state. This means a lot more than merely 3 pounds additional pull weight. (The NY-1 increases the pull to a nominal 8 pounds, which usually measures out to more like 7.75 pounds.) This, plus excellent training, allows NYSP and other departments to have an excellent safety record with these guns.

New York City Police Department initially put some 600 Glocks in the field among specially assigned personnel, ranging from Homicide detectives to the Missing Persons unit. These first guns had the standard 5-pound triggers, and after a spate of accidental discharges, the Firearms Training Unit mandated an even heavier trigger than the State Police had. Thus was born the NY-2 trigger module, also called the New York Plus. This brought the pull up to a stated 12

Top, the Glock 27 holds 10 rounds of .40 S&W ammo; bottom, NAA Guardian holds 7 rounds of .380 ACP. Which would you choose?

pounds, which usually measures about 11.5 pounds on a well broken-in Glock.

This writer personally thinks the NY-2 passes the point of diminishing returns by making the trigger harder to control in rapid fire. Like many, I actually shoot better with the NY-1 at 8 pounds than with the standard pull. The reason is that the different design gives a cleaner "trigger break" as the shot goes off, and the heavier spring better resists "backlash."

Finally, I've found as an instructor that the little S-spring on the standard trigger system is the one weak link in an otherwise ingenious and robust mechanism. I see several break a year. The NY module that replaces that spring is much sturdier and I've personally *never* seen one break. For all these reasons, I have the NY-1 in every Glock that I carry, and strongly recommend it for any Glock carried for duty or defense.

Atop some models sits the other weak link: plastic sights. Retrofit steel sights (the Heinie unit is particularly good) or metal night sights with Tritium inserts that can be ordered on the gun from the factory solve this problem. There is the rare breakage of locking blocks, but that is no more common than cracked locking blocks on Berettas or cracked frames on SIGs, Colts, etc. The finest machines can break when they are used hard and long, and it is no reflection on the product. Outfit your Glock with an NY-1 trigger and good steel sights, and there's nothing left on it that's likely to break.

The Appeal of the Glock

This gun is simple. Most armorer's courses (in which you are taught by the factory to repair the guns) take a week. Glock's takes one day. The pistol has only 30- some components. Almost all armorer's operations can be done with a 3/32-inch punch. You do need a screwdriver to remove the magazine release button.

There is no easier pistol to learn to shoot well! No decocking lever to remember; that's done automatically. No manual safety to manipulate; the safeties are all internal and passive. If your gun was made prior to 1990, call the factory with the serial number and see if it should have the no-

Contrary to popular belief, Glock was not the first auto pistol with a polymer frame. This Heckler & Koch P9S which pre-dated the Glock considerably with a "plastic frame," was not a huge marketing success.

charge new-parts update. Then, like every Glock produced for more than a decade, it will be totally impact resistant and "drop-safe."

Insert magazine. Rack slide. That's it. Now shoot it like you would a revolver, taking care to keep your thumb away from the slide and your firing wrist locked, as you would with any semiautomatic pistol.

If you want a manual safety for weapon retention purposes, or because it just gives you peace of mind after a lifetime with some other brand of pistol carried on-safe, an excellent right-hander's thumb safety can be installed at very reasonable cost by Joe Cominolli, PO Box 911, Solvay, NY 13209.

The Glock is an extraordinarily reliable and long-lived pistol. It is light, fast-handling, and very controllable. The polymer frame can be seen to flex in high-speed photography as it fires, and this seems to provide a recoil-cushioning effect that is enhanced by the natural "locked wrist" angle of its grip-frame. The Hybrid Porting conversion, which reduces recoil by sending several gas jets up through the top of what used to be the slide, will vampire as much as 100 feet per second of velocity and create a louder report, but allows amazing shot-to-shot control. While it seems to take a master gunsmith to make Hybrid-porting work reliably on a 1911, the Glock seems to function perfectly with it installed.

The Glock is southpaw-friendly and lends itself to ambidextrous shooting. A growing cottage industry offers useful accessories for it. Laser sights are available from Laser-Max and Crimson Trace. Models made in the last few years, compact size and larger, have an accessory rail that will accommodate a flashlight. The company has always been scrupulously good about customer service in terms of parts and repairs.

Accuracy is adequate at worst and excellent at best. The only Glocks that seemed to be really inaccurate were the very first runs of the Glock 22, and the company squared that away quickly. I have a Glock 22 that, out of the box, will stay in 2.5 inches at 25 yards with good ammunition; this specimen was produced in 2001. The baby Glocks are famous for their accuracy. This is because the barrels and slides are proportionally thicker and more rigid on these short guns, and also because the double captive recoil spring that softens kick so effectively also guarantees that the bullet is out of the barrel before the mechanism begins to unlock. Modifying a Smith & Wesson auto to have that same accuracy-enhancing feature costs big bucks when done by the factory's Performance Center; it comes on the smallest Glocks at no charge.

The .45 caliber Glocks also seem to be particularly accurate. First, the .45 ACP has always been a more inherently accurate cartridge than the 9mm Luger and particularly the .40 S&W. Second, the .45 barrels are made on different machinery than the other calibers at Glock, and seem to be particularly accurate. The "baby .45," the Glock 30, combines both of these worlds and may be the most accurate pistol Glock makes. My Glock 30, factory stock with NY-1 trigger and Trijicon sights, has given me five-shot, 1-inch groups at 25 yards with Federal Hydra-Shok and Remington Match ammunition.

There is a good reason for the Glock pistol's predominance in the American law enforcement sector and, to a slightly lesser extent, the armed citizen sector. Quite simply, the product has earned it.

Today's Double-Action Autos

Walther popularized the double-action auto with a de-cocking feature in the 1930s. It was seen at the time as a "faster" auto, the theory being that with a single-action auto like the Colt or Browning, you had to either move a safety lever, or cock a hammer, or jack a slide before firing. With the DA auto, it was thought, one could just carry it off safe and pull the trigger when needed, like a revolver.

At the time, most of America felt that if they wanted an auto that worked like a revolver, they would just carry one of their fine made-in-USA *revolvers,* thank you very much. In the middle of the 20th century, 1911 flag-bearer Jeff Cooper applied an engineer's phrase that would stick to the double-action auto forever after. The concept was, he said, "an ingenious solution to a non-existent problem."

Whether or not that was true at the time, a problem later came up to fit the solution. America had become, by the latter 20th century, the most litigious country in the world. With more lawyers per capita than any other nation, the United States became famous for tolerating utterly ridiculous lawsuits that, had they been brought in a country that followed the Napoleonic Code, would probably have ended up penalizing the plaintiff for having brought an unmeritorious case. Two elements of this would have impact on handgun selection in both police and private citizen sectors.

Gun control had joined abortion as one of the two most polarized debates in the land. Prosecutors were either elected by the same folks who elected the politicians, or appointed by elected politicians. Some of them found it expedient to "make examples" of politically incorrect shootings of bad guys by good guys. For this, they needed a hook.

Contrary to popular belief, prosecutors don't get big occupation bonus points for winning a conviction for murder instead of manslaughter. If they get a conviction, they get credit, period. If they bring a case and lose, they lose credibility and political capital. This is why a good chance of a win on a lower charge beats a poor chance of conviction on a higher charge. To convince a dozen people with common sense sitting in a jury box that a good cop or a decent

citizen has suddenly become a monstrous murderer is a pretty tough sell. But to convince them that a good person could have been careless for one second and made a mistake is an easy job, because every adult has done exactly that at

Ruger's P90 beat every other double-action .45 tested and became the issue weapon for author's police department in 1993, along with Safariland SS-III security holster.

some time. A murder conviction requires proving the element of malice, but a manslaughter conviction requires only proving that someone did something stupid. Thus, it came into vogue to attack politically incorrect justifiable homicide incidents with a charge of manslaughter.

It is common knowledge that a light trigger pull – what a lay person would call a "hair trigger" – is more conducive to the accidental discharge of a firearm than a long, heavy trigger pull that requires a deliberate action. Cocking a gun, or pointing an already cocked gun at a suspect, could therefore be seen as negligence. Now, the key ingredient of a manslaughter conviction was in place.

It reached a point where prosecutors would actually manufacture a "negligent hair trigger argument" even in cases where the gun was never cocked. One such case, *State of Florida v. Officer Luis Alvarez,* is mentioned elsewhere in this book. Alvarez' department responded by rendering all the issue service revolvers double-action-only. Some saw this as a weak concession to political correctness. It must be pointed out, however, that if the double-action-only policy had been in place before the shooting, the prosecution never would have had that false hook on which to hang the case, to begin with.

And that was just in criminal courts. On the civil lawsuit side, something similar was happening. Plaintiffs' lawyers realized that the deep pockets they were after belonged to insurance companies, not individual citizens who got involved in self-defense shootings. Almost everyone who

A relic of the early 20th Century, the slide-mounted safety/de-cock lever of Walther PPK inspired designs of S&W, Beretta, and others much later in the "wondernine" period.

shot an intruder had homeowner liability insurance, but such policies specifically exempt the underwriter from liability for a willful tort, that is, a deliberately inflicted act of harm. The lawyers could only collect if the homeowner shot the burglar by accident. Thus was born the heavy thrust of attacking guns with easy trigger pulls, and of literally fabricating the "cocked gun theory of the case." Private citizens who kept guns for self-protection and were aware of these things began to see the advisability of double-action-only autos as well as revolvers for home defense and personal carry.

A two-pronged concern was now in place. Fear of accidental discharges of weapons with short trigger pulls, and fear of false accusation of the same. Police chiefs who had once authorized cocked and locked Colts and Brownings for officers now banned those guns. Detroit PD and Chicago PD are two examples. Many private citizens who carried guns and followed these matters saw the trend, and decided that a design that was double-action at least for the first shot might have an advantage.

Thus was born the interest in DA pistols. The compactness of the Walther .380 had already made it a popular concealed carry handgun. Smith & Wesson's double-action Model 39, introduced in the mid-50s, had captured the attention of gun buffs. It was a good looking gun, slim and flat to carry in the waistband, with a beautiful feel in the hand, and it was endorsed by such top gun writers of the time as Col. Charles Askins, Jr., George Nonte, and Jan Stevenson.

The 1970s saw the development of high-capacity 9mm double-action designs, and of hollow-point 9mm ammo that got the caliber up off its knees. With expanding bullets, the 9mm Luger's reputation as an impotent man-stopper in two world wars was rehabilitated to a significant degree.

These guns became known as "wondernines," a term that was coined, I believe, by the late Robert Shimek. Known to gun magazine readers as an expert on handgun hunting and classic military-style small arms, Shimek was known only to a few as a career law enforcement officer who wore a 9mm SIG P226 to work every day.

These "wondernines" worked. In the late 70s and early 80s, the manufacturers refined the designs to meet the virtually 100 percent reliability requirements in the JSSAP (Joint Services Small Arms Project) tests that would determine the service pistol that would replace the ancient 1911 as the U.S. military sidearm. As a result, they were thoroughly "de-bugged." The prospect of a giant, lucrative government contract proved to be a powerful incentive to "get the guns right."

They would become the platforms of the .40 S&W cartridge in 1990, and of the subsequent .357 SIG cartridge. They would be enlarged, keeping the same key design features, to handle the .45 ACP and the 10mm Auto.

These were the guns that would change the face of the handgun America carried.

Beretta

Beretta snatched the gold ring when the ride on the JSSAP merry-go-round was over, winning the contract as the new primary service pistol of the U.S. armed forces. There were a few broken locking blocks and separated slides. Though some of these involved over-pressure lots of ammo that would have broken any gun, and others involved sound suppressors whose forward-levering weight didn't allow the locking blocks to work correctly, jealous manufacturers who lost the bid amplified the "problem" to more than it was. Almost without exception, military armorers and trainers who monitor small arms performance in actual conflicts have given the Beretta extremely high marks for its performance in U.S. military service.

It has also stood up nobly in the U.S. police service. For many years now the issue weapon of LAPD (almost 10,000 officers) and Los Angeles County Sheriff's Department (some 7,000 deputies), the Beretta 92, 9mm has given yeoman's service. Thanks to its open-top slide design, it is virtually jam-free, and one of the very few pistols that can equal or exceed the Glock in terms of reliability.

The glass-smooth feel of the action as you hand-cycle the Beretta is the standard by which others are judged. The 92F series, with combination manual safety/decocking lever, may have the single easiest slide-mounted safety to operate. Two large departments, one East Coast and one West, mandate that their personnel carry the Beretta on-safe. Each department has logged numerous cases in which the wearers' lives were saved by this feature when someone got the gun away from an officer, tried to shoot him or her, and couldn't because the safety was engaged.

The Beretta is also a very accurate pistol. Five rounds of 9mm commonly go into 1-1/2 inches at 25 yards from the standard Model 92. The Model 96, chambered for .40 S&W, passed the demanding accuracy tests of the Indiana State Police and was adopted as that agency's standard issue sidearm. The state troopers of Rhode Island, Florida, and Pennsylvania joined Indiana and issue the 96 at this writing. The city police of San Francisco and Providence also issue the 96.

In .40 S&W, my experience has been that the Beretta is a notch below its 9mm cousin in reliability. For this reason, Ohio state troopers dumped the 96 for the SIG equivalent.

Beretta's updated Cougar is a good gun. It is the issue weapon of the North Carolina Highway Patrol (in caliber .357 SIG) among others. The latest version, the polymer-

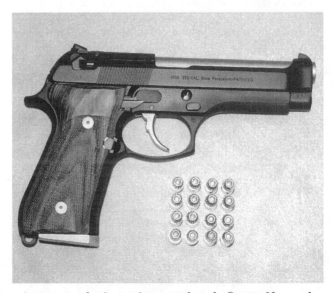

A new wave classic, to mix a metaphor, the Beretta 92 proved to be an utterly reliable 16-shot 9mm, winning the U.S. Government contract and arming countless U.S. police agencies. This is a G-model, customized by Ernest Langdon, who won national championships with such guns.

Colt's Pocket Nine, a 9mm Parabellum the size of a Walther PPK but lighter, was the company's high point in double-action auto manufacture. For reasons explained in the text, it is no longer produced at this writing.

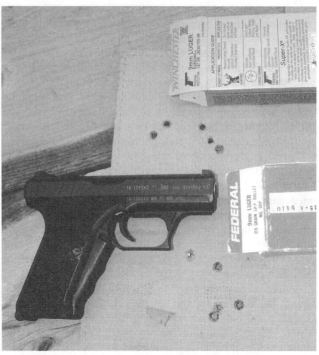

HK's ergonomic P7 shows off its "guaranteed head-shot accuracy" at 25 yards with two of the most accurate 9mm rounds available, 115-grain Federal 9BP and Winchester's Olin Super Match 147-grain, both with JHP projectiles.

frame 9000 series, is not particularly ergonomic and has not been so well received.

Colt

America's most famous producer of single-action autos has not fared well on the double-action side of that table. Their first, the Double Eagle, misfired constantly in its original incarnation. When I broke the story on that, Colt was gracious enough to recognize the problem and correct it. The pistol, however, still looked like what it was: a Government Model with a double-action mechanism cobbled together in a fragile way to get past the Seecamp Conversion patent. It did not fare well and is no longer in production.

Colt's All-American 2000 was a sad and ugly thing. Jams. Misfires. Pathetic accuracy and a horrible trigger pull. Heralded by the newsstand gun magazines as a great leap forward in technology, it soon died a well-deserved death.

Colt's only good double-actions were their last, both DAOs. The little Pony .380 worked, and the Pocket Nine 9mm *was* a breakthrough: a full power, seven-shot 9mm Luger exactly the size of a Walther PPK .380 but 5 ounces *lighter,* utterly reliable, and capable of 2-inch, five-shot groups at 25 yards. While the triggers were heavy, they were controllable. Alas, only about 7,000 Pocket Nines were produced before a patent infringement suit by Kahr Arms shut down production.

Heckler & Koch

HK's 1970s entries in the double-action auto market, the VP70Z and the P9S, did not succeed. The former worked well as a machine pistol and poorly as a semiautomatic. The latter, exquisitely accurate, was before its time. It needed its chamber throated to feed hollow-points reliably, and its decocking mechanism, which involved pulling the trigger, was enough to make police firearms instructors wake up in the middle of the night screaming.

The P7 was much more successful. With an ingenious combination of gas operation and a squeeze-cocking fire control system that the company called Continuous Action, it created a cult following among handgunners. The gun was either loved or hated with no middle ground. A fixed barrel made it deadly accurate, with sub-2-inch groups at 25 yards more the rule than the exception. The squeeze-cocking came naturally and the pistol was super-fast to draw and fire. A low bore axis, plus the gas bleed mechanism, made it the lightest-kicking of 9mm combat pistols. Widely adopted in Germany, it became the issue service pistol of the New Jersey State Police in 1984 as the P7M8, with American style mag release and eight-round magazine. The double-stack P7M13 was subsequently adopted by Utah state police.

Its strength was that it was easy to shoot; its weakness was that it was easy to shoot. Many instructors associated the design with a likelihood of accidental discharge. Cost of manufacturing plus the changing balance of dollar and Deutschmark soon rendered it unaffordable for most civilians and almost all police. Still produced in the M8 format, this unique and excellent pistol is fading from the scene, but still cherished by a handful of serious aficionados, all of whom seem able to shoot it extremely well.

HK tried to get back into the police service pistol market with the gun they sold to the German armed forces, the USP. A rugged polymer-framed gun, it is available in several variants: lefty, righty, double-action-only, single-action-only, safety/decock or decock-only lever, and assorted combinations of the same. Available calibers are 9mm, .40, .357 SIG, and .45 ACP. It was the USP that introduced the now widely copied concept of the dust cover portion of the frame being moulded as a rail to accept a flashlight attachment.

I've found the USP conspicuously reliable, except for occasional jams in the 9mm version. It is also extremely accurate. Though competition versions are available, the standard models, particularly in .45, are tight shooters in their own right. Starting with probably the heaviest and "roughest" double-action only trigger option in the industry, they now have one of the best in their LE module, developed in 2000 for a Federal agency and offered to the civilian public in 2002. The HK USP is approved for private purchase by Border Patrol, and is the standard issue service pistol of departments ranging from San Bernardino PD to the Maine State Police.

Kahr

Brilliantly designed by Justin Moon, the Kahr pistol is slim and flat, comparable in size to most .380s, and utterly reliable with factory 9mm or .40 S&W ammo. The double-action-only trigger is smooth and sweet, and the guns have surprising inherent accuracy. My K9 once gave me a 1-3/8-inch group at 25 yards with Federal 9BP ammo.

The only real complaint shooters had about the Kahr was that, being all steel, it seemed heavy for its size. This was answered with the polymer-framed, P-series guns. Whether the polymer-framed P9 and P40 will last as long as the rugged little K9 or K40, or their even smaller MK (Micro Kahr) siblings, is not yet known. NYPD has approved the K9 as an off-duty weapon for their officers, and Kahrs sell quite well in the armed citizen sector.

The Kahr's controls are so close together, given the small size of the pistol, that a big man's fingers can get in the way a little. By the same token, the gun tends to be an excellent fit in petite female hands.

Improving on the Kahr is gilding the lily, but a few gunsmiths can actually make it even better. One such is Al Greco at Al's Custom, 1701 Conway Wallrose Rd., PO Box 205, Freedom, PA 15042.

Kel-Tec

In the early 90s, noted gun designer George Kehlgren pulled off a coup: the Kel-Tec P-11. With heavy use of polymer and a simple but heavy double-action-only, hammer-fired design, he was able to create a pocket-size 9mm that could retail for $300. At 14-1/2 ounces it was the weight, and also roughly the overall size, of an Airweight snubby revolver, but instead of five .38 Specials it held 10 9mm cartridges. One California law enforcement agency hammered more than 10,000 rounds of Winchester 115-grain +P+ through it with very few malfunctions and no breakage during testing.

The magazine is a shortened version of the S&W 59 series. This means that hundreds of thousands of pre-ban, "grandfathered" 14- and 15-round S&W 9mm magazines exist to feed it. This is handy for spare ammo carry and for home defense use where concealment is irrelevant.

Kel-Tec has made the same gun in .40, but not enough are in circulation for the author to have a feel of how they work. Numerous Kel-Tec P-11s have been through our classes, and the only problem with them is that the heavy trigger pull becomes fatiguing during long days of shooting. However, any competent pistolsmith can give you a better pull for only a small portion of the money you save buying a P-11. Early problems with misfires in the first production runs were quickly squared away.

Perhaps Kehlgren's most fascinating design is his tiny P-32, which will be discussed two chapters subsequent.

ParaOrdnance

When the sharp Canadians who popularized the high-capacity 1911 brought out their double-action-only model,

they called in the LDA. The shooting public automatically assumed it stood for Light Double-Action, even though ParaOrdnance never called in that per se. They didn't have to. The assumption was correct. The pull stroke feels so light that your first thought is, "Will this thing even go off?"

It will. There were some minor problems with the very first LDAs, but the company got them squared away in a hurry. The ones we've seen since, in all sizes, have worked great. Factory throated with ramped barrels and fully supported chambers, they have the slimness and quick safety manipulation of the standard 1911, and in the single-stack models take the same magazines. This .45 is an excellent choice for the 1911 devotee who thinks it's time to go to something in a double-action.

Ruger

Ruger's P-series of combat auto pistols, scheduled to debut in 1985, did not hit the marketplace until 1988. Bill Ruger had shown me the blueprints and rough castings of his original design, an affordable 9mm auto, in the early 1980s and had sworn me to secrecy. Early tests showed some jamming problems with some departments, though the ones we tested were perfectly reliable, but accuracy was sloppy with 4-inch to 5-inch groups being common at 25 yards. The P85 was not a success.

Stung by this, one of the few failures in the history of his company, Bill Ruger and his engineers set to work with a vengeance to correct the problems. The P85 Mark II and later the P89 had total reliability and better accuracy. There would be excellent medium- to service-size .40s and more compact 9mms to come. For my money, though, the triumph of the P-series was the P90 in .45 ACP.

Designed at a time when it looked as if the 10mm would be the best-selling law enforcement round, the P90 was engineered to take a lifetime supply of that powerful ammo. Ironically, it was never chambered for that cartridge commercially, but in .45 the gun was "over-engineered," meaning it could take unlimited amounts of hot +P ammo with impunity. Moreover, thanks to some input from Irv Stone at BarSto, the P90 was the most accurate duty auto Ruger ever produced. One and a half inches for five shots at 25 yards is typical, and with the best ammo, I've seen these guns produce groups under an inch at that distance. There is

Accuracy is a hallmark of the Ruger .45. The author's department-issue P90 has just scored 597 out of 600 points on a PPC course.

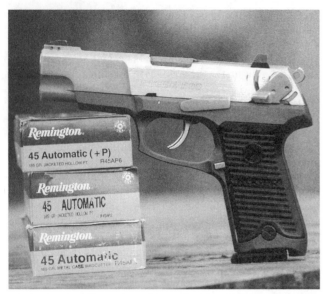

Unlike most 1911s, the "new wave" Ruger P90 feeds reliably with everything from light target loads (bottom) through standard .45 ACP (center) to the hottest +P with 10mm auto power level (top).

Adopted and proven by Huntington Beach (CA) PD, the SIG P220 popularized the double-action .45 auto among America's police and armed citizenry. This is the latest version, all stainless, with 9-round total capacity.

no more accurate "modern style" .45 auto, though the Glock, SIG, and HK USP may equal, but not exceed, the Ruger in this respect.

The P90 is also extraordinarily reliable. In testing for the 1993 adoption of a duty auto, my department found that the Ruger P90 outperformed two more famous big-name double-action .45s, and adopted the P90. It has been in service ever since and has worked fine. Gun expert Clay Harvey tracked .45 autos of all brands used intensively for rental at shooting ranges, and found the Ruger undisputedly held the top spot in terms of reliability. In the latter half of the 1990s, Ruger introduced the P95 9mm and P97 .45 with polymer frames. These allowed production economy that made these guns super-good buys at retail, and both had superb state of the art ergonomics and fit to the hand.

San Diego PD bought large numbers of Ruger 9mm autos and reported excellent results. Ditto the Wisconsin State Patrol, which has issued Ruger 9mm autos exclusively for many years.

SIG-Sauer

Originally imported to the U.S. long ago as the Browning BDA, the SIG P220 .45 was adopted by the Huntington Beach, CA PD. Numerous other agencies followed after learning of HBPD's excellent experience with the gun. And, after decades of ignoring their home-grown 1911 pistol, numerous police departments looked at swapping .38 revolvers for .45 autos. A trend was emerging. When the P226 16-shot 9mm didn't make it out of the finals for the military contract, the police community welcomed the pistol with open arms.

The SIG fits most hands well, and soon there was a short-reach trigger available for those with smaller fingers. The trigger action was deliciously smooth, and the SIG was easy to shoot well. Straight-line feed meant that it fed hollow-points from the beginning. Texas and Arizona troopers went from revolvers to SIGs early, and though both have changed calibers since, neither has changed brand. One of the first

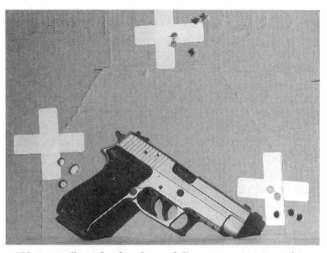

"New wave" combat handguns deliver accuracy users of some of the classics could only dream about. Here are three five-shot groups at 25 yards with different .45 ACP rounds from SIG P220 stainless double-action.

auto pistols approved for wear by rank and file agents, the SIG has been a popular FBI gun ever since. It has long been the weapon of Secret Service and Air Marshals. The troopers of Connecticut, Delaware, Massachusetts, Michigan, Vermont, and Virginia have joined Texas and Aarizona troopers in adopting the SIG. This writer has carried the P226 and P220 on patrol for many a shift and always felt totally confident in the weapons.

With the early P226 and P220, the springs on the side-mounted magazine release tended to be too light, resulting in an occasional unintended drop of a magazine. This was fixed some time ago. One runs across the occasional cracked frame, but SIG is good about fixing them, and the guns are so well designed they keep running even if the frame is cracked. The most annoying problem is a tendency for the grip screws to work loose.

SIGs tend to be very accurate pistols. I've seen more than one P220 group five shots inside an inch at 25 yards with Federal Match 185-grain .45 JHP, and the P226 will go around 1-1/2 inches with Federal 9BP or Winchester's

The double-action-only version of SIG P226 (note absence of de-cocking lever) is in wide use by Chicago PD, NYPD, and numerous other agencies.

John Hall, right, then head of the Firearms Training Unit of FBI, shows the author the Bureau's new S&W Model 1076 10mm in Hall's office at the FBI Academy, Quantico. The year is 1990. Photo courtesy Federal Bureau of Investigation.

OSM (Olin Super Match) 147-grain subsonic. The side-mounted decocking lever is easy to manipulate, and the SIG-Sauer design is more southpaw-friendly than a lot of shooters realize. Your experience, if you buy a SIG, is unlikely to be sour.

Smith & Wesson

The company that introduced the American-made "double-action automatic" took a while to get it right. There were a lot of feed failures and breakages in early Model 39, 39-2, and 59 pistols. Moreover, those guns were not drop-safe unless the thumb safety was engaged. Illinois State Police made them work by having their Ordnance Unit throat the feed ramp areas of all 1,700 or so pistols in inventory.

The second generation was drop-safe, and designed to feed hollow-points. These were characterized by three-digit model numbers without hyphens: the 9mm Model 459, for example, the Model 469 compact 9mm that the company called the "Mini-Gun," and the first of the long-awaited S&W .45 autos, the Model 645.

Ergonomics, however, still weren't great. The trigger pull suffered by comparison to the SIG, and the grips felt boxy and square. The introduction in 1988 of the third-generation guns with four-digit model numbers (5906, 4506, etc.) cured those problems. The only remaining source of irritation on S&W's "conventional style" defense autos is the occasional badly placed sharp edge.

From CHP to the Alaska Highway Patrol, S&W's 12-shot .40 caliber Model 4006 is the choice. S&W .40s are also worn by the troopers of Iowa, Michigan and Mississippi, while Idaho has the double-action only S&W .45 and Kentucky State Police issue the 10mm S&W Model 1076. A number of S&W autos are found in the holsters of FBI agents and Chicago and New York coppers, and S&W 9mm and .45 pistols are the only approved brand in addition to the Beretta for LAPD officers. The Royal Canadian Mounted Police use the S&W 9mm auto exclusively, in DAO models.

In concealed carry, two S&W autos stand out above all others. One is the accurate, super-compact, utterly reliable Model 3913 9mm. Endorsed by every leading female firearms instructor from Lyn Bates to Gila Hayes to Paxton Quigley, the 3913 works well in small hands and its safety features, like those of its big brother, make it ideal for those at risk of disarming attempts. Not only does the standard 3913 have a slide-mounted manual safety, but like the Browning Hi-Power and its own traditional siblings, it has a magazine-disconnector safety. This means that if someone is getting the gun away from you, you can press the release button and drop the magazine; this will render the cartridge in the chamber "unshootable" unless pressure was consistently applied to the trigger from before the magazine was dropped. This feature has saved a number of police officers in struggles over service pistols. It makes sense to security-minded private citizens, too.

The other standout, a genuine "best buy" in the compact .45 auto class, is the Model 457. Compact and light in weight, this 8-shot .45 auto has controllable recoil, delivers every shot into about 2.5 inches at 25 yards, and is a stone bargain because it has S&W's economy-grade flat gray finish. The action is as smooth as that of its pricier big brothers. A whole run of these were made in DAO for the Chicago cops, and they were snapped up immediately. Cops know bargains.

Taurus

In the last two decades of the 20th Century, the Brazilian gunmaker Forjas Taurus doggedly rose from an also-ran maker of cheap guns to establish a well-earned reputation in the upper tiers of reliability and quality. Much of the credit belongs to their PT series of auto pistols. Originally these were simply licensed copies of the early model Beretta 9mm. Over the years, Taurus brought in some design features of their own, notably a frame-mounted combination safety catch and de-cocking lever similar to the one that would later be employed on the HK USP.

We see a lot of Taurus pistols at Lethal Force Institute. The PT-92 through PT-100 models in 9mm and .40 S&W come in, shoot several hundred rounds, and leave without a malfunction or a breakage. Accuracy is comparable to the Beretta, but cost is hundreds of dollars less. Finish may not be quite so nice, nor double-action pull quite so smooth, but these guns are definitely good values. Some find the frame-mounted safety of the Taurus easier and faster to use than the slide mounted lever of the modern Beretta, particularly shooters who come to the double-action gun after long experience with Colt/Browning pattern single-action autos whose thumb safeties are mounted at the same point on the frame.

Taurus has also introduced a high-tech polymer series called the Millennium, aimed at the concealed carry market.

This gun has not yet established the excellent and enviable reputation for reliability that the Taurus PT series has earned.

There are many other double-action autos on the market. These listed above, however, constitute the great majority of what American armed citizens carry, and almost the totality of what American police carry. These were the guns that shaped the double-action auto cornerstone of the new combat handgun paradigm.

Super-Light Revolvers

Combat handguns with lightweight aluminum frames have been with us for more than half a century. Smith & Wesson's Airweights immediately followed the introduction, circa 1950, of the Colt Cobra and lightweight Commander. The aluminum frame became standard a few years later on S&W's 9mm. The 1970s would see Beretta and SIG follow S&W's lead with aluminum-framed duty autos, and of course, Glock popularized the polymer frame in the 1980s.

Great leaps were made in the latter 1990s, however, as Smith & Wesson introduced Titanium and then, at the turn of the century, Scandium to create a generation of light and strong revolvers unseen until this time. Taurus followed immediately with their Ultra-Lite and Total Titanium series. Today, we have medium-sized revolvers in easy-to-carry weights that fire .38 Special, .357 Magnum, .44 Special, .45 Colt, and even the mighty .41 Magnum.

For each such gun that finds its way into the field, there are several small-frame "super-lights" that are being carried in .22 Long Rifle, .32 Magnum, .38 Special, and even .357 Mag. The majority of these are .38s.

The reason the little super-lights are so much more popular than the big ones doesn't have much to do with the fact that they've been around just a little bit longer. It's a convenience thing. There is a huge market among civilians with CCWs and cops already overburdened with equipment. People want small, powerful handguns that don't drag and sag when worn on the body. Let's examine some of the weight standards we're talking about.

Smith & Wesson's Centennial "hammerless" revolver is a case in point. I own them in all four of the different weight configurations. It's interesting to see how they "weigh in," in more ways than one.

Model 640 all-steel

This is one of the first of the re-issued Centennials, produced circa 1990 with the frame stamped +P+. I've always carried mine with the 158-grain +P FBI loads. It shoots exactly where the sight picture looks. It is very accurate, and head-shots at 25 yards are guaranteed if I do my part. Recoil with the +P is stiff; not fun, but not hard to handle either. Shooting a 50-round qualification course with it is no problem. It weighs 19.5 ounces unloaded.

Model 442 Airweight aluminum-frame

As with the 640, this gun's barrel and cylinder are machined entirely from solid ordnance steel. This gun shoots where it is aimed. It is reasonably accurate. A perfect score on the 50-round "qual" course may not be fun with the now distinctly sharper recoil, but it is not my idea of torture, either. A perfect score on the qualification isn't that much harder to achieve. The more visible sight configuration on the newest Airweights helps here. Weight is 15.8 ounces unloaded.

A seven-shot L-frame snubby is a good "envelope" for the ultra-light .357 concept.

A recoil-absorption glove is a most useful accessory when shooting the lightest, smallest-frame revolvers!

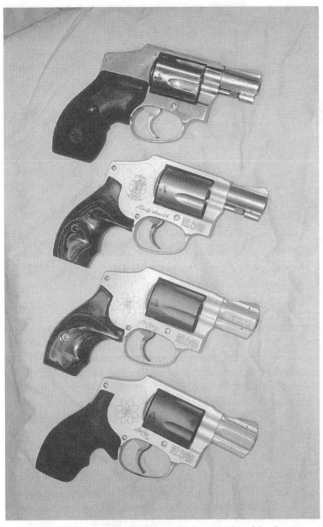

Here are the four S&W Centennials discussed in this chapter. From top: all-steel, Airweight, AirLite Ti, and AirLite Sc.

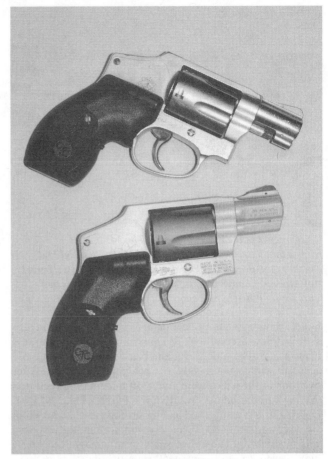

Top, a factory brushed nickel Model 442 Airweight, and below, an AirLite Ti. Both have Crimson Trace LaserGrips. The lower gun is one third lighter, but feels twice as vicious in recoil. The author prefers the Airweight for his own needs.

Model 342 AirLite Ti

This gun's barrel is a thin steel liner wrapped inside an aluminum shroud, and its cylinder is made of Titanium. Like most such guns I've seen, it hits way low from where its fixed sights are aimed. I cannot shoot +P lead bullets (the "FBI Load") in it because the recoil is so violent it pulls them loose. Jacketed +P is the preferred load. The one qualification I shot with this was with jacketed CCI 158-grain +P. Recoil was so vicious I was glad I had a shooting glove in the car. When it was over, I was down two points. Rather than try again for a perfect score, I took what I had. It was hurting to shoot the thing. This gun is not as accurate as the all-steel or Airweight, putting most .38 Special loads in 3-inch to 7-inch groups at 25 yards. Weight, unloaded, is 11.3 ounces.

Model 340 Sc Scandium

Chambered for .357 Magnum, this gun manages not to tear up the FBI load in the gun's chambers, but doesn't shoot it worth a damn for accuracy. Admittedly, this isn't the most accurate .38 Special cartridge made, but the load gives me about 5 inches at 25 yards in my Airweight, versus 15 inches of what I can only call spray out of this gun, with

The little notch at the tip of ramped front sight is an improvement on current S&W J-frame snubbies with all-steel barrels. This is the LadySmith Airweight.

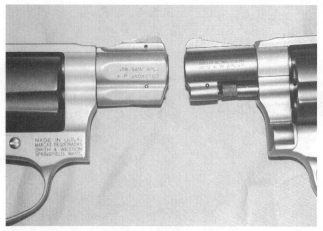

Accuracy is in the barrel assembly. The 342 AirLite Ti, left, has a thin barrel within a shroud, and a too-high sight that makes shots print low. The conventional one-piece steel barrel of Airweight LadySmith, right, delivers better groups and proper sight height puts shots "on the money."

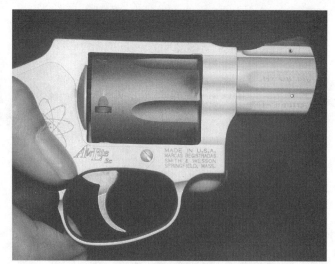

A warning on the barrel shroud of AirLite Sc: it reads, 357 S&W MAG/NO LESS THAN 120 GR BULLET.

bullets showing signs of beginning to keyhole. This gun also shot way low. Recoil with Magnum loads was nothing less than savage. The little Scandium beast was somewhat more accurate with other rounds, but not impressively so. After five rounds, the hands were giving off that tingling sensation that says to the brain, "WARNING! POTENTIAL NERVE DAMAGE." When passed among several people who shoot .44 Magnum and .480 Ruger revolvers for fun, the response was invariably, "Those five shots were enough, thanks." I didn't even try to shoot a 50-shot qualification with it. Unloaded weight is 12.0 ounces.

The thin steel barrel sleeves of the Ti and Sc guns just don't seem to deliver the accuracy of the all-steel barrels of the Airweight and all steel models. All four guns are DAO, so it wasn't the trigger. The same relatively deteriorating accuracy was seen in the super-lights with mild .38 wadcutter ammo and big Pachmayr grips, so it wasn't the recoil. To what degree this is important to you is a decision only you can make.

Now, let's put all that in perspective. In the 1950s when all this ultra-light gun stuff started, Jeff Cooper defined the genre as meant to be "carried much and shot seldom." Alas, the days when we can do that are over, at least in law enforcement. Any gun we carry on the job is a gun we are required to qualify with repeatedly. As I look at my 340 Sc and 342 AirLite Ti, it occurs to me that if I'm deliberately going to do something that hurts like hell, I should go to Mistress Fifi's House of Pain and at least get an orgasm out of the deal.

This is why, for my own small backup revolver needs, I tend toward either the Model 442 or the Ruger SP-101. While the latter gun is even heavier than the Model 640, it fires the .357 Magnum round with very controllable recoil. A qualification with the SP-101 using full power 125-grain Magnum ammo could be called "exhilarating." The same qualification with the same ammo in the baby Scandium .357 qualifies absolutely as torture, at least in my hands.

Different people have different abilities and needs. My fellow gunwriter Wiley Clapp admits that the 342 Sc kicks like hell, but it's his favorite pocket gun nonetheless, even when stoked with Elmer Keith Memorial Magnum ammo. As you look at our differing preferences, note two things.

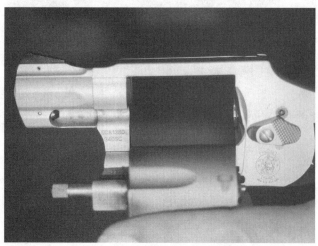

The Model 340 Sc 12-ounce "baby Magnum" was among the first S&Ws to receive integral lock treatment; note keyway above cylinder latch.

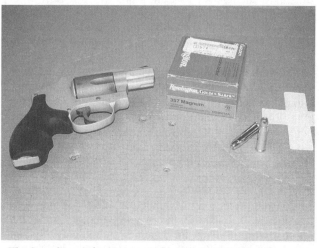

The Scandium J-frame gave 100 percent reliability with Golden Saber medium-velocity .357 Magnum, but uninspiring accuracy.

The grimace on the face of this shooter after firing his first full Magnum round from the Scandium J-frame says it all.

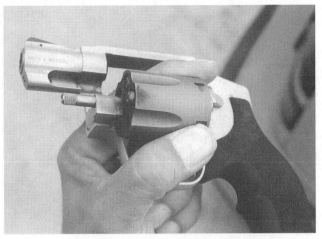

Here's what happens when you use full-power lead bullets in a Ti or Sc S&W. Inertia from the violent recoil pulled the bullet nose of the 158-grain Magnum forward, "prairie-dogging" out of the chamber and preventing rotation.

The Model 340 Sc jammed after the third shot. Note how the bullets of Remington 158-grain SWC .357 cartridges have pulled forward from recoil inertia. At right is a properly sized round from same box for comparison.

First, Wiley is a big, strong guy. I, on the other hand, resemble the "before" picture in the Charles Atlas ads. Second, Wiley is retired from law enforcement and no longer required to qualify at regular intervals with backup guns and their carry ammo. Those repeated qualifications are something I'm still stuck with.

For me, the balance of the super-light versus the Airweight comes out in favor of the Airweight for two reasons. At least in .38 Special, I can use my favorite load, that +P lead hollow-point that would pull loose in the chambers of the lighter guns. Moreover, in my career as an instructor I've seen a whole lot of people conditioned to flinch and jerk their shots because their gun hurt their hand when it went off. I don't want that situation to develop with me especially when I'm into the last layer of my safety net, the backup gun in my pocket. That's why, since I have to shoot a lot with any gun I carry, I want to carry a gun I'm comfortable shooting a lot.

We have more choices than ever, choices that fit some of us better than others. That's a good thing.

There are a great many people who can benefit from the super-light small-frame revolvers. Before you choose, check out the Taurus line. Some are equipped with integral recoil compensators that make them distinctly easier to shoot than a Smith & Wesson of equivalent weight with the same ammo. In fact, the comps take enough oomph out of the kick that the lead bullet +P rounds *don't* start to disassemble themselves in the chambers of Taurus guns so outfitted.

Another option is caliber change. My colleague Charlie Petty recommends the .32 Magnum in these guns. The recoil is much more controllable and the power level will still be more debilitating to an opponent than a mouse-gun. And, speaking of mouse-guns, a considerable number of the AirLite Ti revolvers have been sold as the Model 317, an eight-shot .22 that weighs only 9.9 ounces unloaded.

Let's think about that last concept. No, I'm not *recommending* a .22 for self-defense. But if the person is only going to carry a 10-ounce .25 auto anyway, they're far better served with a top quality eight-shot, 10-ounce .22 revolver. The Model 317 will go off every time you pull the trigger, which is more than you can say for most .25 autos. Unlike most small auto pistols in .22 Long Rifle, this revolver will work 100 percent with the hot, hypervelocity .22 rimfire ammo typified by CCI's Stinger, the cartridge that began that concept long ago. Perhaps because the .22 doesn't generate enough heat to affect the thin steel barrel sleeve, the AirLite .22 will generally group better than the .38 and .357 versions. It will outshoot most any .25 auto going.

More Wattage for the Lite

The super-light revolver comes into a different perspective when you look at the larger models. In the Taurus line, I've found all the Ultra-Lites and Total Titanium models I've fired to be good shooters. The larger frame models come with the company's unique Ribber grips, for which I give great thanks. They soak up recoil better than anything S&W currently offers. Add to that the option of the integral recoil compensator, and you have a much more shootable gun.

Alas, as with the Smiths, all is not perfect with these guns, either. I've run across several Taurus revolvers of this

The finger points to where sights were aimed at 25 yards. The 340 Sc hit far below that, with a poor group.

This federal agent experiences the recoil of a .357 Mag round in S&W 340 Sc.

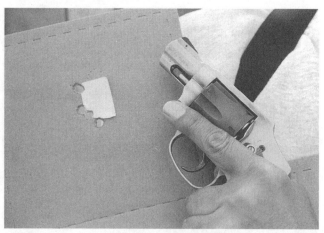

At 7 yards, the J-frame Scandium .357 gave this acceptable head-shot group.

S&W has also sold a number of their Model 396 revolvers, hump-backed L-frames that hold five rounds of .44 Special. The shape of the grip-frame forces you to have your hand low on the gun, and this puts the bore at such a high axis that the gun has a nasty upward muzzle whip. Personally, I can't warm up to this gun. Accuracy is mediocre, in a world where even short-barreled Smith & Wesson .44 Specials have historically shot with noble precision. I tested one next to a Glock 27 on one occasion. The auto pistol was smaller, roughly the same weight, and held 10 rounds compared to the wheelgun's five, in roughly the same power range. The Glock shot tighter groups faster and was actually easier to conceal.

All these guns have a place. The light .357s and the little Taurus .41 make good sense when you're in dangerous animal country and want something very powerful for up-close-and-personal defense, but want to keep the backpack as light as you can.

The big contribution of the super-lights to combat handgunnery is found, nonetheless, in the smallest ones. Easier to conceal on an ankle or snake out of a pocket than a square-backed auto pistol, easy to load and unload and utterly reliable, these little revolvers make up for their

genre whose cylinders were simply too tight and were rubbing against the forcing cone of the barrel, mucking up the trigger pull and binding the action. A quick trip back to the plant to widen the barrel cylinder gap fixes this, however. I've also seen several that didn't shoot to point of aim.

Groups, however, were consistently good. I recall one snubby .41 Magnum Taurus that put five shots into 2-5/16 inches at 25 yards. The ammo was PMC 41A, a full power 170-grain .41 Magnum hollow-point. If the late, great Elmer Keith, the father of the .44 Magnum and co-parent of the .41 Mag, still walked among us, I suspect this little Taurus is what he'd carry for backup.

Both S&W and Taurus have produced L-frame .357 Magnum super-lights. They weigh in the range of 18 ounces, which is about the heft of the old six-shot K-frame Model 12 Airweight .38 snubby. But instead of six .38s, these sleek shooters give you seven rounds of .357 Magnum. Recoil can be snappy, but nothing you can't handle. Use the Ribber grips on the Taurus, and get a pair of K-frame round-butt Pachmayr Decelerator Compac grips for the S&W to take the sting out. These are comfortable holster guns and conceal well under a light jacket, or in a good inside-the-waistband holster under a "tails-out" shirt.

Here is the Taurus CIA (Carry It Anywhere), that firm's answer to the S&W Centennial.

Trainer Michael de Bethancourt shows the aggressive stance required to control "baby Magnums" such as this 340 Sc.

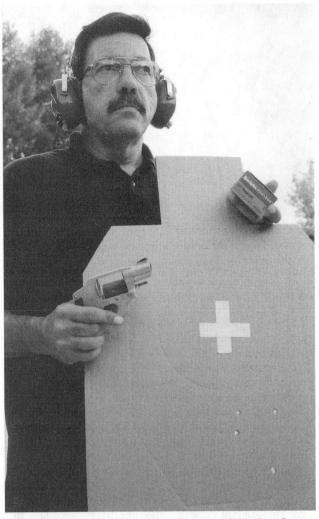

The five gut-shots were aimed at the center of the chest from 25 yards. Ammo was medium-velocity Remington Magnum fired from the 340 Sc. The author is about as pleased as he looks.

vicious recoil with their reassuring presence: being so easy to carry and to access, they're always *there*.

When Bert DuVernay was director of Smith & Wesson Academy, he made the very good point that while revolvers were indeed becoming a thing of the past as mainstream police service weapons, the small-framed revolver with a 2-inch barrel seemed assured a spot in the law enforcement armory as a backup and off-duty weapon. He seems to have called it right.

In states where "shall-issue" concealed carry has only recently been instituted, armed citizens are learning all over again how handy the "snub-nose .38" is as a personal protection sidearm. Many of the permits are going to law-abiding civilians who use these as their primary carry guns. For many of them, the option of the super-light models makes carrying a gun easier. For some, the super-light guns make carrying a gun *possible*. For that reason alone, I am grateful that these good guns exist.

Micro Handguns

First, let's define our terms. How small is small? Smith & Wesson dubbed their 13-shot 9mm pistols of the 1980s, the Model 469 (blue) and 669 (stainless), "Mini-Guns," but they were substantial enough that a number of cops wound up wearing them as uniform holster weapons. Glock's smallest models have been known as the "mini-Glocks" and the "baby Glocks." Kahr Arms dubbed their smallest series with an MK prefix, for "Micro Kahr."

How small is mini, baby, or micro? We can start smaller than that in the world of the combat handgun.

For many years, the tiny .25 auto was considered the quintessential "ladies' gun" and the "gentlemen's vest pocket pistol." There has been the occasional save of a good person with one of these guns because they simply had a gun, and might not have had anything bigger when the attack came. However, we'll never know how many people have been killed or crippled by attackers who

weren't stopped in time by the feeble bite of these tiny sub-caliber guns. As the streetwise martial artist Bill Aguiar put it, "A .25 auto is something you carry when you're not carrying a gun."

Sometimes a .25 is all you can handle. A psycho was beating a single mom in California to death when her little boy, pre-school age, grabbed her Raven .25 auto and screamed, "Get away from my mommy!" When the man did not, the child carefully shot him in the head, killing him instantly and saving his mother's life. I doubt he'll grow up troubled by the act. In Washington, an elderly man with an invalid wife fended off the attackers with the only weapon available, his wife's little .25 auto. As the attackers broke down the door and came at him, he fired once and the men fled. One died a few steps from the back door from a tiny bullet wound in the carotid artery. The other was captured within a few blocks. The grand jury almost instantly exoner-

Comparable in size are the Colt Pony Pocketlite .380 (left), Beretta Tomcat .32 (center) and Seecamp LWS –32, (right). Author picks the .380 for deep concealment.

Tomcat with tomcat, Beretta on left and Scottish Fold on right. Some have job descriptions more suitable for "mouse-guns" than others...

ated the old gentleman, and probably considered chipping in to buy him a bigger gun.

Since the 1970s we've had tiny, single-action, spur-trigger revolvers that harken back to S&W's No. 1 revolver of Civil War vintage, only smaller. They range in caliber from .22 Short through .22 Long Rifle to .22 Magnum. These guns are so tiny they are awkward to manipulate. A fellow on the range recently handed me one to fire. I pointed it downrange too casually, and when I triggered a shot, the gun jumped right out of my hand. I had only been holding it with part of one finger. Embarrassing? Yes, but not nearly so embarrassing as if it had happened in a fight.

Let me be the first to say that there are people who owe their lives to these little guns. In Los Angeles, a woman carrying one was savagely attacked. She pressed the muzzle into her assailant's chest, pulled the trigger, got him just right, and killed him where he stood. The slaying was ruled justifiable. In the south, a police officer was disarmed of his .41 Magnum revolver. The resolute lawman drew his mini-revolver from his pocket and laid into the attacker, who decided that rather than be shot with *anything,* he would give the revolver back. In South Africa, a gang of armed thugs set upon a man outside his suburban house. Rather than let them get in to attack his family, he drew his miniature single-action .22 revolver and opened fire on them. It was rather like sending a Chihuahua to attack a wolf pack,

Both at 14.5 ounces, S&W Airweight .38 Special at left is only slightly larger than Beretta Tomcat .32, right. Author chooses the .38 hands down.

but he pulled it off. He managed to wound one or two of them. Deciding that being shot even with tiny bullets was not nearly as much fun for them as terrorizing helpless people, the attackers fled.

Yes, there are people who have used tiny guns with tiny bullets successfully for self-defense. There are also people who have jumped out of airplanes with non-functional parachutes and survived. It is respectfully submitted that neither is a promising model for the rest of us to follow.

Next up on the handgun ballistics food chain is the humble .32 ACP cartridge. There is no credible authority who will recommend this gun as a primary weapon, but everyone in the business admits that it's a quantum leap beyond .22 or .25 caliber. Evan Marshall's research into actual shootings indicates a significant number of one-shot stops with this cartridge. However, a review of the cases synopsized in his books shows a disproportionate number of these were either gun-against-knife or disparity of force cases. Disparity of force is the legal term for when one or more unarmed men attack someone with such force that likelihood of death or great bodily harm becomes imminent. The attacker's greater size, strength, skill, or force of numbers is treated as the equivalent of a deadly weapon that warrants the use of a genuine deadly weapon in lawful self-defense.

The Winchester Silvertip, the CCI Gold Dot, and the Federal Hydra-Shok are hollow-point .32 rounds developed in hopes of getting the .32 caliber up off its knees. They get all the power out of the round that is probably possible. The problem is, there isn't that much there to start with. We've tested these in the slaughterhouse on smaller hogs and goats. The bullets usually deform. Sometimes they expand and sometimes they don't and sometimes the hollow cavity just turns into a little fish-mouth shape. However, unlike some .380 rounds, they don't seem prone to ricochet. If they don't get the caliber up off its knees, they at least get it up off its belly and onto its knees, and that's *something.*

Jeff Cooper once said that people buy .45s for the powerful cartridge, and buy 9mms because they like the design features of the guns. It follows that people buy tiny guns so they can have some sort of firearm without being inconvenienced by a significant weight in the pocket or by wearing a concealing garment.

Relative sizes, different power levels. Clockwise from noon, S&W Model 3913 9mm, Kahr K9 9mm, S&W Sigma .380, S&W M/640 .38 Special. In the center is Walther PPK .380.

The NAA Guardian .380, center, is barely larger than FN .25 auto, above, or Beretta Jetfire .25 ACP, below. The .380 would be the definite choice here; the Guardian is among the smallest available.

The brilliance of the Seecamp design, the pistol that re-popularized the .32 auto in our time, was that Louis Seecamp was able to conceive a pistol the size and shape of a Czech .25 auto that would fire the larger cartridge. The Seecamp is all the more brilliant in that it *works*. Now, this is the gun of Jeff Cooper's nightmares: double-action for *every* shot, no sights, and only a .32. The mission parameter was for a pistol that would be used at arm's length. Famed officer survival instructor and gunfight survivor Terry Campbell used to call these little pistols "nose guns," because the only way you could count on stopping the fight was to screw the muzzle up the attacker's nose and then immediately pull the trigger.

The supply of Seecamp pistols has never caught up with the huge demand in the marketplace. Other companies entered the field with "Seecamp clones": Autauga Arms, and North American Arms with their Guardian pistol. I never did test the former. The latter wasn't quite as reliable as the Seecamp but was easier to hit with because it had at least vestigial gunsights.

Next up was the gun that quickly became the best seller of its *genre*, the Kel-Tec P-32. One of several ingenious designs from the fertile brain of George Kehlgren, the P-32 weighs an incredible *6.6 ounces* unloaded. No bigger than the average .25-auto and almost wafer-thin, it has tiny little sights that you can more or less aim with, and a surprisingly nice double-action-only trigger pull. Polymer construction is what reduces the weight. By contrast, the NAA Guardian 13.5, and the Seecamp, 10.5 ounces. Each of these guns holds six rounds in the magazine, and a seventh in the firing chamber. All are DAO. The Kel-Tec is the lightest, the least expensive, and has the easiest trigger pull.

I have seen the occasional Kel-Tec that malfunctioned, usually when it was dirty or had at least gone a lot of rounds between cleanings. I've also shot some whose owners swore they had never jammed. Kel-Tec takes good care of their customers if they have a problem.

Perspectives

The young lady in Los Angeles who killed the rapist was in a situation where she simply could not afford for it to be known that she was armed. From undercover cops to private citizens with gun permits who work in anti-gun environments, the same holds true for a lot of people. Yeah, I know, I'm the guy who said "Friends don't let friends carry mouse-guns." But for some people it's that or nothing.

Let me tell you about one of my clients. He was a hunter and target shooter who owned some fine rifles and shotguns. The only handgun he owned was a gift from a friend, a Smith & Wesson .22 Kit Gun. He took it on hunting trips. He would while away the slow times plinking at tin cans from the porch of the hunting cabin, and the little .22 also allowed him to quickly dispatch a downed deer without damaging the skull for mounting. The night came when a burglar alarm went off in his home, telling him a flower shop he owned was being broken into for the umpteenth time.

If he had gone intending to kill someone, he would have loaded his .30/06 auto rifle or one of his 12-gauge shotguns. Thinking about protection, he grabbed his only handgun, the little .22, and loaded it on the way to the shop. Given the lateness of past police responses in this community in which the cops were heavily burdened with calls, it was his intent to frighten away the intruders. But when he got to the scene he was attacked. He fired two shots and the attacker fled.

It reinforced both sides of the issue. *If the guy ran, he wasn't incapacitated.* Yes. I know. That's why I don't recommend .22s. *That guy ran a mile before he bled to death!* Yes. I know. That's why I don't recommend .22s. *If that guy had gone into fight mode instead of flight mode he could have still killed your client!* Yes. I know. That's why I don't recommend .22s. *Then why are you talking about this as if his having a .22 was a good thing?* Because the circumstances were such that a .22 was the only gun he would have had with him…and it saved his life. End of story.

Perspectives

It's all well and good to say, "If you don't carry a .45 or a Magnum, you're a wimp." But there is idealism, and there is what Richard Nixon called *realpolitik*. We have to face reality. I'm fortunate enough that my job, the place I live, and my dress code allow me to carry a full-size fighting handgun almost all the time. Not everyone is that fortunate.

There's another argument in this vein that goes one tier up. I know a lot of cops who are proud of how they look in their tailored uniforms, and don't want the unsightly bulge of a big gun for backup. Shall I tell them if they don't carry a chopped and channeled .45, they deserve to have no backup at all?

I know a lot of armed citizens who already realize what a commitment it is to carry a gun all the time, period. If they're going to carry a second gun – a good idea for civilians, too – their wardrobe may not allow the small revolver

The Guardian .380 is a late-arriving "hide-in-your-hand" pistol barely larger than some .25 autos. A definite "new paradigm" combat handgun.

or baby Glock I favor. For them, the backup weapon might be a Kel-Tec .32, or nothing at all.

When you demand all or nothing, history shows us, you're generally likely to end up with nothing. A tiny, small-caliber handgun is not what you'd want to have in your hand if you knew you were going to get into a fight to the death with an armed felon. But it's at least something. And something is better than nothing.

The finger touches the point of aim. A decent group from the Beretta Tomcat .32 went extremely low at only 7 yards.

The Guardian .380, top, is only the tiniest bit larger than the .32 version (below) that preceded it. Nod goes to the .380.

CHAPTER FOUR

A BLUEPRINT FOR LEARNING THE COMBAT HANDGUN

I was reading the deposition of a man who was being sued for shooting a contractor who showed up at his house early. He thought the man was a burglar. When asked why he shot him, he replied he didn't mean to; he intended his shots to warn, he said under oath. Did he aim the gun? No, he just pointed it. Had he been trained with his home defense gun, or even fired it before the day in question? No, he snapped indignantly, it wasn't like hunting where you needed a training course…

That man ended up paying a great deal of money to the man he shot, to that man's attorneys and to his own. Firing guns at human beings is not something you want to be ill prepared for in a moment of crisis. How does that preparation begin?

Some states have made training mandatory before issuance of a concealed carry permit. A few have even put together specific courses that must be taken. Two of the best are found in Arizona and Texas. Neither lasts long enough to give you anything close to all you need, but they give a solid foundation.

There are doubtless people reading this who have been shooting and carrying handguns longer than I, have forgotten more than I know, and could outshoot me on demand. They and I will both, however, be teaching others who are completely new to this discipline, some of whom are going to buy this book for that very reason. Therefore, let's address this progression beginning at new shooter level.

The Basics

Don't leave the gun shop without having a professional show you how the gun works. Loading and unloading, manipulation of safety devices, even field stripping. Make sure you have an owner's manual with it. Once you have it…READ the owner's manual before going any farther.

If you are new to the gun, don't go out shooting by yourself. It's like a new pilot starting solo, or trying to learn to swim all alone. Find someone who knows this stuff.

Focus at first on safety…and keep that focus for as long as you own firearms. We bought a combat handgun to provide safety for ourselves and those we're responsible for. Whether or not we ever have to draw that gun on a dangerous felon, we know that we will spend the rest of our lives with that gun. Putting it on, wearing it, taking it off…loading it, unloading it, checking and cleaning it…sometimes when we're distracted or tired or stressed…*in proximity to the very people we bought the gun to protect.* The price of gun ownership is like the price of liberty: eternal vigilance.

It's always a good idea to start with a basic handgun safety class. The National Rifle Association has tons of instructors all over the country. Check locally – your gunshop will know where you can get training. This is one reason to buy your gun at a dedicated gunshop instead of a Big

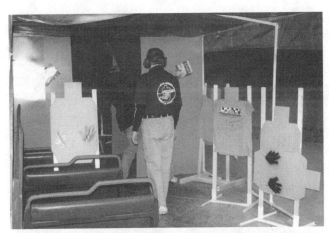

Match sponsors have the wherewithal to set up more complicated scenarios than most of us can on our own. Here a range officer follows a shooter through a complex stage at the S&W Mid-Winter IDPA Championships, 2002.

Police Chief Russ Lary tries his hand with his off-duty compact S&W .45 at the IDPA Mid-Winter National Championships, 2001.

The author awaits approval of the range officer (back to camera, wearing body armor) before ascending the stairs in Jeff Cooper's "Playhouse" simulator at Gunsite.

Box Monster Mart where today's gun counter clerk is yesterday's video section clerk. Another excellent source of information is your local fish and wildlife department, which generally has a list of basic firearms safety instructors as well as hunter safety instructors.

You may not be ready yet to compete, but you're always ready to learn from the best. Find out from the gunshop what local clubs are running IPSC or IDPA matches. Contact those clubs. See about joining. *Ask about safety classes offered by the IPSC and IDPA shooters!* These will focus on important elements like drawing and holstering that might get short shrift at a basic firearms safety class. Find out when they're having matches, and go a few times to watch. Remember to bring ear and eye protection. Watching skilled practitioners handle their handguns gives you excellent early role models.

Be A Joiner

Definitely join a gun club. You'll like the people, you'll enjoy yourself, but more importantly, you'll now be exposed to a whole group of seasoned shooters who have ingrained good safety habits. Never be afraid to ask questions. These folks enjoy sharing a lifestyle they love, and are always ready to help a new shooter get started.

Another good thing about joining a club is that on practice nights, there's usually an opportunity for people to try one another's guns. Finding out that the Mark II Master Blaster Magnum isn't nearly as controllable as the gun magazine said it would be is much more painless at the gun club trying a friend's, than after you've shelled out a thousand bucks for your own. This factor alone can more than make up the cost of your membership and range fees.

Formal Training Begins

I truly wish that shooting schools like the many available today existed when I was in my formative years. It would have saved me a lot of wasted time learning as I went. Unfortunately, the boom in concealed carry permits has drawn out of the woodwork a swarm of get-rich-quick artists who smelled a fast buck, took a few courses, and declared themselves professional instructors. As Jeff Cooper once commented on the matter, "There are a great many people teaching things they haven't learned yet."

Left to right: Cat Ayoob, Peter Dayton, and Mas Ayoob pause between stages at the National Tactical Invitational, 1996. This event has always been a useful training experience.

Shooting under the eye of experienced shooters is a fast track to improved skill. This is an LFI class in progress at Firearms Academy of Seattle.

This shooter puts his 1911 to work from behind a realistic barricade during an IDPA match at the Smith & Wesson Academy.

Local police officers experience role-playing training set up by Lethal Force Institute students, who are playing the bad guys and bystanders in this scenario.

Using a dummy gun, this role-player takes another student hostage in live-action scenario training at LFI.

When you inquire for particulars at a shooting school, request a resume of the person who will be the chief instructor at your course. If he gets indignant and refuses, he's told you all you need to know. Keep looking. Once you get the resume, do what you would do with any other prospective employee's resume, and check it out to make sure he's been where he says he's been, and has done what he says he's done. (You're hiring him to perform a service for you, right? Of course, he's a prospective employee.)

If in the early stages the prospective instructor is patronizing or condescending, move on. One of the truly great officer survival instructors, Col. Robert Lindsey, makes a profound point to his fellow trainers. "We are not God's gift to our students," Lindsey says. "Our students are God's gift to us."

Nationally known schools may be more expensive, but they are generally worth it. If a cadre of instructors has been in business for 15 or 20 years, it tells you that there aren't too many dissatisfied customers. Particularly in the time of the Internet, word gets around. The various gun chat rooms on the 'Net are also a good source of customer feedback. The best, however, is advice from someone you know and can trust who has already been to the school in question.

Once you get there, *be a student*. Soak up all you can, paying particular attention to the explanation of why the instructor recommends that a certain thing be done a certain way. Litmus test: If he says, "We do it that way because it is The Doctrine," add more than a grain of salt to whatever you're being asked to swallow. Try it the instructor's way; you're there to learn what he or she has to teach. You wouldn't throw karate kicks at a judo dojo; don't shoot from the Isosceles stance if the instructor is asking you to shoot from the Weaver.

Don't be afraid to ask for a personal assessment or a little extra help. Any instructor worth his or her title will take it as a compliment that you asked, not as an imposition.

Journeyman Level

You have progressed. You're into this stuff now. You want to get better. *Yes!*

Remember at this stage that revelatory, life-changing experiences tend to come one to a customer. After you've become a reasonably good shot, further improvement will probably be incremental. In your first few schools in a discipline, you're trying to absorb it all and wondering if you're a bad person because you might have missed some small point. As time progresses and you get more courses under your belt, some of what you hear at successive schools will sound familiar. That's OK. It never hurts to reinforce and validate something positive that you've already learned.

You'll be all the more appreciative when you do pick up something new, and all the more insightful when you put that new knowledge to use.

The instructor can't do it all for you. Skill maintenance is the individual practitioner's job. Martial artists and physiologists tell us that it takes 3,000 to 7,000 repetitions to create enough-long term muscle memory that you can perform a complex psycho-motor skill, such as drawing and firing a pistol, in the "automatic pilot" mode that trainers call Unconscious Competence. One intense week a year at the gym, and 51 weeks as a couch potato, won't keep your body in shape. That kind of regimen won't keep your combat handgun skills in shape, either.

By now you should have found at least one gun/holster combination that works well for you. Stay with it for a while. Don't try to buy skill at the gunshop. Buy ammo or reloading components there instead, to better reinforce and enhance the skills you already have.

This is a good time to be thinking about some sort of practical shooting/action shooting/combat shooting competition. Doing well gives us motivation to get better. Being exposed to others who've been to different schools and shoot with different styles will broaden your horizons and give you new ideas you can put to good use. Sometimes even more importantly, this will introduce you to a new cir-

Self-defense training goes beyond shooting. Do you know self-treatment for a gunshot injury if you're alone and wounded? Paramedic and LFI Staff Instructor Bob Smith demonstrates for a class.

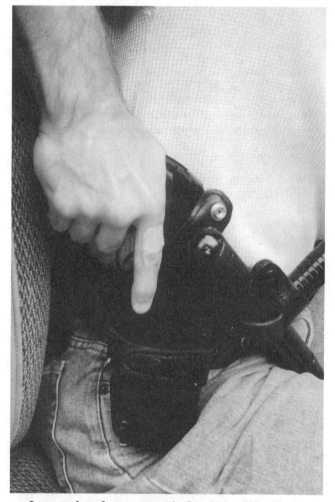

Learn to draw from compromised positions. This officer clears an issue DAO Beretta Model 8040 from a Safariland 070 security holster while seated in vehicle.

Sometimes intense training can hurt. Allan Brummer takes a full power hit of OC pepper foam…

… and proves he can "fight through it," drawing a dummy gun and issuing commands while carrying out tactical movement.

Here the author rinses out his teenage daughter's eyes after she has taken a hit of pepper spray.

cle of friends and acquaintances who have the same self-defense values as you. Even if the thrill of the competition wears off, the pleasure and value of the friendships you make there will stay with you.

Remember as a journeyman that safety still has to come first. You're shooting enough now to be a high profile potential victim of the "familiarity breeds contempt" syndrome. Avoid that at all costs. The carpenter is more skilled with a hammer than the home craftsman, but he can still hit his thumb. The reason is that he uses it more, and is that much more exposed to that danger. So it is with us. Remember…eternal vigilance.

In The Land Of The Experts

When you get really deep into this, and really good at it, improvement comes even more slowly. When Mike Plaxco was the man to beat in combat competition, he told me, "I get slumps just like everybody else. When I do, I change something in my shooting style. It makes me focus again, makes things fresh again, and makes me work at it again." Good point.

We're not going to preach here, but there are a great many people in this country who need to know these things, and not all of them can afford to travel to shooting schools to learn them. There comes a time when giving back is almost a moral obligation, like courtesy on the road. Con-

Can you draw weak handed if your dominant hand is taken out? Here the author clears a Glock 22 from Uncle Mike's duty rig.

A Blueprint For Learning The Combat Handgun • 47

Wearing protective gear and using Code Eagle modifications of S&W revolvers that fire only paint pellets, these students act out a car-jacking scenario.

Ambush waiting! The Beamhit system uses guns modified to non-lethal function and vests to carry the sensors which register only stopping hits.

sider teaching. Helping at a course at your local club, or volunteering to help someone who has once trained you, is a good place to start.

When you teach something, it forces you to see the forest for the trees. I can remember taking classes in things I didn't care about, but needed the course credit for. It was as if my mind was a tape recorder that held the information long enough to play it back on the final exam, and then erased the tape once the chore was done. That wasn't "life learning," and I regret it now. There were times when I took a class just for myself, saw something I liked, kept it, but didn't really get into the details of why I did it that way. If we don't understand why we're doing what we're doing, even if it works for us, we don't truly command the skill. I regret those learning experiences now, too.

Have you learned how to return fire from disadvantaged positions if wounded? Here, LFI-II students go through one of several such drills.

I learned that I didn't really command a body of knowledge until I had been certified to teach it. "Hey, wait a minute, people are going to be asking me why we do it this way, and why we don't use technique X instead? I have to explain that? Hey, Coach, brief me on that one more time…"

Teaching not only ensures that we have it down, it puts the final imprimatur of understanding on our own performance in that discipline, sharpening us like the double-stamping of a coin. Since the inception of ASLET, the American Society of Law Enforcement Trainers, I've been chair of its firearms committee. ASLET's motto is *qui doscet, disket.* Translated loosely from the Latin: "He who teaches, learns." Thousands of my brethren and I have learned the truth of that through ASLET and similar organizations such as IALEFI, the International Association of Law Enforcement Firearms Instructors.

You're not comfortable with public speaking or perhaps some other element of formal teaching? That's fine, but if you look around there will be people in your family, your neighborhood, your workplace or somewhere else in your ambit who are interested in acquiring a defensive handgun or have already done so, and desperately need to know these things. Take those people to the range. Be patient. Be supportive. Give them what you wanted to get when you began in this discipline.

If nothing else, you'll make a good deposit in the karma bank and you won't come back as a dung beetle.

Final Thoughts

Read on the topic. Watch the new generation of combat shooting videos. It's one thing to read about it, and another to actually see masterful speed shooting in action. One thing videos can do that even experience cannot is deliver instant replay in slow motion, showing subtleties of technique frame by frame.

Learn from your mistakes. Losing a match or a having bad day at the gun class doesn't mean you're a bad person

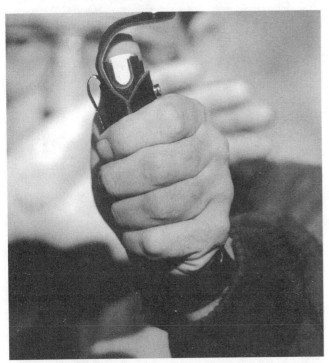

Make sure your self-defense training is not confined to just the gun. OC pepper spray requires training to use to its best advantage.

On qualification day at an LFI-I class, the instructor's target…

and you need therapy. Winning gives you warm fuzzy strokes, and it also gives you positive reinforcement, validating that you're doing it right. But losing is where you learn. Think about it: How many of life's lessons did you learn by messing something up? Sometimes, that's the strongest reinforcement of the learning experience. On days when you win, you can say to yourself, "A day well spent. I'm on the right track." On days when you lose, you can say to yourself, "A day well spent. I've learned a lesson, and I will *not* repeat the mistake I made today." Sometimes, the "instructional days" are a lot more valuable than the "positive reinforcement days."

It has been said that experience is the collected aggregate of our mistakes. But wisdom, said Otto von Bismarck, is learning from the collected aggregate of the mistakes of others. That's why we read and study and reach out beyond our own experiences.

How do you best practice? This way: Stop practicing! This doesn't mean that you don't shoot or drill in your movement patterns or perform repetitions of tactical skills. It means that if before you practiced, now you *train!*

Practice can easily turn into just hosing bullets downrange. Often, you wind up reinforcing bad habits instead of enforcing good ones. Training, on the other hand, is purpose-oriented. Where practice can easily degenerate into "just going through the motions," training sharpens and fine-tunes every motion. If practice was going to be a couple of hundred rounds downrange, training might be as little as 50 rounds, but all fired with purpose. You, the box of ammo, and the electronic timer (one of the best investments you can make in your own skill development) head to the range. Instead of creating 200 pieces of once-fired brass, your goal is 50 draws to the shot. Each will be done in a frame of time that satisfies you and results in a good hit, or you'll analyze the reason why not and correct what's going wrong.

…has become the traditional award for the most-improved shooter. The staff, whose collective vote determines the recipient, signs it. Here John Strayer waits his turn to sign as Steve Denney pens some words of encouragement to the winning student.

Training should give you fallbacks for worst-case scenarios. Here, author drills on weak-hand-only with his Glock 22.

Don't assume that statistics are right, and you'll only be in a gunfight at point-blank range. Here bodyguard Lars Lipke deploys his HK P7M13 at 50 yards, from standing position...

Shoot in competition. It hones the edge. A gun club that's enthusiastic about IDPA or IPSC (see the chapter on Combat Competition) will be able to set up complicated and challenging scenarios that you or I might not have the time or the money to construct. You'll get to watch top shooters in action and pick up subtle lessons from how they handle various tactical problems.

If there's no competition near you, or not as much as you like, shoot with a buddy or a loved one. Personally, I find I put forth my best effort against someone who shoots about the same as I do. When I shoot against world champions, it's exciting, but I know I'm not really going to beat them. When I shoot against someone who's had a lot less opportunity to develop skill, I'm not challenged. Someone who's at the same level seems to bring out the greatest internal effort.

Go ahead and side-bet with each other. That's a good thing, too. It conditions you to the reality that every time you pull that trigger, something rides on the outcome. You'll pay for a bad shot and be rewarded for a good one. Soon, shooting under pressure becomes the norm.

Your partner is not as good a shot as you are? Pick a course of fire and each of you go through it a couple of times and determine an average score. Subtract the one from the other, and give the difference to the lower scoring shooter as a handicap.

Let's say it's a course of fire with 300 points possible. You average 299 and the partner averages 230. Give the partner 69 bonus points as a handicap. Now he or she is challenged: beating you is within striking distance, where before it seemed hopeless. This will encourage the partner to really focus and put forth his or her best effort. Before, you weren't challenged, but now you know that the newer shooter with the faster learning curve only has to get a little better to beat you. You, in turn, are now motivated to shoot a perfect score, the only thing that will keep you from losing the bet.

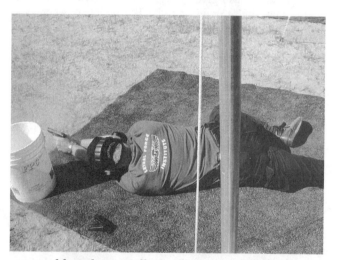

...and from the more effective Chapman Rollover Prone.

At Lethal Force Institute, we have the instructors shoot what we call a pace-setter drill on the last day. Just before the students shoot their final qualification test, the staff will shoot the same course of fire as a demonstration. This does several good things. First, it lets the students see what's expected of them. Second, watching us do it helps them "set their internal clock" which in turn helps them make the times required for each string of fire. Third, it gives them a mental image of what they are supposed to be doing.

Bob Lindsey, the master police officer survival instructor, noted in the 1980s that a number of cops who were losing fights would suddenly see in their mind's eye an image of an instructor performing a technique. They would act out that image, make it work, and prevail. He called it "modeling."

Learn to make tactical movement as thoroughly ingrained as stance and trigger press. Here Justine Ayoob, 15, performs a tactical reload while moving behind cover at the New England Regional IDPA championships.

This is the main reason we do the pace-setter drill. Until then, I had followed the advice I'd been given in firearms instructor school. "Don't shoot in front of the students," I had been told. "If you're as good as you're supposed to be, it will make some of them despair of ever reaching your level. And if you blow it, you lose your credibility."

That had made sense. If a student asked me back then, "When do we get to see *you* shoot," my standard answer was, "When you go to Bianchi Cup or Second Chance. You're not here to see how well I can shoot. You're here to see how well *you* can shoot."

"Simunitions" has ushered in a new dimension in reality-based training. This Glock has been factory modified to fire only the Simunitions paint pellet rounds.

Be able to shoot effectively from non-standard positions. National IDPA champ Ted Yost shows his form with a "cover crouch," which gets him down behind the rear of a car faster than conventional kneeling.

Lindsey's research changed my opinion on that. It was after hearing Bob's presentation on modeling that we started the pace-setter drills at LFI. Since we've been doing it, the scores of the students have gone up, and fewer of the students have had problems getting all their shots into the target before the cease-fire signal.

One thing we added was an incentive. Whatever score I shoot, if the student ties me he or she gets an autographed dollar bill with the inscription, "You tied me at my own game." If the student beats me, it's an autographed $5 bill that says, "You beat me at my own game." It's the cheapest investment I can make in their shooting skill, and it pushes them to do their best. It's natural for a student to want to exceed the instructor…and frankly, accomplishing that is the highest compliment a student can pay to a dedicated teacher.

My favorite award to give out is "most improved shooter." This award is the instructor's target, signed by all the staff. Often, the student who has accelerated "from zero to 50" has accomplished more than the already-skilled student who came to class at 100 miles an hour and was only able to get about 5 miles an hour faster.

In the end, it's up to you. Your skill development will be proportional to how much time you're prepared to spend training yourself, and acquiring training from others. Getting good training is cost-effective, because despite tuition and travel expense, it saves you re-inventing the wheel. Yes, it takes a lot of years to get a Ph.D. in nuclear physics, but it would take you a helluva lot longer to figure out nuclear physics by yourself. Shooting isn't nuclear physics, but you don't need years in the university to learn it either. A few well-chosen weeks, backed up by your own commitment to a training regimen of live fire when you can and dry fire the rest of the time, will be the best investment in skill development you can make.

I do this for a living, as a full-time teacher and part-time cop, part-time writer, and part-time everything else. I'm supposed to have "arrived." But it's never wise to kid oneself. This sort of thing, at its greatest depth, is a life-study. As soon as you think you've "arrived," you stop moving forward. That's why I budget a minimum of a week a year for myself to take training from others. It keeps me sharp, and keeps the mind open. The old saying is true: Minds, like parachutes, work best when they're open.

THE HEART OF THE BEAST:

Mastering Trigger Control

Agreed: What kind of bullet we're firing doesn't matter unless the bullet hits the target.

Agreed: The bullet doesn't have to just hit, it has to hit something vital.

Agreed: The bullet doesn't have to just hit something vital, it has to hit something so immediately vital that the person can no longer continue to attack.

Agreed: We'll have a very short time frame in which to accomplish this.

Agreed: As much as we might rather have a rifle, a shotgun, or a submachinegun to deal with this problem, the tool we're most likely to have with us is a handgun.

If we can agree that all these things are predicates to stopping a deadly fight with a combat handgun, then we are agreed that accuracy is extremely important. It's like high school Logic 101: If A is true and B is true, then AB must be true.

A lot of things will impact our ability to deliver accurate shots rapidly while under stress. Will you use a one-hand or two-hand hold on the gun? Two-hand is more accurate, but one-hand is sometimes more expedient. Will you use Weaver or Isosceles stance? There are times when it can matter, but they are relatively rare. Any basic marksmanship instructor will tell you that once you've brought your gun on target, there is one key element to making the shot fly true: *You must pull the trigger in such a way that the gun is not jerked off target.*

We know that because the bullet flies in a relatively straight path, any deviation of the sight alignment is magnified in direct geometric progression. If your trigger pull jerks the muzzle off target by the tiniest fraction of an inch, the shot may hit in the white of the target, but not the black

of the center scoring area at 25 yards. "Hah," say the clueless. "That's a target shooter talking! Those increments don't matter in a close-range gunfight!"

Ya think? Then, consider this.

You and I start the fight at the distance of only *one yard*, 36 inches torso to torso. You have drawn to shoot from the hip so I can't reach your gun. Let's assume further that your pointing skills are perfect today and your gun is dead center on my torso. You now jerk your trigger, moving the gun muzzle a mere inch to your strong-hand side. *Only one yard away, your shot will miss my main body mass.* It might go through the "love handle" and give me a .45 caliber suction lipectomy, or it might even hit my arm if it's hanging to the side, but it won't do anything to effectively stop me from harming you.

That's why, in real world combat shooting and not just match shooting, trigger control is so important. *The trigger is the heart of the beast! If you don't control the trigger, you don't control even what should have been the most perfectly aligned shot!*

How can we hope to control the trigger under extreme stress? By being trained and conditioned to do it beforehand. Is it easy? No, and that's why we've devoted a whole chapter to the concept.

Understanding The Mission

Too much combat handgun training has been borrowed from the world of target shooting. While some of the concepts survive the translation from range to street, some don't. One that doesn't is the *targeteer's* concept of trigger activation.

Trigger control need not sacrifice speed. Here, Marty Hayes is firing four rounds in a fraction of a second from a prototype Spectre pistol. Note two .45 ACP casings in mid-air above the gun, a third below, and the muzzle flash of the fourth round.

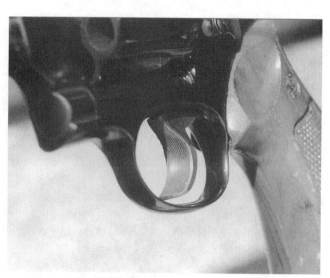

S&W's wide, serrated "target trigger" is the best type for single-action target shooting, but the worst choice for double-action combat shooting.

S&W's "Ranger" trigger has smooth surface so the finger can glide across it during fast double-action work without pulling the muzzle off target.

In the old days, shooters tried to "stage" double-action revolvers, especially Colts like this snub Python. Today's more knowledgeable shooters use a straight-through trigger pull. Note the distal joint contact on the trigger.

We are told that we should contact the trigger with the tip or the pad of the trigger finger. When asked why, we are told that this is the most sensitive portion of the finger and therefore the part most suited to this dextrous task. That makes sense as far as it goes, but let's analyze the target shooter's task versus the defensive shooter's.

In bull's-eye pistol matches, the core event is shot with the .22 caliber. You have, let's say, a High Standard .22 match pistol. It weighs 48 ounces, more if you have it scoped, and it has a crisp 2-pound trigger pull that needs to move only a hair's breadth. The gun is loaded with standard velocity (read: low velocity) .22 Long Rifle, which kicks with about as much force as a mouse burp. In this course of shooting events, "rapid fire" is defined as five shots in 10 seconds. All well and good.

But let's put ourselves somewhere else, perhaps a darkened parking lot. Our 260-pound assailant, Mongo, is coming at us with a tire iron. We are armed with a baby Glock, the G33 model that weighs only about 19 ounces. Its New York trigger gives us a pull weight of almost eight pounds over 3/8 of an inch. The power of its .357 SIG cartridge is that of some .357 Magnum revolver rounds, generating significant recoil. For us, "rapid-fire" has just become five rounds in *one* second, before Mongo reaches us with the tire iron.

Let's see, we have a few things to think about: a 3-pound gun with a 2-pound trigger, versus a 1-1/4-pound gun with an 8-pound trigger. We have 1/10 of an inch of movement versus 3/8 of an inch. We have almost no recoil versus sharply noticeable and palpable recoil. We have five shots in 10 seconds versus five shots in one second. Have the mission parameters changed for the trigger finger?

Obviously, the answer is yes. We're going to need a stronger finger, a finger with more leverage, to achieve the necessary results.

Placement And Fit

You'll find that you have much more control of a longer, heavier combat trigger pull if you contact the trigger with *the palmar surface of the distal joint* of the index finger. It is at this point that the digit has the most leverage to draw the trigger rearward with the most speed and the least effort.

At LFI, we developed a simple test to allow you to see and feel this for yourself. Open this book and set it down where you can read it with your hands free. Take your nondominant hand, turn its palm away from you, and extend the index finger. Stiffen it up: this finger is going to be a trigger with a heavy pull.

Now, with the index finger of your shooting hand, try to pull that "trigger" back, using the *tip* of your trigger finger. You'll have to use great effort – enough effort to probably distract you from focusing on much else – and when the finger does start to give, it will move in fits and starts.

Now try it again, making contact with the *pad* of your trigger finger. The pad is defined as the center of the digit, where the whorl of the fingerprint would be. You won't feel much difference.

Now, for the third and final portion of the test. With your "finger/trigger" still rigid, place your trigger finger at the same spot. Make contact with the crease where the distal phalange of the finger meets the median phalange, as shown in accompanying photos. Now, just roll the stiffened finger back against its force. Feel a huge difference? This is why the old-time double-action revolver shooters called this portion of the trigger finger the "power crease." It is here that we gain maximum leverage.

Of course, for this to work the gun must fit your hand. In the early 1990s, when gearing up to produce their Sigma pistol, Smith & Wesson paid some six figures for a "human engineering" study of the hands of shooters. It turned out my own hand fit exactly their profile of "average adult male hand." Not surprisingly, I found the Sigma to fit my hand perfectly.

Gaston Glock did much the same. However, he went on the assumption that the shooter of an automatic pistol would be using the pad of the finger. When I grasp the Glock properly in every other respect, my finger comes to the trigger at the pad. To make it land naturally at the distal joint, I need the grip-shape slimmed and re-shaped, as done by Robar (21438 N. 7th Ave, Suite E, Phoenix, AZ 85027) or Dane Burns (700 NW Gilman Blvd, Suite 116, Issaquah, WA 98027). On a K-frame S&W revolver whose rear grip strap has not been covered with grip material, my trigger finger falls into the perfect position. Ditto the dou-

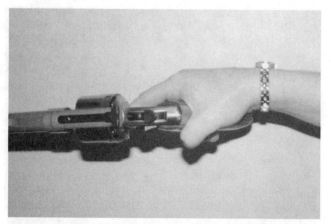

This is the hand of a petite female on a gun that's too big for her, a Model 625 from S&W Performance Center. Note that she has been forced to use the "h-grip," in which the hand and forearm are in the shape of lower case letter h. One can get better trigger reach with this method, but at the expense of weakened recoil control.

Many prefer the short-reach trigger on a 1911, particularly those with small hands or those who use distal joint contact on the trigger as the author does. This is a 10mm Colt Delta Elite customized by Mark Morris.

ble-action-only S&W autos, and ditto also the Browning Hi-Power with standard trigger and the 1911 with a short to medium trigger.

Proper grasp means that the web of the hand is high on the back of the grip-frame, to minimize muzzle jump and stabilize an auto's frame against the recoiling slide. The web should feel as if it is pressing up into the grip tang on the auto, and should be at the very apex of the grip frame of the revolver. The long bones of the forearm should be directly in line with the barrel of the gun. This properly aligns skeleto-muscular support structure not only with the handgun's recoil path, but also with the direction of the trigger pull. The trigger finger, we mustn't forget, is an extension of the arm.

When the gun doesn't fit and the finger can barely reach the trigger, it will tend to pull the whole gun inboard. That is, a right-handed shooter will tend to pull the shot to the left. If the gun is too small for the hand and the finger goes

Although the Glock was designed to be shot using the pad of the trigger finger; the author finds he has better control in extreme rapid fire with his finger deeper into the trigger guard.

into the trigger guard past the distal joint, the angle of the finger's flexion during the pull will tend to yank the shot outboard, i.e., to a right-handed shooter's right.

This is why gun fit is critical. The key dimension of determining the fit of the gun to the hand is "trigger reach." On the gun, it is measured from the center of the backstrap where the web of the hand would sit, to the center of the trigger. On the hand, it is measured from the point of trigger contact (distal joint suggested) to the center of the web of the hand in line with the radius and ulna bones of the forearm.

Avoid if possible the expedient hand position called the "h-grip," intended for adapting a too-small hand to a too-large handgun. In it, the hand is turned so that, with the hand at the side, hand and forearm would resemble a lower case letter "h." This brings the backstrap of the gun to the base joint of the thumb and brings the index finger forward far enough for proper placement on the trigger.

While this can work with a .22 or something else with light loads, it's a matter of robbing Peter to pay Paul. What is gained in getting the trigger forward is lost by a weakened hand grasp on the gun. Recoil now goes directly into the proximal joint of the thumb. Doctors tell me that this is a quick short-cut to developing artificially-induced arthritis in that joint. Such a grip was one of the "remedial" techniques employed by FBI instructors in the late 1970s for small-handed female agent recruits firing +P ammunition. It not only failed to work, it beat up their hands. It was one reason that in the landmark case of *Christine Hansen, et. al. v. FBI* we won reinstatement and compensation for a number of female agents who had been fired because they couldn't qualify with the old-fashioned bad techniques. The same court ordered FBI to "revise and update its obsolete and sexist firearms training."

Distal joint contact works well even for single-action autos. Even when the pull weight is relatively light, "leverage equals power, and power controls the pistol." This placement of the finger eliminates the old shibboleth of double-action first shot pistols that said one had to change finger position between the double-action first round and the

With DA-to-SA pistol, like this Beretta 92G, placing finger at distal joint will give good control with both types of trigger pull.

Trigger control is all the more important with more difficult tasks like one-handed double-action work with a light gun, such as this Colt Magnum Carry .357 snub.

single-action follow-up shots. Place the distal joint on the trigger for the first heavy pull, keep it there for subsequent shots, and all will be well.

Rolling Pace

From here on, it's a matter of pace. Learn trigger control as you would develop any other physical skill. Remember what I call "Chapman's Dictum": Smoothness is 5/6 of speed. Crawl before you walk, and walk before you run.

Start slowly. Do lots of dry fire. Watch the sights as they sit silhouetted against a safe backstop. *Do not let the sights move out of alignment at any point in the trigger stroke, particularly when the trigger releases and the "shot breaks."* Then, gradually, accelerate the pace.

Generations of combat shooters can tell you: accuracy first, speed second will develop fast and accurate shooting skills much more quickly than a curriculum of speed first and accuracy second. If you stay with it for several thousand repetitions, you will find that you can roll the trigger back as fast as your finger will go, without jerking your sights off

target. Put another way, we can learn to hit as fast as we were missing before.

The key to trigger manipulation under stress is to *distribute the trigger pressure*. A sudden 4-pound jerk will inevitably pull a 2-pound gun off target. Smooth, evenly distributed trigger pressure done at the same speed will fire the gun just as quickly, but without moving the alignment of bore to target. The key words here are *smooth* and *even*.

Generations of shooters and gunfighters have learned to talk themselves through the perfect shot. They chant it to themselves like a mantra. "Front sight! Squeeze the trigger. *Squee-e-eze...*" One instructor says "squeeze," another says "press"; this writer uses "roll." To me, the word "roll" con-

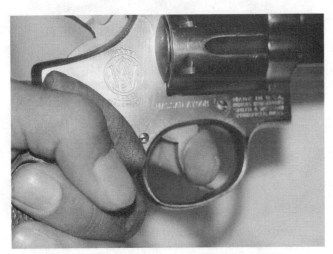

Proper trigger finger placement for DA work with K-frame S&W .357.

A smooth double-action trigger stroke is bringing the next .357 round under the hammer of this S&W Bodyguard.

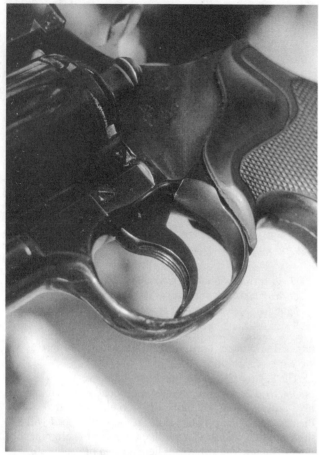

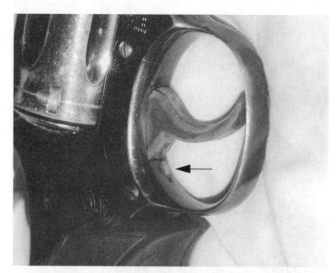

Note S&W's internally adjustable trigger stop, coming down into trigger guard at a point behind the trigger. Because there is a remote chance it can come out of adjustment and block the trigger…

…it is usually removed from a duty gun, as it has been from author's S&W Model 66.

A workable solution. This Colt Python has a serrated trigger, usually undesirable for double-action work, but the ridges between the serration grooves have been polished glass smooth, solving the problem.

notes the smooth, even, uninterrupted pressure that I want. The word doesn't matter so much as the concept.

Don't try to "stage" or "trigger-cock" the pistol. This is fine motor intensive, and our fine motor skills go down the drain when we're in danger and our body instinctively reacts. Such skills just won't be with you in a fight. Learn from the beginning to keep the stroke smooth and even, executed in a single stage.

A word on "surprise trigger break." Marksmanship instructors tell us to let the trigger go off by surprise so we don't anticipate the final release and jerk the gun. However, if you say in court that the shot went off by surprise, it sounds to anyone without your training as if you didn't mean for it to go off. That can turn a justifiable, intentional shooting into a negligent act of manslaughter. *We don't begin pressing the trigger back – we don't even* **touch** *the trigger – until the intent to immediately fire has been justifiably formulated!* The only surprise should be in what fraction of an instant the deliberate shot discharges.

Trigger Mechanicals

A light trigger pull is, more than anything else, a crutch for bad trigger technique. It is also "plaintiff's counsel's guaranteed employment act" in the civil liability sense. On a defense gun, you don't need a *light* trigger pull, you need a *smooth* trigger pull.

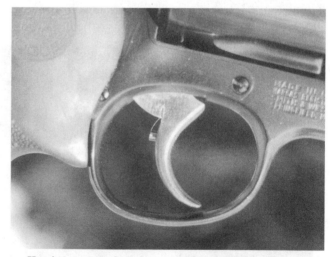

Here's a true combat trigger stop. It is welded in place. It can't move and cause problems, yet it cures aim-disturbing trigger overtravel. Installed on author's S&W Model 25-5, in .45 Colt, by Al Greco.

The surface of the trigger should be glassy smooth, with rounded edges. Grooves, serrations, or checkering on the trigger will trap the flesh of the finger and translate any lateral finger movement to undesirable lateral gun movement. As the finger moves back, it may change its exact contact point with the trigger very slightly, and if that happens, we want the finger to be moving smoothly and easily across the frontal surface of the trigger. On revolver triggers in particular, it's also a good idea to round off the rear edges of the trigger, to keep the flesh of the finger from being pinched between the trigger and the back of the trigger guard at the end of each firing stroke.

Beware of "backlash." This is the movement that occurs in the instant between when the sear releases, and when the rear of the trigger comes to a stop. Because spring pressure resisting the finger has just been released, there is a tendency for the finger to snap back against the rear of the trigger guard, possibly jerking the muzzle off target. An "anti-backlash device" or "trigger stop" is a good idea, *if* it is constructed in such a way that it cannot come out of adjustment, move forward, and block the trigger from firing. This problem was known to occur in the old "built-in" trigger stops of Smith & Wesson's target and combat-target revolvers (K-38, Combat Magnum, etc.) and it got to the point where departments ordering such guns would specify that the trigger stop device be left out entirely. A good pistolsmith can weld up a stop on the back of the trigger or the back of the trigger guard, then grind or file it to a point where the trigger will always be operational.

Power stance in action. Dave Sevigny, National IDPA champion, shows winning form with a Glock 34 at the New England Regional Championships.

Smaller people need the power stance more than big bruisers. Justine Ayoob is 15 in this photo as she wins High Novice in the enhanced service pistol class at the New England Regional IDPA championships. Note power stance as she delivers head-shots with a Novak Custom Browning 9mm.

Lost Secrets Of Combat Handgun Shooting

Evolution of doctrine is a strange thing. Sometimes, we do something after we've forgotten why we started doing it. Sometimes, we forget to do things we should be doing.

There are secrets the Old Masters of combat handgunning knew, secrets that have been lost to most because they weren't incorporated into this or that "doctrine." Just because they are lost doesn't mean they don't still work. Let's look at a few of them.

Lost Secret #1: The Power Stance

In true *combat* handgun training, as opposed to recreational shooting, you are preparing for a fight. This means you should be in a fighting stance. Balance and mobility can never be compromised in a fight. Accordingly, your primary shooting stance should be a *fighting* stance.

When the body has to become a fighting machine, the legs and feet become its foundation. You can expect to be receiving impacts: a wound to the shoulder, a bullet slamming to a stop in your body armor, and certainly the recoil of your own powerful, rapidly fired defensive weapon. Any of these can drive you backward and off-balance if you are not stabilized to absorb them and keep fighting.

The feet should be at least shoulder-width apart, and probably wider. Whether you're throwing a punch or extending a firearm, you're creating outboard weight, and your body has to compensate for that by widening its foundation or you'll lose your balance.

We have long known that humans in danger tend to crouch. It's not just a *homo sapiens* thing, it's an erect biped thing. The same behavior is observed in primates, and in bears when they're upright on their hind legs. In his classic book "Shoot to Live," Fairbairn observed how men just on their way to a dangerous raid tended to crouch significantly. Decades before Fairbairn had noticed it, Dr. Walter Cannon at Harvard Medical School had predicted this. Cannon was the first to attempt to medically quantify the phenomenon called "fight or flight response" as it occurs in the human. While we know now that Cannon may have been incorrect on some hypothesized details, such as the exact role that blood sugar plays in the equation, we also know that on the bottom line he was right on all counts.

When threatened with deadly danger, the erect bipedal mammal will turn and face that danger, if only to observe and quantify it before fleeing. Its torso will square with the thing that threatens it. One leg will "quarter" rearward. This is seen today in the boxer's stance, the karate practitioner's front

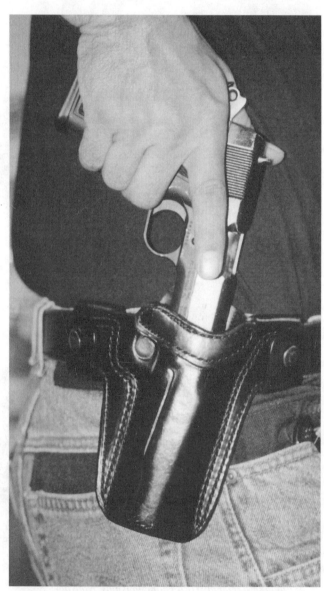

A high-hand grasp is best taken with the gun still in the holster, as shown here pulling a Para-Ordnance .45 from Alessi CQC holster.

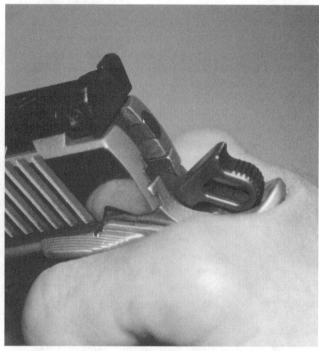

A high-hand grasp on a Kimber Gold Match .45; note the "ripple of flesh" at the web of the hand.

A high-hand grasp on a revolver. Note that the top edge of the gripframe is higher on the "hammerless" S&W Centennial (AirLite version shown), affording the shooter more control than a conventionally styled revolver. Note also the white-nailed "crush grip."

stance, the Weaver stance of pistol shooters, and the "police interview stance" taught at every law enforcement academy.

The head will come forward and down, and the shoulders will seem to hunch up to protect it. The knees will flex, lowering the center of body gravity, and the hips will come back, coiling the body for sudden and strenuous movement. The feet will be at least shoulder-width apart laterally. The hands or paws will rise to somewhere between waist and face level.

This, and not the exaggerated "squat" of the ancient FBI training films, is the true and instinctive "combat crouch." The body is balanced forward, rearward, left and right, its weight forward to both absorb and deliver impact.

There is no good reason for the combat shooter not to stand like this. Indeed, there is every reason for him or her to do it.

A key element of the power stance as we teach it at Lethal Force Institute is the application of the *drive leg*. In the martial arts, you generate power in a punch by putting your whole body behind it. Whichever leg is to the rear is the drive leg. Beginning with the knee slightly flexed, the practitioner digs either the heel or the ball of the foot into the ground, straightening the leg. This begins a powerful turn of the hips. The hips are the center of body gravity and the point from which body strength can most effectively be generated. The punch and extending arm go forward along with the hip. The forward leg has become the weight-bearing limb; it needs to be more sharply flexed than the rear leg because as force is delivered forward, it will be carrying well over half of the body's weight.

Lost Secret #2: The High-Hand Grasp

It's amazing how many people come out of shooting schools and police academies not knowing the most efficient way to hold a handgun. The primary hand's grasp, which some instructors call "Master Grip," needs to be able to stand by itself. In a shooting match that calls for a two-handed stage, we know we'll always be able to achieve the two-fisted grasp. In the swirling, unpredictable movement

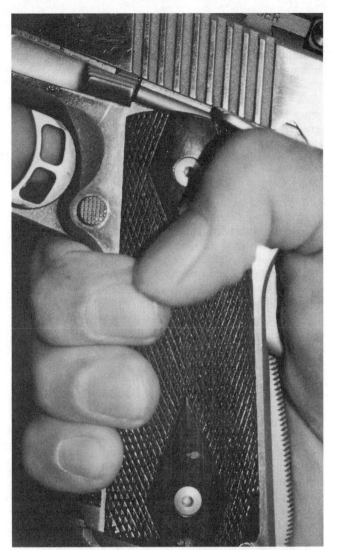

The crush grip in action on a Kimber .45. Note that the fingernails have turned white from max-force gripping pressure.

that occurs in close-range fights, however, we can never be sure that the second hand will be able to get to its destination and reinforce the first. It might be needed to push someone out of the way, to ward off the opponent's weapon, or simply to keep our balance. That's why the initial grasp of the handgun with the dominant hand must be suitable for strong control of one-handed as well as two-handed fire.

The hand should be all the way up the backstrap of the grip-frame. With the auto, the web of the hand should be so high that it is not only in contact with the underside of the grip tang, but pressed against it so firmly that it seems to shore up a ripple of flesh. On the revolver, the web of the hand should be at the highest point of the grip-frame's backstrap. There is only one, easily fixed potential downside to a high hand grip. If the grip tang has sharp edges, as on the older versions of the 1911, this can dig painfully and even lacerate the hand. Sharp-edged slides on very small autos, like the Walther PPK, can do the same. Simply rounding off sharp edges or installing a beavertail grip safety fixes that.

Now let's count up the many advantages of the high-hand grip. (1) It lowers the bore axis as much as possible, giving the gun less leverage with which to kick its muzzle up when recoil hits. (2) It guarantees that the frame will be held as a rigid abutment for the auto's slide to work against. With too low a hold, the whipsaw recoil that follows moves the frame as well as the slide, dissipating some of the rearward momentum needed to complete the cycle. The result is often a spent casing caught "stovepiped" in the ejection port, or a slide that does not return fully to battery. (3) On most handguns, this grasp allows a straight-back pull of the trigger. If the gun is grasped too low, a rearward pull on the trigger becomes a downward pull on the gun, jerking its muzzle – and the shot – low. Draw is hastened because (4) the grip tang of the auto is the easiest landmark for the web of the hand to find by feel.

Pick up a gun magazine with one or more stories on action shooting championships, and watch how the winners hold their guns. The webs of their hands will be riding high. Now you know why. The champions know what so many other shooters have missed.

Lost Secret #3: The Crush Grip

In target pistol shooting, light holds are in vogue. The bull's-eye shooter is taught to let her pistol just rest in her fingers with no real grasp at all as she gently eases the trigger back. The IPSC shooter is taught to apply 60 percent strength with the support hand and 40 percent with the firing hand (occasionally the reverse, but 50 percent of available hand strength in any case).

Common sense tells us this will not do for a fight. For one thing, it is dexterity intensive, and dexterity is among the first things we lose in a fight-or-flight state. For another, the genuine fight you are training for always entails the risk of an opponent attempting to snatch your gun away. We know that action beats reaction. If you're holding your handgun lightly or with only half your strength and it is forcibly grabbed or struck, it will probably be gone from your grasp before you can react. But if you have conditioned your hand to always hold the gun with maximum strength, you have a better chance to resist the attack long enough to react, counter with a retention move, and keep control of your firearm.

A third tremendous advantage of a hard hold, one that world champion Ray Chapman always told his students, is that it's the ultimate consistency in hold. "40 percent hand strength" is one thing in the relatively calm environment of the training range. It's something else when you're at a big match shooting for all the marbles, and it's something a league beyond that when you're fighting for your life. One effect of fight or flight response is that as dexterity goes down, strength goes up precipitously. Even in target shooting, marksmanship coaches agree that a consistent hold is a key element of consistent shot placement. There are only two possible grasps that can be guaranteed to stay truly consistent: no pressure at all, or maximum pressure.

A fourth big advantage for the crush grip is that it prevents "milking." When one finger moves, the other fingers want to move with it. The phenomenon is called "interlimb response." As the trigger fingers tighten, so do the grasping fingers, as if they were milking a cow's udder, and this jerks the shot off target, usually down and to one side. But if the fingers on the gripframe (NOT the trigger finger!) are already squeezing as hard as they can, they can't squeeze any more when the index finger separately pulls the trigger, and milking is thus made impossible.

Finally, the hard hold better controls recoil. If you had me by the throat and were holding me against a wall, and I was struggling, would you relax your grip or hold harder? The harder you hold me against the wall, the less I can move. Similarly, the more firmly you grasp your gun, the less *it* will move in recoil, in terms of both overall gun movement and the stocks shifting in your hand.

Detractors of the concept call this "gorilla grip," and warn that it interferes with delicate movement of the trigger finger and can cause small tremors. Those of us who advocate crush grip answer, "So what?" Delicate manipulation of the trigger disappears once the fight is on. The hands are going to tremble under stress anyway, and the shooter might as well get used to it up front in training. If the sights are kept in line, the gun's muzzle won't tremble off a target the size of a human heart.

Lost Secret #4: Front Sight

Every marksman who is accomplished with open sights remembers the day he or she experienced "the epiphany of

The front sight is the key to good hits. In close, even an image like this, well above the rear sight, will put the shot where it needs to go.

The most precise, almost surgical, accuracy comes when the eye focuses on the front sight, with the rear sight in secondary focus and target in tertiary focus.

A smooth roll of the trigger becomes more critical as the shooting problem becomes more difficult. With the 11-ounce .357, double-action, and weak-hand-only, you can be sure the author is focusing on this trigger stroke.

the front sight." The phrase "watch your front sight" doesn't mean just have it in your field of view. It doesn't mean just be aware of it. It means focus on it as hard as possible, making sure it's on target, and that it's not moving off target as you stroke the trigger. Pistol champions and gunfight survivors alike have learned that this is the key to *center* hits at high speed under pressure.

As discussed in the chapter on point shooting, you don't need the perfect sight picture of the marksmanship manual. But remember that the handgun is a remote control drill, and it must be indexed with where we want the hole to appear, or the hole will appear in the wrong place. The sights, at least the front sight in close, will be the most reliable such index.

Lost Secret #5: Smooth Roll

A smooth, even, uninterrupted roll of the trigger, as discussed in the last chapter, is critical if the shooter is going to break the shot without jerking it off target.

Note that the last two elements, "front sight" and "smooth trigger roll," are not listed as "to the lines of secrets four and five, prior." This is because it's debatable whether they are really lost secrets, and if so, who lost them. Every competent instructor will teach the students how to use the sights and how to bring the trigger back. The problem is, these things are very easy to forget until the student develops the discipline to first think about doing them, and then finally ingrain the concepts through repetition so they are done automatically.

Power stance. High hand. Crush grip. Front sight. Smooth roll. I try to go through it in my mind like a pre-flight checklist before I even reach for the gun.

You don't even have to think about it all at once. As soon as you know there may be a stimulus to draw the gun, slip into a power stance. It might be a thug giving you the bad eye as you wait for a bus, or it might be that you're on the

Power stance, high hand, crush grip, front sight, smooth roll. The author, foreground, brings it all together as he wins a shoot in the Northwest. Note that spent casing is in the air above his STI, but gun is already back on target despite recoil of full power .45 hardball. Photo by Matthew Sachs.

range awaiting the "commence fire" signal. If you're in the position to start, you don't have to think about it any more.

Condition yourself to always begin the draw by hitting the high hand position. Once it's there, it's done and you don't have to think about it any longer.

Crush grip? I tell my students to think of the eagle's claw. When the eagle sleeps, it does not fall from its perch because its claws automatically clutch it with a death grip. If we condition ourselves to do this whenever we hold the gun, it'll happen on its own when we need it without us having to think about it.

Power stance…high hand…crush grip…front sight…smooth roll. Recover these "lost secrets" and apply them…and watch your combat handgun skill increase.

CHAPTER FIVE

"MAXING" QUALIFICATION AND COMPETITION

The master gunfighters of the 20th century – Bill Jordan and Elmer Hilden of the Border Patrol, Jim Cirillo and Bill Allard of the NYPD Stakeout Squad – all felt that shooting in competition sharpened your ability to shoot under stress in defense of your life. If you haven't tried it, you should.

Just in case you haven't competed, let's see what it's like. Come with me and shoot a match. I can't make it up for you. I don't do fiction. The only way to do it is for you and I to "channel" together, as the Yuppies say. It's June 5, 2001. We're at the Cheshire Fish & Game Club, the host range for the event, sponsored by the Keene, NH Police Department. The occasion is the annual conference of the New Hampshire Police Association, and the combat shoot that accompanies it is the *de facto* state championship in police combat shooting for cops in the Granite State.

You want a gun and ammo that you know will work. With the Glock 22 (NY-1 trigger, Meprolight fixed sights) and Black Hills EXP ammo, you have both.

Getting Ready

Bad news: you're stuck doing it with me, a "geezer cop" in his fifties. Good news: this particular geezer knows this particular beat, and you and I are prepared to compete on a level playing field.

Rules are that you have to compete with the gun you carry on duty. No tricky recoil compensators or optical sights. Holsters must be suitable for police wear, with retaining devices not only present but fastened before each draw. Ammunition must be suitable for law enforcement use.

My department issues a traditional-style double action .45 auto that is justly famous for both its accuracy and its reliability, two things I appreciated when I won this match with my issue weapon last year. For the whole second quarter, I've been in plainclothes – actually allowed to wear a beard, which I can't in uniform – because I'm a captain who handles primarily administrative and training tasks. These include test and evaluation of new equipment, etc. I've been assigned to test two new uniform security holsters that are about to come into the field. Since the Glock pistol is by far the most common in law enforcement today, it is what these new holsters were initially made to fit. My chief has given me permission to carry one on duty for testing purposes. It's the Glock 22, .40 caliber, the single most popular Glock thanks in large part to police sales, and at the same time, the single most popular police service handgun in the U.S. today. It is as it came from the factory: bone-stock, equipped with the 8-pound New York (NY-1) trigger and Meprolight fixed night sights.

The new security holsters haven't come in yet, so my gray whiskers and I have a reprieve for a while yet in plainclothes, but I'm carrying the G22 to get bonded with it beforehand. It's a good little pistol, particularly with the ammo my department issues for off-duty or plainclothes wear with that caliber, the Black Hills EXP. It sends a 165-grain Gold Dot hollow-point out of the barrel at an honest 1,150 feet per second, a .357 Magnum power level, and it is loaded to match-grade quality specifications. When we sighted in this gun/ammo combo for the first time at 50 yards, aiming for the head of a silhouette target, we jerked one shot down into the neck and didn't count it. But the other four shots were in the head in a *one and seven-eighths inch group.* Is *this* gonna be accurate enough for the B-27 target with competition scoring rings, where the tie-breaking center X ring measures 2 inches by 3 inches? *Oh,* yeah!

We're wearing what we wear to work these days. BDU pants (loose, comfortable, lots of pockets, great for strenu-

Each shooter finds his own pace. The hands of the shooter in the background are beginning to separate as he prepares to reload his Beretta while transitioning from standing to left-side kneeling; the officer at right is already in a kneeling position and has just fired the first shot from that position with his Glock.

ous things like going prone and running, which we'll have to do here.) Polo shirt with the department patch logo on it, one size large to help conceal the bullet-resistant vest. (We wear the vest on duty; we'll wear it here.) Handcuffs in a Galco quick-release plainclothes carrier. The dress gun belt is by Mitch Rosen, as are the first magazine pouch and the holster. The rig fits us perfectly, as it should; it's the one Rosen called the ARG for Ayoob Rear Guard. It rides comfortably inside the waistband behind the strong side hip, secured by a thumb-break safety strap. Backing up the Rosen pouch with its 15-round Glock "law enforcement only" G22 mag are two more pouches, both Kydex, one by Blade-Tech and one by Ky-Tac. This match will have some stages where two reloads are necessary, and then we'll have to reload to "hot" condition before refilling magazines, etc. Hence, the need for four magazines on the person, including the one in the gun.

Let's get our head right. We're going for the title of top dog, or in this case, top law-dog. That engenders pressure. There's a little more of that on you and me than on most of the others. One person has to be the defending champion from last year, and that raises the price of the ego investment bet on the table. That person, right now, is us.

We get the briefing on the course of fire. There has been a last-minute change in rules. At the barricades, we cannot touch the wall with either gun or hand to stabilize for the shot. OW! Particularly at 50 yards, this hurts accuracy: we're firing free-hand instead of with support. The good news is everyone has to do the same. It's fair, a level playing field. We are *awfully* glad, you and I, that we have a lot of experience shooting at long range with a pistol held in unsupported hands from the standing position.

50 Yards

We'll have exactly 60 seconds to go prone, fire six, reload, stand, fire six from one side of the barricade (no support, remember), reload again, and fire six more from behind the wall on the other side without actually touching that wall. We MUST be effectively behind cover or we'll be penalized.

We load the Glock 22, holster, fasten the safety strap, and stand by, hands clear of the holster. On the signal, we draw and drop into the rollover prone technique you and I learned from world champion Ray Chapman so many years ago. AAUUGGHH! There's grass between us and the target, obscuring aim! We scoot to the side, get a clear shot, and begin shooting. The readjustment of position has put us behind the other shooters from the get-go.

We fight the urge to hurry. Front sight is dead in the center of the target. We carefully press the trigger back until the shot breaks. Then again. And again.

Those six are done, and the clock is ticking. We feel the shots went right in where we wanted them. A review of the target in a couple of minutes will prove us right. But now, as we leap to our feet, our right thumb punching the Glock's magazine release as our left hand snatches a fresh mag from behind the left hip and snaps it home, the left thumb pressing down on the slide lock lever to chamber a fresh round, there is a sense that we are behind the others in time. This is a quick stage. Normally in police combat shooting, 24 shots are fired from this 50-yard distance, all of them supported either by the barricade or in the sitting or prone position, and you have two minutes, 45 seconds. That works out to 6.875 seconds per shot. We've just fired the only *six* shots where we'll have support, that of the ground in the prone posture, and we're firing at a rate of 3.33 seconds per shot, faster than double speed.

The first shot from standing feels perfect. But on the second we feel ourselves jerk the trigger, actually *see* the front sight dip in the notch as the shot breaks. The sight hasn't gone down that much, but there's a geometric progression here. The slightest drop of the front sight means a bullet *way* low by the time it reaches its mark half a football field away.

Firing prone from 50 yards. Note that each officer has a slightly different technique.

Fifty yards seems a long way off, even when firing prone.

We finish about 10 seconds ahead of that unforgiving clock. We reload and holster, set about refilling our magazines, and then prepare to go forward to score. Jerry St. Pierre of the Keene Police is leading the host team. He knows how easily the whole target can be missed from this far away. He's going to score and mark the 50-yard hits before we go any further.

As we approach the targets, we see something in the pelvis of our silhouette target. Oh, *please,* let that be a staple or something! No such luck. The shot we jerked would have been a take-down hit on a man, and would have been worth three out of five points if the target was scored in the police qualification fashion. But this is the police *competition* scoring system, and that shot is counted as a miss. Ten points gone for one bad shot!

In a regular PPC match, that would ruin you. The master class shooters here get 580 and 590 out of 600 scores routinely with their match guns at standard time, and 10 points gone for one of the 60 shots would tank you out of the match for good. Fortunately, here *everyone* is shooting at double speed and using service guns. The playing field is still level…*but you and I can't afford any more mistakes!*

25 Yards

We start with six shots kneeling. Then fire, six from the left side of the barricade, standing, and six more from the right, the same way, with a mandatory reload between each stage. The latter is done to level the playing field for any shooter who has a revolver or a low-capacity auto. This is the first year I've been here where not a single wheelgun is in evidence. In this state, the transition to the service pistol is virtually complete. You usually have 90 seconds for this stage in a Police Combat match, and can stabilize your support hand on the barricade. Here, we can't use anything to steady on, and time is only 60 seconds. Only two-thirds the time, and at least double the difficulty.

Officers fire over the barricade at 25 yards, and also from around both sides. Duty pistols are Glock in the foreground, Beretta 9mm at left.

Brain cells front and center! We have to tighten up! Consciously, we harden our hold to better stabilize the gun (since there's nothing but our bare hands to stabilize it at all) and dig our rear leg into the ground to drive our body forward. This will let our body weight help better to snap the gun down out of recoil and back into line with the target, giving us fractions of a second more time per shot to "hold and squeeze."

Those six are done. Speed reload. We're back on target with not a lot of time left, standing just behind the cover on the other side of the barricade. We chant to ourself consciously but silently, "Power stance! High-hand grasp! Crush grip! Front sight! Smooth ro-o-oll of the trigger."

Rather than brace an elbow at the knee, these officers use "speed kneeling" around replicated cover at 25 yards.

On signal, officers sprint forward from 25-yard line…

The timer sounds. We draw first, then drop to kneeling – even at speed, we don't cross a bent lower leg with the muzzle of a loaded gun – and lock in our front sight. The gun was sighted to hit dead on at 50 yards and this means we have to hold a tad low in close, taking a 6 o'clock sight picture that balances the "X" on top of the front sight.

We are thinking "front sight, smooth roll…front sight, smooth roll" for each shot. The reloads, practiced so many times, seem to happen on automatic pilot. There is just time enough to "ride the link" of the Glock trigger, to fire each shot, let the trigger come back forward just enough until we feel the click of the mechanism resetting, and then we draw the trigger back again, feeling the smooth subtle movement of the Glock pistol's cruciform sear plate until each subsequent shot is released.

We make the time. That's no sweat. Under pressure, things go faster than you think. Glance downrange. There are a very few shots out in the 9-point ring, but the rest have gone true to center. Life is good.

Now comes what, for some, is the toughest stage. You stand at 25 paces facing the target, hands at your side. On the signal, you draw and fire six shots…in ten seconds, including reaction time. Getting the shots off is no problem. Making the hits in that tiny center ring is the problem.

You and I breathe deeply as we hear the command sequence begin, holding the air in and letting it hiss slowly out. It's the internalized version of that "breathe into the paper bag" trick we cops always use with people in crisis who are hyperventilating. Ya can't do the bag on the range or in a fight, though. Some call it "crisis breathing." You and I learned it decades ago in a karate dojo where they called it *sanchin* breathing.

The signal comes. We draw, lock in, get the front sight on target, and roll the Glock's trigger back. Our head is forward and down, like a vulture's, the way humans stand when in the grip of "fight or flight" response. This helps us stay focused on the front sight ("target identified, missiles locked on target, launch, maintain target lock for next missile…"). We finish a good second before the cease-fire signal is sounded. We glance downrange as we reload. There aren't any more errant hits outside the 10/X rings than there were before.

… to 15 yards, where they draw and fire. Note safety officer moving in behind the firing line.

15 Yards

Reloaded, we begin standing at the 25-yard line. On the signal, we have to run forward to the 15-yard line, draw, and fire two shots, all in only six seconds. The horn sounds. We lunge forward. Time slows down. As we approach the line we use a trick we learned from World Champion Ray Chapman: a little jump in the air, then land at the finish point on flexed and coiled knees as the gun comes out, as is only now

Note individualized versions of the low ready positions as officers await command on the firing line…

…to react, bring up the gun, and score two hits at 15 yards, all in two seconds.

The officer at left is down on his right knee behind left side cover; the officer on right has chosen the left knee for better balance with slight leftward lean.

allowed. There isn't much time left. We snap it to line of sight in an Isosceles hold, and instead of using the usual post in notch sight picture, we just align the three big dots of the Meprolight fixed night sights that came on our service Glock, and roll the trigger back, fighting the urge to hasten the shot. Bang, bang, *beep!*

We've made the time. Not everyone else has been so fortunate.

Now we go to a low ready stance. Three more times, the signal will come to shoot, and each time we'll have only two seconds to raise our service weapon, align it, and get two shots into that heart-sized center ring. We must start with our finger outside the trigger guard. Most are holding it straight on the frame: safe, but slower than it needs to be. Not all of them make the time. Many are starting with their fingertip on the front of the trigger guard. Fast, but tricky: under stress, this position holds the trigger finger taut, and when it snaps into the trigger it hits with impact, often breaking the shot prematurely. That's tragedy on the street, and it's a bad hit here on the line. Some others learn that today the hard way.

You and I start with our trigger finger flexed, the tip of the finger touching the takedown niche on the side of the Glock frame. Now, on the signal, as we raise the gun we can thrust the finger swiftly into the trigger guard *across* the trigger, until we find that sweet spot where the distal joint of the finger feels virtually centered on the trigger so we have maximum leverage for a fast, straight-back pull that won't move the muzzle off the target. BAM-BAM! We're in! And again, BAM-BAM. We're doin' OK.

With the six-round magazines that are demanded (to level the playing field between the different service guns styles), we're at slidelock, and we quickly reload. Some of our brother and sister officers have come to grief at this point, and they're out of the running. Their guns jammed. When you have only two shots left, and two must be fired, and your pistol locks up in the middle of that, two seconds simply isn't time enough to recognize the malfunction, clear it, reload, and fire another round. Fortunately, you and I

One-hand-only stages at 7 yards are the cruncher for time.

This state trooper is at 7 yards as he draws and fires five shots strong-hand-only with his issue S&W .45 auto…

have a Glock with Black Hills ammunition, two exemplars of reliability, and that disaster does not befall us.

7 Yards

This is the final stage. The cruncher. The one where cops are most likely to fail to get their shots off in time. In PPC, it's 12 shots in 25 seconds, including the reload, in a two-hand stance. But here in New Hampshire, you draw strong-hand-*only,* fire five shots, reload, then shift the gun to your other hand and fire five more shots weak-hand-*only,* all in only 15 seconds.

We're ready. We've practiced this. We start in a fighter's stance, not a target shooter's stance, and on the start signal we draw and bring the gun into the target like a Shotokan karate fighter throwing a punch. The body weight behind the Glock keeps it on target with the stout recoil of the hot Black Hills load, the three dots already back at center in the time it takes to re-set the trigger. The gun goes to slidelock. Speed-reload, hand change. We sense the clock ticking and, losing our sense of time we fire faster than we should, finishing the whole thing in about 10 seconds. But all ten of those last shots are inside the 10 and 10-X rings, and our job is done.

…he ducks down to reload (good survival training in action!) and then…

It Ain't Over

Now you stand by your target and await the official scorer. Smoke 'em if you got 'em and cope with the stress. It's like waiting for the biopsy to come back from the lab. The stress isn't *nearly* over yet.

We check the target along with the scorer. We don't like it, but he has it right. It's not the best we have ever done. On the other hand, it *is* the best score on the first relay, and we're in the lead.

The match sponsors have announced that each shooter can get one second chance over the course. However, *as soon as they fire the first shot of their second try, their first score becomes null and void.* You and I immediately go over to the registrar, pay an entry fee, and book a slot to shoot again if we have to.

…fires the last five shots weak-hand-only.

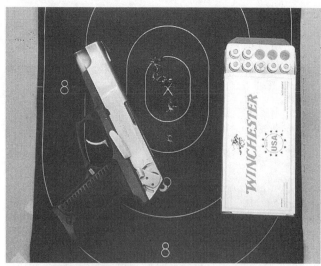

This is the combination that won the year before: Ruger P90 with fixed IWI night sights and Winchester USA 230-grain .45 hardball.

Now comes a war of nerves and ego. You and I don't like that score, particularly the 10 points down shot from 50 yards. We want to try again, strut our stuff, shoot better than we did before. That's understandable. However, ego must come second to The Job. I represent my police department here. My chief wants our department to keep the title from last year. If I get beaten, I'm ready to shoot again…but if my chief of police ever finds out that I had victory solidly in my hand, then shot again to feed my ego *and lost what I already had locked up,* he is going to start wondering whether I should really keep command authority after making such a stupid decision. Soon I will be walking foot patrol in the sanitary landfill or something.

So we must wait these tension-filled moments, you and I who are shooting together, until the scores are in and "last relay" is called.

Several have tried twice. None have beaten the top score on the board. That score is ours.

The end of the match feels almost anti-climactic. It is announced that you and I have won. We shake hands with the match director, Officer Jerry St. Pierre, and some kind person takes a photo.

You and I have won the state shoot. Our prize is a Glock 27 pistol, donated by Riley's Sport Shop in Hooksett, NH. It's identical to the one that has been strapped to our left leg the whole time in an Alessi ankle holster, a fallback in case something goes wrong with the Glock 22 and we quickly need a gun to finish the match. The Glock 27 will take the Glock 22's magazines that are already on our belt.

But we'll leave with some lessons even more valuable than that excellent Glock pistol.

Focus on the task, not the goal. The task was to shoot perfect shots, 60 of them. We dropped our focus on one and blew the shot. Our 59 decent hits turned out to be enough to get us through the "trial." If we focus on the goal, we'll neglect the tasks necessary to achieve it, but if we focus on the tasks, the goal will achieve itself.

You need a damn good gun with damn good ammo for something like this. With the Glock 22 and the Black Hills EXP .40 ammo, we had both. Others who might have beaten us failed when their equipment failed. Ours didn't.

All draws begin with the safety devices fastened.

Match director Jerry St. Pierre, right, congratulates the author on winning the title.

The trigger is the heart of the beast. When you control the trigger, you control the shot. You and I just experienced living proof that a heavy trigger isn't uncontrollable. Those 8 pounds of pressure were manageable enough. In my experience, the New York trigger gives a cleaner trigger break and less trigger backlash. It's a win-win thing, and that's why I have a New York trigger on every Glock I ever carry for anything serious, like this one, which is, for now, my police service pistol.

One in the hand really is worth two in the bush. Right brain warring with left brain, I desperately wanted to shoot the course again to get a better score. But logic won out over ego, as it always should. You don't throw away a locked-in victory for a mere *chance* at a more spectacular victory. This is just one example of many of how competition teaches us how to make life decisions.

Self-coaching works. Often times, you'll be coaching a friend and watching him miss the plates. You yell, "Front sight!" and then comes, BANG-CLANG, and the hit is achieved. You don't need a separate coach if you're constantly reminding yourself of what to do. Works in a match, works in a fight, works in any life crisis.

Combat competition isn't gunfighting. You know you won't die if you fail. But it's as close to a microcosm of a gunfight as you can come in training as far as pressure is concerned. I've done my share of Simunitions and similar realistic role playing, and I can tell you the stress is more in a big match.

Anything that conditions you to shooting under pressure can help you stay alive with a gun in your hand. Combat competition is the most cost-effective, most readily available avenue to getting used to the pressure.

Combat Competition

There are those of us who can remember when we shot bull's-eye pistol matches because, in part, we wanted to stay sharp with the guns we carried for self-defense. Why? Because it was the only game in town! Today, things are a lot better.

Let's take a look at the combat shooting competition that is currently available to the law-abiding private citizen in the United States. It's not that any one has it all over the other. Each element will have a piece of the puzzle.

IDPA

Bill Wilson and some others who felt that available defensive handgun competition had become more of a game than a training tool founded the International Defensive Pistol Association in the mid-1990s. It has been the fastest-growing shooting discipline of its kind since. For the author's money, it's the "best game in town," but it still doesn't have everything.

You need a "street gun" in a "street holster," which in most stages will be concealed when the start signal comes. The holster must ride behind the hip, and hide under the concealing garment. The ubiquitous 1911 .45 auto and its 10mm sister compete in CDP (Custom Defense Pistol) class. A Browning Hi-Power or other cocked-and-locked 9mm, .38

Super or .40 pistol will be used in ESP (Enhanced Service Pistol). A double action auto or a Glock would enter the single most popular category, SSP (Stock Service Pistol). For wheelgunners, there is SSR (Stock Service Revolver). Even with high capacity guns, the shooter is limited to 10-round magazines in the interest of a level playing field.

A shooter who does not use available cover will be penalized. Just like in a gunfight, only in a match, the penalties aren't nearly as harsh. Often, the shooter is required to move while shooting, and will be penalized if he comes to a stop to fire.

A stage may begin with the practitioner seated in a car, lying in bed, even sitting on a toilet. Don't worry; they'll let you keep your pants up. Failure to neutralize a bad guy target gains a penalty. Hitting a no shoot target is a BIG penalty. In these things, again, IDPA is reflecting real world values.

There will be a penalty for leaving live ammo behind or making a reload on the run. As in real life, IDPA figures it's healthier to stay behind cover and only move if you have a fully reloaded gun already in hand. While I think the emphasis on tactical reloads over speed reloads is a bit excessive, that's just one participant's opinion.

The target is reasonably realistic, a cardboard silhouette with an 8-inch maximum point "A-zone" in the center of the

When he carried the S&W 4506 on duty (top), the author had Wayne Novak make him up a custom single-action version for matches (center), and later had another crafted in .45 Super by Ace Custom (below). However, as time wore on...

...experience taught him to just shoot the duty gun in matches. He did OK.

Four flavors of Glock .40. From top, G35, G22, G23, and G27. The author has seen them all used in matches by people who actually carried them on the street.

chest. Some targets will be steel knock-downs. I've seen events where the targets were on their sides, simulating a pack of wolves or wild dogs. Protecting yourself from vicious animals is legitimate self-defense too, one too often neglected in the other shooting disciplines.

If you've been to a lot of matches, you've seen chronic whiners and "gamesmen" who aren't there to learn, just there to win, and sometimes they are there to take their insecurities out on others. IDPA has an answer for that. Anything that smacks of cheating or bad sportsmanship earns a "failure to do right" penalty that is so massive it blows the offender out of the match. It has served to keep egos well in line.

To see what it's all about, to find a club offering IDPA events within reach of you, or to see about starting up such matches yourself, check out the website at www.idpa.com

IPSC

The International Practical Shooting Confederation was founded in the mid-1970s under the direction of Jeff Cooper, who had created "replicated gunfight" matches as early as the 1950s with his "Leatherslaps" and the founding of the Southwest Combat Pistol League in California. Until then, the efforts of Cooper and company were exotica that we read about, but couldn't share unless we moved to the West Coast; now, it was available to all.

The early days of IPSC were much like IDPA today. "Real" guns. "Real" scenarios. I had the privilege of running the first IPSC Sectional Championship in the United

These officers shot the Washington State Championships with the .45s they carried on duty. Left, Bill Burris with street-tuned Para-Ordnance; right, the author with his issue Ruger P90.

Bill Fish shoots an IDPA match with his Glock 34. The skills transfer…

States, with Col. Jeff Cooper and section coordinator Jim Cirillo present, in 1976. The event was weighted toward larger caliber guns with "Major/Minor" scoring. A hit in the center ring was worth five points with either a 9mm or a .45, but outside that ring, you lost twice as many points if you were shooting 9mm instead of .45. The Colonel said that this appropriately rewarded the more competent gun handler, who was dealing with more recoil and wielding a "more serious" weapon.

That made sense a quarter century ago, when high efficiency ammunition for medium calibers such as 9mm and .38 Special was just coming in. Today, however, a 115-grain 9mm at 1,300 feet per second will kill a criminal just as dead as a 230-grain .45 ACP at 850, and might actually cause more tissue damage. This is why IDPA chose to avoid major/minor, instead instituting a "power floor" in each caliber and having like guns shoot against like guns.

I was there over the years when IPSC seemed to change course. The first big switch to the "race guns and space guns" came when John Shaw had pistolsmith Jim Clark build him a Colt .45 auto with forward muzzle weight. The gun was originally for the Second Chance bowling pin shoot, which is why that genre became known as "pin guns," but John quickly found it advantageous in IPSC and promptly won the national championship with it. The race was on: Mike Plaxco, Bill Wilson, and other master shooters with gunsmithing skills soon built expansion chamber recoil compensators to further tame the recoil.

Then Rob Leatham discovered that he could hot-load the .38 Super to make major, and the intense pressure of the redline-loaded cartridge created more expanding gas for a recoil compensator to work with. Muzzle jump was now nil. Then Jerry Barnhart proved that with an Aimpoint red dot sight, one could see the aiming index and the target on the same visual plane and hit faster. Next thing you knew, every gun had a big "can" on top for the shooter to aim through. Holsters for these guns evolved into super-fast skeletons carried at the front of the belt, with such a precarious hold on the pistol that Barnhart was successful selling a device he called a

…to the Glock 19 and Glock 26 he carries. In fact, he is known to compete with all three. Note the identical "Glock socks" on each.

"walk-through strap." This was a strap that would keep the gun from falling out of the holster while the range officer walked the competitor through the course! Clearly, the "Practical" element of IPSC was coming into grave question.

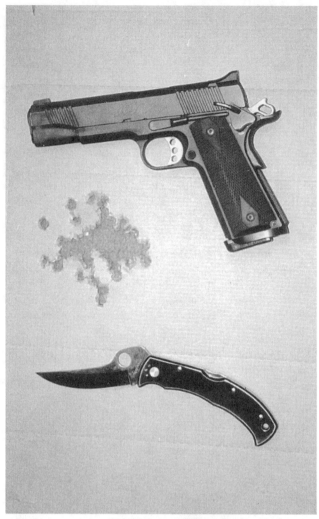

Many combat handguns are accurate enough for competition yet reliable enough for carry. This out-of-the-box Kimber Custom II has shot a perfect score on a 60-round qualification, in a 4-inch group as measured by the Ayoob Spyderco knife. Ammo was full power .45 hardball.

This shooter fires from behind cover at 20 yards in the IDPA National Mid-Winter Championships at the S&W Academy. The pistol, drawn from thumb-break concealment holster, is his daily carry gun, HK P7 9mm,...

...which he reloads tactically behind cover, a hallmark of IDPA, before he continues shooting from opposite side of the barricade.

Next, pioneered by Para Ordnance, came the wide-body "fat guns" that held huge magazines. I saw .38 Super pistols with extended fat mags that could fire more than 25 shots without reloading. By now shooters were using triggers with as little as 28 ounces of pull – an accident waiting to happen in a real-world stress situation, but a winner's edge in IPSC. Competing against a pistol that didn't need to be reloaded and had a trick sight and no recoil and a telekinetic trigger left a cop with a department issue nine-shot double-action .45 asking himself, "Why bother?"

The sport began to stagnate. People broke off and formed things like IDPA. Gun expert Andy Stanford wrote in *American Handgunner* magazine of what he called "The Lost Tribe of IPSC," people like Bill Wilson and Ken Hackathorn and Walt Rauch and myself who had been in at the beginning, but had become disenchanted with IPSC.

The typical IPSC course is a "search and destroy" assault in which the shooter runs through a maze of targets and shoots the ones who are supposed to be bad guys, suffering only a 10-point penalty for shooting an innocent bystander. It is little wonder that the cops started to back away. That was a shame, because the realism of the early IPSC days

Bill Wilson, founder of IDPA (center) explains the target's scoring system to the author and an unidentified IDPA member.

The owner of this target grade HK P9S 9mm has carried it on police patrol, worn it concealed, and shot it at the Bianchi Cup.

had done wonders when grafted into the training of forward thinking police departments like that of Orlando, Florida.

This is not to say that one might not *need* a dollop of "run and gun" as they prepare their training recipe for real-world defensive handgunning. In January 2002, a Palestinian terrorist whipped an M-16 out from under a long coat and opened fire at a bus stop in Jerusalem, killing two innocent women and wounding at least 14 more people. Nearby, a plainclothes Israeli police sergeant named Hanan Ben Naim, dressed in jeans and tennis shoes, drew his Jericho and gave chase. At the end of the foot pursuit Naim faced the terrorist at a range of 20 feet and fired with the Jericho, a 9mm pistol that resembles the Czechoslovakian CZ75, as the terrorist opened up on him with the M-16. The assassin missed. The brave young sergeant didn't, and his pistol fire killed the machinegun-armed terrorist where he stood.

Today, IPSC is trying to return to its roots with a Revolver class, a Production Class, and a class called Limited-10. The latter is an iron-sight pistol with no compensator and a magazine that can hold no more than 10 rounds. Production Class is geared to Glocks and double action semiautomatics. At this writing, it has not taken off like IDPA, but perhaps it needs more time for the word to get out.

IPSC in the United States is governed by USPSA, the United States Practical Shooting Association. For information contact their website www.uspsa.com.

PPC

Get a bunch of police pistol team types together in a bar after a match, and it's about a two-beer argument whether "PPC" stands for "Practical Police Course," "Practical Pistol Course," or "Police Pistol/Combat." Some of the run-and-gun types suspect it stands for "pretty pathetic crap" because the shooting goes slower than they like.

Going back half a century, this course of fire began with police officers using revolvers and ammo loaded one car-

tridge at a time out of belt loops or pouches. With speed-loaders for revolvers, let alone magazines for semiautomatic pistols, there's no question that the times in PPC may be overly generous. 25 seconds to draw, fire six, reload, and fire six more, two-handed, from 7 yards? Come on. NRA, the governing body of PPC shooting, has brought that down to 20 seconds, which is a start.

NRA has never let civilians shoot this match under their auspices; for reasons of political correctness, they don't want the negative publicity of citizens shooting at "pictures of human beings," as reporters like to call the B-27 silhouette target. Nonetheless, many gun clubs offer PPC shooting matches to civilians.

I started shooting bull's-eye. I went to PPC, known locally as "Police Combat," as soon as I could because it was faster, more relevant, and frankly more fun. I jumped from there to IPSC when it became available. By comparison, PPC was old and slow. Many years later, I came back to it. For one thing, *I* was now old and slow.

This shooter runs a PPC match from standing right-hand barricade position.

The Para-Ordnance pistol, top, will kick harder with the same .45 ammo than match Colt Government with D.R. Middlebrooks JetComp compensator, below, but manipulation will be similar.

It's obsolete in terms of shooting speed, but PPC offers some good things. It puts more emphasis on use of cover than any other kind of combat shooting competition. Consider the microcosm of PPC, Match Five, also known as the National Match Course. You'll fire 12 shots from 7 yards, 18 from 25, 24 from 50 yards, and the last 6 at 25 again, this time standing without cover and support. The 18 at 25 are all from behind a vertical wall called a barricade: six kneeling strong hand, six standing weak hand, six standing strong hand. At 50 yards, it's six each from sitting, prone, left barricade and right barricade. The low positions replicate taking cover behind something like an automobile. This means that of 60 shots, all but 18 – more than two-thirds – train you for shooting from behind cover.

The cover rules are strict. You'll be penalized if your foot steps past the barricade's edge, because that would have put some of your main body mass out into the field of fire. By contrast, IDPA allows up to 50 percent of your body to be exposed before you're penalized for failure to use appropriate cover. In the real world, the single tactical failure that gets most good guys killed is failure to use cover that was available before the fight started.

Don't write off the 50-yard shooting as irrelevant; the distances at which the cops engaged the gunmen exceeded that in both the North Hollywood bank robbery shootout and the Columbine incident, two infamous case studies in the need for intensive marksmanship training on the part of the good guys. Another good point for PPC is the B-27 target they use.

It's not my favorite target. Originally known as the Prehle target, it came about many years ago when a smart trainer named Prehle superimposed the scoring rings of the Olympic Rapid Fire target over the old Colt silhouette.

The center rings are too low, focusing on the solar plexus area instead of the heart. However, the 10-ring is almost exactly the size of a human heart. The IDPA target with its 8-inch center circle and the IPSC Brussels target with its 6-inch wide by 11-inch high center rectangle are altogether too generous. In either, what in the real world would be a "lung shot" has the same match scoring value as a "heart into spine" shot. That's simply not practical.

Even before IPSC, PPC evolved into an equipment race with "space guns." In open class, the weapons you need to win are "PPC revolvers" with massive barrels and sight ribs, or long-slide autos with similar sights. Both would be impractical to carry. Fortunately, NRA has been emphasizing stock gun classes for revolver, auto, and "off-duty guns," and I think these will be the salvation of the sport. Last year's National Championship in the stock service pistol event, I'm told, was won by a Richmond (VA) cop with the *SigPro* pistol he was issued by the department, and department-issue 125-grain CCI Gold Dot ammo, caliber .357 SIG. This is a good sign.

If you're a full or part-time police officer or security professional or in the military with an MOS in law enforce-

Using guns modified for non-lethality, Chris Edwards and the author shoot each other as the latter opens a closet door during a force-on-force stage at National Tactical Invitational. Ayoob recommends the NTI as a learning experience for any who haven't tried it.

In this stage, officer Jerry Lashway rushes forward to snatch a "baby" from high chair and pull her to "cover"…

Practical matches replicate practical situations. This IDPA stage begins with pistol lying on "toilet tank" in "restaurant rest room." Shooter will begin seated on replicated toilet. In the interest of dignity, pants won't be dropped.

…as he returns fire weak-hand-only with his Les Baer .45 auto. The scene was part of the 2002 Smith & Wesson MidWinter Championships.

ment, you're eligible for PPC shooting under NRA's auspices. Contact the National Rifle Association and direct your inquiry to the Police Competitions division. If you're a private citizen, you'll have to check around with the gun shops and gun clubs to see who in your area offers PPC shooting to the public.

Tactical Shooting

My fellow LFI instructor Peter Dayton and I were the only two men to compete in all six of the first National Tactical Invitational shooting events. It was a concept developed by three well-qualified men, Chuck Davis, Skip Gochenauer and Walt Rauch, to truly test tactical skills in not only shooting but building search and related disciplines. We loved it. Alas, in the mid-90s, it took a different direction. Rauch and Davis were no longer really in the picture. It ceased to be a competitive skill test and became more a learning experience, in which the sponsors were teaching the lessons. That is certainly useful for some people. It was simply no longer what Dayton and I and some others were looking for, so we went elsewhere.

I've been told that the NTI has gotten better since then. It is certainly a good learning experience. Follow *Combat Handguns* magazine for information on how to apply for the next NTI; the group that runs it usually makes their announcements there.

Pin Shooting

In the late 1960s, armed citizen Richard Davis won a gunfight with three armed robbers. He was hit twice himself during the fracas. As he recovered from his wounds, it occurred to him that there had to be something better to stop bullets with than one's own body. He invented the concealable soft body armor he called Second Chance. By January of 2001, more than 2,500 identified good guys and gals had been saved by the concept, more than 800 by Richard's Second Chance brand alone.

In the early days, he had to overcome the myth that the blunt trauma of a bullet striking the soft armor would render the officer helpless. He needed a visually dramatic target that would show the truth. He set up a table on a dirt firing range in Walled Lake, Michigan, on which he placed a couple of blocks of Roma Plastilena modeling clay (then used to demonstrate bullet effect before the coming of improved ballistic gelatin). He also set up a few bowling pins.

What happened next, as a home movie camera whirred erratically, was law enforcement history. Davis loaded a Colt .357 Magnum with hot Smith & Wesson brand .38 Special ammo that was the forerunner of today's +P, and he blew up the clay blocks with a couple of rounds.

Then he turned the gun on himself … and shot himself in the midriff.

Match gun? Street gun? Two guns in one! The author used this S&W Model 625 in .45 ACP to shoot a personal best at Second Chance (faster than he'd ever shot a comp gun) and to make Master at the IDPA Mid-Winter National Championships in 1999...and it is the gun he would carry on duty if he was required to switch back to a service revolver tomorrow.

Immediately, to show that the impact of the slug had not impaired his ability to fight, he spun back toward the table and with the three rounds left, shot the three bowling pins. A few years later, already a millionaire from his invention, Rich wanted to give something back to the cops who had made him successful. He decided to create the Second Chance Street Combat Shoot, in the mid-1970s. He invited a few friends to the first one for a "test drive," and then opened it up to all cops in 1976.

I was there. I found it a lot tougher than it looked. If you think about it, a bowling pin is a very anatomic target. The neck/head area of the pin roughly duplicates the human cervical spine. The pin widens at the same place and to about the same width as the human heart, and truncates at about where the xiphoid process would be on a human sternum. A powerful bullet that hits the pin anywhere would pretty much do the job on a human antagonist.

Richard's Second Chance match became a regular stop on the "professional tour" of handgunning...and more. If the big shooting matches were rock concerts, Second Chance was Woodstock. It was a "happening." Free food and barbecues, parties, fireworks, and a smorgasbord of shooting that was sort of like a carnival midway, except that the games weren't cheating you and if you performed well, you won guns. There were people who went to the eight-day festivities who didn't even compete anymore, and just came to be with other like-minded shooters. A few years into the experience, Richard had remembered his roots as an armed citizen and opened it to civilians.

Second Chance, sadly, was discontinued in 1998, a victim of fear of civil liability on the part of the corporate board. But it had left a legacy. There are hundreds and hundreds of "pin matches" held now at local clubs around the country. Check at your gun shop or gun club and find out where they're happening near you.

The range is close, 25 feet. However, just as in real life, only center hits count. The object is to blow each bowling pin all the way back off its 3-foot-deep table. Whoever gets all the pins off fastest, wins. If you hit more than an inch off

So inexpensive it's a best buy, the reliable Ruger P90 is accurate enough to win combat matches.

center with a powerful bullet, the pin will spin sideways instead of falling back, and you'll have to shoot it again. It will roll in unpredictable directions and you'll have to track it carefully to shoot it once more and finally blow it away. But if you hit it dead center, it's "out of the fight."

Richard and I got together some years ago and wrote a book on how to do this, called "Hit the White Part." The joke went around that it was my combat shooting book for black guys. In fact, the title came from the single most common question/answer sequence Richard had to go through with new shooters. They would ask arcane questions like, "Where on the bowling pin should I aim?" Richard would reply, "Don't overcomplicate it. Just hit the white part." The book is available for $11.95 +$4.90 shipping from Police Bookshelf, PO Box 122, Concord, NH 03301, or you can order from the website, www.ayoob.com.

Advice in General

I went through the whole thing with the race guns and space guns and PPC guns. They're still in my gun safe. They hold pleasant memories, and they're good investments, but I never seem to shoot them anymore. I retired from the "pro tour" in 1981, and have since shot matches just to keep my hand in. The matches are my personal "pressure laboratory," to see how well a given technique works under stress, and to constantly keep testing myself for self-defense ability.

How deeply you get into it is up to you. Even when I was into it deeply, I made a point of shooting a gun that was analogous to what I carried. When my department issued the K-frame S&W Combat Magnum, I shot a K-frame S&W PPC gun that had been tuned by Ron Power. I won my share of matches and trophies and guns with it, and every stroke of the trigger in competition was pretty much the same as what I had with the revolver I carried on police patrol.

When my match gun was a Plaxco or Middlebrooks Custom .45 tricked out with a recoil compensator, my carry gun on duty and off, and the gun I kept by the bed, was a Colt Government Model or Commander .45. The same feel, the same trigger, the same manual of arms.

In a time when I could carry my Colt Python on duty, I had Austin Behlert put a heavy match barrel and sight rib on a Colt that I shot in open PPC matches. I used the 4-inch duty gun in NRA Service Revolver, a 6-inch Python in the NRA's Distinguished event, and a 2-1/2-inch Python tuned

This shooter tests his skill with his Glock carry gun against the ringing targets of the Steel Challenge.

These two S&W target-grade .38s complement one another. Top, Combat Masterpiece Model 15 for carry; below, 6-inch Model 14 with BoMar sight rib, for PPC shooting. Identical frames, actions and Hogue grips allow strong skill translation from match gun to duty gun.

by Reeves Jungkind (who also did my PPC gun's action) for the snubby events. I won the state championship in police combat two or three times with the 4-inch Python, which had been slicked by Jerry Moran, and once with the snub-nosed Jungkind gun shooting against the 4-inch revolvers. I never felt handicapped when I didn't have the crutches of the heavy barrel and the massive sight rib.

When my department issued the S&W 4506, I dedicated myself to that gun. Bob Houzenga slicked up my personal duty pistol, and I bought another 4506 and sent it to Wayne Novak, who made it single action and put in a Model 52 match trigger for competition. I shot that for a year or two, and then realized the trigger wasn't the same and I was kidding myself, so I just competed with the 4506. One year at Second Chance I shot the target version in the Pin Gun event and the duty gun in the Stock Gun class, won a gun with each, and discovered to my surprise that I had shot a faster time with the gun I carried on duty than with the target pistol. Not long after that, my team won the four-man state championship in a bowling pin event called "Rolling Thunder." One contestant shot a rifle, one a pistol, one a pump shotgun, and one an auto-loading scattergun. I

anchored on pistol with my duty 4506, double-action first shot and all, and we took home the big one.

The lesson is this: *compete as much as possible with the gun you actually carry.* This way, you'll maximize the effect of "shooting the match as training." If you think about it, one definition of "training" is the LFI definition: "authentically replicated experience." The more you shoot matches with the gun you're likely to actually have in your hand if you have to fight for your life, the more each of those matches becomes a true, relevant training experience.

A lot of times, I'll shoot a match with whatever gun I'm testing for a gun magazine at the time. Testing guns is part of my job. How it works in human hands under stress is one of the things I test for, and that's why when the scheduling permits I'll shoot a match with whatever handgun I'm writing up. I don't do that for myself. I do it for the readers of the test.

There are also times when I'm shooting a match to win, and I know I'm up against stiff competition who are all equipped with the best guns, and I'd be a damn fool not to have the best gun myself. In those events, I might indeed use a high tech, state-of-the-art custom match pistol if one is allowed.

But the ones I like most are the matches where you *have* to use the gun you carry. Our state championship for cops is like that where we live. I've found that whether you carry a K-frame or a Python, a Ruger .45 auto or a Glock, doesn't make that much of a difference. If you've bonded to the gun, as you should with the weapon you carry to defend your life and the lives of the innocent, you'll do OK with it.

Competition with the defensive handgun is one of the strongest avenues to developing the skills that will save your life. It has been my experience that the only people who say otherwise are those that haven't tried it, and therefore don't have a right to the opinion, or those who shot so badly in competition that they're desperately trying to deny the future they saw when they failed on the range that day.

CHAPTER SIX

COMBAT HANDGUN CONTROVERSIES REVOLVER VERSUS AUTO

They've never stopped arguing about this one...and they've rarely made the most cogent points for either side!

In days of yore, gun magazine editors who ran out of fresh ideas could always get another few pages out of the "revolver versus auto" thing. The auto guy would write about "wave of the future" and "firepower!" The revolver guy would warn about the hazards of untrustworthy jam-amatics compared to "our trusted friend, the six-shooter" and point out that since most gunfights were supposed to be over in 2.3 rounds, if you couldn't do it with six you couldn't do it at all.

What happened? Basically, things changed. In those days, about the only reliable autos were the Colt .45 and the Browning 9mm, and then only if you fed them ball ammo. Round-nose, full-metal-jacket was an adequate stopper in .45, though it didn't optimize the cartridge's inherent potency, but it was woefully inadequate in 9mm. When loaded with hollow-points, most of the autoloaders of the mid-20th century *did* jam, if not epidemically then at least enough to worry about.

In the 1970s, when police departments and armed citizens started switching to 9mm high-capacity pistols, someone coined the term "wondernine" for this new hardware.

There was nothing wondrous about a 9mm auto with a double-stack magazine; the classic Browning Hi-Power had been around since 1935. What was wondrous was that this new breed – Beretta, Heckler & Koch, SIG-Sauer, second-generation Smith & Wessons – actually *worked* with JHPs. In 1985 came the Glock, just as reliable and even simpler to operate, and the dominance of the modern auto became a *fait accompli.*

The revolver remains the choice of handgun hunters, who but rarely go after game with their .44 and .50 Magnum Desert Eagle and .45 Magnum Grizzly autos, but that's a topic for a different book. The wheelgun is by no means dead in the combat handgun world. Bert DuVernay, the master instructor who once ran the Smith & Wesson Academy, said that the revolver would remain strong as a backup and off-duty gun among police. The years have proven him correct on that.

The cylinder gun also remains the choice of most experts when outfitting novices who won't necessarily be getting the structured training and in-service refresher time that a cop

Better hit potential under stress seems to be a cardinal advantage of the self-cocking auto pistol with its short, light trigger stroke, such as this Beretta 9mm.

It's easy for a new shooter or someone with weak hands to open the cylinder of a double-action revolver like this Colt Detective Special and check to see if it's loaded or not.

will get with his duty automatic. That's a good place to start when listing the real-world attributes of each design concept.

Revolver Advantages

Ease Of Administrative Handling. The routine loading, unloading, checking, and cleaning that a combat handgun demands is more easily accomplished with the revolver. That's particularly true if the user is debilitated or injured, or lacking in strength in the hands and upper body. There's no tough recoil spring to muscle a slide against, and no hidden firing chamber where a live cartridge can secrete itself while an amateur thinks the removal of the magazine has unloaded the gun. Even a little old lady with osteoporosis can activate a cylinder release latch, push a cylinder out of a frame, and check to see if the revolver is loaded or not.

Simplicity Of Function. No magazines to worry about. Nothing that you need to run a revolver can get separated

Street cop and six-time national champion Bob Houzenga carries a department issue Glock .40 as primary duty gun…

…but prefers a revolver, specifically this S&W Model 642, for backup for reasons explained in the text.

from it except for the ammunition. Load gun, point gun, pull trigger. If cartridge misfires, pull trigger again. That simple.

Reliability. Yes, revolvers can jam, and yes, some of our modern autos are splendidly reliable. That notwithstanding, if you take *all* auto pistols currently in defensive use and compare them to *all* modern revolvers, the autos are at least slightly more likely to malfunction. The auto requires maintenance, particularly lubrication. The auto's magazine springs can take a set after being kept loaded for too long. A Smith & Wesson hand ejector model of 1899, if kept in a cool dry place for more than a century and then loaded with fresh ammunition, would undoubtedly fire. Few of us would want to stake our lives on the functionality of a 1911 pistol whose magazine spring had been fully compressed since before WWI.

Ammo Versatility. Your revolver will run blanks, snake-shot or rat-shot, light target loads, standard service rounds, or Monster Magnum cartridges. No alteration is required when you change ammo. Your auto, however, was designed with a slide mass/spring compression rate geared for a certain range of duty ammunition. Too light a load won't run the gun. Too hot a load may actually cycle the slide so fast it closes again on an empty chamber because the magazine spring didn't raise the next cartridge fast enough to be picked up. A bullet profile with too flat a nose or too short an overall cartridge length may compromise your auto's feed reliability, too. None of that compromises the turning cartridge wheel from which the revolver draws its nickname.

A wide mouth guarantees these Federal 125-grain Magnum loads will expand when fired from this S&W 686 revolver, but few auto pistols would feed such ammo reliably.

Intimidation Value. When a homeowner points an automatic pistol at an arrogant intruder, he may believe it's a toy. He might convince himself it's your grandfather's war souvenir with cobwebs instead of cartridges in the chamber. If that makes him go for his gun, or for yours, he might get lucky. But if you're pointing a revolver at him, he will almost certainly see something else: the heads of live cartridges pointing right at him. The sight of these missiles poised for launch may make the difference in convincing

Most autos are easier to shoot well under stress than most revolvers. In this qualification shoot, Tracy Wright (left), the author, and Bob Smith (right) have all shot perfect scores with 1911 Tactical .45s tuned by Mark Morris, standing at rear.

For those who wear ankle holsters, there's something else to consider. The gun is inches above the ground, with dirt and grit being kicked up around it with every step. This is why an "ankle gun" is generally covered with a fine film of grit after you've been out and about wearing it for a few days. The finely-fitted moving parts of most small auto pistols won't take that. We've had cases from California to Florida where the good guy drew a small auto from an ankle holster, got off a couple of shots, and suffered a malfunction at the worst possible time. A quality revolver, by contrast, will shoot even if it has dust bunnies in it.

Shooting from right to left, John Lazzaro smokes a table of pins with his modified S&W 1917 .45 revolver. With only five pins, a shooter this good won't need more than six shots.

him that you're not running a bluff, and result in his deciding not to attack. No guarantees, but if something even *might* work to your advantage, it's worth considering.

Barricade Advantage. When you have to fire from behind cover, you want to maximize that cover. With an auto pistol, the gun has to be out away from the wall or its slide can jam from friction. This means your head has to come out that much more from behind cover to aim, and where your head goes, your body follows. With the revolver, you can lay the barrel right against the barricade. This also steadies your aim somewhat (though it also increases felt recoil), but mainly, it brings you in deeper behind protective cover.

Low Maintenance. Unless you've rusted it shut or crapped it up so much there's a layer of carbon binding the cylinder's rotation past the forcing cone of the barrel, or debris built up under the ejector star, your revolver will probably do OK without a cleaning. An auto, even if pristinely cleaned after its last firing, should be lubricated regularly. The long bearing surfaces of slide and frame require lubrication for reliability. When the gun is carried in a holster, the liquid lubricant drains out. It can also evaporate. This can lead to a jammed-up pistol. The revolver, in my opinion and that of many experts, actually shouldn't be lubricated inside. Doesn't need it. That means a person who doesn't clean and lube his revolver regularly is not susceptible to gun lock-up when they need their handgun most, but the auto shooter most certainly is in danger of that.

Deep Concealment Access. When you carry in a real hideout location – ankle rig, pocket, belly band, or Thunderwear – the gun is pressed tightly against your body. The flat sides of the small auto's grip frame will be so close to your flesh that, in a fast-draw emergency, your fingers almost have to claw to gain a solid drawing grasp. But the rounded profile of a small revolver's grip-frame guides the firing hand right into drawing position. Deep concealment is slow to draw from anyway; using a revolver there minimizes that problem.

Cost/Value. Look in the catalogs of companies that produce both revolvers and semiautomatic pistols. Taurus and Smith & Wesson are good examples. You'll generally find, grade for grade, that the revolvers are significantly less expensive.

Accuracy. As noted elsewhere in this book, accuracy can be more important in a combat handgun than many traditionalists believe. We can get by with the accuracy of any of the auto pistols recommended in this book, but more never hurts. The revolver, by and large, is more accurate than an auto pistol of similar quality grade.

In 1988, the department I then served became the fourth in the nation to adopt Smith & Wesson's third-generation .45 automatic, the Model 4506. It was a splendid gun. Ours averaged about 2.5-inch groups from the bench at 25 yards. However, the S&W Model 13 .357 Magnum revolvers we traded in for them were capable of holding the same size group at twice the distance.

Autoloader Advantages

High Hit Potential Under Stress. When the Illinois State Police adopted the Smith & Wesson Model 39 semiautomatic in 1967, they were ahead of their time. They and other cops with revolvers of the period were hitting bad guys with about 25 percent of the bullets they fired in

Even the finest auto pistols can jam. This is a failure to eject with the Kahr P9.

Though complicated for a novice to handle, the HK P7 pistol is extremely easy for most people to shoot fast and straight once they are familiar with it.

action. With the adoption of the 9mm auto, hit ratio sky-rocketed to somewhere around 65 percent.

The auto pistol is more ergonomic. Most revolver users who knew their stuff put after-market grips on their wheelguns as soon as they bought them. In the 1990s, S&W and Colt wised up and put the after-market grips (Uncle Mike's and Pachmayr, respectively) on their own guns at the factory. "If you can't beat 'em, join 'em."

The auto's lower bore axis reduced recoil. Most autos have a shorter trigger pull, at least after the first double-action shot, which means that shooter panic is less likely to muscle the gun barrel off target as the defender jerks at the trigger. It is significant that ISP noted a lot of those 35 percent misses were the first double-action shot.

It should also be noted that the best hit potentials in the field have been with *single-stack* (8- or 9-shot) pistols. With high-capacity guns – especially when the cops were told the new pistols had been bought for "firepower" – the firepower seemed to become a *raison d'etre* that led to a "spray and pray" mentality. Significantly, ISP troopers' hit percentages in the field reportedly went down when they went from single-stack Model 39s to higher capacity guns.

Proprietary Nature To The User. We have case after case on record of suspects getting the gun away, trying to shoot the officer, and failing because the snatched weapon was a semiautomatic pistol carried "on safe." Most tests on this over the last 20 years (the first was published circa 1981 in *Police Chief* magazine, the journal of the International Association of Chiefs of Police) have resulted in the unfamiliar person taking an average of 17 seconds to figure out which little lever "turned on" the pistol.

Many auto pistols don't have this feature. Many double-action models are in the hands of people who don't choose to use this feature. This feature *can* be retrofitted to some revolvers: the Murabito safety catch conversion, and the "smart gun" conversion called MagnaTrigger. That said, the ability to serve as proprietary to the user is primarily a function of the semiautomatic pistol.

Firepower. Purists will tell you that you can't call it "firepower" until you get into belt-fed weapons. Realists know that since the first two cavemen started throwing rocks at each other, whoever threw the most rocks the fastest and straightest had an advantage.

The degree of advantage varies from gun to gun. If you go from a five-shot .38 revolver to a seven-shot Micro Kahr 9mm, it's a 40 percent increase. When California Highway Patrol went from six-shot .38 service revolvers to 12-shot S&W Model 4006 autos, they doubled their firepower. When any department went from six-shooters to the 18-shot Glock 17 in 9mm, they had 300 percent the firepower they had before. And that's just the in-gun reservoir of ammo. The auto pistol is also faster to load (in case a gun is kept unloaded for home defense), and faster to reload, especially under stress.

There's that firepower thing. An auto will still be shooting when revolver is reloading and, with both starting empty, the auto will be shooting sooner than the revolver, all other things being equal.

You can get awfully fast at refilling a wheelgun with speedloaders. You may get to where you can reload a revolver faster than I can reload an auto pistol. But you'll never get to where *you* can reload a revolver faster than *you*

Not every .45 auto will handle this broad range of ammo without a malfunction, though this SIG P220 stainless passed the test.

reign police instructors made officers qualify with the same rounds they loaded for work, but you still see that "practice with light loads, carry with heavy loads" thing with armed citizens.

Ya can't do that with an auto pistol, gang. Go below the threshold of what the gun was designed for, and your auto pistol won't work. That means the auto forces you to use ammo that's at least reasonably close to the power of what you'd carry on the street. That means its design enforces more relevant training.

This Colt 1911A1 .45 auto is locking open after the last shot. A shooter can reload it faster than a revolver.

can reload an auto pistol, assuming the same amount of practice with each gun.

Times have changed. We're seeing more multiple offender assaults, more and more perpetrators involved in professional armed robberies. In the horror of September 11, 2001, we saw hijack teams of up to six terrorists. If hit potential might be as low as one out of four shots in the stress of combat, and multiple opponents are increasing, you don't need to be a math major to see the advantage of a defensive weapon with more firepower.

Add to that the fact that the bad guys are using small-unit guerrilla tactics (fast movement, and cover) and are more likely than ever to be wearing body armor. Both of these factors mean you're likely to have to fire more shots before one takes effect. Firepower is more important today than when revolvers ruled.

Relative Compactness. A semiautomatic is flatter than a revolver of equal power. That makes it easier and more comfortable to conceal discreetly. That goes double for spare ammo: speedloaders for revolvers have as much bulge as another whole revolver's cylinder, but flat spare magazines for autos "carry easier."

Relevant Training. That "takes any ammo that fits its chamber" thing is sometimes an advantage for the revolver, but it became a disadvantage under the old paradigm of cops training with .38 wadcutters that kicked like mouse farts, yet actually carrying Elmer Keith Memorial Magnum rounds for serious business. Revolvers are gone from the police scene now for the most part, and toward the end of their

Lower Muzzle Flash. Large-bore auto pistols generally have less muzzle flash than large-bore revolvers. The .357 SIG auto round doesn't flash as much as the .357 Magnum revolver round, and most 9mm auto ammo flares less at the muzzle than does equivalent .38 Special revolver ammo. We are in the time of low flash powders for premium ammo for both types of gun, so this is not as huge a difference as it was in the old days...but the difference is still there, and it favors the auto pistol. A gun whose muzzle flash blinds you when you fire it at night is not conducive to your being able to see the sun rise the next morning.

Conclusions

There are still very real revolver advantages versus auto advantages. As Bruce Lee said, each practitioner of the given martial art must assess her own strengths and weaknesses, and choose what she will fight with accordingly.

When in doubt, carry one of each. For most of my adult life, I've carried two guns. The primary was usually (but not always) a service-size semiautomatic pistol. The backup was usually (but not always) a small frame snub-nosed revolver. The main fighting weapon gave me improved hit potential and all the other factors when it was an auto. The backup revolver gave me fast access and certain function from deep concealment, and also allowed me to arm a compatriot with a gun whose manual of arms I wouldn't have to explain when there wasn't time.

I always figured if I carried a revolver *and* an auto, when I got to the Pearly Gates I'd be covered, whether Saint Peter turned out to be a Jeff Cooper fan *or* a Bill Jordan fan.

DAO Versus DA/SA

The DAO SIG E26 fired the top group at 25 yards. An older DAO P226 fired the second group down. A DA first shot with four SA follow-up rounds from a conventional P226 delivered the third group, followed by the bottom group, the same gun fired single-action for all five shots.

The double-action auto pistol in its conventional style – i.e., self-cocking itself after the first DA shot and becoming single-action for each shot thereafter until de-cocked – at first seemed hugely logical for police and armed citizens. Many think it still does.

Later came DAO, or double-action-only. This, in effect, was a mechanism that allowed the gun to "de-cock" itself after every shot. Some, especially in the higher echelons of law enforcement, believed this was safer for the rank and file. It has become hugely popular in policing, somewhat less so among the private citizenry.

Jeff Cooper said that *any* double-action auto was "an ingenious solution to a non-existent problem." He considered double-action-*only* autos to be anathema to good shooting as he knew it, and at one point forbade such guns from his famous shooting school, Gunsite. A gunwriter once remarked, "Double-action-only is so stupid, they're making jokes about it in Poland." Meanwhile, three of our six largest law enforcement agencies mandate DAO auto pistols: NYPD, Chicago PD, and the Border Patrol.

Who's right? Let's hash out the arguments and decide.

In 1990 I found myself teaching a class for the DEA Academy at Quantico. DEA shares the same facility as the FBI Academy. They call each other "the guys down the street." I took some extra time to spend with John Hall, then the chief of the FBI's Firearms Training Unit. They were in the news big time because they were then in the process of implementing the adoption of a gun they had designed with Smith & Wesson, the Model 1076 10mm. 10mm Auto was the hot ticket during that period.

If you've already fired a shot under stress, and aren't deeply familiarized with your weapon, you may not remember to de-cock. In such circumstances, this lady is well served with DAO Kahr K9 as she covers the threat zone from behind cover while calling 9-1-1.

Some departments were already going over to the DAO concept. I asked John why he and his agency didn't buy into that. The reply was clear and succinct. The rationale of the double-action trigger with its long, heavy pull, John explained, was to reduce the likelihood of accidental discharges under stress. He and the Bureau accepted that. This was why it was only DA first shot autos that were approved for the Bureau's then approximately 7,000 agents. Only the *crème de la crème,* the elite Hostage Rescue Unit, was allowed to carry single-action autos. At the time the HRU had Browning Hi-Power 9mms customized by Wayne Novak, and local-office FBI SWAT teams had the DA/SA SIG P226 9mm.

Hall continued his explanation. "Almost all accidental discharges are one-shot events," he said. "After the first shot, if he needs to continue shooting, the agent is in a gunfight." Hall and company wanted that agent to have the easiest possible job of making those subsequent shots count under stress. The self-cocking trigger was deemed the best way to achieve that obviously worthwhile goal.

This made sense to me. I had always been an advocate of a broad weapons policy that let officers pick, within reason, the guns that worked best for them. As the motorcyclists say, "Let those who ride, decide." I still believe that. But, two years before, my new chief had decided that we would all carry the same gun, and all I had left to say about it was

Don't tell a seasoned shooter that a good DAO auto isn't controllable. The author shot this 60-round qualification group with Beretta 96D Centurion and full power .40 S&W ammo. The "D" suffix after a Beretta model number means double-action for every shot.

Genesis of DAO

In the early 1980s, police chiefs became increasingly aware of accidental discharges caused by the "hair trigger" effect created when officers cocked their service revolvers. LAPD started what became a trend, an alteration of the revolver's mechanism (the simple removal of the cocking notch of the hammer) that rendered the gun double-action only. Sure enough, when no one could cock the gun, cocked gun "accidentals" disappeared. Miami PD, NYPD, and Montreal PD soon followed suit.

Bill Laughridge lines up the DAO auto that may be the easiest of all to shoot well, the Para-Ordnance LDA.

I can tell you the inside story on two of those last three. Miami made their S&W Model 64 .38 revolvers DAO after the controversial killing of Nevell "Snake" Johnson in an inner-city video arcade by Officer Luis Alvarez. It was a cross-racial shooting that triggered the second largest race riot in the city's history. Janet Reno was then the State's Attorney (the chief prosecutor) for Dade County, which encompasses Miami. The city needed a scapegoat. Alvarez was offered up. He was charged with manslaughter. The prosecution's theory was that Alvarez had cocked the hammer of his gun to show off as he arrested Johnson for possession of an illegal weapon, and that the resultant hair-trigger effect had caused the gun to accidentally discharge because Johnson, while turning to surrender, unexpectedly startled Alvarez. Since it was against regulations to cock the gun for a routine arrest, this theory created the element of negligence, a necessary ingredient to the state's formula for manslaughter conviction.

There was one small problem. The story was all BS. Alvarez never cocked the gun. His defense lawyers, Roy Black and Mark Seiden, retained me as an expert witness. We were able to *prove* that he had never cocked the gun. The jury learned that Johnson had spun toward Alvarez and his rookie partner and had reached for the stolen RG .22 revolver in his waistband, with the obvious intention of killing both cops. At that moment, Luis Alvarez had instantly and intentionally done the right thing: he shot and killed the gunman.

The trial lasted eight weeks, the longest criminal trial in Florida history. It ended with an acquittal after only two hours of jury deliberation, including dinner. The acquittal triggered the *third* largest race riot in Miami history, but

what gun it would be. I had been instrumental, in 1988, in selecting an issue gun very much like what Hall came up with: the Smith & Wesson 4506.

The reasons Hall had cited were there. So was the fact that our people had to patrol in some nasty winters, and for a third or more of the year would have to manipulate guns with hands impaired by either numbing cold or feel-blunting gloves. With the gloves, a lot of double-action-only guns – including the S&W .357 Magnum revolvers we issued up until then – could have their trigger return blocked by the thick glove material on the trigger finger. This could turn the six-shot .357 into a single-shot. With the DA/SA Smith auto, once they fired the first shot, the trigger would stay in a rearward position until all further necessary shooting was done. Then, with the trigger finger removed from the guard, the officer's thumb could easily manipulate the slide-mounted de-cocking lever. It seemed the safest and most practical method.

Frankly, it still does. Well over a decade later, I now serve another department. We've had similar guns, the Ruger P-series .45 autos, as standard issue since 1993. The previous department, last I knew, still had their conventional style S&W autos. I note a point: *neither department, in all those years, had an accidental discharge with those "traditional style" DA/SA semiautomatic pistols!*

that's another story. This trial comprises one fourth of famed defense lawyer Roy Black's superb book, *Black's Law*, if you want to read more about it.

The point is, the city had all their revolvers rendered DAO between the shooting and the trial. The local cops called them "Alvarized" guns. Though it was nothing more than a concession to political correctness, it's entirely possible that later, down the road, this alteration did have some positive safety benefits. I can't say either way. If nothing else, it kept unscrupulous prosecutors from throwing any more innocent cops to the wolves with the bogus "cocked gun" theory.

The Montreal decision to go DAO came after the case of *Crown v. Allan Gossett*. Canadian firearms training of the period was at least 20 years behind that of the U.S., and Gossett had become a constable of the Montreal Police when they were still taught to shoot a revolver by cocking the hammer and squeezing off single-action shots at bull's-eye targets. The night came when he was in pursuit of a felony suspect, and had to draw his issue S&W Model 10 .38 caliber service revolver. As the suspect spun toward Gossett, the constable was seen to jerk as if startled, and his gun fired. The violent jump of the gun with mild .38 recoil, and the look of shock on Gossett's face as it discharged, were noted by witnesses and tended to confirm the fact that it was an unintentional discharge.

"New" doesn't always mean "progress." The author found in testing of these two Berettas that the newest Model 9000-D, below, didn't hold a candle to older Model 96D, above. Both are DAO in caliber .40 S&W.

It was believed that the gun was cocked. Gossett didn't remember cocking it. I believed him and so, in the end, did those who tried the facts, the only ones whose beliefs counted. The Crown, as the prosecution is known up there, charged him with manslaughter on the same grounds as Reno had charged Alvarez. It was their theory that negli-

gence (intentional cocking of the gun), plus death (which obviously took place) equals manslaughter.

I testified for Gossett, too. Like Alvarez, he was ultimately acquitted. We believe that one of two things happened: he went back to his original training reflexively and in those high-stress moments cocked the gun without realizing it, or the hammer had become cocked by accident. We'll never know which. At the time, Montreal issued a crappy holster that appeared to be living proof that you could tan the hide of a chicken and make gunleather out of it. The safety strap went over the back of the trigger guard instead of over the hammer. The unprotected hammer could thus snag on seat belts, coat sleeves, or just about anything else and become cocked while still in the holster, unnoticed by the constable wearing it.

After Gossett's ordeal, Montreal got some decent gunleather and ordered the Model 10s made DAO.

What does all this have to do with auto-loading pistols? Glad you asked. It *is* a long story.

Shortly after the Alvarez trial, the Miami street cops and their union went to the chief in Miami and asked for high capacity 9mm autos to replace their .38 six-shooters. They were confiscating an increasing number of high-cap autos from dopers – their city was then the illegal drug capitol of the nation – and they sought parity. Sure, the chief said, you can have hi-cap autos...*if* you can find one that's double-action for every shot!

The union (and the city firearms instructors) pleaded with Beretta, SIG, and S&W to make a 9mm auto that was double-action for every shot. The companies thought the idea was stupid and blew them off. At about that time, the Bureau of Alcohol, Tobacco, and Firearms declared the Glock pistol's mechanism, which its inventor designated Safe-action, to be "double-action only."

It was delicious. The chief who hadn't wanted autos for his troops was "hoisted by his own petard." In desperation, seemingly impossible torture tests were ordered for durability. The Glock passed them. To cut to the chase: Miami became the first really big, high-crime city to adopt the Glock. They were the flagship of the fleet, and soon Glock was outselling all the rest combined. Beretta, SIG, and S&W *now* felt the impetus to come out with DAO guns...but they were too late to stop the huge momentum Glock had developed in the police market.

Today, Miami PD still issues the Glock, having upgraded from the 9mm to the .40 S&W caliber. Montreal, when they went to autos, went DAO too, as did virtually all of Canadian law enforcement. While most provincial and municipal agencies in Canada chose the .40 caliber, the Royal Canadian Mounted Police and the Montreal PD went with DAO Smith & Wesson pistols in 9mm.

The Decision Today

There are shooters who prefer DAO because having only one trigger pull to work with for every shot is easier for them. I won't argue the point. I've seen too many shooters for whom that was true. If you anticipate the shot and jerk the trigger when you're working with a gun that has a short, light pull, the DAO is something you should try.

There are departments that can't devote as much time and money as their instructors would like to train the rank and file with handguns. NYPD (40,000 officers) and Chicago PD

(13,000 cops) are well known for being in that situation. Both of them require that all personnel, except for older officers who are "grandfathered" with permission to carry double-action revolvers, carry DAO auto pistols on duty.

I've seen people under stress "lose it" to the degree that after they had fired one or more shots, they forgot to de-cock their conventional DA autos before holstering. In one case in California, an officer did this with his Beretta 92F 9mm after shooting an attacking pit bull. He had not only forgotten to de-cock, he had forgotten to take his finger off the trigger. As he put the gun back in his holster, his finger caught the edge of the leather that was designed to cover the trigger guard, and came to a stop. However, the gun kept going, driving the trigger against the finger. BANG! He shot himself in the leg. Now even more stressed than before, he tried to shove the gun into the holster again. BANG! He shot himself a second time in the space of only a few seconds. The unique "partially open front" design of his department's trademark holster had allowed the Beretta to cycle while partially holstered.

Some believe this is a training issue. For the most part, it is, but the fact remains that the harder it is to pull the trigger, the harder it is to pull the trigger *accidentally*. When you have a light, easy, single-action trigger, there is good news and bad news. The good news is it's easy to shoot. The bad news is it's easy to shoot. It's the situation that will determine whether a certain type of trigger pull is a good thing or a bad thing.

Design Features

All DAO handguns are not created equal. The ParaOrdnance LDA (an acronym its users have determined stands for "Light Double-action"; the manufacturer never actually spelled it out) has a deliciously easy trigger pull. Some police departments (such as North Attleboro, Massachusetts) have already adopted it for standard issue. Some others (such as the San Bernardino Sheriff's Department) have approved it for duty if deputies wish to buy their own.

Next up on the "ease of manipulation" ladder are the DAO guns of Kahr Arms and Smith & Wesson. Both are extremely smooth and easy to shoot well. The Kahrs are

small, reliable hideout guns; the S&W line encompasses small to large and includes duty-size service pistols.

The DAO Berettas tend to be lighter than the regular Berettas in the big 92 and 96 series guns, but heavier than LDAs, Smiths, or Kahrs. The absence of a single-action sear removes a friction point, and I believe the springs are a bit lighter. On the other hand, Beretta's little Model 9000 polymer gun has a nasty double-action pull.

The theory is that transitioning to DAO gives you one less manipulation to worry about, that is, de-cocking after the shooting is over. That's true as far as it goes. On the other hand, a great many people find a shorter, lighter trigger pull is less likely to jerk shots off target, particularly when firing under great stress and at great speed.

Personally, I can live with either style. I've explained why I'm partial to the "conventional" style, the DA/SA. That's not a habituation thing, that's an "I've looked at everything I and my people need where we are" thing. But my people and I aren't you and yours, and we may be in two different places in more ways than one, with two distinct sets of needs.

I serve a small police department where we can train intensively. Whether or not we're all likeable, we're all demonstrably competent. What if I had to take responsibility for training 40,000 personnel, most of whom were not interested in spending a minute to develop confidence and competence with the gun if they weren't being paid for it? What if I could only pay for a couple of days a year of that training? In that case, the double-action-only concept would look very good, indeed.

Don't say DAO autos aren't accurate. Illinois State Rifle Association president Rich Pearson, right, holds a cutout group he watched the author shoot at 25 yards with hot Triton 115-grain/1,325 fps 9mm ammo from this SIG P226 DAO.

When the police instructors and supervisors pick a gun for their officers, two commandments must be kept in mind. *Know thy specific needs,* and *Know thy personnel.*

When a law-abiding citizen makes that decision between these two common types of semiautomatic pistol, a similar process makes sense. Before you decide whether you want a DAO pistol, or a "conventional" DA pistol, or perhaps something else, there are again two commandments: ***Know thy specific needs*** and, perhaps more important, ***know thyself.***

Beretta's 96D in double-action only (short barrel Centurion model shown) has earned a good reputation in the field.

On-Safe Versus Off-Safe

Pick up a standard model S&W, Beretta, or Ruger auto pistol. Manipulate that little lever at the rear of its slide. If two typical firearms instructors are standing one on each side of you, ask them, "What *is* that lever?"

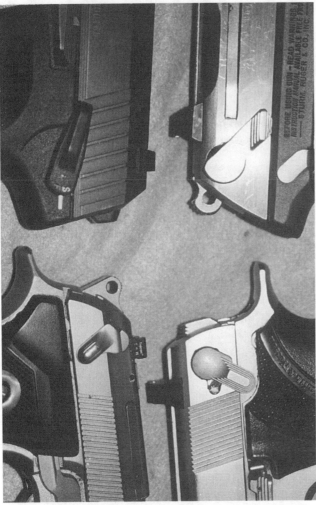

Four popular combat handguns with safety/de-cock levers. Clockwise from noon, those of Ruger, S&W, and Beretta are slide-mounted, while that of HK USP is mounted on the frame.

On a typical day, one might answer, "It's the safety." The other would be likely to scream, "That's not a safety, it's a de-cocking lever!"

And if a firearms engineer was there, he'd probably sound like the Doublemint Twins. "It's two levers – *two* levers! – two levers *in one!*"

Who's right? In a greater or lesser way, all three.

Popularized on Walther pistols developed in the 1920s and coming to prominence in the 1930s, refined by Smith & Wesson on their first 9mm pistols in the mid-1950s, this dual-purpose lever may be the single most misunderstood piece of equipment that you'll find on any combat handgun. If you look at the patents, Smith & Wesson's for example, you'll find it listed as a "safety/de-cock" lever.

I was very much a part of things when autoloaders began pushing revolvers out of the law enforcement handgun picture in the mid-1980s. I saw some scary things, some of which still exist. A few others and I had been voices in the wilderness crying out in the early and mid-1970s that these "automatics" had some advantages that might make them worthy of replacing our ancient "service revolvers."

Most of the police chiefs back then didn't know from guns. They relied on their firearms instructors for input on that. The problem was most of their firearms instructors only knew the revolver. Such an instructor had a set of pat answers when cops came to him asking why they couldn't carry autoloaders.

"Those autos will jam on you," the instructors would say. "Besides, the revolver is loaded and ready to go when you're in danger! Just draw and shoot! With an automatic, you'd have to slow down and take the safety off – if you remembered!"

Then, in what must have seemed to some of them like a cataclysmic change of worlds, the union guys had won, and the chiefs were giving them the autos they had asked for. Groping desperately to catch up with technology they had spent their firearms training careers trying to pretend didn't exist, a lot of these instructors had no *clue* how to manipulate the slide-mounted safety on firearms coming into service. Some examples included the Ruger auto the Wisconsin state troopers had adopted, the Beretta that had been chosen by LAPD, and the Smith & Wesson chosen by the Illinois State Police before any of the rest.

Rather than teach its manipulation, it was easier to pretend that it didn't exist. "It's not a safety catch, it's a de-cocking lever" became the mantra. Now, had this gone to court, I can say as both a police prosecutor and an expert witness that the argument would probably have been destroyed in less than a minute of cross-examination.

"Sir, you are the department's designated firearms expert, correct?"

"Yes."

"And you say this part is not a safety, it's strictly a de-cocking lever?"

"Yes."

"Sir, I show you these two documents. Exhibit A is the patent for the gun you issue your department. Exhibit B is the nomenclature sheet produced by the factory that manufactured the gun you issue to your officers. Can you tell the jury what the part in question is called by these authoritative sources in these documents?"

"Um, it says 'safety/de-cocking lever'…"

"Nothing further."

You can't say something isn't what it obviously is, just because you want it to be so. That's Stalinist revisionism. It didn't even work for Stalin.

It is possible for departments to lose their own sense of institutional history. When you forget where you came from, it's always a bad thing. Case in point: the Illinois State Police, who in 1967 became the first major police department in the USA to issue autoloading pistols.

Here's the real story. ISP at the time let the troopers buy their own Colt or S&W, .38 or .357 revolvers. They were required to be armed off duty, and virtually all carried small-frame snub-nose .38s. The department wanted them all to qualify with the off-duty guns as well as the duty weapons. The scores with the snubbies were pathetic. Let's face it, guns like that were tough to shoot on courses of fire that emphasized 25-yard shooting at the time. The superintendent tasked Louis Seman, then head of Ordnance for the department, with finding a solution.

The solution was the Smith & Wesson Model 39. Weighing only 26.5 ounces, it was midway in heft between a 19-ounce off-duty Chief Special and a 34-ounce K-frame service revolver. It was flat in silhouette, easy to conceal in plain clothes. It reloaded more quickly – *way* more quickly – than loose revolver shells from the dump pouches of the time. While it lacked the inherent accuracy of the guns it replaced (you were doing well to get a 4-inch group at 25 yards), its beautiful hand-fitting ergonomics made the Model 39 9mm autoloader easy to shoot. Maybe it wouldn't equal the revolvers in a machine rest, but you could *put* all its shots into that 4-inch group at 25 yards, and that meant a perfect qualification score.

A decade or so later, I came to Illinois under the auspices of the Troopers' Lodge 41 of the Fraternal Order of Police, the entity that represented the troopers in bargaining. I did the first poll of the troopers on this gun. Some 87 percent of them wanted to go to something else. These 1,700 or so people resented having an alien concept foisted upon them by what they perceived to be one Ordnance Corporal and one desk-bound superintendent.

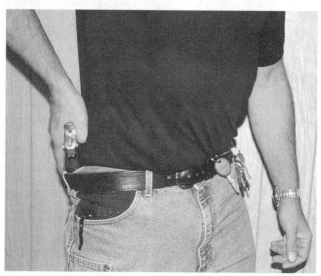

The draw begins. The S&W 4506 is carried on-safe in an LFI Concealment Rig…

But, an interesting thing showed up in all that research. Those troopers had been in a bunch of deadly encounters, and I was given *carte blanche* by the administration to study them. Even though the majority of the troopers at that time wanted to go back to the revolver, there was overpowering evidence that Seman had made the right choice.

I was able to identify **13** troopers who were alive because they'd had the S&W automatic, and would have probably been killed if they'd been armed with six-shot revolvers. I could find **no** case where a trooper armed with the 9mm was shot by a criminal and would not have been shot if the trooper had been armed with a revolver instead.

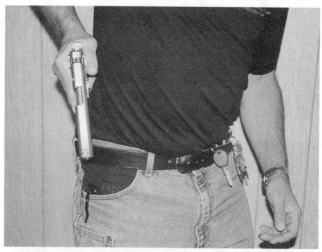

…At about the time the gun clears the body, the thumb has pushed the lever into "fire" position…

… Since the action was accomplished during the draw, there has been no significant time loss in getting a ready-to-fire .45 up on target. Note that the lever is in the "fire" position with the red warning dot exposed.

Everyone thinks firepower is the *raison d'etre* for an auto instead of a revolver. It certainly was a factor, but not the main factor. I found two officers who survived because either the seventh or eighth shot put down the attacker. Trooper Ken Kaas was facing a charging attacker who had a 20-gauge auto shotgun, and a man who had already shot people and was wielding a 12-gauge pump was charging Trooper Les Davis. Both fired their last couple of shots and dropped their would-be murderers. Troopers Lloyd Burchette and Bob Kolowski both ran dry and needed quick reloads to keep up the pace of fire that finally saved their lives in a sustained firefight.

That was four. Of the remaining nine, a few, who were in struggles for their guns were able to hit the magazine release button, and thus activate the magazine disconnector safety. This is the feature seen on the standard S&W auto, the Browning Hi-Power, and some other guns that renders weapon unable to fire, even with a cartridge in the chamber, if the magazine has dropped out of place. In each of those cases, when the suspect finally got the gun away from the trooper, the attempt to shoot the officer failed.

However, the overwhelming majority of those "auto pistol saves" were cases in which the suspect got the gun away from the trooper, pointed it at him, and pulled the trigger…*and the gun did not go off because the trooper had been carrying it on safe.*

From 1967 until well into the 1980s, Illinois troopers were given the option of carrying their gun "on safe" or "off safe." They were shown how to flip off the safety as they drew. The decision was then left up to them.

Then, in the 1980s, some personnel changes took place in the Ordnance Section. Seman was long since retired. Now it was time for the wise senior men who had replaced him, Bob Cappelli and Sebastian "Bash" Ulrich, to take their well-earned retirements too. As transfers, promotions, and retirements would have it, some new people soon flooded into ISP Ordnance. The department thought it best to send them to an outside instructor school.

The school they went to was a famous one that will remain nameless. The instructors were told at that school, "It's not a safety catch, it's a de-cock lever. The gun should be carried off-safe at all times, because it's too awkward to move the lever under stress."

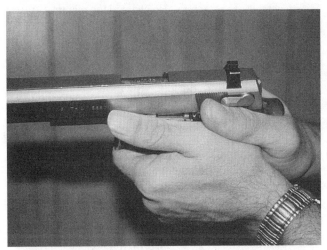

This ergonomic grasp, widely used by combat champions, is perfectly compatible with disengaging a slide-mounted manual safety.

Never mind that in the history of the department, no Illinois State Trooper had ever been hurt because he couldn't get his gun off-safe in time. "The Word From Afar" now became "The Doctrine." Troopers were now *mandated* to carry their S&W autos off-safe. This situation continued until the late 1990s, when the department switched from the S&W 9mms they carried – 16-shot third-generation models by that point – to the Glock 22 pistol, which has no manual safety at all, and requires no decocking lever.

I suppose that's one way to deal with the problem…

The Lessons of Engineering…

Certain auto pistols *must* be on-safe to shield the user from unintended discharges. No logical, sane, and experienced firearms instructor would argue that a single-action auto pistol should be carried off-safe. There is simply too much danger of its easy, short-movement trigger being unintentionally activated.

The Colt .45 and all the many clones of that 1911 design, the Browning Hi-Power, the Star FireStar, and other such designs, are all carried cocked and *locked* by any professional worthy of the name.

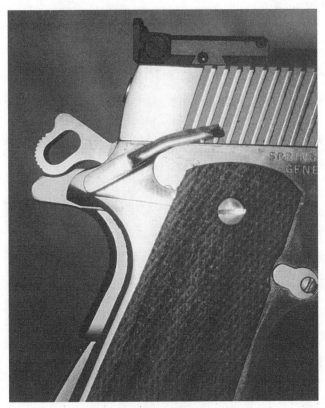

The many 1911 fans think having to carry their gun on-safe is a tactical advantage. The author thinks they're right. Here's the easily manipulated ambidextrous safety of Ayoob's cocked and locked Springfield Trophy Match .45.

When such guns are drawn, the safety is flicked down into the "fire" position as the gun muzzle comes up into the target, after the intention to immediately fire has already been formulated.

There are also certain double-action autos that are not "drop-safe" if the manual safety is not engaged. These include all Walther PP and PPK series guns, and all first-generation Smith & Wesson double-action autos. Two-digit primary model numbers distinguish the latter. The Model 39, 39-2, 59, etc., do not have internal firing pin locks. This makes them and the previously mentioned Walther designs subject to "inertia firing" if dropped or struck on the muzzle or the rear of slide. The firing pins on these guns are only "locked and/or blocked" if the manual safety is engaged.

An officer with an off-safe Model 59 in his holster was carrying a large box of evidence out of the police department. His hands being full, he tried to activate the bar that opened the front door by hitting it with his hip. His pistol's hammer was the contact point, and – BANG! The pistol fired in the holster.

A couple tried to carry a loaded, off-safe Walther .380 into the house along with several bags from a shopping trip. The gun slipped and fell, landing on the floor on its hammer. BANG! The pistol discharged and struck one of the spouses, producing a grave gunshot wound.

...and the Lessons of History

Gun retention is the big advantage of on-safe carry. Gun retention is the corollary science to gun disarming. It is the defeating of the disarming attempt.

Washington: The suspect jumps a cop, gets his cocked and locked 1911 .45 away from him, tries to shoot him. Nothing. Suspect, still with gun, runs. Cop commandeers passing car, takes suspect at gunpoint with 2-inch .38 revolver, and suspect surrenders. A cop-killing was prevented.

Practice plus proper technique equals fast, sure draws to the shot with a double-action pistol carried on safe.

Indiana: Armed robbers take a gun shop owner at gunpoint, relieve him of his HK P7 pistol, take him into back room to murder him. The suspect with the P7 tries to shoot: no effect. He has not fully squeeze-cocked what might be called the "safety lever" at the front of the gun. The gun shop owner grabs a secreted .357 revolver, shoots down two robbers and survives.

Alabama: A suspect being arrested grabs an officer's S&W 9mm from the holster, aims at him, pulls trigger. Nothing happens; gun is "on-safe." The officer draws a back-up Taurus .38 from his ankle holster. The terrified suspect drops the gun and surrenders. No blood is shed.

Illinois: Two suspects attack, disarm, and beat a state trooper. One suspect takes his gun and tries to shoot him. He can't because the S&W Model 39 is on-safe. At this point a second trooper arrives, orders men to stop; suspect points gun at this trooper and pulls trigger. The S&W still won't fire. Second trooper shoots and kills gunman, saving both troopers' lives.

Utah: Many witnesses watch as an officer is sucker punched and knocked unconscious. The attacker pulls the gun from the uniform holster, points it at the officer, and pulls the trigger. Nothing. The S&W 9mm was being carried on safe. The suspect jacked the slide, ejecting a live round, aimed and attempted to shoot again. Nothing. The suspect then fiddled with the slide release lever trying to find the safety, aimed at the officer, and pulled trigger. Nothing. The suspect pressed the button behind the trigger guard and the magazine dropped under a car where it was found later. The suspect again tried to shoot the cop. Nothing. Finally finding the safety lever, the suspect tried again to

shoot the cop. Nothing. The magazine disconnector safety had been activated, preventing the firing of the round in the chamber. The suspect then threw the gun at the prostrate officer and fled. The officer survived.

Florida: A suspect has stolen a Smith & Wesson 9mm auto that is fully loaded with round in chamber, but has been left on-safe. As he robs and attempts to murder cab driver, the gun does not fire. When the cab driver sees the suspect pulling the trigger, he goes for his own gun, a cocked and locked Colt .45 automatic. Since he owns the gun, the cab driver knows where *his* safety is. He shoots and kills the robber, saving his own life.

The list goes on...

Know Thy Weapon

The choice is yours. But be sure it is an informed choice. Look at all sides, weigh all the risks, then decide what works for your balance of need versus risk.

It pains me to see cops and law-abiding citizens giving up a life-saving tactical advantage because their instructors don't know how to operate their tools. More than a decade ago, I was at a seminar where one of the instructors who told those Illinois State Police instructors to give up their safety catches was teaching. He chanted the mantra: "It isn't a safety, it's a de-cocking lever."

I just said the truth to him. "On my department, the chief has mandated that we carry our S&W .45 autos on-safe. Show us what you think is the best way to do that."

He stood there for a moment fumbling with an S&W, wiggling the last digit of his thumb off its median joint as if he was trying to shoot marbles. He said, "You can't. See?"

I didn't want to attack him in public, but he was wrong. You *can,* and I *can* see, and so can you.

With the slide-mounted safety, where the lever has to be pushed up, certain guns are awkward. The little Walther is a case in point. Its lever is at the wrong angle for mechanical advantage. It's one of many reasons I don't carry that tiny .380.

But with the S&W, the Beretta, or the modern Ruger, it's a piece of cake. Simply *thrust the firing hand's thumb up, at a 45-degree angle, as if you were trying to reach the ejection port. Unless your thumb is very short or bends outward to an unusual degree, this will pop the safety catch into the fire position.*

This 45-degree straight angle thrust of the thumb of the firing hand is the most efficient way to disengage a slide-mounted manual safety.

With some holsters, the thumb strap or strap paddle may get in the way. While it would be dangerous to off-safe a single-action auto in the holster, I'm comfortable doing that with a double-action; hell, everybody else is telling you to carry it off-safe to begin with! Videos and high-speed photos of me when I'm drawing showed me that I disengage the safety lever at about 45 degrees of muzzle angle as I'm coming out of the holster. I win my share of matches, and have outdrawn my share of scumbags, and all I can say is, "It works for me."

I'm prepared to test this under pressure. I've done it already. Smith & Wesson owns videotape of me in police uniform doing it, in a film made but never released after my old department adopted the 4506 and Tom Campbell, then an S&W staffer, brought me down to do the flick. S&W Academy's great instructors Bert DuVernay, Brent Purucker, and Tom Aveni were all present when I went to an advanced instructor school there and beat everybody else on the draw to accurate shot, using a 4506 carried on-safe. There were lots of witnesses when I won the 2000 New Hampshire state shoot for cops, on a fast 7- to 50-yard combat course using an on-safe Ruger P90 .45 drawn from a fully secured Safariland 070/SSIII holster.

The techniques are there. The safety catch factor in weapon retention is there. If you find the techniques don't fit your hands, so be it, but make your decision of "off-safe" instead of "on-safe" an informed decision, not just a blind acceptance of something you were told by someone who might not have known how to do it.

The life on the line is your own.

Point Shooting Versus Aimed Fire

For more than a decade, this is a topic that has been guaranteed to not only sell gun magazines, but to generate a flurry of angry letters to the editors. Gun expert Dave Arnold was the first to make a key point about it. "A lot of this argument," Dave said, "is simply a matter of terminology."

As one who has been in or around the center of that debate since 1990, I'll certainly buy *that!* Let's see if we can't quantify our terms at the very beginning so we're all working off the same sheet of music.

Firearms instructor Andy Stanford explains the cone of shot dispersal and the importance of indexing the gun on target. In his hand is a Ring brand dummy gun with Ashley Express high-speed sights.

Two concepts need to be understood first: *index* and *coordinates.* Index is what lines up the gun with that which is to be shot. Coordinates are the things we have to accomplish to achieve index.

There are perhaps three possible indices by which we can line up our gun with the target or the threat:

Here's a situation where hip-shooting will work. The target is at the height of the driver in an average-size car. If the driver pulled a gun during a traffic stop, the officer's hand already on a backup gun in his pocket could give him a fighting chance with this technique.

Body Position Index. This would be the situation where you can't see where the gun is aimed, so you're using a certain body position to align the gun with the target. In the obsolete FBI crouch, the coordinates are backside low, upper body forward, gun punched forward to keep it from going too low. In the speed rock, discussed elsewhere in this book, the coordinates include leaning the upper torso all the way back to bring the forearm lateral as the gun is fired immediately upon levering upward away from the holster. In pure hip-shooting, you are relying on either long-term muscle memory developed through exhaustive practice, or by a degree of talent few of us could ever hope to possess. I would define any type of body position index as "point shooting."

This is a StressPoint Index. It is almost as accurate at close range, and much faster than a conventional sight picture, especially if eye focus is on the threat instead of on the defense gun.

Visual Index. This is where you are indexing by seeing the gun or the gunsights superimposed on the target. If you can see the gun is on target, I consider this aimed fire. Whether you are superimposing the silhouette of the whole gun over the target, or looking over the top of it, *or* taking a classic sight picture, the only question remaining is whether it's coarsely aimed fire or precisely aimed fire.

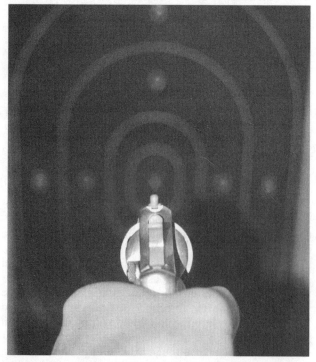

The front sight doesn't have to be in focus to index the shot when it is sitting up out of the rear notch. The revolver is S&W Model 64.

Artificial Index. This would be something like a laser sight. Let's say you have a ballistic raid shield in one hand, and a gun in the other. It will be awkward and difficult to bend the arm into a position where you can aim through the Lexan view port using the regular sights. If you reach your gun around the side of the shield and see your red dot on target, the artificial mechanism of the projected laser dot has indexed the weapon for you, rather than you visually aligning the gun or aligning it by body position index.

Since the laser sight is by no means universal, this argument of point shooting versus aimed fire really comes down to an issue of body position index versus visual index.

The middle road position is, "practice both." That saves controversy, but if you're teaching cops or others with limited time who can't waste even minutes on useless stuff because you don't have as much time as you need to give them key life-saving skills, you can't afford to save controversy any more. A great many police departments have either gotten away from point shooting entirely, or given it very short shrift. The reason is that their cops get into a lot of shootings, and they can quickly find out what works and what doesn't. Departments that have learned to re-emphasize sighted combat fire include LAPD and NYPD, to name but a few. Both saw a significant jump in hit percentages in actual gunfights after renewing their emphasis on visually indexing the duty sidearms.

A gun must "point" for you if you're going to hit with true "point shooting." If the natural hold is center for you with this customized Glock 23...

...then you'll probably shoot high with this slim-gripped S&W Model 60 revolver...

... and way low with this Beretta Model 21 pocket pistol.

A book could be written on this topic – some have been, and more will be – but let's cut to the chase. The bottom line is this; a lifetime of studying real-world gunfight dynamics has taught this author that true point shooting simply doesn't work, except for a handful of extremely skilled and highly practiced shooters.

Perhaps the easiest way to proceed directly to the bottom line is to debunk the myths that have developed, particularly in the past 15 years or so, about point shooting.

Myths of Point Shooting

"Point shooting worked for Capt. William Fairbairn of the Shanghai Police, who survived over 600 gunfights shooting this way." **WRONG.** If you read Fairbairn's classic book "Shoot to Live," you'll see that the *entire 1,000 man Shanghai Police force* was involved in some 660 gunfights during the 10-year period in question. While it's entirely possible that in a violent city Fairbairn might have had his gun out of the holster 600 times on the street, he was not in 600 gunfights and never claimed he was. If you think about it, Fairbain would have killed more opponents than were accounted for by Sgt. Alvin York, Audie Murphy, and Carlos Hathcock combined.

End of argument. Rex Applegate demonstrates his point shooting technique for Ayoob's camera with Ayoob's Beretta 92. Note that you could draw a line from the pupil of his eye to the front sight to the target. This, the author submits, is coarsely aimed fire, not point-shooting.

"The great Col. Rex Applegate taught point shooting and quantified statistics showing that it worked for the OSS!" **MISINTERPRETED.** Col. Applegate was indeed a great man. I knew him. I was there to congratulate him when he won his long overdue Outstanding American Handgunner of the Year award, and he was there to congratulate me when I won mine a few years later. We both spoke before the Joint Services Small Arms Project on the Personal Defense Weapon project, at Oak Ridge.

Unlike many who quote him, I had the privilege of him showing me his technique. A photo of that experience accompanies this article. You can see that he has brought my Beretta pistol up to arm's length, and you can draw a line from the pupil of his eye to the front sight to the target.

Ed Lovette demonstrates the Applegate-based point shooting he learned from Lou Chiodo. This style will work, because the gun and its sights intrude into the cone of tunnel vision and the weapon can be visually indexed.

Rex *called* it point shooting to distinguish it from the precise, focus-on-the-front sight concept taught in the traditional marksmanship manuals. But, make no mistake, Rex had the gun up where the eye couldn't miss it, even in the tunnel vision state of fight or flight reflex. That's why his technique worked, and that's why shooting that way still works, as Sgt. Lou Chiodo and the California Highway Patrol have proven. It's just not really "point shooting." Again, we're back to Dave Arnold's point: a lot of this is semantic quibbling.

"Point shooting can be learned in 50 shots live-fire, or even just by dry firing in the mirror!" **UNTRUE.** This has been set forth in print by two separate point-shooting advocates, neither of whom to my knowledge has actually ever run a live-fire shooting class. Both have repeatedly turned down invitations to demonstrate their skills in public. One has produced a video in which, if you look carefully, he can be seen to be scattering his shots all over a huge target at close range with his point shooting techniques. The other caused to be published a photo of himself dry-firing at a mirror. If you look carefully at the picture and lay a ruler over the gun barrel, you can see that he is performing the almost impossible feat of missing himself in his own mirror. The shot would have gone over the reflected image's shoulder. Shooting at a mirror is a false approach to learning body-position index shooting anyway, since the eye can see where the mirror image is pointing and automatically correct, which would never happen in real life.

A shooter attempts point shooting. Note the widely scattered hits even at very close range.

"Aimed fire was proven useless when NYPD had only 11 percent hits with it." **WRONG.** That low hit potential figure attributed to aimed NYPD fire is taken from the single worst year in more than 30 years of the department's SOP-9 study. Standard Operating Procedure Number Nine is the intensive debriefing of all officers on that PD who fire a shot with their duty or off-duty weapons other than on the range. The low hit percentage years turned out to be due primarily to officers *not* seeing their sights when they fired. This led John Cerar to institute a "back to basics" training program when he took over NYPD's Firearms and Tactics Unit, which emphasized the use of the front sight. Soon, progressively, hit percentages crept upward and with more officers

using their sights when they fired "for real," actual hits in street gunfights tripled over the previously quoted figure. The people who incorrectly applied that statistic obviously never contacted the NYPD. I did. The facts are there, documented with excruciating thoroughness, for anyone who wants to seek the truth.

*"The effects of epinephrine dumping into your body under stress will make it impossible for your eyes to focus on your sights, so you **have** to point shoot!"* **UNTRUE, and proven so.** In experiments conducted by the Olympic Training Center and the U.S. Army Marksmanship Training Unit (1981) and at Lethal Force Institute (1998), shooters were injected with doses of epinephrine calibrated to equal the "fight or flight state." In all cases, the shooters were able to see their gun sights with crystal clarity, and to hit what they shot at aiming that way.

"I've read of people who fired and hit and don't remember seeing their sights." **UNFOUNDED ARGUMENT.** You've also read about people who didn't remember firing, but they did. A large percentage of gunfight survivors didn't hear their shots, but that doesn't mean their guns were silent. Some remember seeing their sights, and some don't. That doesn't mean they didn't see their sights, any more than not remembering consciously pulling the trigger means they didn't pull it.

Problems With Point Shooting

Dennis Martin, the martial arts and small arms expert who for some time was Great Britain's coordinator for the International Association of Law Enforcement Firearms Instructors, has little use for point shooting. He told me, "When the SAS had as their primary mission the eradication of enemy soldiers in combat, they taught point shooting with a high volume of gunfire. But as soon as their mission was changed to include hostage rescue, they switched from point shooting to Col. Cooper's concept of the 'flash sight picture.' Now they had to shoot through narrow channels between innocent people, and it would have been irresponsible to do that without aiming their weapons."

This is as clear an explanation of the problems with point shooting as I've ever seen. As an expert witness for the courts in weapons and shooting cases for more than 20 years, I realized early on that again and again, point shooting was culpable when the wrong people were hit by the good guy's fire. One case is mentioned elsewhere in this book. The man "pointed" his .38 for a warning shot and hit, crippling for life, a man he said he was trying to miss. More common are people hitting those other than the ones they're trying to hit. I was retained on behalf of one police officer who "point-shot" at the tire of a car that was going toward a brother officer and instead hit in the head and killed a person inside the vehicle. I was retained on behalf of another who, at little more than arm's length from a murderer trying to shoot him, resorted to the point shooting he had been taught and missed with all but one shot. The one hit, almost miraculously, nailed the bad guy in the arm and cut the radial nerve, preventing his attacker from pulling the trigger. But one of his misses struck, and horribly crippled for life, an innocent bystander – one of the potential victims the officer was trying to protect.

You don't need too many cases like that to understand why true point shooting, firing without being able to see where the gun is oriented, can quickly pass the point of diminishing returns. Law school students are taught that the exemplar of recklessness is a "blind man with a gun." A person who is firing a gun when they can't see whether or not it's on target is, in effect, a blind man with a gun. It could be eloquently argued in court that, *ipso facto,* firing without being able to see where the gun is aimed creates recklessness. In turn, recklessness is the key ingredient in the crime of Manslaughter and in a civil court lawsuit based on Wrongful Death or Wrongful Injury.

Enough said?

Point Shooting Alternatives

If there isn't time for a precise, perfect marksman's sight picture, at the closer distances it will suffice to simply be able to see the gun superimposed over the target. As noted earlier, if you can see the gun, it's aimed fire. Now it's just a matter of how precise the visual index is. Let's analyze the precision, from the most precise on down.

A classic marksman's sight picture, with that 1/8-inch-wide front sight visible in the rear sight's notch, level on top and with an equal amount of light on either side, is absolutely "do-able" in combat. Countless gunfight and military battle survivors have proven it. In Jim Cirillo's most famous gun battle, his strongest memory was seeing the front sight of his S&W Model 10 in such stark clarity that he was aware of every imperfection in the tiny grooves machined across its surface. In that gunfight, he shot three men in three seconds, and he shot one of them out from behind a hostage. Bill Allard was the one guy on the NYPD Stakeout Squad who

shot more armed criminals in the line of duty than Jim, and he told me he always saw his sights. His strongest memory of *his* most famous gunfight, a pistolero and a rifleman that he took out in a hail of bullets, was seeing the front sight of his handgun so sharply that he could have counted the grooves in it. Ed Mireles, the hero of the infamous 1986 FBI shootout in Miami, told me that among his most vivid memories were the giant white ball that was the front sight of his Remington 870 12-gauge shotgun, and the giant orange front sight of his S&W Model 686 revolver, as he fired the shots that blew away the two cop-killers in question.

Next down the list of precision is the "flash sight picture" popularized by Jeff Cooper. The sights are more or less in line, but you're not trying for a perfect image. You just quickly verify that they're on target and break the shot. It can be done at surprisingly high speed.

Ratchet down one more notch on the coarseness level to the StressPoint Index, a concept I developed in the 1970s and published in the 1980s. You're focused on the target – something you always have to be prepared for because nature makes us look at what threatens us – and over the spot on the threat you want to hit, you see superimposed the image of a front sight sitting on top of a rear sight. Break the shot, and if you're inside 7 yards or so, that spot you're

Firearms instructor and combat pistol champ Andy Cannon has just shown an entire class of students that their guns are sighted in close enough...

An instructor demonstrates the protected gun position at National Tactical Invitational at Gunsite.

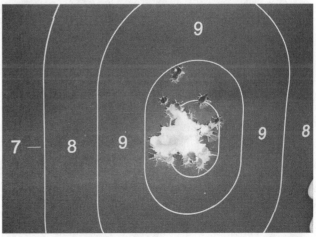

...by putting six shots from each into this heart-size group. Try that with point shooting!

focused on is exactly where you'll see the bullet strike. Todd Jarrett rediscovered this concept later, calling it "shooting out of the notch" to describe the front sight's orientation with the rear, and he won national and world championships with it at super-speed.

One more notch down and you have what master gunfighter Jim Cirillo calls the "silhouette" technique. You see just the silhouette of your gun superimposed over the target. If you know your gun, you can tell instantly from the shape if it's "on." The rear of the cylinder will be round instead of oblong, and the "safety wings" of a Smith & Wesson or Beretta standard model auto will be silhouetted. Don't hesitate, break the shot. You're there.

The better shooting technique systems that have been called "point shooting," the ones that actually work such as Applegate's, all bring the gun up to the line of sight so high that it will intrude into the cone of tunnel vision. As Cirillo has said, you'll see it subliminally even if you don't see it consciously. That will let you hit at close range. That will give you a good chance of getting through the fight.

Bottom Line

If the gun is where you can see it at close range, you can hit. You're visually indexing your gunfire. You're aiming. Perhaps you're aiming crudely instead of precisely, but you're aiming. If the gun is where you cannot see it, it can be argued that you are not really in control of it. You're relying on a body position index. There are problems with that.

Author can point shoot when he has to, as in this required stage on three targets in tight time frames at first National Tactical Invitational. He finished in the top 10. The pistol is a Colt Government Model stainless by D.R. Middlebrooks.

The body position index only works on a static range. You can get yourself set up exactly with the target, then go through the motions and repeat the alignment. But this is false to reality. On the street, the opponent may be above or below you. As soon as he moves laterally, as he undoubtedly will unless he has a death wish or is terminally stupid, all the coordinates will break and you'll be back to being a "blind man with a gun."

The ultimate boast of shooters is, "If I can see it, I can hit it." This is admittedly a bit over the top. You and I can both see the moon and the sun, but neither of us can hit them with a bullet. But there is a corollary here: *if we can't see the gun in relation to its target, we probably can't hit the target.*

We live in a world where if we fire for real and don't hit the target dead center, it can remain hostile long enough to murder us or those we love. We live in a world where if we launch a deadly bullet when we can't see the predictable course it will take, we can not only expect to perpetrate a tragedy, but expect to pay dearly for it in both criminal and civil court.

One rationale the author can see for hip shooting: you've been manacled behind your back with your own cuffs and have sneaked out your backup gun. This is a great argument for a laser sight! Note that one shot has gone low right out of the vital zone.

That's the problem with point shooting. If you are truly convinced that your main plan of action should be to fire in self-defense without being able to see where your gun is pointing, do yourself a favor and at least equip the weapon with a laser sight.

CHAPTER SEVEN

DEFENSIVE HANDGUN AMMUNITION SELECTION

Morgue Monsters And Jello Junkies

Handgun "stopping power" has been a topic of heated debate for more than half a century. The debate shows little sign of fading away.

On one side are those concerned primarily with field results. In their forefront are Evan Marshall, a retired homicide detective and SWAT instructor from the Detroit PD, and his colleague Edwin Sanow, a trained engineer who has been accepted by the courts as an expert on the topic. Marshall's research of several thousand shootings has been compiled in books from Paladin Press including *Handgun Stopping Power* and *Street Stoppers*, co-authored by Sanow. Their research indicates that in certain calibers, medium- or slightly lighter than medium-weight bullets at high velocities have the most immediate effect on felons who are shot. Those calibers include 9mm Luger (115-grain JHP at +/- 1,300 fps) and .357 Magnum (125-grain SJHP at +/- 1,400 fps). They have also found that in some calibers, the heaviest projectiles normally encountered, moving at moderate velocities, did the best job. These include .38 Special (158-grain LHP at +/- 850 fps) and .45 Auto (230-grain JHP at +/- 850 fps).

On the other side of the fence are those led by Dr. Martin Fackler and an organization he created called International Wound Ballistics Association (IWBA). Fackler's theory, based largely on measurement of wound paths in a specific 10 percent formula of ballistic gelatin that he created, is that penetration of at least 12-inches in the human body is essential to hit vital organs. This favors the heaviest available bullet, traveling at moderate velocity. In .45 Auto and .38 Special, both sides are in agreement. In 9mm Luger, they are not, with Fackler and his colleagues recommending the subsonic 147-grain JHP at +/- 970 fps.

Those who follow the street research believe that if lab research isn't proven by what happens in the field, the lab research, by definition, must be flawed. Those who believe in the lab research cite its repeatability, noting that every shooting is at least subtly different from every other.

Before the bullet matters, it must hit the target. A stock Ruger P90 .45 has just put five rounds of inexpensive Remington-UMC training hardball into about 1-1/4 inches, center to center, at 25 yards.

Who is right? Each side has a piece of the puzzle. The laboratory research can explain to us why certain rounds may work better than others. It can predict a round that will dangerously over-penetrate, or which will break up so soon it won't reach vital organs in time to stop a murder attempt. But field results assembled over time do, quite definitely, point to certain trends. When we ignore what happens in the real world, we do so at our peril.

Vern Geberth, who wrote the authoritative text on homicide investigation, felt that all 9mm rounds were highly lethal. Shown is SIG P226 with 115-grain hollow-points.

The Scope of the Task

How a gunshot wound causes a violent human being to cease hostilities is a much more complicated question than it sounds. IWBA feels that only three such mechanisms exist, and only two can be reliably counted upon. Disruption of the central nervous system can do it. So can the effect of hemorrhage when it reaches the point that there is insufficient flow of oxygenated blood to sustain consciousness. IWBA indicates that any "stop" not attributable to one or the other of these two mechanisms must be attributable to psychological surrender; basically, the opponent wimped out after he was shot.

Both sides of the ammo controversy agree that .25 autos like this Beretta Model 21A are insufficiently powerful for self-defense.

Central nervous system (CNS) impairment will certainly work. So, obviously, will massive hemorrhage, though the latter will take time. Most physicians agree that if the brain is fully oxygenated at the moment of the shot, the patient can maintain consciousness and perform physical action for up to about 14 seconds *even if the heart stops completely at the shot.* Thus, the great many instant one-shot incapacitations that we have on record in which the bullet's path never touched brain or spinal cord cannot be explained away by blood loss. Many of these individuals were hard fighters, impervious to fear, and it is most unlikely that a psychological dread of being shot caused them to faint.

Dr. Dennis Tobin, a neurologist, has hypothesized that a mechanism called "neural shock" can cause collapse from a gunshot wound even when vital organs are not permanently damaged. Others believe that the temporary cavitation around the wound track, which becomes larger as velocity increases, has the effect of stunning organs that sustain no permanent, quantifiable damage. This flies in the face of the IWBA theory that only tissue actually destroyed by the bullet's passing will materially contribute to incapacitation. Yet it has happened too many times to ignore.

Chuck Karwan, who wrote *The Complete Book of Combat Handgunnery* two editions ago, did an absolutely excellent essay on this concept in those pages. A military combat veteran and advanced martial artist, he noted that blows to

many parts of the body could cause instant incapacitation, yet leave no permanent wound cavity per se. Since many of the men so incapacitated were hardened, trained fighters willingly in the ring, it is hard to imagine that they fainted or otherwise experienced a "psychological stop" because someone punched them.

Bullet designer and multiple gunfight survivor Jim Cirillo believes bullet design is critical. Here he shows the importance of a sharp-shouldered bullet when a projectile strikes hard bone on an oblique angle.

Those who disagree with Sanow and Marshall attack their statistics and their interpretation of them. Statistics can be argued. Reality cannot. During the period the Indianapolis Police Department issued the 125-grain .357 Magnum hollow-points at about 1,400 feet per second, some 220 violent felony suspects were shot with that round by IPD officers. City officials told me there was never an effective return of fire from a felon hit with one of these bullets in the torso. The Kentucky State Police had essentially the same experience with the same load. The Illinois State Police for almost 20 years carried the 115-grain +P+ hollow-points at 1,300 fps velocity. It worked so well in their troopers' many gunfights that it became known as the Illinois State Police load among the nation's cops and gun enthusiasts.

Yet because both rounds are designed to penetrate 9 to 11 inches and stop, after having created a massively wide wound path, both are seen as inadequate by the IWBA because they do not meet IDPA's mandatory 12 inches of penetration in the gelatin used to simulate muscle tissue. One memorable gelatin test of the early 1990s gave the 9mm 115-grain/1,300 fps load a wound value of zero, even though it had caused the wound cavities with the largest volume, because by design none of the projectiles reached the foot-deep penetration mark! The bullets instead averaged between 9 inches and 10 inches of bullet penetration. This is about the depth of the average adult male chest, front to back. That interpretation would have been laughable enough, had it not been for the fact that the same report listed a .380 hollow-point as having a "minus" wound value. Presumably, if you were shot with it you would feel better than had you not been shot at all. Such interpretations destroy any value of the underlying work that went into the testing, which is a shame.

Most would agree that the .480 Ruger, a powerful, deep-penetrating cartridge intended for hunting large game, is probably too hard to control and penetrates too deeply for most to consider for self-defense against humans.

Dr. Bruce Ragsdale at the Armed Forces Institute of Pathology embedded pig aortas in Fackler gelatin. He noted that when a round like the ISP load passed close to the vessel without actually striking it, the stretch cavity was still sufficient to transect the aorta – that is, to tear it apart. He presented those findings at a bona fide wound trauma conference. A senior IWBA official, who was present, never uttered a peep…but continued to write that, at handgun velocities, only tissue actually touched by the bullet and damaged by it would contribute to incapacitation. Hmmm…

More than a decade ago I sat down in an outdoor café with a physician who is an apostle for the "deep-penetrating bullet" theory. I gave him the names of personnel at the Indianapolis Police Department and the Kentucky State Police who would confirm the real-world performance of the 125-grain Magnum ammunition he said was over-rated and ineffective. He replied that there was no need to do so, because the gelatin told the whole story.

It was this attitude that caused Evan Marshall to coin the term "Jello Junkies" for those who would not venture beyond the laboratory environment to correlate their theories with real-world findings. It was a gun magazine editor who coined the term "Morgue Monsters" for those who felt that only the results of actual shootings would tell the tale. The two sides have remained at odds with one another ever since, with some very acrimonious comments being issued. Interestingly, most of the personal attacks have been by followers of the IWBA dogma attacking Marshall and Sanow. Make of that what you will.

The problem with this dichotomy is that both sides have authoritative backgrounds. When two experts disagree, who is the layman to believe? The person who carries a gun for serious self-defense is now in the position of a juror assessing conflicting expert testimony in a court case. It becomes necessary to compare the arguments and weigh them in light of logic, common sense, and life experience.

That's what we'll attempt to do in the following pages.

Recommended Loads

There are so many different calibers and loads that we can't cover them all here. That would take a separate book. In fact, Marshall and Sanow have written more than one book on the topic and they still haven't covered all the load combinations! Therefore, let's stick with the most popular and most effective of the self-defense calibers.

We won't be working with .480 Ruger, .454 Casull, or .50 Desert Eagle. These big boomers are hunting rounds and generally too powerful for personal defense. Nor will we work with cartridges so tiny and notoriously impotent that most police departments forbid their officers to carry them even as backup. The .22 and the .25 auto can certainly kill, but they can't always *stop,* which is a different thing altogether. Such small rounds require literally surgical bullet placement, with the primary point of aim being deep brain. However, both are notorious for ricocheting off human skulls, so where does that leave you?

.32 Auto. It is a little known fact that NYPD became the first police department to issue semiautomatics early in the 20th century, with a quantity of Colt .32s. They got away from them in part because they were too feeble, and the department standardized on the .38 Special revolvers instead, many of which remain in service. European police departments issued .32s for decades because the sidearm was seen as a badge of office, and these small autos were convenient and had a low-key look. Then terrorism and violent crime struck Europe, and the cops needed real guns; they switched en masse to .38 Special revolvers and 9mm autos.

The Seecamp .32 auto was made to work with Silvertip ammo, which is as good an ammo choice as any in that caliber.

Today, thanks to the defining Seecamp LWS-32, pistols the size of .25s are now available in this caliber, and it has become an in-thing to carry them. Various hollow-points are available. All open sometimes. None open all the time. The Winchester Silvertip was the .32 cartridge the Seecamp was built around, and has the best track record. The Marshall

Study shows a surprisingly high one-shot stop rate, but also includes a disproportionate number of strong-arm robbers and rapists or attackers with clubs and knives instead of guns, who may have simply given up after realizing they were up against a gun and had already been shot once. Still, the Silvertip has the most established track record, and when I carry my own Seecamp .32, it's the round I choose.

.380 Auto. Known in Europe as the "9mm Short," this round seems to constitute the acceptable minimum dividing line in defensive handgun potency. Some experts will say it's barely adequate, and the others will say it's barely inadequate. The ball rounds penetrate too deeply and can ricochet, creating narrow, puckered wounds in the meantime. The hollow-points, when they open, may not go deep enough.

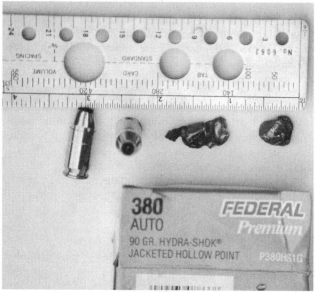

This is what a .380 Hydra-Shok looks like after being fired into living tissue.

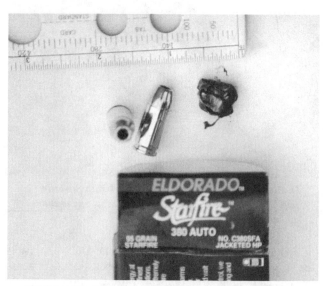

PMC StarFire's bullet, designed by Tom Burczynski, is as dynamic an expander as you will find in .380 caliber. This one was retrieved from a slaughterhouse test.

In some of our advanced classes, we have the student kill a large animal with their carry gun and load, then dissect the wound to see what it did. Seven times now I've seen .380 JHPs either stop in the frontal wall of the skull or ricochet around the skull to the ear. Not impressive. These days, for students with the smaller gun, we use very small swine to prevent torturing the animal. All animals used in this way were destined to be slaughtered for meat on the given day anyway, but a clean and painless death is ethically required here. The .380 doesn't seem to deliver that reliably.

I haven't run across an actual shooting yet with the Remington Golden Saber, which at 102 grains is the heaviest bullet available for the .380. I did shoot a hog with it on one occasion. The bullet just got through the frontal wall of the skull and barely touched the brain. Most JHPs weigh 85 to 90 grains. Winchester Silvertip and Federal Hydra-Shok seem to lead the pack and perform about the same.

.38 Special. This is the universally accepted minimum or above-minimum load for self-defense. With certain loads, it's far below minimum. The classic example is the old 158-grain lead round nose. It provides too much penetration and too little stopping power. For most of the 20th century, this round was the police standard, and only the commanders who issued it had anything good to say about it. Street cops called it "the widow-maker" because so many times, an officer would empty it into his attacker, and the assailant would live long enough to still make the cop's wife a widow.

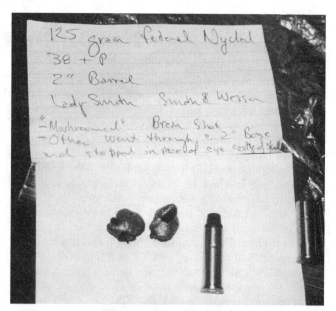

Federal Nyclad Chief Special load, a standard pressure, nylon-jacketed 125-grain hollow-point, gives the most dynamic bullet performance the author has seen in a low-recoil .38 Special cartridge. Note the significant expansion even when fired from 2-inch barrel into living flesh and bone.

Hollow-points work better, but not all hollow-points are created equal. Where low recoil is imperative – a very light revolver, or a .38 in a very frail hand – the best of the standard pressure, mild-kicking loads seems to be the Federal NyClad Chief Special. As the name implies, it was expressly designed for small, light revolvers. The soft lead bullet begins to deform as soon as it hits. We've never seen it fail on large animals in the slaughterhouse, and it showed up well in the Marshall study. The nylon-jacketed bullet weighs 125 grains.

Head and shoulders, the best .38 Special is the old "FBI load," developed by Winchester in 1972. It is comprised of an all-lead semi-wadcutter bullet with a hollow point at +P velocity. FBI, RCMP, Metro-Dade Police in Miami, St. Louis, Chicago PD, and a great many others used this round in countless gunfights, out of snubbies and service revolvers alike. They all had excellent results with it. Because there is no copper jacket that has to peel back, a design feature that seems to require considerable velocity to work, the soft lead slug seems to open even when fired at lowered velocity from short barrels and even when fired through heavy clothing.

Recoil is snappy in the small, light guns, but very easy to handle in a service revolver. The "FBI load" is a legendary man-stopper. It delivers the performance ammo makers were hoping for with the 147-grain subsonic 9mm at 970 fps. Alas, the copper jacket of the 9mm round didn't always open up the way the lead slug of the .38 FBI load did.

Most brands give reasonably similar performance, though over the years the Winchester has used the hardest lead and the Remington the softest, with the Federal brand in the middle. Evan Marshall's observation that the .38 Special FBI load hit about like GI .45 hardball seems to have been proven out in 30 years of extensive field testing.

Federal's 9BP 115-grain load is the most effective standard-pressure 9mm cartridge the author has found. It worked very well for many years for the New Jersey State Police in their HK P7M8 pistols such as the one shown.

cartridge produced with top quality has been available for some time as the Pro-Load Tactical, and the Triton Hi-Vel is very similar.

124-grain "hot loads" at about 1,250 feet per second also have a good track record. The Gold Dot in this format has worked splendidly for NYPD since its adoption in 1999, and is also the 9mm load of choice for the Denver Police Department.

Many older guns won't stand up to these high pressure loads in constant shooting, and some people don't like the little extra jolt of recoil they give. In the same size gun, a +P or +P+ 9mm kicks about the same as a standard pressure .40 S&W load. In a modest recoil 9mm, history has shown us that you can't beat the Federal Classic 9BP, a 115-grain JHP at about 1,150 feet per second. It is standard issue for Philadelphia PD and New Jersey State Police at this time; both have had many shootings with it, and been satisfied with the results.

There is no more proven .38 Special load, even for snubbies like this Taurus Model 85, than 158-grain lead semi-wadcutter hollow-point at +P velocity.

9mm Luger. Illinois State Police were not the only ones to prove that the +P+ 115-grain JHP at 1,300 feet per second was the best man-stopper in this caliber. U.S. Border Patrol and Secret Service found the same in extensive study of real-world experience. ISP used mostly the Winchester brand, Border Patrol the Federal, and Secret Service the Remington. There was little difference between the brands, which had one other thing in common: all were sold to police only, and not to the general public.

However, CCI Speer has recently released this load to the law-abiding public with the Gold Dot bullet. An identical

The Remington 115-grain JHP 9mm proved accurate in this STI Trojan pistol, but higher-velocity versions of the same round have been more dynamic "on the street."

Most law enforcement agencies that adopted the 147-grain JHP subsonic, as noted above, have gotten away from it after disappointing results in the field. Expansion failures and overpenetrations occurred too often. While some departments, such as Las Vegas Metro and Jacksonville simply went to faster-moving 115-grain JHPs, others simply bought more powerful guns that fired the .40 Smith & Wesson, the .357 SIG, or the .45 ACP. LAPD, LA County and Chicago PD got around the 147-grain subsonic's perceived weaknesses by authorizing privately-owned .45 autos for those who didn't trust the slow-bullet 9mm ammo.

.40 S&W. Conceptualized by Paul Liebenberg and Tom Campbell at Smith & Wesson and created by them and Winchester, the .40 Smith & Wesson was simply a 10mm Short. Indeed, the sarcastic called it the .40 Short and Weak when it was introduced in 1990. Intended to be a bridge between the 16-shot 9mm and the 8-shot .45, the 12-shot .40 proved to be a viable compromise. Within a few years it was the most popular law enforcement cartridge as measured by new gun orders.

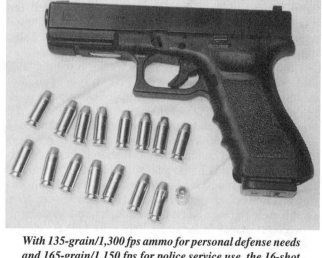

With 135-grain/1,300 fps ammo for personal defense needs and 165-grain/1,150 fps for police service use, the 16-shot (with pre-ban magazines) .40 caliber Glock 22 is a potent sidearm indeed.

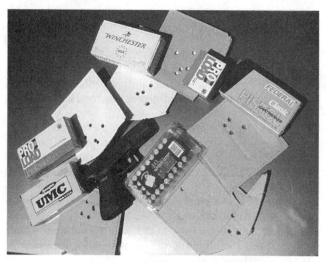

Accuracy of given load in given gun is a definite factor. These are assorted .40 S&W cartridges, fired from Glock 22 at 25 yards.

Federal's standard 155-grain JHP .40 has proven itself well in the field in pistols like this Beretta 96D Centurion.

With its original load of a 180-grain subsonic bullet at 980 fps, it was indeed a viable compromise, and it worked out better than many of us feared it would, though it still had some tendency to overpenetrate. As new loads were developed that performed better, many saw the .40 as upscaling from compromise to optimization.

The 165-grain bullets at 1,150 fps and 155-grain slugs at 1,200 or better, dubbed "cruiserweights" by gun expert Dean Spier, passed all the FBI barricade and gelatin tests and still expanded and created significant wounds. Border Patrol reports excellent results with the 155-grain Remington and Federal JHPs, Nashville has experienced extraordinary performance with the Winchester taloned hollow-point weighting 165 grains The 165-grain Gold Dot bullet as loaded by Speer delivers similar performance, and when the same projectile is loaded as the hot EXP by Black Hills, performance plus match-grade accuracy is achieved.

Dick Kelton conceptualized the 135-grain .40 caliber hollow-point at 1,300 fps in the early 1990s, and I convinced a small ammunition company to manufacture the load after extremely impressive slaughterhouse testing results. When the first field shooting report came in, it was from a coroner's office asking what sort of explosive had been put in the bullet! Striking in the abdomen a man who was attempting to stab a police officer, the 135-grain JHP had flung him back and to the ground. He was clinically dead within 10 seconds, a result not explainable by an abdominal wound, however massive this one was.

The 135-grain/1,300 fps combination is now available with excellent quality control in the Pro-Load Tactical and Triton Hi-Vel lines, using the same well-proven Nosler projectile. Its 10-inch wound depth, however wide the wound, does not excite police who want their ammo to pass FBI 12-inch penetration/barrier protocols, but is ideal for armed citizen self-defense scenarios as they generally unfold.

Winchester Ranger 165-grain high-velocity .40 load has been spectacularly successful for Nashville (TN) Metro Police. Greg Lee of that department demonstrates with an issue Glock 22 service pistol.

.357 SIG. What is, in essence a .40 S&W cartridge necked down to take a 9mm bullet, the .357 SIG was an attempt to gain .357 Magnum power level in a moderately sized auto pistol. It clearly succeeded. The cartridge is now in use by the state troopers of Delaware, New Mexico, North Carolina, Texas, and Virginia. It replaced the +P+ 9mm ammunition of the Secret Service and the Air Marshals. Simply put, the latter two agencies liked what they got out of a 115-grain 9mm bullet at 1,300 fps, and figured they'd get more of it with a 125-grain 9mm bullet at 50 to 100 feet per second greater velocity.

Speer Gold Dot 125-grain .357 SIG has given dynamic street performance in many shootings. The pistol is full-size P226.

They were right. With the cartridge in use for several years, uniformly excellent results have been reported. Richmond, VA has had seven shootings at this writing, all very fast stops. In only one was the suspect shot several times, probably because he was attempting to murder a downed officer and brother officers hosed him as fast as they could pull the triggers of their *Sig Pro* pistols. In a Texas shootout, a veteran trooper shot at the gunman ensconced in a semi-tractor trailer, but the bullets from his .45 did not go through. His rookie partner's SIG P-226 spat a .357 SIG Gold Dot through the cab and through the gunman's brain, killing him. Richmond noted that despite 16-inches of penetration in gelatin, all the 125-grain .357 SIG Gold Dots they've fired into men have stayed in the bodies, or in the clothing on the opposite side.

One Virginia trooper told me that what impressed him the most about the .357 SIG was that it dropped offenders instantly even when hit in non-vital areas like the abdomen. Numerous officers noted that it delivered instant one-shot stops on pit bulls, when in the past they'd had to pump round after round of 147-grain 9mm subsonic into similar animals. While 115-grain through 150-grain loads exist, virtually all shootings on record have been made with the 125-grain round. The Gold Dot is the most proven.

The .357 SIG has drawn the wrath of at least one critic, who insisted that it was no better than 9mm subsonic and that its massive temporary wound cavity surrounding the bullet's path was irrelevant. The cops just rolled their eyes, reviewed their dynamic real-world results, and kept carrying their .357 SIGs.

.357 Magnum: Amply represented in police gunfights since its inception in 1935, the original 158-grain flat-nose bullet load immediately earned a reputation for excessive penetration that continued when hollow-point bullets of the same weight were introduced. Not until Super Vel introduced a high velocity 110-grain hollow-point did law enforcement have a .357 round that would stay in a felon's body and use its energy effectively. When Remington introduced the 125-grain hollow-point at 1,450 fps, the round hit its stride. With a wound channel 9 inches to 11 inches deep and massively wide, it set the all-time standard for one-shot stops in actual field shootings. The price, however, was a nasty kick, an ear-splitting blast, and a blinding muzzle flash. Nonetheless, the full power 125-grain remains the clear winner of the .357 Magnum defense load sweepstakes.

10mm Auto. Touted in the mid-1980s as the long-sought "ultimate man-stopper," the 10mm's popularity got a shot in the arm when the FBI adopted the caliber in the late 1980s. Unfortunately, to make recoil more controllable they watered down the power to the level of a .40 subsonic. The FBI load for 10mm was jokingly called a "minus-P". Prior to that, most of the ammo available for the 10mm was hard-jacketed, deep-penetrating stuff better suited to hunting hogs than anti-personnel work. When people were shot with it, it tended to go all the way through without having much immediate visible effect. Interest had waned in the caliber before the really promising anti-personnel ammo, 155 grains at 1,300 fps or 135 grains at 1,450 fps, had a chance to be represented in actual gunfights.

Flat-shooting and accurate, the 10mm like the .41 Magnum never had a chance to prove itself. The author carries one frequently as a personal weapon, generally loaded with 155-grain JHP at 1,300.

.45 Auto. All those 20th century gunwriters weren't exaggerating when they called the .45 ACP (Automatic Colt Pistol) round a "legendary man-stopper" even before hollow-point bullets became available for it. Hollow-points just made it more effective and less likely to dangerously over-penetrate.

There are 165-grain JHPs available for it at a screaming 1,250 fps, but to my knowledge no one has ever been shot with one and its real-world ability remains unproven. However, Remington's 185-grain +P at 1,140 fps and similar loads by other makers have been well proven in the field, and are among top choices in the caliber. What you're losing in extra recoil, you're gaining in a flatter trajectory. The +P 185-grain .45 shoots like a full-power 10mm and allows easy hits on man-size targets out to 100 yards and beyond. This would be the load of choice if the mission profile included likelihood of long shots. Because short-barrel .45s lose velocity dramatically, some feel the +P load is a logical compensation when loaded in a "snubby" auto of that caliber.

For typical pistol distances, jacketed hollow-points with the same ballistics as the GI ball round proven for more than nine decades (230-grain bullet at 830 to 850 fps from a 5-inch barrel) have earned undisputed top dog status. With the high-tech hollow-points, more shootings have occurred with the Federal Hydra-Shok than any of the others, but we also get excellent reports on the Winchester SXT, the Remington Golden Saber, and CCI Gold Dot. In one slaughterhouse test, the PMC StarFire outperformed all of them by a slight margin. There are many good loads to pick from here. The high-tech modern bullets mentioned in the last couple of lines were all expressly designed to open even at reduced velocity when fired from short-barreled guns.

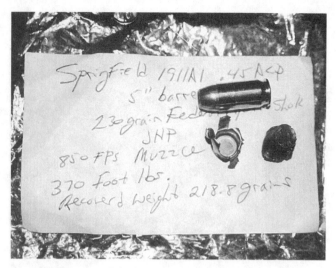

Federal's 230-grain Hydra-Shok is seen by many as the "gold standard" for .45 auto rounds at regular pressures. This is what one looks like after impacting living flesh and bone. The pistol used was a Springfield Armory, with a 5-inch barrel.

Another advantage of the 230-grain standard-velocity round is that once you know the full-price hollow-points will feed in your weapon, practice with relatively inexpensive "generic hardball" gives you the exact same recoil and point of aim/point of impact as the duty load.

These are the rounds this writer would personally recommend. Some go more toward the Fackler side of the house, and some more toward the Marshall/Sanow side. What do you do when you're advising someone who is torn between those two authoritative sources? Why, you find something both sides agree on, and we'll look at that next.

Compromise Ammo

When life just isn't black and white, a shade of gray is often the real-world middle ground. Sometimes we just have to compromise.

Let's say it's the early 1990s, and you are the head of firearms training for a 100-officer department. The chief wants to go to one standard pistol for all armed personnel. Half your guys and gals like the firepower of the typical 16-shot 9mm. The other half are more concerned about per-shot power, and want eight-shot .45s. The solution, of course, is the 12 shot .40 S&W. Each side gives a little, gets a little, and can claim to have won the argument. Now everyone is free of the controversy and can focus on what really wins gunfights: mindset and preparedness, proper tactics, and shooting skill.

But what if the caliber has already been selected, and the argument is what load to select? If the troops have been reading the gun magazines or are on the net, and you have 50 of them in the Marshall/Sanow camp and 50 on the Fackler side, a decision for one side will tick off the other. Far worse, it will leave half your troops with a lack of confidence, and confidence is always one of the cornerstones of competence.

The author's department issues Black Hills 230-grain .45 ACP for their Ruger P-90 duty weapons...

The trick is to find rounds that both sides agree on. Believe it or not, they exist. Let's look at the serious calibers only.

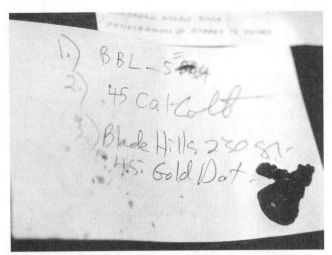

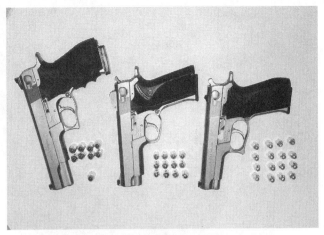

Caliber is one of the compromise options. You could choose (from the left) a nine-shot .45, a 12-shot .40 or a 16-shot 9mm. The .40 splits the difference. These are all S&W pistols; the 4506, 4006 and 5906.

...and this is one reason why. Massive expansion of the Gold Dot bullet has caused a large wound at the proper depth in living tissue. Both sides of the stopping power argument agree on a 230-grain JHP at 850 fps.

.38 Special: The old FBI Load. Previously, we discussed the .38 Special lead semi-wadcutter hollow-point at +P velocity. This is the round recommended for the .38 Special by the group Dr. Fackler founded and leads, the IWBA. It has also been at the top of the Marshall/Sanow list in the caliber more times than not. There has been the occasional year where lighter, faster bullets seemed to be working better in recently compiled shootings, but over all the years Marshall's work has been published, it has led the pack in .38 Special. This has been true with snub-nose revolvers as well as service-size guns with longer barrels.

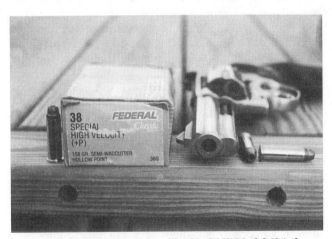

For a .357 Magnum revolver like this S&W Model 686, the only defense load both sides agree on is the old FBI .38 Special round, a +P all-lead semi-wadcutter hollow-point.

When *these* two warring factions agree on something, it's got to be good. The consensus is almost universal among serious professionals. The lead SWCHP +P is street-proven *and* lab-proven as the best .38 Special self-defense load there is.

.45 ACP: 230-grain JHP. Both sides find this type of cartridge the top choice in the caliber. They seem to differ only on the brand choice. The Marshall Study has consistently put the Federal Hydra-Shok ahead of other rounds of its

type, though not by much. Fackler has stated that he considered the old Winchester Black Talon (which in .45 ACP was a 230-grain at standard velocity) to be the greatest advance in handgun ammo since the hollow-point bullet.

Personally, I've found the Hydra to open a little more consistently than some others, and to be truly match-grade in accuracy, for whatever that's worth in combat ammo selection. But the FBI uses the Remington Golden Saber in 230-grain. I've seen 230-grain Gold Dots dug out of human flesh, and the mushrooming was impressive. My own department issues that bullet in the accurate Black Hills duty round, loaded to hit 850 feet per second from the 4-1/4-inch barrels on our issue guns, and I'm extremely comfortable carrying it. As noted in the previous chapter, one test I performed comparing hi-tech 230-grain .45 ACP JHP in the slaughterhouse resulted in the PMC StarFire showing very slightly more tissue disruption than in any of the others. Really, it's almost a coin toss.

The point is, both sides agree. The issue is resolved. The .45 Auto shooter can now move on to those things mentioned above that will *really* win the fight.

.40 S&W: 180-grain subsonic JHP. IWBA recommends the original 180-grain subsonic. Marshall and Sanow list other rounds, notably the full-power 135-grain and 155/165-grain loads, as having slightly more stopping power. However, the Federal Hydra-Shok 180-grain subsonic is very close to the top of their .40 charts, and certainly on the list of recommended loads.

Again, the only difference is in the details. Where Evan and Ed rate the Hydra-Shok tops among the subsonic .40s, Marty seems to clearly prefer the Winchester. While I have to side with Sanow and Marshall on the best 9mm and .357 loads simply because my field research comes out yielding the same top rounds as theirs, I have to go to Fackler's side of the line in brand selection among 180-grain subsonic .40 S&W offerings. I've run across several shootings with Winchester's talon-style Ranger load. All but one stayed in the body. All have opened up exactly like a Winchester publicity photo. All have stopped hostilities immediately. The one that exited the offender involved a slender female who was

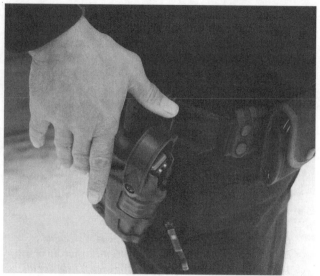

When you can't decide on a 9mm load you like, reach for a .40 caliber of the same make and model! Both sides of the argument are satisfied with the 180-grain .40 subsonic JHP, though the author loads hotter ammo into his Glock 22, carried here in a Safariland Raptor snatch-resistant duty holster.

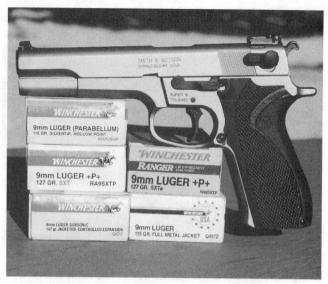

Which of these 9mm loads is the best? The debate continues. Of those shown, the author would take the 127-grain +P+. The pistol is the S&W Super 9, made for the European market and seldom seen in the U.S.

trying to murder an officer. The bullet that punched through her left a massive exit wound and instantly stopped her attempted cop-killing.

Unfortunately, the Ranger load is currently offered only to law enforcement. Fortunately, there is not all *that* much difference. The California Highway Patrol has issued the ordinary Remington 180-grain subsonic (not the hi-tech Golden Saber version) for most of the time since their 1990 adoption of the .40 S&W cartridge. CHP's thousands of highway patrolmen collectively log a great many shootings. The agency has pronounced itself quite pleased with the performance of that ammunition as well as the performance of their chosen sidearm, the Smith & Wesson Model 4006.

In other calibers, there seems to be no such common ground between the two camps. This is not to say that compromise is not possible.

Let's say your choice of handgun is the .357 Magnum revolver. There is simply no Magnum round on which both sides agree. But any .357 Magnum revolver will fire .38 Special +P ammunition. A logical choice presents itself: Load with the FBI .38 Special formula, and you're good to go.

The 9mm Luger remains one of our most popular caliber choices. There is no 9mm round on which both sides agree; indeed, this caliber has probably been the focus of more argument between the two camps than any other. So, the logical compromise in a 9mm is ... the 180-grain subsonic .40 S&W.

Think about it. Almost any modern handgun you want to buy in 9mm is also available in .40 caliber, sacrificing only one to four rounds of magazine capacity. Beretta, Glock, Kahr, SIG, Smith & Wesson, Taurus ... even if you prefer the 1911 or the Browning Hi-Power; if the company makes that gun in 9mm they make one identical or almost identical to it in .40 caliber.

Sometimes compromise isn't possible. Sometimes, though, it's a necessity. And sometimes it's a good thing,

because it gets us past the small arguments so we can focus on more important matters.

The placement of the shot will be more important than the "wound profile" of the bullet we launch. Tactics that put us where we can shoot the offender more quickly and easily than the offender can shoot us, may be even more important than shot placement. And being alert enough to see danger signs in time to avoid being shot at all might be more important still.

That said, the ammunition in our gun is one of the few variables in a violent encounter that we can control before the fight starts, and we'd be fools not to load the most effective ammunition for the purpose. One thing that is not examined enough is tailoring the ammunition to its "mission profile."

You wouldn't hunt small antelope and moose with the same ammunition. Different jobs require different tools. If you were a police officer on rolling stakeout, tracking armed offenders and pulling them over at opportune times, it would be reasonable to expect that you would often have to fire through auto bodies and auto glass, and you would want ammo with deep tactical penetration. If you were the court security officer in a crowded Hall of Justice designed by an architect who thought marble was the key to structure, you have much greater concerns about over-penetration and ricochet, and this could and should alter your approach to ammunition selection.

Pick something suitable for the task, something that has already been proven on the street as well as tested in the laboratory. Don't be "the first on your block" to get the cool new ammo that is the subject of full page ads in gun magazines, but has never been used for its intended purpose and thus, in real world terms, remains untried. Let someone else be the guinea pig. In this discipline, the price of failure is simply too great.

Getting bogged down in one corner of a multi-dimensional discipline will not serve you well. There is a legal maxim that is on point to this: *De minimus non curat lex.*

The law does not bother with trifles.

CHAPTER EIGHT

DEFENSIVE GUNLEATHER TODAY

Concealment Holsters

Thanks to the enlightened and widespread adoption of "shall-issue" concealed carry legislation, more ordinary American citizens are carrying guns in the 21st century than at any time in the 20th. As determined by Professor John Lott, and others, to a point that can no longer be realistically questioned, this seems to have improved the public safety.

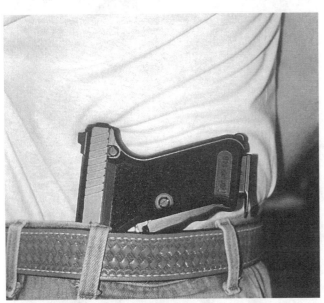

Carrying a handgun loose in the waistband is never the best idea. This HK P7M8 has shifted position and accidentally released its magazine.

We have more good concealment guns and concealment holsters than ever before. The term "gunleather," once the catch-all for belt, holster, ammo carrier and related accoutrements, must now be expanded to include leather-look synthetics like Uncle Mike's lightweight Mirage, Kydex holsters by countless makers, other related "plastic" technology as exemplified by Fobus, and fabric units ranging from ballistic nylon to Cordura.

Before looking at where the holster goes, let's look at what it's made of.

Leather has among its good points tradition, style, and pride of ownership. With the potential for perfect fit, it remains for many the preferred choice. Downsides: requires a modicum of care, may be tight when new and loose when very old, and may squeak if not properly cared for.

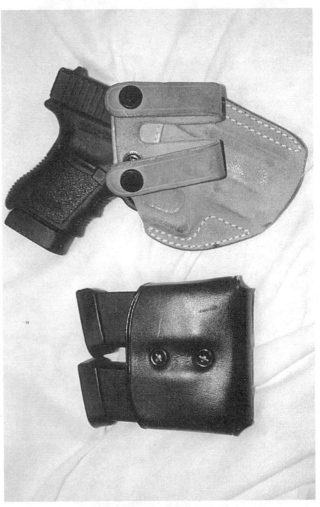

Here a Glock 30 rests in a leather IWB holster, with a double spare magazine pouch, all by Galco.

Plastics, whether Kydex or polymer or whatever, require no break-in. They generally fit perfectly from the start. They are *very* fast, so much so that synthetic holsters now rule all the combat shooting events that include quick-draw. Downsides: they can break, particularly in a struggle for the holstered gun. With rare exceptions like the suede-lined Hellweg, they make a distinctive grating sound when the gun is drawn, which can hamper a surreptitious draw in certain danger situations. They are dramatically cheaper than leather as a rule, quality level for quality level.

Dave Elderton, founder of Ky-Tac, left, discusses his super-fast and super-concealable Kydex holsters with a satisfied customer and national champ, Bob Houzenga.

Uncle Mike's holsters drove the market price downward in Kydex rigs, and work fine. This one holds a Kimber target grade .45 auto with Pachmayr grips.

Strong-Side Hip Holsters

For plainclothes police and armed citizens alike, particularly males, this is overwhelmingly the most popular concealment holster site. On the male body, a pistol just behind the hip bone tends to ride very comfortably, and is naturally hidden by the drape of the concealing garment in the hollow of the kidney area. Just behind the ileac crest of the hip is the best location. At the point of the hip, the holstered gun will protrude obviously on one side, and dig at the hip bone on the other. The dominant hand is very close, being on the same side, which is conducive to a tactically sound fast and efficient draw. The dominant-side forearm is in a position to naturally protect the holster.

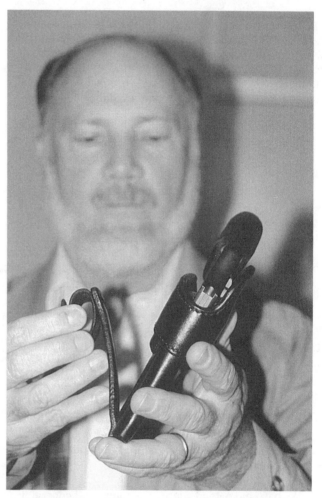

NRA director and firearms instructor Mike Baker examines the first "tuckable" holster, designed by Dave Workman. The deep area between the belt loop flap and the holster body allows the shirt to be tucked in around a holstered gun. A key chain on the belt loop makes it look harmless. Draw is done with a Hackathorn Rip. This may be the most widely copied of the new concealment holster designs.

Fabric "gunleather" is generally the cheapest of all. It rarely offers a perfect fit, but does generally allow silent draw. Now, let's look at the most street-proven holster styles for lawfully concealed handguns.

The higher, more flaring hip of the typical female, plus her proportionally shorter torso, makes the strong-side hip holster work against her. A disproportionate number of females choose to carry their guns in other locations.

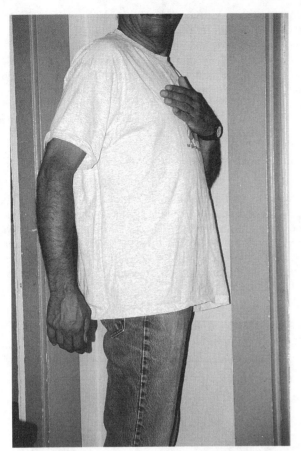

Untucked T-shirt, one size large, completely conceals...

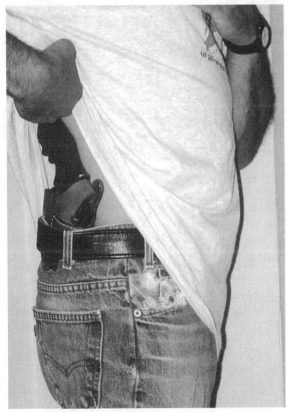

...a 4-inch square butt, Hogue-gripped S&W .357 Combat Magnum in Bianchi #3 Pistol Pocket holstered inside the waistband.

Crossdraw Belt Holsters

Whether you see it spelled crossdraw, cross-draw, or cross draw, it's all the same. We're talking about a belt-mounted holster mounted butt-forward and requiring the dominant hand to reach, to at least some degree across the abdomen for access. Hence, the terminology "crossdraw."

Many female shooters are more comfortable with crossdraw holsters. This one has done well with hers.

Good news: This is very fast for a seated person, particularly if the gun is forward of the off-side hip. It is particularly well suited to males who have rotator cuff problems or other conditions that limit the mobility of the strong-side shoulder. For reasons discussed above, it also works better for females than for males as a rule. The typical female's arm will be proportionally longer and more limber vis-à-vis her more narrow torso. The crossdraw tends to conceal better for women than for their brothers, and to be more accessible. Bad news: For most males to be able to reach the gun they must have it forward of the hip, which causes concealment problems. In a face-to-face struggle, the butt of the gun in a crossdraw holster is presented to the opponent and may be actually more accessible to him than to you.

Shoulder Holsters

The gun is suspended under the weak-side armpit by a harness that goes around the shoulders, hence the name of this rig. A shoulder holster draw is a form of crossdraw. Broad-chested, broad-shouldered men may have difficulty reaching the gun, though buxom women don't seem to have the same problem. For a number of reasons, shoulder holsters tend to be more readily detectable under a supposedly concealing garment than many other types.

Good news: Cops in particular like "shoulder systems," a concept developed by Richard Gallagher, founder of the old Jackass Holster Company and today's gunleather giant Galco. If you are right-handed, the handgun rides under your left arm and pouches containing spare ammunition and handcuffs ride under the right. This provides balance and comfort despite the added weight. More to the point, it

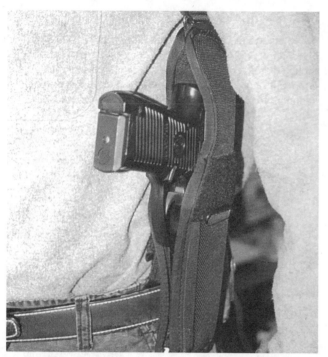

The upright shoulder holster works particularly well with large guns under heavy winter coats. This is author's Bianchi Ranger, holding a Ruger P97 .45 auto.

allows you to put on all your gear at once as quickly as putting on a jacket, and taking it all off just as easily.

A particularly useful variation of the shoulder holster is the type of rig that attaches a small handgun to the opposite armpit area of a "bulletproof vest." Noted Officer Survival authority Jim Horan designed the very first of these.

Unusual, but useful, is this security shoulder system by Strong Holster. From their Piece-Keeper series, it has a unique two-way safety strap release that's easy for the legitimate user to operate, but tough for a snatcher. This one holds the author's department-issue Ruger P90 .45 auto with IWI night sights. In the belt pouches are spare magazines and OC pepper spray.

Women seem partial to shoulder holsters. They solve the problem of having to wear a heavy-duty belt that is incongruous with the typical professional woman's wardrobe.

Bad news: Many find shoulder holsters uncomfortable, and as noted, they are not the easiest to keep discreetly concealed. A jacket or some similar garment must be kept on at all times. If the harness is not secured to the belt, the holstered gun and magazines will bounce around and hammer the rib cage mercilessly if you have to run.

Small of Back Holster

Often called SOB for short, this holster carry is thought by some to earn that nickname in more ways than one. The pistol is carried at or near the center of the lumbar spine. The theory is that even if the concealing garment blows open, it will not be visible from the front. It is reasonably fast with a conventional draw and particularly easy to access with the weak hand, an attribute shared by the crossdraw and the shoulder holster.

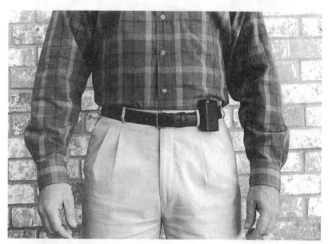

This individual doesn't appear to be carrying a gun...

...until he pulls up his Pager Pal holster with AMT .380 auto. With this draw, be careful the muzzle doesn't cross the support hand. Photos by Pager Pal.

Good news: Excellent concealment from the front and fast access when standing. Bad news: Almost impossible to reach from a seated position, especially with seat belts in place. A gun in this position is extremely difficult to defend against a gun snatch attempt. The gun tends to catch the rear hem of the concealing garment and lift it up in such a way that the wearer can't see or feel it, but everyone behind him or her sees the exposed gun. Finally, any rearward fall guarantees the equivalent of landing on a rock with your lumbar spine.

Belly Band Holster

This is a 4-inch-wide elastic strip with one or more holster pouches sewn in. It is ideal for wear with a tucked-in shirt or blouse and no jacket. The belly band is worn "over the underwear and under the overwear."

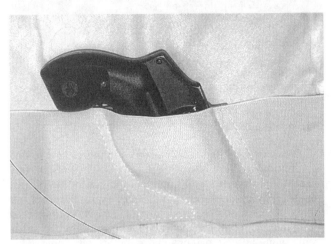

The belly band is often the most practical concealed carry system in a business environment. This one, by Guardian, holds a Model 442 Airweight S&W .38 Special with Crimson Trace LaserGrips.

Most advertisements for such products show them being worn inefficiently. For the male, these rigs work best at belt level, with the handgun just to the side of the navel, butt forward in what has been called "front crossdraw" carry. To speed the draw, the second button above the belt may be left undone. A necktie will cover this minor lapse of fashion protocol.

Many women prefer to wear the belly band just below the breast line. Natural fabric drape hides it well.

Good news: Unbeatable for discreet carry under business clothing. This holster is faster than it seems and can be combined with a money belt.

Bad news: Some find this carry uncomfortable. The wearer is, practically speaking, limited to a fairly small gun. A small-frame, short-barrelled revolver with rounded edges is particularly suitable for belly band carry.

Pocket Holster

At this writing, loose-fitting pants of the Dockers and BDU persuasion are in style, and literally cover the wearer in situations from "tie and jacket" to "tailgate party informal." All are well suited for small handguns in the pockets. The larger cuts will allow pistols up to the size of baby Glock autoloaders. Tight jeans, on the other hand, may limit you to the tiniest "pocket autos."

This is not to say that the wearing of a pocket gun is entirely "fashion dependent." Fortunately, certain "timeless" styles lend themselves to pocket carry. These include police and security uniform pants, military style BDUs, and the seemingly eternal men's "sack suit."

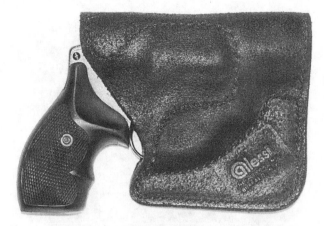

A pocket holster is essential for pocket carry. This one, by Alessi, holds a S&W Centennial Airweight with Uncle Mike's affordable version of Spegel Boot Grips.

Just dropping the gun in the pocket is not enough. It will shift position, often winding up with its grip-frame down and the muzzle pointed straight up, a nightmare if you need a reasonably fast draw. In the pocket, "the naked gun" will also print its shape obviously to the least discerning eye, and will tend to wear holes in the pocket lining.

A pocket gun needs a pocket holster. This product serves to break up the outline, protect pocket lining and thigh alike from chafing, and to assure that the handgun is always oriented in the same, appropriate position. The front side trouser pocket is almost universally deemed the pocket of choice for "pistol-packing."

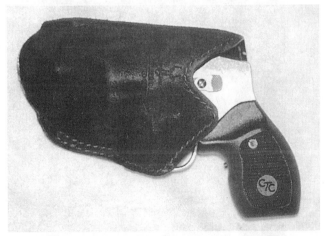

The author's favorite pocket holster is the Safariland, here holding a S&W Model 640 Centennial with LaserGrips.

Good news: The hand can be casually in the pocket and already holding the gun. The draw can be surprisingly fast. A jacket can be removed with impunity if the gun is carried in the pants.

Bad news: The gun can be lost from all but the best pocket holsters when rolling and/or fighting on the ground. It is difficult for the weak hand to reach if necessary and limits the user to a fairly small handgun.

Ankle Holsters

Fobus ankle holster can conceal this baby Glock .40 if the pant legs are loose enough.

Since the first horseman stuck a pistol in his boot-top, this method of carry has been with us. It is somewhat fashion-dependent. Peg-bottom jeans or Toreador pants just weren't made for ankle rigs. On the other hand, "boot-cut" jeans, "flares," and the old bell-bottoms were perfect for ankle holsters. Standard cut men's suits and uniform pants adapt to this carry well.

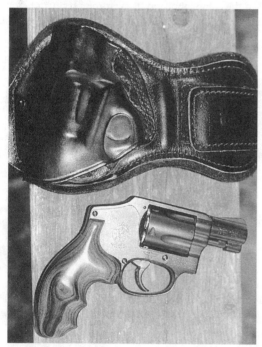

Alessi is the author's choice in an ankle holster for all-day wear. This one holds a Gunsite Custom S&W Model 442 Airweight with Hogue grips.

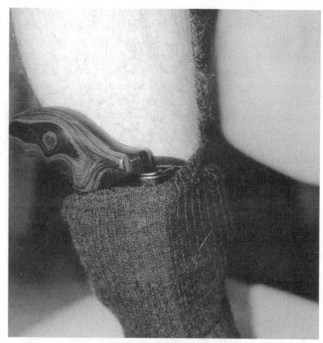

Pulling a sock up over the ankle holster distinctly enhances concealment.

The ankle rig is the holster people are most likely to find uncomfortable. Very few of them fit well. The holster body wants to be firm and well-fitted, but the part of the rig that touches the leg needs to be soft and supple. All-wool felt lining seems to be the best interior surface option; even those allergic to wool can cure the problem with hypoallergenic white all-cotton socks under the holster. Some ankle rigs are available with sheepskin lining.

It takes about a week of constant wear to become accustomed to the new weight and constriction at the ankle. Hint: It conceals better if the sock is pulled up over the body of the holster, leaving the butt exposed for a quick draw. Also, because running through brush or simply crossing your ankles can release a safety strap, it is imperative that an ankle holster's scabbard portion fit the gun tightly enough to keep it in place during strenuous activity.

Good news: Ankle rigs are among the fastest holsters to access while sitting and are perhaps *the* fastest to access when you're down on your back. Since the legs no longer bear the body's weight, you can simply snap the ankle up to the reaching hand. Most users find that wearing it on the ankle opposite the dominant hand, butt to the rear, works best.

Bad news: These are among the slowest to draw from when standing and can be uncomfortable. Weight and particularly constriction around the lower leg can aggravate phlebitis and any number of medical conditions where impaired circulation to extremities is a concern.

Fanny Pack

From the defining DeSantis "Gunny Sack" to the Second Chance "Police Pouch" that opens up into a bullet-resistant shield, belt packs designed to contain firearms have become ubiquitous, particularly in hot climates. Some in the world of the gun believe the fanny pack is the ultimate tip-off to an armed person. If so, they'll get awfully paranoid at the beach or Disney World, where every second person seems to be wearing one.

Fanny packs aren't the fastest way to get to a gun, but are often the most convenient way to carry one. This one is home to a Kahr K9 compact 9mm.

Good news: These are very convenient. When you have to leave your gun in the car to comply with the law, simply locking the fanny pack in the trunk draws no attention.

Bad news: Fanny packs offer a very slow draw. Weight can cause problems with lumbar spine for some wearers. The fanny pack is seen as the location of a wallet and folding money and may thus become the very focus of a criminal attack.

Off-Body Carry

Since handguns have existed, people have carried them in saddlebags and purses, suitcases and briefcases, mounted on saddles or in the glove boxes of automobiles. Today we have all manner of purses, attaché cases and day planners designed to contain hidden handguns. Particularly useful is the Guardian Leather "legal portfolio," which contains a panel of body armor along with the hidden sidearm.

... helps organize survival by also concealing a Micro Kahr pistol.

Here is one of several variations of a briefcase...

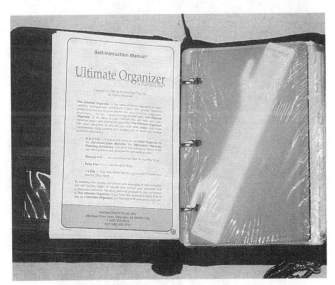

Designed to work (and function) as a personal organizer, this handy little unit...

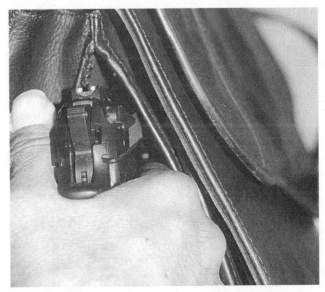

...with hidden pockets that can easily carry this full-size Beretta service pistol.

Good news: These options are very convenient and are not fashion-dependent, meaning the gun might be along when it would otherwise have been left at home.

Bad news: When you've set it down, security has disappeared. People in other countries where loss of a firearm is considered presumptive evidence of criminal negligence have gone to jail for leaving their gun-bearing purse or case behind in a restaurant. Leave the room where you're visiting, and ask yourself if the host's child might wander in and pick through the purse you left beside your chair. Once again drawing from almost all these devices is painfully slow. Besides, the attack on you might revolve around a mugger or purse-snatcher grabbing the very object that contains your firearm.

Common Questions

"Should my holster be inside or outside the waistband?" Inside the waistband is certainly more concealable. The drape

...and securing to the belt with J-hooks.

of the pants breaks up the outline of the holster, and the concealing garment can come all the way up to the belt without revealing the holstered gun. For comfort, however, the pants should be about 2 inches larger in the waist than what one would normally wear. If you have tried inside the waistband (IWB) carry and found it uncomfortable, try it again for a week, but this time leave the top button of the lower garment undone. If it's now comfortable, you can buy new clothes with wider waistbands or let out the ones you have. (We could also lose weight, but hey, let's be realistic here.)

This Kydex holster by Sidearmor holds a Glock 30 compact .45 comfortably inside the waistband...

...protecting its finish against sweat thoroughly, thanks to the built-up inside surface...

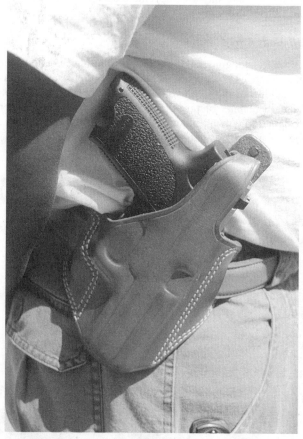

A safety strap is always a good idea on a defensive holster. This scabbard with a thumb-break is by Galco and holds an HK USP.

"Should my concealment holster have a safety strap or other security device?" It is a myth to believe that you'll never have anyone try to snatch your gun because it's concealed and they don't know you have it. The gun might momentarily become visible. The attacker might be a disgruntled employee you've fired, who not only knows that you carry a gun, but knows where you carry it. And any physical fight is likely to reach a point where the opponent grabs you around the waist to throw you, at which time he'll feel your gun and grab at it. Therefore, at least one "level" of retention, such as a simple thumb-break safety strap, is desirable. More snatch-resistant holsters than that are available in concealable styles, such as the Safariland 0701 or the Piece-Keeper from Strong Holsters.

"Is quick access really important?" Frankly, yes. When the general public sees a uniformed police officer with a gun in his hand, they're not afraid of him, they're afraid of the situation that made him draw his gun and they get out of the way. When the general public sees an ordinary person with a gun in his hand, panic often ensues and someone may try to be a hero and disarm him. There will be some situations where responding police officers might also mistake an unidentifed armed citizen for "the bad guy," setting the stage for a mistaken-identity shooting. Thus, the armed citizen is often wise to wait 'til the last possible moment to draw, meaning that speed of presentation is all the more important.

The author has become particularly partial to these Toters ™ jeans designed by Blackie Collins especially for gun carriers. All pockets are reinforced for small handguns, cuffs are cut for ankle rigs, and the "mature cut" waistband works well with belly bands and IWB holsters.

Police Uniform Holsters

Through the late 19th century, most police officers bought their own handguns and their own means of carrying them. Many Eastern officers simply put their revolvers in a coat or trouser pocket. The Western lawman generally carried a heavier six-gun, normally in whatever scabbard was available at the gunsmith's shop or the saddle-maker's place of business.

...the legendary S.D. Myres company.

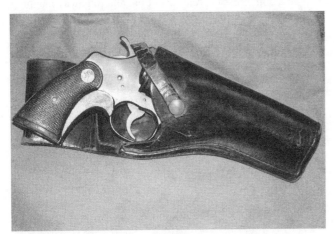

Dating to the first third of the 20 century, this duty holster was made for a 5-inch Colt service revolver by...

The mid-1890s purchase of the Colt New Police .32 revolvers by the police departments of New York City and Boston began the trend of departments issuing guns and, inevitably, holsters in which to carry them. The earliest police holsters were simply gun pouches with something to hold the gun in place. Some departments opted for a simple safety strap to perform the latter function, while others preferred a military style flap. The rationale for the latter was three-fold. First, the flap holster had a military look that went well with the whole concept of uniformed police as a paramilitary structure during the early part of the 20th century. Second, it gave the department-owned gun some protection from rain and snow when the cop was out there walking the beat. Third, some saw the flap as more impediment than the strap to a suspect gaining control of the officer's sidearm.

As the years rolled along, advocates of the "strap" won out over advocates of the "flap." S.D. Myres' holster company was one of the early pioneers in designing sparsely cut, fast-draw scabbards that need only have a strap over the hammer added to placate the security demands of police chiefs. Berns-Martin's radical break-front holster of the 1930s was the first effort in really giving a cop a fast duty rig that was also secure. The gun came out the front, in keeping with the theory of the time that a draw should be a forward swing that ended with the revolver being fired from below line of sight.

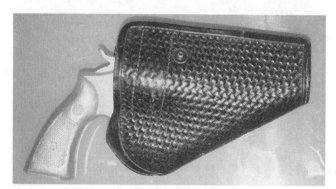

High-tech, in the 1930s, was embodied by the Berns-Martin holster. Shown here with a K-frame Odin Press dummy gun...

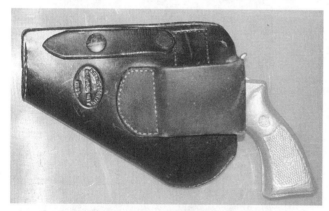

...the Berns-Martin was generally carried with its frontal strap fastened thus out of the way for a quick draw.

Time went on. By the 1970s, three significant developments had taken shape. Bill Jordan's rigid steel reinforcement of the Myres type scabbard had become hugely popular. Jordan, the Border Patrol's most famous gunslinger, had redefined the paradigm. He had designed the holster to be worn unfastened, with the strap out of the way

and fastened only when a cop was going into a bar fight or about to undertake a vigorous foot pursuit.

The thumb-break holster, pioneered at about the same time by the Bucheimer Company in Maryland and brilliant gunleather designer Chic Gaylord in New York, made so much sense that it took cops by storm. Don Hume, the sole licensed producer of the Jordan holster (though everyone seemed to make copies) offered the classic with a thumb-break attachment. This allowed the strap to be kept fastened with virtually no sacrifice in drawing speed.

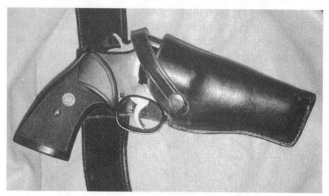

By the 1970s, this was the paradigm: A S&W Model 10 (or Combat Magnum for the lucky ones) in a simple Jordan-style holster.

The 1970s also saw the return of the Berns-Martin concept in John Bianchi's updated break-front holsters, the first of which was the Model 27. The first design had a major in "fast" and a minor in "secure." The Bianchi break-front reversed the priorities. It had a major in "secure" and a minor in "fast." It quickly earned a reputation for saving lives, and the holster industry geared up for "security rigs" to attack Bianchi's dominance in the lucrative police gunleather market.

Along the way, several "gimmick" holsters came and went. Appearing primarily on the West Coast, especially popular with the LAPD, was the clamshell holster. A button was "hidden" in front of the trigger in the exposed trigger guard. When pressed, the spring-loaded holster flipped open like the shell of a clam. It was very fast, but since the trigger finger had to be working at the trigger area just to get the gun out of the holster, it lent itself to unintentional discharges under stress. Legend has it that smart-aleck kids learned to run up behind a cop, press the release button, and run away laughing when the service revolver clattered to the ground. Most episodes of the old TV cop series "Adam-12," still shown on some "oldies" channels, show the clamshell in use.

The Audley duty holster never gained much popularity except on the East Coast.

On the opposite coast, the Audley holster was regionally popular for decades. Like the clamshell, the trigger and guard were exposed, and the shooter had to reach past the trigger to release the gun. The Audley lock was a simple spring tongue that pressed against the inside front of the trigger guard. Like the clamshell, it was implicated in numerous accidental discharges.

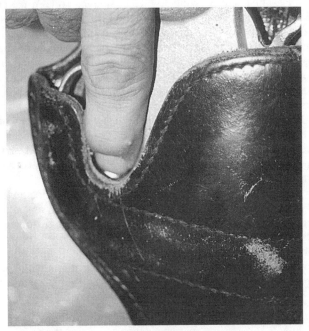

The trigger finger had to be pressed into the trigger guard to release the revolver from the Audley holster.

If the Audley was an Eastern Seaboard phenomenon, the Jay-Pee holster developed for the NYPD had few fans beyond that city. Selling at one time for $12 per holster, it had an inner welt of leather that secured at the rear of the revolver's cylinder. A twist of the revolver in a certain direction released it for draw. At least, it had a covered trigger guard. All three of these holsters normally left the hammer spur unsecured, where it could be accidentally caught and drawn back, becoming cocked in the holster and setting the stage for unintentional discharges. This is one reason LAPD, and later NYPD, eventually ordered service revolvers altered department-wide so they could not operate in single action.

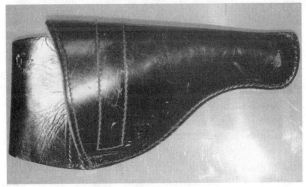

Though ugly, cheap, and made of less than premium materials, the Jay-Pee NYPD holster was credited with saving multiple lives.

Enter the Autos

As the competition rushed at the Bianchi break-front, new designs emerged such as the "split-front." Typified by the Security Plus from Smith & Wesson's then-popular leather division and also by Bianchi's own Hurricane, this was seen as a less radical alternative to the break-front with similar security function. Instead of sweeping the whole gun out the front of the holster, the officer would release the thumb-break, rock the gun forward to clear the rear trigger guard shield, and then draw straight up and out. Truth to tell, this could also be done with the breakfront.

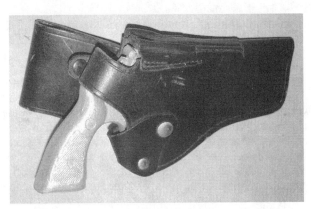

Smith & Wesson's Security Plus holster was extremely popular during the last days of the police revolver era, and defined the "split-front" as opposed to "break-front" design.

By the 1980s, more and more departments were going to auto pistols. Bianchi spent a then-unprecedented $100,000 in research to design the snatch-resistant Auto-Draw holster. It was difficult to draw from, but extremely retentive, against a disarming attempt. Meanwhile, an FBI veteran named Bill Rogers had designed a holster he called the SS-III. The officer had to break two safety straps and then rock the gun in a certain direction to release it for draw. The good news was it was so ergonomically designed that any committed officer could learn to make the draw quickly. The SS-III was to become the most successful security holster ever. By the year 2001, some 20 years after its inception, over a million had been sold. Early on, Safariland had bought out Rogers, kept him as a consultant, and renamed the SS-III holster the Model 070.

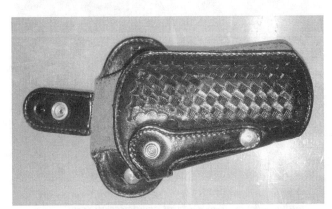

This was the Bianchi Auto-Draw. The author carried one on duty with a Colt .45 for years.

A cutaway of the new Raptor security holster shows its state-of-the-art mix of modern features. The gun is a dummy Glock by Ring's.

Rogers gilded the lily in 2001 when he came out with a higher-tech version called the Raptor. It effectively addressed what many police tacticians saw as the one weakness in the 070 design. While an officer could learn to quickly draw from the 070, it took a few seconds to re-fasten the two safety straps. This could be a problem when the officer had to holster and secure his weapon for a foot chase or to handcuff a temporarily compliant suspect. With the Raptor, the securing

The Safariland SS-III/070 is the "gold standard" in police security holsters. This one carries a Ruger P90 .45 auto.

The Safariland 070 is standard-issue for officers on the author's department. Old vets and newer officers appreciate its balance of high security with good speed of draw.

device at the rear locked automatically as the gun was inserted into the holster, and the forward device locked back in place with a flick of the finger. This had been borrowed directly from a popular mid-1990s Rogers/Safariland development, the SLS (Self Locking System).

Duty Belts

The first police gunbelts were simple, soft strips of leather. After WWI, the military Sam Browne belt became almost universal issue among American police. More than 2 inches wide, it much better distributed the weight of the officer's equipment. The Sam Browne concept included an over-the-shoulder strap, which helped to bear the weight of the service revolver and other gear. To this day, some departments still use the diagonal Sam Browne shoulder strap. Officers also learned to wear belt keepers, simple loops of leather that snapped over both the "underbelt" – the officer's regular pants belt, usually a Garrison style – and the heavy belt that went over it. This held them together and prevented the duty belt from shifting during strenuous activity.

In the last 30 years of the 20th century, new refinements became popular. "Buckle-less" belts, using Velcro or sometimes hooks, were seen by some agencies as more streamlined and less evocative of Santa Claus (who also was usually depicted with a Sam Browne style belt, albeit without the shoulder strap). Some officers felt that removing the polished belt buckle also removed a "bull's-eye" that an opponent could aim at in a dark alley.

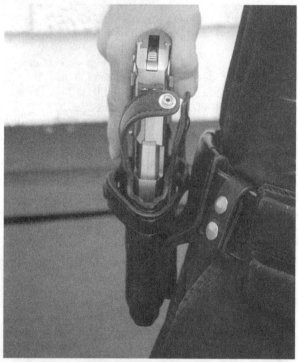

Despite triple-level security, the draw is quick from the author's department-issue 070 holster. On-safe carry adds one more level of retention capability.

Safariland pioneered Velcro-lined belts that mated with under-belts with an outward Velcro surface. This did away with belt keepers. The result was a more streamlined belt, and several seconds taken off the time it took a cop to dress for work and remove the belt at the end of the shift.

Meanwhile, the police belt was beginning to resemble Batman's "utility belt." Photos of American police (and depictions of them in old movies) in the first half of the 20th century show them wearing a revolver, perhaps 12 spare cartridges, and a handcuff pouch. By the 1960s and 1970s, it came into vogue to wear a baton on the belt. Portable radios had become standard issue, and these, too, were belt-mounted for the most part. Streetwise officers learned to carry a second pair of handcuffs. In the 1980s and 1990s, awareness of the dangers of blood-borne pathogens made latex and nitrile gloves standard issue. While these didn't weigh much, their pouch took up more of the decreasing space on the duty belt. First Mace and then pepper spray became standard issue, and another pouch had to be added to the belt.

State-of-the-art today is the Levitation duty rig system from Safariland. Velcro lining mates with a Velcro underbelt…

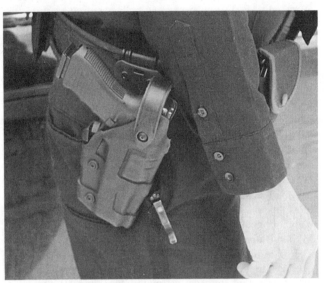

Many consider the Rogers-designed Raptor holster to be the police duty rig of the future. The author tests this one on patrol with Glock 22.

…and a unique Bill Rogers attachment design prevents inner edges of the attachment loops from digging against wearer's body, yet…

Police unionization was growing, and with it came more concern for occupational hazards. Studies finally quantified what had long been suspected: One of the occupational hazards of police work is lower back problems, much of it traceable to the massive equipment belt worn around the waist for eight to 10 hours a day. An officer with a heavy radio and a heavy police flashlight at his waist might have a belt that weighed 18 to 20 pounds.

There was a strong demand to lighten the load. With it came another concern, that blood-borne pathogen thing. Leather is organic and can absorb blood. It is very difficult to clean after it has been bloodstained. Enter the fabric duty rigs!

These were lighter. That was more comfortable. They were softer and more supple. That was more comfortable too. If they were splashed with blood, they could simply be machine-washed. But some departments didn't feel anything less than leather was professional-looking, so Uncle Mike's set the pace with their synthetic, leather-look "Mirage" line.

Female officers were particularly hard-hit by belt comfort and weight problems. The 1970s saw the development of an orthopedic curved belt that was instantly dubbed the "Sally Browne" style. It flared at the hip to better distribute

…the system is strong enough that this NYPD officer can hang from his gun butt without pulling the holster loose from the Levitation belt.

the weight of the equipment load. Shortly after the turn of the century, Bill Rogers made another leap forward with his Levitation belt. As light as the lightest synthetic, it incorporated soft, rubbery tubes on the top and bottom edges to cushion the weight and pressure of the belt. It was determined that the belt shank of attached equipment pouches in general and of holsters in particular, tended to cause nerve damage after pressing into the body for a long period of time. Bill Rogers developed an ingenious new locking mechanism that secured the holster and accessories to the top and bottom edges of the belt. This left only a soft, smooth surface facing the officer's body. This writer has worn the Levitation belt system on uniformed duty and believes it may be the wave of the future in police duty equipment.

Another concept to emerge in the late 1990s was "duty suspenders." Pioneered by Magnum Software under their Orca brand and popularized by Uncle Mike's, these distributed the weight of the duty belt across the shoulders. They have become regionally popular, particularly in the Pacific Northwest. There is the possibility that they give a physical attacker something else to grab hold of to throw the cop around; that was always a concern with the Sam Browne shoulder strap as well. On the other hand, they make good "drag handles" for pulling a wounded brother officer out of the line of fire.

Some trends developed in combat shooting matches, proved themselves there, and were then gradually accepted into day-to-day police work. Revolver speedloaders and semiautomatic pistols are two cases in point. However, some concepts that were successful in matches and even in real-world concealed carry just didn't make the jump into law enforcement. The Kydex holster is a case in point. Its anchoring on the belt has proven too weak to stand up to a determined gun snatch attempt, in most models. While certain plastics, like Safariland's "Safari-Laminate," have stood the test of time on patrol, most others have not.

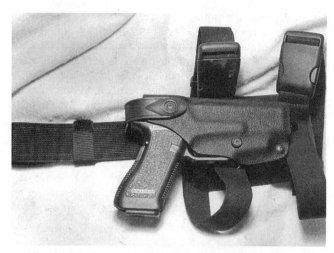

The thigh holster is a concept borrowed from the military that has found favor with police tactical units. This one is a Safariland SLS style, shown with a Glock 17.

If the first borrowing from the military was the flap holster and the second was the Sam Browne belt, the third – much later – was the tactical thigh holster. Popularized by the British SAS, it carried the holstered handgun down out of the way of heavy, hardshell body armor and load-bearing vests worn by SWAT officers. Thigh holsters do not give the officer good leverage to defend against a gun-grab. However, a lunge for the holstered police pistol is not likely to happen when a SWAT cop and at least four of his colleagues blow open a door with explosive entry, throw in a "flash-bang" concussion grenade, and then charge in wielding MP5 sub-machineguns or M4 assault rifles.

Police duty "leather" has come a long way in the last century. Indeed, the term itself is becoming archaic. By many informed industry estimates, less than 50 percent of police duty belt gear is now actually made of leather.

Ammo Carriers

A gun without spare ammunition is a temporary gun. This is why combat competition puts significant emphasis on the ability to quickly and efficiently reload. But you can't reload if you don't have ammo, and if you don't have a comfortable, convenient way of carrying it, you *won't* have it when you need it. Once you have it, you need to be able to access it quickly and get it into the gun. Because revolvers and semi-automatic pistols reload in completely different manners, they'll be treated separately.

Revolvers

Belt Loops. Belt loops go back almost to the dawn of the self-contained cartridge. It their time, they were awesomely efficient. Even today they're not too shabby.

In cowboy days, the loops were sewn directly to the belt. Today, whether for concealed carry or for uniformed personnel equipped with revolvers, the loops are on a slide that attaches to the belt. The first thing a professional looks for is to see that the loops are at the very top edge. This will allow the rounds to be plucked out much more quickly. Only amateurs (or those issued the cheapest equipment bought on bid)

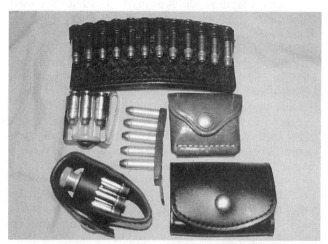

There are half a dozen options for spare revolver ammo. Clockwise from noon: shell loop slide (Don Hume), dump pouch (Bianchi), 2X2X2 carrier (DeSantis), Rogers-style speedloader carrier w/HKS speedloader (Safariland), .45 full-moon clip in Shoot-the-Moon carrier. Center: Bianchi Speed Strip downloaded by one round as the author suggests.

Loading with belt loops. The revolver is a Ruger SP-101 with Bob Cogan recoil reduction venting. The belt slide is by Don Hume...

...and, inserted on this slight angle for greater speed...

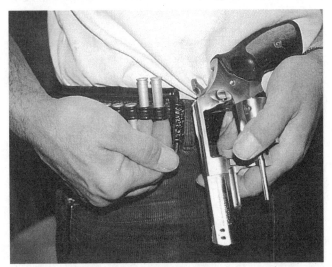

...the Hume loops sit out from the slide, making it easy for two fingers to pop up two rounds...

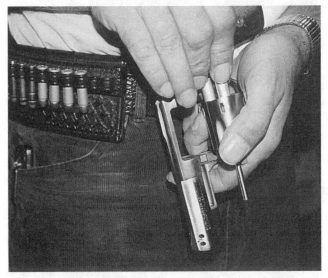

...snap them into the chambers. The thumb then rotates the cylinder to receive the next "ammo delivery" while the dominant hand is returning to the belt loops.

...that are now easily plucked up by the first two fingers and the thumb...

use carry loops that are sewn to the middle of the belt slide. You practically need tweezers or forceps to get the cartridges out of the latter.

It is no trick to load two cartridges at a time. Use your dominant hand: This is a dexterity-intensive function, and Mother Nature demands that you use your dexterous hand if you want to accomplish it under stress. Carry the loops on your strong-hand side. As your hand comes down, palm toward you, use the tips of your index and middle fingers to push up the bullet noses of two rounds. This will bring the bases of the cartridges up clear from the loops. Now, grab them at the base with those two fingers and the thumb. Angle them slightly as you feed them into adjacent revolver chambers, and you can load two-by-two. I've seen very practiced people who could load three cartridges at a time this way.

Cartridge Pouches. Slim, flat, and streamlined, these looked good on police duty belts. Stamped with a single die and then sewn together, they were cheap to make and always won low bid. This is why they were almost standard by the 1960s. Pouches as a rule are the slowest method of reloading. Some "dump pouches" were designed to flip down and spill the rounds into the officer's palm; as a result, they were also known as "spill pouches." Trouble was, leather can shrink over time. Many of us can remember seeing officers claw desperately to get their rounds out of these

The Bianchi dump pouch is small and unobtrusive, but not the fastest of reloading devices…

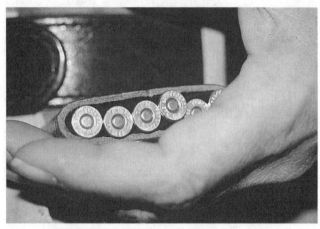

… available. The author uses it by spilling the contents into the palm of the non-dominant hand …

…and using the palm as a "loading tray" as the dominant hand inserts the cartridges into the cylinder.

pouches, or jumping up and down trying to shake them loose. That wouldn't work if you were down on your knees behind cover. Some resourceful cops learned to take tin shears to a license plate and cut liner strips for the inside of their spill pouches so the cartridges would actually spill.

John Bianchi was a young policeman during the years when the cartridge pouch was the dominant spare ammo system for cops. He later became a master holster designer, and he also designed the brilliant Bianchi Speed Strip, a little rubber thing that would hold six .38 or .357 cartridges in line inside the pouch. Once you got your Speed Strip out of the pouch and learned how to use it, you could reload about as fast as with belt loops, which was reasonably fast.

The best of the stand-alone pouches were the "2X2X2" style. These became standard issue for FBI in their last years with revolvers. The pouch would tilt out to about a 45-degree angle when its flap was opened. The cartridges were held in three pouches of two each. This could be about as fast as using Speed Strips or loops, but the added leather required by the design made for a bulkier unit that was harder to conceal, though less obvious if it became exposed.

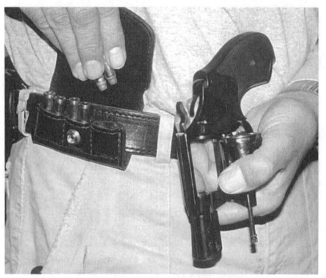

Here is a DeSantis 2X2X2 pouch in action, loading two at a time. The revolver is a .38 Colt Detective Special with Pachmayr Compac grips.

Bianchi Speed Strip. Developed to augment the belt pouch, the Speed Strip was also a stand-alone device. It was exactly the right size to fit in the watch pocket of a pair of jeans, or that little business card pocket you often find inside the right outside suitcoat pocket. This made spare ammo convenient to carry, especially for concealed revolvers.

This writer discovered over the years that the fastest way to use a Speed Strip was to load it one round down from capacity, leaving the sixth hole near the handling strip empty. Instead of six rounds flopping on the end of a soft tab, you had five rounds that you could quickly stabilize for a positive, fast reload. The middle finger would curl around the space left by the removed cartridge, and the index finger lined up along the spine of the Speed Strip. This is the way most surgeons hold their scalpels, with the index finger along the back, and in both cases it gives tremendous accuracy. Feeding of the five remaining cartridges into the chambers is faster and more positive.

The author developed this grasp of the Bianchi Speed Strip shortly after it came out. The round near tab is removed beforehand, allowing the middle finger to lock there securely while the index finger takes a scalpel position on the back of the strip...

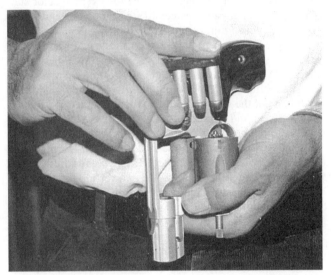

...the top two rounds will enter the S&W AirLite's cylinder first...

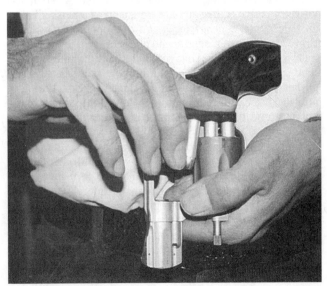

... with the index finger snapping them into the chambers...

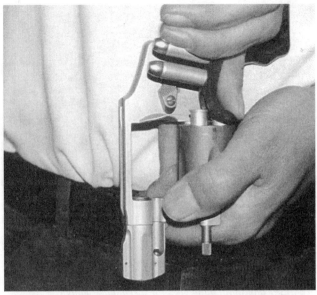

...and the Strip is peeled off the cartridge rims as shown...

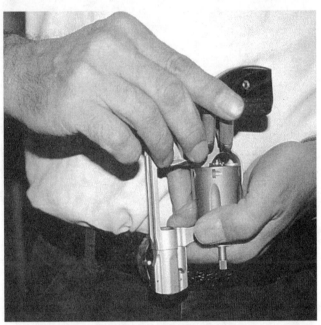

... with the process repeated until all five rounds are in the gun.

In the old days when auto pistols weren't as reliable as current ones are today, law enforcement justified its reliance on the revolver with the principle, "six for sure beats 14 maybe." This method with the Speed Strip gave you five for sure, positive and fast, instead of six with fumbling. Today, a huge number of revolvers carried for self defense are small-frame five-shot guns anyway, so the concept comes together better than ever.

Speedloaders. There were six-shot charging units for the first Colt revolvers with swing-out cylinders in the 1890s. The concept did not catch on with combat shooters until the 1960s. Even then, because each loader was the width of a revolver's cylinder, the pouches in which they were carried bulged on the belt and were seen as "unsightly" and "unprofessional."

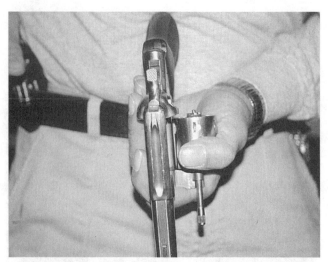

Here is how to speed-reload the revolver. Once the empties have been punched out, the weak hand holds the gun thus as the dominant hand goes for speedloader pouch...

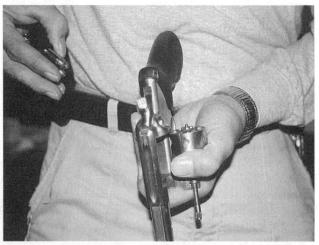

... the fingertips are extended past the bullet noses to help guide the loader into the cylinder of this Sile-gripped Ruger .357...

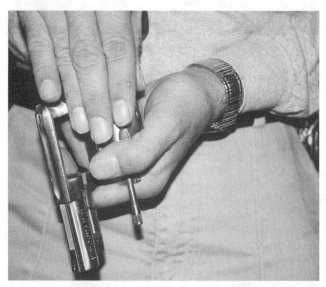

... and insertion is accomplished thus. Release the payload, let the empty loader fall away, close the cylinder, and go back to business.

Then, in 1970, came the Newhall Massacre. Two heavily armed robbers in the course of a felony car-stop in Newhall, California, killed four young California Highway Patrolmen. The last survivor was down on his knees, wounded through the chest and both legs, desperately trying to reload his revolver. He had to take one cartridge at a time out of his pouches, access to which was partially impaired by his kneeling position. He had been taught to fire six, reload six, fire six more, and had reverted to training under enormous stress. He was just closing the cylinder on the fresh load when one of the killers completed his stealthy approach, screamed "Got you now, (expletive deleted)," and shot him in the head. In the wake of this tragedy, the CHP became the first major department in the nation to authorize, and later issue as standard, speedloaders for duty wear. Not until 20 years later would CHP adopt a semiautomatic pistol, the .40 Smith & Wesson Model 4006, which carried 12 rounds and offered a fast reload.

Numerous speedloader designs have come and gone. Two have remained: the HKS and the Safariland. The latter is faster, being a one-stroke unit. It releases as the center hub of the unit hits the center of the revolver's ejector star. The HKS is a two-step device; after insertion, it requires the second step of turning a release knob.

Does a second step make it second rate? Not at all. The HKS is by far the most rugged speedloader ever put on the market. Years ago, this writer loaded some up with .357 Magnum hollow-points and put them in an empty paint can, and then put the can in a Red Devil paint mixer and flipped the switch. (And, admittedly, took cover.) When the cycle was over, the paint can had been torn apart, and all the bullets had expanded back to their case mouths. However, the HKS speedloaders still worked. Other brands turned into plastic dust under the tremendously powerful vibrations.

Safariland makes three variations of speedloaders. Their smallest and oldest, the old JFS design, is called the Comp I. It is very compact and very fast, but John Farnam has noted that after about 500 reloads, it will break. I also found it breakage prone. Since no one counts their reloads, and no one throws away equipment that still seems to be functioning, this unit is an accident waiting to happen. The Comp II is proportionally larger and proportionally sturdier, and just as fast. The Comp III is huge. Modeled after the old Austrian Jet-loader, it is shaped like an old German "potato masher" hand grenade. Duty pouches for it are disproportionately large. However, it is extremely fast and does not seem to break. The trick is concealing it. This writer did find that the shape is such that when it is tucked into the right side of a right hip pocket, with a handkerchief in the same pocket to keep it in position, it tucks into the natural hollow of the gluteus maximus. Carried thus, the Comp III is reasonably concealable and comfortable, and very accessible.

Lining up six or so cartridges with as many same-size holes is a dexterity task, and once again Mother Nature demands that we use the dexterous hand to perform it. Keep the speedloaders on the dominant hand side. After ejecting the spent cartridges, I like to grab the revolver around the front of the frame with my left hand, using the left thumb to hold the cylinder out, and bring the gun butt in to touch the center of my abdomen. This creates a felt index that keeps the gun in the same spot all the time, and also orients the muzzle downward so I can take maximum advantage of gravity to help insure that the fresh cartridges fall all the way in and don't tie up the cylinder.

Years ago, a speedloader designer named Kubik came up with the most effective grasp of such a device. Hold it with the fingertips ahead of the bullet noses. This shapes the fingers to the shape of the cylinder. Even in the dark, as your fingertips feel the cylinder, all you have to do is give the loader a light jiggle and all the rounds should slide into place.

When the cartridges release, let the loader fall away. Close the cylinder before you bring the gun up, so centrifugal force doesn't throw a round backward as the cylinder is closing and jam things up. Once the cylinder is closed, return to firing position.

Moon Clips. Half-moon clips were developed by Smith & Wesson to adapt rimless .45 auto cartridges to revolvers, for their 1917 Model, in WWI. It would be more than 50 years before someone would figure out that a single "full-moon clip" of six cartridges would be far more practical than two "half-moon clips" of three cartridges each.

The full-moon clip is, without question, the fastest way to reload a revolver. There is nothing to release, and no empty loader to cast aside. You simply shove the whole thing in and close the cylinder. With a .45 ACP sixgun and a moon clip of round nose jacketed ball, you can literally throw the loader into the cylinder!

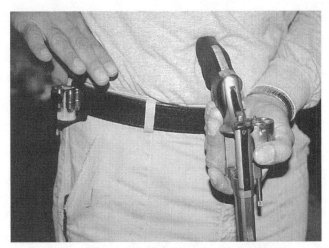

Reloading with a moon clip. The spent "moon" has been ejected from this S&W Model 625, and the dominant hand goes for the loaded moon ...

A full-moon clip goes right into the gun with the ammo.

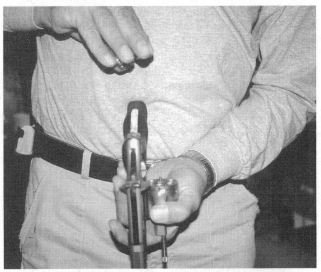

...with the fingertips ahead of the bullet noses to interface with the cylinder, the fresh charge is on the way ...

How fast is fast? Jerry Miculek holds the record for firing six, reloading, and firing six more from a double-action revolver (and hitting the target with every shot). He used a Smith & Wesson Model 625 and full-moon clips. The time? 2.99 seconds!

The only down side of moon clips is that they can become bent, which renders them inoperable in the gun. This means that they must be carried in a rigid, protective pouch of some kind. On a duty belt, a pouch that will hold one N-frame .357 or .44 Magnum revolver speedloader will hold *two* short, efficiently sized moon clips of .45 ACP. A compact, protective unit suitable for concealment that holds the moon clip with the bullet noses toward the wearer's body is available from leathermaker Chris Cunningham at 1709 5th Ave., West Linn, OR 97068.

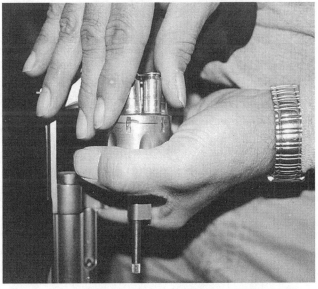

...and the whole kit and kaboodle goes into the gun, making it the fastest of all revolver reloads.

A combination magazine pouch and flashlight carrier (Glock and SureFire, respectively) was first conceptualized by gunwriter Dean Spier. This one is produced by Blade-Tech.

Unlike a revolver, the auto doesn't need to be brought down to the ammo supply at the belt. It's faster to do as the author does with this Colt Government in this multiple exposure, and keep the auto in your line of sight as you reload.

Autoloaders

Many see firepower as the auto's cardinal advantage over the revolver and this certainly holds true in reloading. You can easily get so fast with a speedloader that you'll refill your sixgun faster than a criminal can recharge his stolen autoloader. You can even get so fast that you can reload your revolver faster than the average trained cop can reload his service pistol. But you'll never get so fast with the revolver that you can reload it faster than *you* can reload a semi-automatic pistol with the same amount of practice.

Reloading the revolver is a fine motor skill that requires dexterous manipulation by the dominant hand. Shoving a large magazine into a large receptacle and thumbing a lever or jacking a slide are simple gross motor skills, much more easily learned and more easily applied under stress.

Magazine pouches are available in leather (Bianchi, top right), "plastic" (Safariland, bottom right), and fabric (Bianchi, left).

The spare magazines should be on the weak-hand side of the body. The frame of the pistol should be held in the dominant hand, using the support hand to perform most or all of the reloading function. Most fabric magazine pouches are floppy and slow, hard to conceal because they lean out from the belt, and require an action-slowing flap to hold them in place. Leather pouches can be too tight when they're new, and stretch to become too loose after extended wear. Kydex pouches, properly made, are "just right." They hold the

magazines friction tight when you run or even somersault, yet give you maximum speed of access.

Police, soldiers, and outdoorsmen have traditionally used flapped pouches to protect the equipment, which is worn exposed, from rain and snow, and from mud when the wearer goes prone out there in the elements. The concealed pouch is protected by the garments over it, and is normally worn behind the hip for concealment, eliminating concerns of mucking it up if one dives to one's belly. Thus, most concealment pouches, like most competition magazine pouches, are open-top.

Left hand magazine ejection: The trigger finger of a southpaw can probably reach the magazine release button faster than the thumb of most right-handed shooters.

Worn vertically on the weak-hand side with bullet noses forward is the orientation that the overwhelming majority of experts and shooting champions prefer. This allows the support hand to drop down to the magazine, with the palm touching the floorplate. Thumb and middle finger, the two strongest digits on the hand, grasp the inside and outside surfaces of the magazine respectively, while the index finger takes a position outside the pouch and pointing down. Now, the hand pulls the magazine out and rotates to a palm up position. The magazine is correctly oriented toward the

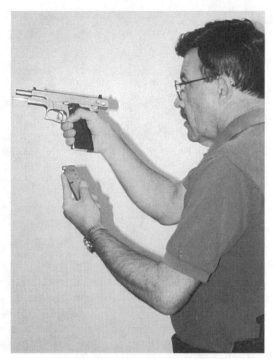

...and the palm rotates upward as the fresh magazine approaches the butt...

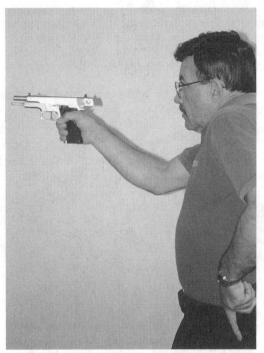

Here is a speed reload of an auto pistol. The support hand goes for the spare magazine as the thumb of firing hand moves to the magazine release button...

...with the index finger guiding it in as the shooter watches the threat zone...

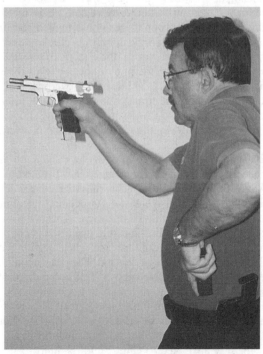

...as soon as the hand is on the fresh mag, the depleted one in the gun is ejected...

magazine well in the butt of the gun, and the tip of the index finger is under the nose of the topmost cartridge.

This allows the index finger to do its job and *index,* literally pointing the fresh magazine into the gun. The reason for the bullet noses being forward in the pouch now becomes apparent: At the moment of insertion, the entire line of the forearm's skeletal support structure is directly aligned with the magazine, virtually guaranteeing a positive, full insertion. A tip: With most pistols and magazines, it will be smoother and

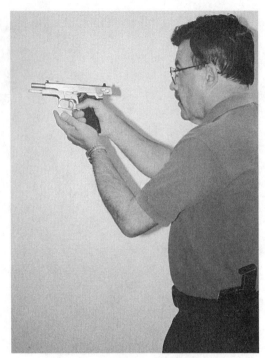

...the palm drives the magazine firmly home, and the support hand prepares to return to its two-hand grasp position...

...thumbing down the slide stop and chambering a round on the way. The S&W .45 is now reloaded, cocked, and ready to continue firing.

faster if you allow the flat back of the magazine to make contact with the flat back of magazine well as the insertion begins.

If the pistol has been shot completely dry, its slide will probably have locked back, and the speed reload or emergency reload must be completed by bringing it back into battery. Instructors seem to split down the middle on this.

One camp holds that thumbing the slide lock release lever is the preferred method, since it is much faster and can be done as the support hand is returning to the two-hand firing grasp. This also guarantees that the support hand doesn't "ride" the slide, which could cause a failure of the first round to chamber. The other school of thought holds that vigorously jerking the slide back and letting it slam forward is more positive and more "do-able" under pressure. Lethal Force Institute injected volunteers with enough epinephrine to equal a "fight or flight" state and then ran them through a double speed combat course in 1998. We saw that simply thumbing the slide release lever was much faster and less fumble prone in the shaking hands of the volunteers.

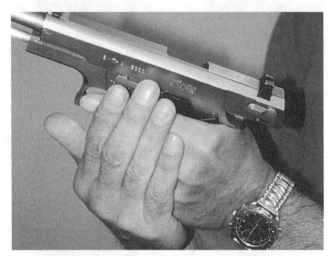

Slide release for southpaws. After the supporting right hand has slapped in the magazine, it is positioned to "spear-hand" up with the fingertips and quickly release the slide stop before sliding back into firing position.

As noted, the above protocol was the "speed reload," sometimes called an "emergency reload." It is the logical technique to employ when the gun has emptied and there is still immediate shooting to be done. A useful but less necessary, technique is known as the "tactical reload." This maneuver is done when the practitioner believes the shooting is over, or that there is at least the proverbial "lull in the action." It makes sense to use this time to fully reload the pistol in case a need to fire resurfaces, but the shooter does not want to throw away the partial magazine of live ammo still in the pistol.

Every instructor seems to have his own signature method of the tactical reload. Some are dangerously overcomplicated. Let's look at just a couple of techniques that are easy to learn.

International Defensive Pistol Association encourages a technique it calls "reload with retention." This is the simplest to learn. The shooter pulls the partial magazine out of the pistol and places it in a pocket or some other location where it can be quickly recovered on demand. Then the shooter inserts a fresh magazine as outlined above. This is the simplest such technique, and the easiest to learn and teach. However, many tacticians feel the "down-time" is too great. That is, there is too much time in which the pistol can fire only one shot or, if it has a magazine disconnector safety, cannot fire at all.

A method attributed to Clint Smith is almost as easy to learn and results in a fully reloaded pistol much more quickly. Smith reportedly developed it while chief instructor

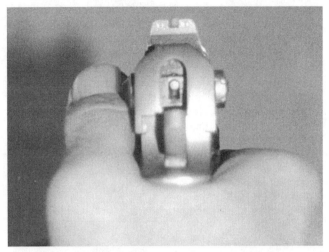

Tactical reload, seen from shooter's eye view. There are some unfired rounds in the gun that you want to save; the double-action S&W is cocked and off safe…

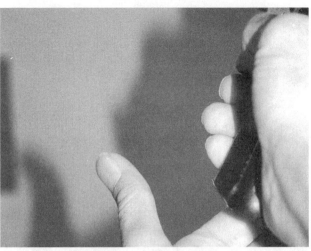

…but now the fresh magazine goes between the index finger and the middle finger as the hand maneuvers into position…

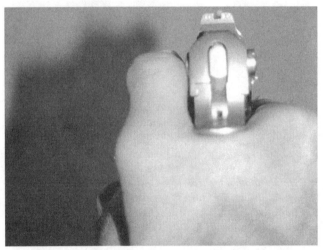

…the first move is to get the finger out of the trigger guard and decock. Note that the lever is down and the hammer is forward. Immediately push the lever back up so you can fire if necessary…

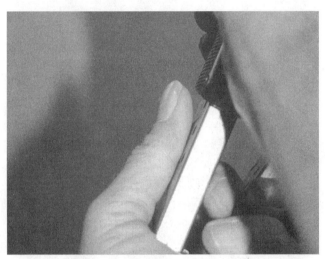

…to catch the spent magazine's floorplate at the base of the thumb, with the thumb and index finger grasping it…

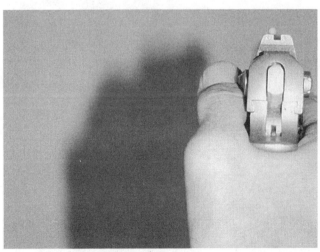

… the spare magazine is brought up to the gun as if for the speed reload…

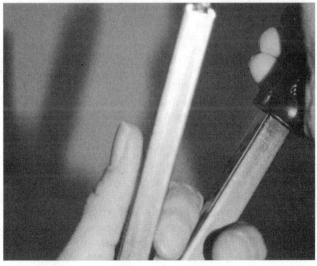

… the spent mag is pulled free and the hand rotates slightly to insert the fresh magazine…

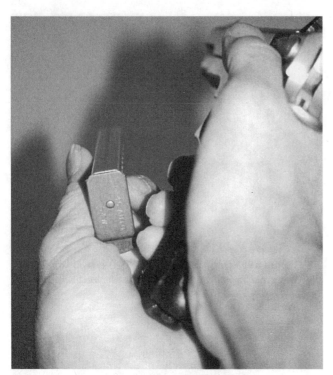

... the palm slaps the fresh magazine home...

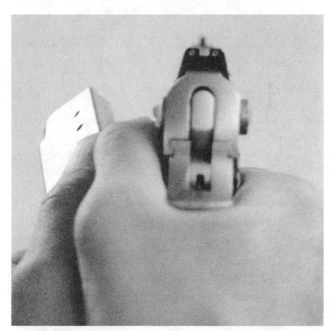

... and, still holding the depleted magazine, the support hand takes a firing hold in case the sound of the reload has brought on a second attack. When all is secure, the free hand will put the spare magazine away.

at Gunsite before moving to his own school, Thunder Ranch, and it is still taught at both facilities. It goes like this.

First, remove your finger from the trigger guard. I suggest you also decock or on-safe the pistol, since a tactical reload can be a fumble-prone procedure. Draw the fresh magazine as if you were going to perform a speed reload. As the support hand comes up to the gun, move the full magazine over "one finger." That is, where the index finger was under the bullet nose, the magazine should now be

between index and middle fingers. With the now-free index finger and the thumb, pull the partial magazine out of the gun and keep it between those two digits. Rotate the support hand and shove the fresh mag into the pistol, taking care to roll the fingers forward so they don't block insertion. You now finish in a good approximation of a two-hand hold, with the partial magazine between the thumb and forefinger of the support hand. Scan your area, put the partial magazine away, and carry on.

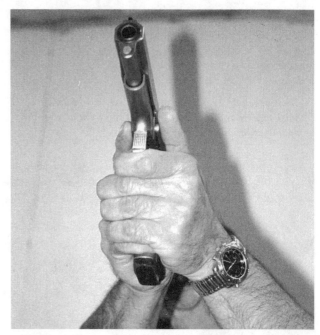

Here's another tactical reload technique the author is fond of. As always, the index finger leaves the trigger guard before anything else. A single-action is put on safe and a double-action is decocked...

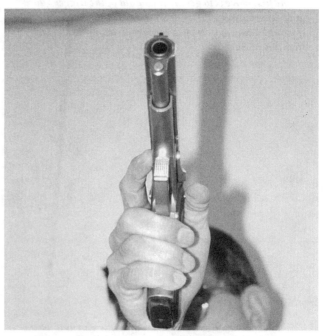

... the support hand drops to grab a fresh mag in the normal fashion...

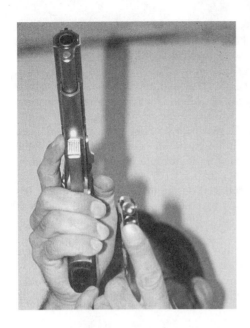

… as the support hand comes up as if to do the speed reload, the hand rotates under the butt as shown…

…and pluck it out, holding it in place as the hand rotates the fresh magazine (with ball ammo) up to insert it the same way as in the speed reload …

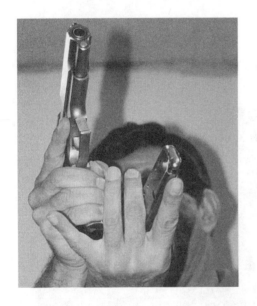

… the ejected magazine is caught at the heel of the palm. The little finger splays out…

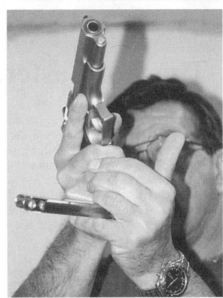

…slapping the fresh mag into place…

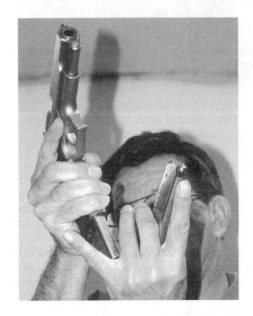

…and the little finger and ring finger are now in position to wrap around the ejecting magazine…

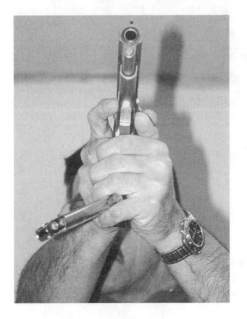

… and the hands resume a very strong firing hold. The magazine held as shown is not in the way. Once it is determined that there is still no further need to fire…

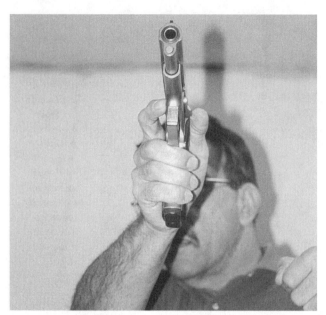

... the S&W 4506 is held on target as the free hand puts the partial magazine away.

Let's discuss a few points on tactical reloads. 1. As noted above, they are difficult to accomplish. 2. In an actual fight, a tactical reload sounds like some poor SOB trying to reload an empty gun. You have just given a wounded rabbit call to the coyotes! This is a high-risk time for a secondary attack, which is why minimized downtime is so important. 3. Be sure the partial magazine is someplace where you'll reach for it under stress if you *do* need it later. If you put the partial in your pocket, spend some practice time retrieving it from the pocket and reloading. Conversely, if you carry only one spare magazine, you can simply put the depleted one in the now-empty pouch. It's where you're used to reaching, and with the one fresh magazine now in the gun, there's nothing for it to get mixed up with.

Fast reloading isn't always needed in actual defensive shootings, but it happens often enough that being able to quickly and positively reload is an important skill. Make sure you've practiced it sufficiently that you can do it in the dark.

Tips For Faster, Smoother Draw

Defensive handgunning isn't all about quick-draw, but that's a definite component. We've all heard the bad joke about the guy who brought a knife to a gunfight. More than one good guy has died because he didn't get his gun to the knife fight in time. The person not readily identifiable to all in sight as a good guy (off duty cop, or armed citizen with carry permit) may not be able to draw his or her weapon in public as soon as a uniformed officer when the danger is not yet clarified. Thus, drawing quickly is important.

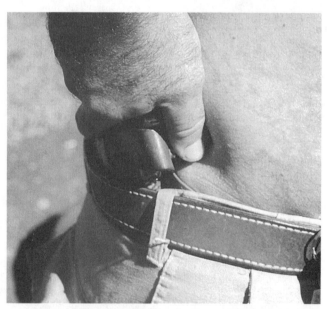

... the gun hand is executing a perfect thumb-break movement with the safety strap version of the classic Bianchi #3 Pistol Pocket inside-the-waistband holster designed by Richard Nichols. The revolver is a 3-inch S&W Model 65.

A draw breaks down into two steps: access and presentation. *Access* is actually the hard part. This is where the hand makes its way to the sidearm, takes a firm firing grasp with everything but the trigger finger and, perhaps, the safety-manipulating thumb, and releases all security devices that keep the gun in the holster. *Presentation,* by contrast, is a simple gross motor skill. This is where the already-grasping hand pulls the gun from the holster and brings it into line with the target or the threat.

Dennis Luosey demonstrates the Hackathorn Rip, the most effective technique for drawing from a hip holster that is worn under a closed bottom garment. As better seen in close-up...

Ray Chapman, the first world champion of the combat pistol, was an engineer in his first career and a master small arms instructor in his second. He brought his engineering mindset to both careers, and his ability to analyze things was what made him such a great teacher. Chapman said, *"Smoothness is five-sixths of speed."* I first heard him say that in 1979, and nothing I've seen since has caused me to question the validity of his advice. Go for smoothness, and the speed will take care of itself. Go for speed, and all you're likely to get is a faster foul-up.

Let's go through each type of draw, step by step.

When the gun is under a closed-bottom garment, you may not have both hands to do a Hackathorn Rip. In that case, the author recommends...

... this one-handed draw. The author's thumb is pointed inward, tracking up the peroneal nerve and lifting the shirt hem to allow the left-handed draw of a baby Glock .40.

Strong-side Hip

Access. You always want to be prepared to make the draw from concealment. Assuming that the concealing garment is an open-front jacket, begin by letting all four fingertips of the dominant hand touch your abdomen at midline. Now immediately sweep the hand back to the gun. The fingers will automatically brush the coat back without you having to think about a separate movement.

The hand immediately falls to the gun in a firing grasp with all but the trigger finger, which should be kept clear of the trigger guard area. The web of the hand should be press-

Access is the tough part. Six-time national champ Bob Houzenga has achieved that and is halfway through presentation when he pauses at low ready, awaiting the signal of the author's PACT timer...

... and when it comes, completion of the presentation and the first shot with a Glock 23 are almost instantaneous.

ing firmly into the grip tang of an auto pistol, or located high on the backstrap of the revolver's frame. The thumb now presses straight in toward the body to release the safety strap if one is present.

During this, the support hand has been brought in to the centerline of the body at about solar plexus level. If the inside of the wrist touches the body and the fingertips point straight ahead of you, you're in the strongest and safest possible position. 1.) That hand is poised to fight off a close-range physical assault or a felon's grab for the gun. 2.) That hand now will not be crossed by the gun as it is drawn. 3.) The support hand is in place to most efficiently join its mate in a two-hand hold as the draw continues.

Presentation. Lever back on the gun butt and bring the muzzle up level with the downrange target or threat as soon as it clears leather. This movement, called a "rock and lock," allows you to most quickly engage a fast-closing threat if necessary. Thrust the pistol straight forward to the target,

...the firing hand takes a high grip, with the thumb breaking the safety strap, and all fingers but the index taking a firm hold on the handgun...

A straight draw from the hip with an open-front concealment garment...

...the pistol is cleared with this "rock and lock" motion...

...begins as four fingertips of the drawing hand touch the centerline of the body. As the hand tracks to the gun, the coat will automatically clear. Meanwhile, with fingers pointed forward for better self-defense ability, the heel of support hand also touches the centerline of the body...

...and the support hand comes in from the side and behind the muzzle to meet the firing hand. Note that the trigger finger has at no point entered the trigger guard...

letting it come up to line of sight naturally. *After the muzzle has safely passed the support hand,* it (the support hand) thrusts forward and takes its position to complete the two-hand hold.

...and the shooter flows into the preferred firing stance. If the need to fire is present, it is now that trigger the finger enters the guard, as shown.

As you draw, *be sure to keep your elbow straight back!* This creates the strongest alignment of the arm's skeleto-muscular support structure, giving you more leverage and thus more speed, strength, and efficiency. It is doubly essential with "directional draw" security holsters.

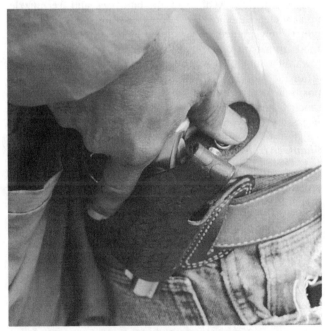

A thumb break holster is useful for gun retention, and takes almost no additional time to release if done properly. Here the author draws a short-barrel Ruger .357 from a Bianchi Black Widow belt holster.

If the concealing garment has a closed bottom, like a sweatshirt or pullover sweater, an alteration is needed. Ken Hackathorn developed the most efficient draw for use with this garment. For what is called a "Hackathorn Rip," the right-handed shooter uses the left hand to grab the bottom edge of the garment at about appendix level, and jerk it upward to the shoulder. This pulls it clear and allows the gun hand to draw as above. The garment may not have enough stretch to reach the shoulder, but if you try for the shoulder you should at least get it up high enough to allow the gun to clear. It's kind of like, "If you aim for the stars, you at least hit the moon."

In case the support hand is needed to fend off a contact-distance assault, you also want to practice a one-handed version. Let the thumb of the gun hand point toward your body and track upward, on a line level with the trouser seam or the common peroneal nerve of the leg. This will catch the hem of the waist-length closed-bottom garment and lift it enough to let the hand reach the gun. Throw your hips straight to the side away from the gun; that is, to the left if you are right-handed. This will give you more range of movement to complete the draw.

Crossdraw

The across-the-body-draw is not efficient if done facing the threat squarely. Crossdraw holsters are banned from most ranges and many police departments because of their tendency to cause the muzzle of the loaded gun to cross a shooter standing beside the practitioner on the firing range. A crossdraw can also be very easily blocked at contact distance. Finally, with the butt forward, if you stand square to the opponent it is easier for him to reach and draw from your holster than it is for you.

A crossdraw from a belt holster begins...

...with a step-back of the gun side leg to blade the holster side of the body. Simultaneously, the free arm rises in a blocking position, for protection against close-range assault and to clear it from the path of the muzzle, as the firing hand knifes through the opening in the garment to grasp the holstered gun...

...the draw path is straight back instead of a crossways sweep, putting the muzzle on target almost immediately...

... as the pistol is thrust forward toward the threat (note that the finger is still away from the trigger) and the support hand moves in from above and behind muzzle...

...and the two-hand hold is achieved and the shot can be fired at this point, as indicated by the finger on the trigger of this S&W 4506. The classic Weaver stance shown lends itself to crossdraw work.

So, before the draw begins, turn your body edgeways so the holstered gun is toward the threat. Make sure your arm on the holster side is up out of the way where the gun muzzle won't cross it.

Access. Point all fingers straight, like a martial artist's "spear hand," and keeping the palm close to your torso, knife the hand in to the gun. This will help you reach through partially closed coat fronts, a situation where a crossdraw can be advantageous to the wearer. Take a firm grip and release the safety strap as with the hip draw, above.

Presentation. Again rock the butt back and the muzzle up as it clears the holster; if you are standing edgeways, the gun is now immediately pointed at the threat and can be fired from here if necessary. Now thrust the gun forward toward the target, letting the gun rise to eye level if possible. After the muzzle has passed it, the support hand takes its position for a two-hand hold. This gets the gun on target much faster than a swing across, which would have been necessary, had you not bladed your body.

Shoulder Holster

Drawing from a shoulder holster is much like executing a crossdraw, but with a slight variation. Because the gun is higher in relation to the arm, and literally located under the armpit, it is important to take extra measures to make sure you don't cross your own support arm with the gun muzzle.

Access: As with the crossdraw, blade the body with the holster side toward the threat. *Raise the support arm sharply until the elbow is shoulder high and pointed toward the threat.* It also creates a simple and extremely effective block to a punch or bludgeon attack, developed decades ago by police martial artist Kerry Najiola. Let the drawing hand "knife" in to the gun's gripframe through the garments as with a crossdraw. Take a firm grasp and release the safety strap, as above.

A shoulder holster lends itself to use with heavy winter clothing. The shoulder draw begins…

…note that the muzzle is pointed toward the threat even before the heavy coat is cleared…

…with backward step of the strong-side leg to quarter properly. The free hand rises in a blocking position as the gun hand "spears" through the opening in the coat to the grip-frame of the holstered weapon…

…once cleared, the gun thrusts forward toward the threat as the support hand begins to drop down…

…as the gun hand draws the pistol straight across the chest, the support arm has already risen to the "Najiola block" position. This not only protects the head from close-range assault, but clears the upper arm from the path of the muzzle during the draw…

…and the firing hold is achieved. The classic Weaver stance as depicted works particularly well with a shoulder holster draw.

Presentation: As with the crossdraw, bring the gun out and back across your chest so it is immediately pointed at the threat. Now thrust it forward toward the threat, bringing the gun to the line of sight if possible. The support hand comes to the firing hand from above and behind to safely take a two-hand hold. Note: With the crossdraw hip holster or the shoulder holster, it will generally be fastest to draw to a Weaver or Modified Weaver/Chapman stance, since the body is already pre-bladed for that position.

Safety point: When reholstering, you may have to turn your body with your back to the target to keep the gun down-range, particularly if the shoulder holster is the horizontal or upside-down type.

You play like you practice. Bill Fish demonstrates his practiced draw of the Glock 19 he usually carries. Note the support hand coming in from behind the muzzle of the gun...

...and he does it the same way under pressure at an IDPA match with his Glock 34, showing the value of getting the core movements down!

Small of the Back Holster

In essence, this is same as strong-side hip. Be aware of the following, however.

Many SOB holsters rake so sharply that a draw crosses a practitioner standing next to you on your weak hand side at the firing line. It may also cross a range officer behind you. The same can happen upon reholstering. This, and reasons cited in the chapter discussing that holster, explains why so few professionals choose this mode of carry.

Belly Band Holster

In the usual front crossdraw position, draw as if with a crossdraw holster at the same point on the belt. If the gun is carried on the strong hand side, use strong-side hip draw techniques as above, with Hackathorn Rip.

Pocket Holster

Use a"spear hand" to get into the pocket. Since locking the thumb in a firm firing grasp creates a fist that can snag coming back out of the pocket, place your thumb on the back of the hammer or slide. This narrows the profile of the hand, and causes the thumb to act as a "human hammer shroud," thus minimizing snag potential in two ways. Otherwise, this is the same as strong side hip holster draw.

Ankle Holster

There have been many techniques taught for this the most difficult to reach of holsters. Some look like the strange mating dances of demented storks. The following technique was developed at Lethal Force Institute and is the fastest we've seen.

The ankle holster is particularly easy to draw from when supine...in a relaxed position like this, or knocked down on your back in a fight.

Access. Plant the leg to which the handgun is strapped. Use the support hand to grab a fistful of trouser material above the knee, and pull it sharply upward. Step widely outward with the free leg, and perhaps also back. (The gun-side leg is stationary; you don't want to move the gun away from the reaching hand.)

Rather than bending at the waist, bend sharply at the knees so you can watch what is going on in front of you. With the dominant hand, grab the gun's grip-frame in a proper firing grasp as above and release the holding strap if necessary.

Presentation. Rock the muzzle forward as soon as it clears and thrust the gun toward the target. Support hand can come in for a two-hand hold at this point. You may fire immediately from this deep crouch, or if time permits, rise to your preferred stance.

... and the shooter can either fire from a low cover crouch as shown, or rise to a preferred firing stance if time allows.

The author demonstrates the high-speed/high-mobility ankle holster draw he developed at LFI. The first move is for the weak hand to grab the weak-side trouser leg and pull up. The non-holster leg takes a deep step back, and the pelvis drops as the gun hand begins the reach...

Option: If you are down on your back, orient yourself so the sole of your holster-side foot is toward the target or opponent. Snap the ankle up toward the reaching gun hand and take firing hold, releasing the strap if necessary. As the gun is pulled, stomp the foot forward and *down* to clear it from your line of fire as you prepare to shoot from the supine position, one- or two-handed.

Fanny Pack

If the fanny pack is worn toward the strong-side hip, use a strong-side draw. If the pack is worn at the front of the torso or toward the opposite hip, use a crossdraw. The support hand may be needed to open the fanny pack. If so, practice intensively ripping it open and then getting that hand immediately out of the way so you won't cross it with your own gun. Spend half your practice time with the support hand in a position to fend off the attack, using the gun hand to both open the pouch and make the draw.

Off Body Carry

Carry the purse, briefcase or whatever in the non-dominant hand or slung from the weak-side shoulder. When the time comes, swing the whole thing to body center, blading your body so that your weak side is toward the threat. Now draw as if from a crossdraw holster, keeping the muzzle downrange. With some guns, this will allow you to fire through the container if necessary, and with all handguns should allow you to get one shot off. Hold the container with the hand high to minimize crossing that hand with the gun muzzle. You can now drop the container and go to your preferred two-hand hold. If the container includes a panel that can stop bullets, press it flat to your torso with the weak hand and pivot at the hips so that it is squarely between you and the incoming fire as you prepare to shoot back one-handed.

...which allows a fast draw as the S&W Model 442 clears the Alessi ankle rig. The support hand is now free to move to a two-hand hold...

Final Advice

A combat *match* shooter may spend 100 percent of drawing practice time on the draw to the shot, automatically finishing each presentation with a pull of the trigger. The real world defensive gun carrier can't do that. It conditions you to fire every time you draw, and history shows that "we play like we practice." Most of the time, police and armed citizens alike do not have to fire the guns they draw to ward off a criminal threat.

If it turns out that you do need to immediately fire as soon as you draw, you'll know it. There should be no perceptible loss of speed. As a general rule, those who carry guns "for real" probably should make at least 90 percent of their drawing practice a draw to "gunpoint," not a draw to the shot.

… and the shooter can finish with a one-handed or two-handed firing posture.

The author begins the draw of a backup gun with his weak hand. Note that the index finger is straight and clear of the trigger guard, and the thumb is over the hammer area to lower the profile of the hand for a more snag-free draw…

As in all dry fire practice, make sure the gun is always oriented toward something that can safely stop the most potent round the gun is capable of discharging. A "dummy gun" of similar weight to the real one is an excellent practice tool for this.

In regular dry fire, our watching of the sights will tell us if we had the trigger press down pat or not. A draw is more complicated. If you can't do it with a friend to critique each other, take a video camera to the practice session and set it up on a tripod, and critically review your performance on tape later. Finally, while practicing in front of a mirror is over-rated in terms of most types of firearms training, it is an excellent way to learn smoothness and economy of movement as you drill on access and presentation.

CHAPTER NINE

CLOSE QUARTERS BATTLE

Conventional CQB Techniques

Most gunfights don't occur in the middle of Main Street at high noon. Most gunfights take place with the participants within 7 yards of each other, and the majority of *those* are at more like 7 feet. The conventional response has always been to shoot from the hip or some other position below line of sight that hopefully keeps your weapon out of the close-range attacker's reach. There is good news and bad news with this. Good news: for a brief moment, at least, you've kept your firearm beyond the attacker's grasp. Bad news: if you can't see to aim, you probably won't hit what you want to hit.

Consider this real-world case in point, from the book "A Cold Case" in which author Philip Gourevitch shares the recollection of a New York City beat cop who had to kill a criminal named Sudia. For our purposes we'll call this brave lawman "Officer 1."

Close quarters combat shooting is often taught like this. However, there is a possibility that at this angle, the heavy winter coat could block the auto pistol's slide.

"Officer 1" told Gourevitch, "They were heroin addicts, and deserters from the Marine Corps, and they'd got in a shooting in the Hotel Whitehall on 100th Street and Broadway. I didn't know it. I was standing down on Riverside drive, a new cop, on what they call a fixer. That's a fixed post. You have to stand there. This was December, a cold December night, and for some reason they decided to run toward me. I could hear them running down the street. There was no one else around from West End Avenue to the Drive, just a lot of doctors' cars. I figured they'd broke into a car, no big deal. So when they got abreast of me, I stepped out and had my arms out with my nightstick. Sudia put a pistol to my head and said, 'You c---sucker, hand me your gun, or I'll kill you.' So – I'm not sure of this exchange, but I'm pretty sure – I said, 'OK, OK.' And I went into my coat. We had big heavy coats that you're too young to have seen. They wrapped around you. Terrible heavy coats. If you could stand up in them all night, you were lucky to walk home. Anyway, when I cleared the holster, I fired through my coat. I shot at him six times. You know how many times I hit him? Twice. Once in the heart – he had a tattoo of a heart on his heart – and once in the knee. The others passed through his clothing, and our noses were touching, so I guess I was frightened. He was dead by the time his head was by my knees."(1)

This account is worth some time to digest for all its learning points. First, we are dealing with one *very* lucky police officer. Even being so close to his attacker "our noses were touching," only two out of six shots actually took flesh, striking 3 feet apart on the offender's body. Only one of those hits was really dynamic, the heart shot, unless the knee hit came first and buckled the would-be cop-killer's body down into the path of the gun to allow for the cardiac shot.

Let's contrast that with a shooting some years later involving another NYPD officer. We'll call him "Officer 2." He was off duty in a subway car, also in the winter, with his 4-inch Model 10 .38 under his suit coat and overcoat and his 2-inch Colt Detective Special .38 in his right hand coat pocket. Suddenly, two men sat down on either side of him. The one on the right pulled a knife, and the one on the left drew a Sterling semiautomatic pistol and placed the loaded gun to the officer's head, demanding his wallet.

Like Officer 1, Officer 2 feigned compliance, reaching with his right hand into the coat pocket as if for a billfold. Then, in a single fast move, he brought up his left hand and slapped the gun away from his head, his palm staying in contact with the attacker's wrist and the back of his gun hand to keep the weapon diverted. At the same time, he swung the snub-nose .38 up with his right hand until he could see it in peripheral vision and fired one shot into the gunman's brain, killing him instantly. He spun to engage the armed felon on his right, who leaped away. The pair had timed the robbery just before a stop to facilitate escape, and the second offender was able to run through the opening door and escape into the crowd. He was subsequently captured and sent to prison.

In both cases, the officers had loaded guns held to their heads. Both exhibited great valor and tenacity, and both prevailed and emerged unhurt. Clearly, though, if we are going to emulate one or the other, the second is the role model. The first officer fired six shots with one immediately stopping hit and one wounding hit, a 33 percent hit delivery and 16.7 percent delivery of "stopping hits." The second officer delivered 100 percent on both counts.

With the gun hand rotated out 45 degrees the slide will be clear of body and clothing, and Kimber .45's muzzle will be angled in more to the center of your opponent's body.

He did two things differently than the first officer. For one thing, *Officer 2 waited the tiniest fraction of an instant until he could see his gun in peripheral vision, to target the shot, before he fired.* Investigators were impressed to note that the single .38 Special bullet had struck the gunman squarely between the eyes. Perhaps more importantly, *he diverted the suspect's weapon before he did anything else.*

We need to remember our priorities. Shooting the attacker is not the object of the exercise. Not getting shot is the object of the exercise. Shooting the attacker is certainly one legitimate way of accomplishing it, but if we get the goals confused, we do so at our peril. With the assailant's weapon unrestrained in the first case, the officer had to fire blindly and desperately, and was lucky to score the hit that saved his life. With the weapon at least momentarily diverted from him, the second officer was able to take the

tiny extra fraction of a second to put the first shot where it would immediately end the deadly threat to him.

Analyzing Conventional Techniques

We are taught that all we have to do to hit something with a gun is point it as we would point our finger. The problem is, the gun does not always point in the direction of your finger. When the gun is pulled back, away from the attacker, our gun naturally points low.

This is a critical problem with "hip-shooting," either Bill Jordan-style or with the technique called the "speed-rock." Bill Jordan was my friend and one of my mentors. I witnessed his awesome display of point shooting skill in which, from the hip, he shot aspirin tablets at a range of 10 feet with wax bullets! Interestingly, the targets were mounted somewhat low.

Look at pictures of Bill shooting. You'll find them in his classic, must-read 1966 book "No Second Place Winner," now published by Police Bookshelf, PO Box 122, Concord, NH 03302. You'll see that his revolver barrel appears to be angling downward. In the book, he also makes reference to the effectiveness of "a bullet judiciously applied to the region of the belt buckle." He later confirmed to me that this was his point of aim for gunfighting. "Seems to hit a man like a solar plexus punch," he drawled. Now, you have to remember that Bill Jordan was a long drink of water who stood about 6 feet, 7 inches tall.

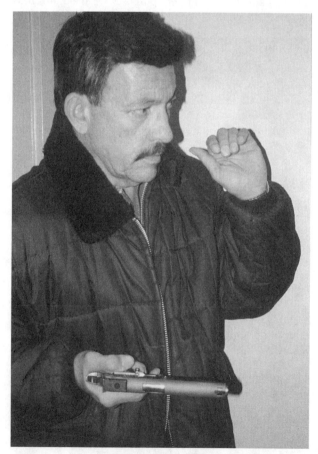

This sometimes-taught technique angles shots inward to the opponent's center, but takes shooter's wrist to the end of it's range of movement and leaves him vulnerable to being disarmed.

Put that all together. Bill is taller than his opponent. His gun arm is pointing downward enough to strike the shorter opponent at waist level. You and I are the same height as our assailant, or perhaps our attacker is taller. Our gun is angling in the same downward direction. We're likely to deliver a leg shot, not a fight-stopping hit.

The fast draw artists of the 1950s, who learned to compensate for it by rocking their upper bodies backward at the hips to bring the gun more level, noted this tendency to shoot low. The problem is, rocking back hyper-extends the back and takes the shooter completely off balance. If there is still aggressive forward movement by the opponent – even if he falls into us – he's going to plow right into our off-balance bodies and take us to the ground with him. And he'll be on top, pinning us under his weight. Not good.

Does this mean you shouldn't get some practice shooting from the hip or using the speed rock technique? No. If the attacker has you backed up against a wall with his forearm across your throat, hip-shooting may be the only option you have left. If he has you bent back over the hood of an automobile, he has already put you into a speed rock. Either of these techniques will work well for a cop making a traffic stop on a typical passenger sedan, because the seated driver is now right in line with the cop's duty gun belt and the hip shot or the speed rock will be most effective.

When practicing either technique, get up close and personal with a cardboard silhouette target in a soft wooden frame. Don't use a steel target frame. Until you have it down pat, you can wind up like that first New York cop and put some of the shots wide even at the closest range. If the lead bullet strikes the steel frame it's going to send some vicious particles your way, enough to cause penetrating gunshot-like injury.

Here's a tip for handgunners in general and auto pistol shooters in particular: you might want to rotate your gun hand about 45 degrees to the outside when doing this. We tend to practice on sunny days in T-shirts, but may have to fire on a cold, rainy night when we're wearing a billowing raincoat. If the auto pistol is oriented straight up, the slide may foul on the garment and jam the pistol. A very over-weight male or large-busted female can stop the slide's mechanism against his or her own body. The outward rotation of the pistol prevents these mishaps, because the slide now clears both body and loose garments.

The outward rotation has another advantage. If you are face-to-face, squared off with one another, and you're right-handed, a shot from the hip with the gun straight up will strike the far left side of your opponent's torso. You don't want to hit the love handles; you want to put the bullet in the boiler room. The outboard rotation angles the muzzle proportionally inward, and within arm's length is more likely to put your shot in the middle of his torso, at least in terms of windage if not elevation.

Don't go overboard with the angle. I have to disagree with those who teach rotating the gun all the way over on its side, i.e., so the right side of the slide is toward the ground in a right-handed man's grasp. This brings the gun hand's wrist to the very end of its range of movement, and weakens the joint against upward pressure. If the opponent tries to shove your gun up away from him, it will point right up into your face. With the wrist at a 45-degree angle, you'll have a much stronger lock and a better chance of resisting that ploy.

The gun is angled the wrong way here, and highly likely to jam when the slide is fouled in a coat or blocked by the body after first shot.

The Step-Back

It is widely taught that you should step back, possibly striking your opponent first, then draw your gun and come up to an extended-arms stance and shoot. This works much better on still targets than on moving attackers. Another school of thought holds that you should back-pedal, firing as you go.

The problem here is that in the real world, dealing with a living, thinking, reacting, and homicidal human aggressor, *you can't back up faster than the aggressor can move forward.* The human body isn't built to move rearward as effectively as it moves forward.

Excellent videotape exists graphically proving this point. Offered by Paladin Press, it was put together by a friend and graduate of mine who is an accomplished police trainer, named Ralph Mroz. In live action sequences using non-lethal guns, Ralph vividly shows how quickly you can be overrun by an aggressive man with knife or club when you try hip-shots, speed-rocks, step-backs, and shooting while backing up.

Ralph found only one technique that worked, the same CQB principle that we've taught for years at Lethal Force Institute. It's a parrying movement off mid-line that "changes the structure of the game." We'll look at that principle next.

Gourevitch, Philip, "A Cold Case," New York: Farrar, Straus and Giroux, 2001, pp. 16-17.

ADVANCED TECHNIQUES

In the early 1990s, I met Reynaldo Jaylo at an American Society of Law Enforcement Trainers seminar. Rey has been involved in more than two dozen shootings. The Manila newspaper at the time credited him with killing some 23 criminals in gunfights, most of them at point-blank range. Working in the Philippines for their equivalent of FBI, he was a very senior commander who "led from the front." Many of his shootings had occurred at arm's length distances during drug buys.

I asked him what technique he used. "Point shooting," he replied. I asked him to demonstrate. I used a Spyderco Police knife as Rey demonstrated with my carefully unloaded Colt .45 auto. As I moved toward him, he parried to my weak hand side, brought his weapon to eye level at arm's length, and instantly "fired" directly into my chest. I observed that he lowered his head in line with the gunsights as if to verify a sight picture.

Rey Jaylo confirmed that this was exactly what he was doing, and this was what he meant by point shooting. He explained that this close, if you didn't get the other man dead center immediately and shut him off, he was certain to kill you.

The LFI circling parry is demonstrated. Snow falls as the officer, at 6 o'clock, confronts a suspect at 12 o'clock, who suddenly produces a weapon. With the gun side hip back, the suspect is out of reach of a smothering disarm...

... The officer's left hand now takes control of the shoulder, "monitoring" movement and helping to keep himself behind bad guy, as the officer's right hand draws the service pistol...

...and the officer's right hand goes to rear of shoulder joint on the non-gun side. The suspect is simultaneously spun toward the gun side as the officer takes a deep step behind him. The object of the combined movements is to get the good guy behind bad guy so the bad guy, at least for a moment, will have to shoot through his own body to hit the good guy...

... and parity has now been restored. If the suspect does not immediately drop the gun, officer is justifiable in firing because in a fraction of a second, suspect's gun can again be pointed at the officer.

This is unarguable logic, and Reynaldo Jaylo is living proof that it works. It was absolute validation of what many others and I had been teaching along that line.

At close range, it's not a shooting contest; it's a fight. Specifically, it is a gunfight at knife-fighting range. This means it's not so much a shooting thing as a martial arts thing, and the martial arts are where you have to look to find the answer.

No practitioner of any martial art will tell you to lean back off balance to escape your attacker, nor to try to back-pedal from him. As the opponent is seen to commit to a line of force – whether he's projecting it with his fist or the muzzle of a gun – the only proven counter is *lateral movement away from the midline of the attack.* If you are on the antagonist's weapon-hand side, as with Officer 2 in the previous chapter, logic says that you should strike the weapon hand aside. If his weapon hand is out of reach, as mine was when Rey Jaylo demonstrated, then you should move in a circular pattern around his non-weapon side, toward his rear. In a fistfight, this would put you beyond the range of that fist. In a knife fight, it would put you for a moment beyond the blade's effective field of action, a knife fighter's term for what a boxer calls reach. If the opponent has a gun, you have for this instant made him unable to shoot into the center of your body without hitting the edge of his own. This is what buys you time to draw, index your weapon, and make the hit that stops the fight.

Note how the bladed hand strikes exactly at the point where the arm meets body, from the rear. This seems to be a high-leverage "pivot point" for moving a resistive adult's torso.

Action/Reaction Paradigms

Keys to understanding the reality of such encounters are the action/reaction principles. Principle I: **Action beats reaction**. If the two of you are very close together and he moves first, he will complete his move before you can react to evade what he's sending your way. This works even if he is less skilled than you, less swift than you, and armed with a less suitable weapon. This is why master combat firearms instructor Clint Smith makes the point we'll call, for the moment, Principle II: **Proximity negates skill.**

If proximity negates our superior skill, we need to negate the proximity to restore dominance. We need to create **reactionary gap.** Space buys time, and time allows us to react and stop the threat. Thus, Principle III: **Time and distance favor the trained defender.**

Plan A for applying this, of course, is never allowing the belly-to-belly confrontation in the first place. A police officer

has to get close to a suspect; how else can he handcuff and search him? The alert citizen can more easily see danger signs and evade such close-quarters traps, in most cases.

When you and your opponent have opposite hand dominance, the circling parry is done thus. Mark Maynard (right, in attacker role) uses his left hand to draw first on defender Mike Briggs...

Briggs uses his left hand at the rear joint of Maynard's non-gun-side shoulder to turn him as he simultaneously steps to the "safe side" and draws...

That alertness is the key. The mightiest air armada is useless if it has no radar to alert it to the approach of enemy bombers that can destroy it on the ground. The radar is useless if no one monitors it for warning signals. The warning signals are useless if no one on the ground responds to the alert of impending danger. So it is in individual conflict.

...and is able to perform a head shot barely ahead of opponent's ability to stay on target. Rationale of the shot to the head is the instant cessation of action, and best guarantee that the defender doesn't shoot his hand in the real-world swirl of violent movement. Note that the control hand remains at shoulder.

This is why most training programs in this discipline follow Jeff Cooper's "color code" principles. Cooper used four different color codes; some of us use five.

Condition White is unprepared. If you are caught off guard, you are likely to be too far behind the power curve to ever catch up in time.

Condition Yellow means relaxed alertness. You're not checking around corners with a periscope, but you make a point of knowing where you are and who's around you. At any given time, you could close your eyes and point out lanes of access or egress, and objects nearby that could be used for cover. You don't have to be armed to be in "yellow," but if you are armed that should certainly be your mental status.

Condition Orange means an unspecified alert. Something is wrong, but all the details aren't confirmed yet. You now focus acutely on sensory input and other intelligence that will help you determine what is going on.

Condition Red is, in essence, an armed encounter. The threat is identified, and dangerous enough for you to draw your weapon and take the suspect(s) at gunpoint.

Condition Black means the presence of maximum danger, as on the pigment color scale black is the presence of all colors. This means that you are under lethal assault. At this point, your response is to unleash the deadly force you held at bay in the gunpoint situation, and return fire.

Alas, not every human being can maintain a perfect and continuous alertness scan. If the Plan A of seeing the danger in time to avoid or outflank it doesn't work, and we're trapped in that unforgiving arm's length range of deadly danger that instructors have come to call "the hole," we need a Plan B. The studies of Ralph Mroz mentioned in the previous chapter, centuries of martial arts experience, and simple common sense tell us that Plan B is to move quickly off the line of attack, if possible parrying or controlling the opponent's weapon, as we counterattack with an encircling motion.

Training Problems

Why are these principles not taught more? They take some time, they don't lend themselves to mass practice like square range shooting drills, and they are not particularly fun.

Shooting is fun. Even shooting while moving backward can be fun, if it is done safely under careful supervision. The circling parry movement and similar drills require you and a practice partner to be grabbing arms and slapping shoulders, and that starts to hurt. If you're not into martial arts, this action soon ceases to be fun.

Always use dummy guns in this type of training! **Left, an actual Smith & Wesson .40 caliber Sigma SW40F. Right, an identical copy rendered in "dead metal" by Odin Press.**

Shooting from the hip or while moving backward or whatever can be done en masse. A circling parry, which can be as much as 180 degrees of movement, is all but impossible to arrange on a firing line with more than one shooter and one coach. It is not time and cost effective for large training groups. It should only be done with people who already have a very strong grounding in firearms safety, quick presentation of the firearm, and decisive confidence in their shooting skills. At our school, we don't get into circling parries and similar CQB drills until the second level of training.

This training should be done primarily with dummy guns and live partners, in a gym or dojo environment. It can be done that way 100 percent. On the range, some of these techniques will end up with muzzle contact shots, which quickly tear apart paper or cardboard targets, and muzzle contact shooting will swiftly ruin expensive three-dimensional targets.

Nonetheless, these techniques are your most certain route to survival of an aggressive, real-world lethal force assault that begins at arm's length.

We must heed the warning of Abraham Maslow: when the only tool we have is a hammer, every problem begins to look like a nail. We are conditioned that if the opponent has a deadly weapon, we must respond with a deadly weapon. That is often the case. It is the case more often than not when some significant distance separates the parties at the moment of truth. But there are times at very close range when, even if you are armed with the best fighting handgun and are extremely skilled with it, there might be a better option for you than to draw and fire. We'll examine that option in the next chapter.

Close Quarters Battle

Disarming

One more time, is the object to shoot the other guy, or is it to not get shot? Correct, it is the latter! With that in mind, continuing at the distance my friend Cliff Stewart, the master bodyguard and martial artist calls WAR (Within Arm's Reach), let's look at a non-shooting option.

You are facing the other person a yard away. He goes for his gun. You go for yours. You are good at this: you can react, draw from concealment, and get off a shot in 1.5 seconds. Hell, let's say you're *extremely* good at this and can do it in a second, flat.

You're still behind the curve. The best you can hope to do, realistically, is shoot him just before he shoots you, or shoot each other simultaneously. Only if your bullet has hit upper spinal cord or brain will you be certain of interdicting the message his brain has already sent to his trigger finger, and then only if you fired first.

He is already past the apex of the power curve by the time you can react. His hand is already on his gun, completing the tough part of the draw, the access. Now all he has left to do is the simple gross motor skill part, the ripping the gun up, shoving it toward you, and jerking the trigger. Even if he's a bozo with a stolen gun he has never fired before, he can do this in half to three-quarters of a second. You are so close you have to assume you'll take a hit. Remember what Clint Smith said in the last section: "proximity negates skill."

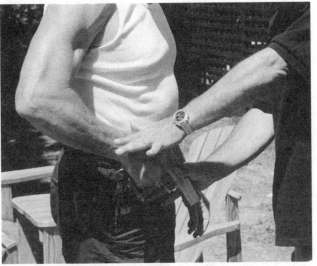

...and the good guy's forward-thrusting hands block the gun as it is coming up. The lower hand seizes the barrel/slide of the pistol as the upper hand seizes the opponent's wrist...

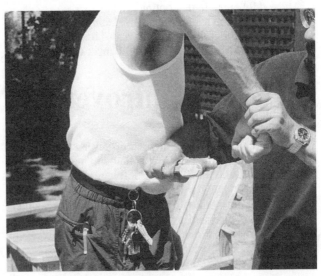

...and as the wrist is pulled out to the side, the gun muzzle is levered toward opponent's body and almost effortlessly stripped from his hand. In this close, disarming works faster than a reactive draw, if you know how to do it. Note: such techniques should always be practiced with dummy guns. This is an Odin Press model of S&W 5946.

Bad guy at left begins his draw. Good guy at right is behind the curve. However, human instinct is for the hands to attempt to smother the threat...

Even with your one-second draw and lightning reflexes, there is an excellent chance that his shot will go off a quarter-second ahead of yours. Have there been men who could "beat the drop," and outdraw even a drawn gun? It has happened in the field. Post-fight analysis usually indicates that the man who started with the drawn gun didn't think his opponent would be crazy enough to resist, and when he did, was so surprised that he had a long reactionary gap. The person who outdrew that drawn gun got inside that gap.

However, this is not an overconfident schmuck holding you at gunpoint and making demands. He's an angry homicidal criminal, trying to draw a gun and shoot you as fast as he can, and his attempt to do so is already underway. That's why you're behind the curve.

A handful of human beings have been fast enough to react and shoot first even in this situation. The late Bill Jordan is on film reacting to a visual start signal and accomplishing a draw/fire/hit sequence with a K-frame Smith & Wesson double-action revolver in 0.27 of one second, including the reaction time. My friend and holster-designing colleague Ted Blocker established the world fast draw speed record with a single-action revolver out of a speed rig of his own making at 0.25 of one second.

But I know I'm not nearly that fast, and you may not be either, and that's why in this situation the best we can hope for, realistically, is that we shoot the bad guy an instant after he shoots us.

Dying together in the same ambulance is not victory. This won't work.

Why couldn't you catch up? Remember what we discussed earlier: the drawing and firing of a pistol is a complex psychomotor skill, a chain of events in which each link must be accomplished with something close to perfection if we're going to make that 1.0 to 1.5 second time. Our reaction time to an anticipated stimulus, based on Lethal Force Institute's extensive research, will be about a quarter second, on the average. Perhaps as little as 0.17 second in the athletic young adult, maybe even faster than that in people like Bill Jordan with uncanny reaction speed. A quarter second into things, we begin a chain of dexterity-intensive events against a man who only has to perform the easier, faster, gross motor skill of "present and fire."

Suppose we had the option of responding with a simple gross motor skill ourselves. Suppose further that ours was easier to accomplish than the opponent's. Would we now have a fighting chance to beat the draw he has already begun? Yes, absolutely.

And, oddly enough, that option exists.

If you are an arm's length apart and facing one another, as he goes for his gun, *you go for his gun too!* It is instinctive for humans to use their hands to ward off danger coming toward them at close range. Let your hands do what is instinctive. Depending on how fast your opponent is your hands should interdict his gun and gun hand as the weapon is coming out of the holster or just after it has cleared leather.

This movement will "stall the draw" or "smother the draw." It will keep his gun muzzle pointed down away from you for an instant. You have just bought yourself time. You have just created reactionary gap. You have just kept him from shooting you, at least for the moment.

Now, finish what you began. With your lower hand, firmly seize his gun and with your higher hand, grab his wrist. Ideally, against a right-handed opponent, you'll have more leverage if your left hand is topmost to grab the wrist, and your right hand is just below it to grab the gun, but this hand placement is not absolutely essential.

There is a principle of human body movement that comes into play here. "If he's moving north and south, he has no resistance east or west." That is, once an opponent has committed himself to move in a certain direction, he cannot immediately resist lateral force delivered from a 90-degree angle.

The "north and south" line of force here is his bringing the gun up toward you. The "east and west" movement is what you need to do now. Your left hand, holding his wrist, pulls to your left as your right hand, holding his gun, pulls to your right. You will feel an almost effortless release as his hand separates from his gun.

Where you go from here is up to you. Run away with his gun. Shift his gun to your other hand as you create distance between the two of you and draw your own gun. Options are wonderful. But the point is, you have stalled his draw and disarmed him faster than you could have drawn your own gun and shot him…*and you haven't been shot!*

Controversial New Techniques

The search for a better mousetrap never stops. Sometimes the quest is for a hardware fix that will make a dangerous task less so. Sometimes a software fix is a better approach to reducing long-recognized dangers, or new dangers that have emerged with changing patterns of encounter.

Some new approaches work. Some just plain don't. Some are so new that field testing and training analysis are still underway, and the jury simply isn't in yet.

Let's review some current "hot-button topics."

Finger On Or Off The Trigger?

All the way through the early 1990s, FBI agents were taught to place their fingers on the trigger as a part of the draw process. Countless TV programs and movies showed everyone from cowboys to cops with their fingers on their triggers as they went into danger.

In the last few years, properly trained police and the best-trained armed citizens have learned to keep their fingers off the trigger until the actual moment to fire has arrived. The reason is, we know a lot more than we used to about sudden, convulsive movements as they relate to unintended discharges of firearms with potentially fatal results. In the 1990s, the work of a brilliant physiologist named Roger Enoka was widely circulated through the professional firearms training community. Dr. Enoka's study of accidental shootings had shown that the startle response, postural disturbance, and

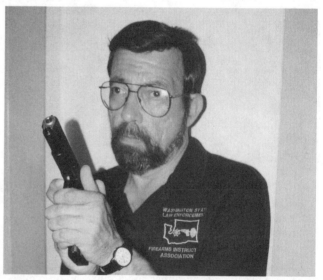

Sometimes derided as the "Sabrina Position," named after the character on the old "Charlie's Angels" TV show, the tactical high ready position seen here can actually be the best choice in some scenarios. The operator can easily scan a dangerous scene looking past the pistol, but with the muzzle in line with the eye, and can come on target faster. If the gun is grabbed, this is the most defensible start position for such a struggle. The pistol is an STI.

interlimb response were the primary culprits. When we are startled, our muscles react, and at least in the human hand (if not in the anti-gravity muscles of the legs), flexor muscles are stronger than extensor muscles. This is why if you're startled with a gun in your hand, you are far less likely to drop the weapon than you are to fire it unintentionally. When we lose balance or fall (postural disturbance) similar reactions can occur, triggering an unwanted shot. When the support hand closes (as when grabbing a suspect or applying handcuffs) the primary hand sympathetically wants to close with it. BANG! Another accidental discharge tragedy.

A strange and atavistic article appeared a few years ago in a privately published newsletter that sometimes resembles a medical journal and sometimes resembles a parody of one. A leader of the organization in question co-authored an article on a "study" that purported to show significant difference in lag time if the officer did not already have his finger on the trigger if a suspect held at gunpoint chose to attack. Ironically, though this organization attacks others for not performing studies to sufficiently scientific standards, this "study" they did themselves did not quantify the experience or training of the officers involved, the types of handguns used, nor the technique of holding the finger off that was used in the testing. The writer in question issued a strong editorial urging police to have their fingers on their triggers when making gunpoint arrests or performing dangerous searches.

The professional community reacted with predictable anger and strong criticism. The people who published the deeply flawed "study" backpedaled quickly, but their credibility with professionals had taken a severe hit.

Real professionals, such as Manny Kapelsohn, had done more scientific studies that showed you would probably lose no more than a tenth of a second of reaction time by having your finger outside the trigger guard instead of on the trigger. There is an undeniable history of many cases of tragic accidental discharges in which a finger prematurely on the trigger was a culpable factor. There is also the unassailable logic of Dr. Enoka's research. This is why any credible instructor today will tell you to keep your finger off the trigger until you have actually decided to fire.

Different takes on how to keep the finger off trigger in a "ready" grasp. The finger at the ejection port, recommended by some, is awkward for many hands and can weaken primary grasp of pistol...

... the finger straight along the frame is most commonly taught, and is acceptable...

...the finger straight at the front of the trigger guard is dangerous. The author believes the finger can be held taut and can snap back to the trigger and fire an unintentional shot...

...for reasons described in the text, Ayoob prefers this technique, with finger flexed and indexed on the frame. The demo pistol is a Kahr K40.

That old bugbear, combat semantics, enters the scene again. It became common to teach "on target, on trigger; off target, off trigger." This was good enough for the range but not sufficient for the dynamic realities of the street. When the suspect was taken at gunpoint, the good guy subconsciously considered himself "on target," and therefore went "on trigger," bringing us back to square one and re-setting the stage for tragedy.

The principle needs to be, "keep the finger outside the trigger guard *until the intent to fire immediately has been formulated.*"

Where To Place The Finger

Any good concept can be carried too far. Some have advocated keeping the fingertip so high that it touches the flat of the slide or even the barrel of the auto pistol. The problem with this is that in many if not most combinations of hand and gun, this can bring the finger up so high that it breaks or at least weakens the grasp, and lowers the muzzle to an extreme degree. This may be going too far.

The finger on the front edge of the trigger guard *is not safe!* The problem is that with a long guard and a short finger, the fingertip may not be in firm contact. The extended finger is "held taut" in this position, and when there is a startle response, a postural disturbance, or an interlimb reaction, the finger can snap back toward the trigger with so much force that there is a high likelihood of unintended discharge.

The most commonly taught technique is to keep the index finger straight along the frame above the trigger guard. This is better, but still not perfect. There are four problems identified with this grasp. 1) If there is a lateral strike to the gun, the most common opening gambit of an expert disarming attempt, the extended index finger is now hyperextended. It has to let go or break, and the other three fingers sympathetically release as well. 2) If the hand-to-gun interface involves a long finger and a short trigger guard (i.e., a big hand on a 1911 pistol), the frontal portion of the trigger guard may get in the way and slow the finger's access when it does become necessary to fire immediately. 3) If the finger does somehow get into the guard, it has again been held taut, and therefore is again likely to strike the trigger with rearward impact. 4) With some guns (1911, P-35, some S&W autos, and many other guns) a right-handed shooter will inadvertently be applying leftward pressure to the exposed stud of the slide stop, which might also be called the takedown button. If this part is moved to the side by this pressure, the gun can lock up after the first shot has been fired.

All four of these problems are remedied by the StressFire (TM) technique that goes back to the 1970s. Here, the trigger finger is flexed, and the tip of that finger is placed at an index point on the side of the frame. On a revolver, the index point would be the sideplate screw. On a P7 pistol, it would be the forward edge of the grip panel. On a Glock, it would be the niche of the takedown lever, which due to the Glock's design cannot inadvertently begin takedown. On a 1911, Browning, or Smith, the fingernail is placed behind the slide stop stud, where it can now exert pressure in any direction without doing harm.

Fingerpoint Technique

One fellow on the Internet and some of his friends are responsible for a rather aggressive campaign pushing a radical technique. The shooter points the usual trigger finger, the index finger, at the target, and uses the middle finger to actuate the trigger. The primary advocate of this technique admits that he has little handgun experience, and that when he shot better than he thought he would firing this way he had the epiphany that he had discovered the ultimate shooting technique. He recommends and all but requires a finger shelf attachment that affixes to the pistol's frame to facilitate this technique.

Problems with the radical "fingerpoint" shooting technique include: only two fingers around grip-frame to secure the gun in case of snatch attempt; the index finger can block ejection port; and the muzzle of gun is radically lowered, impairing "pointing" characteristics. This pistol is an SW99, cal. .40.

This group is not the first to suggest this shooting style. The famous photos of Jack Ruby murdering Lee Harvey Oswald in Dallas in 1963 show Ruby using his middle finger to trigger the single fatal shot from his hammer-shrouded Colt Cobra .38 Special revolver. Some assassination buffs decided that this was a secret technique of master gunfighters that showed that Ruby must have been a professionally trained hit man. Actually, the reason Ruby fired his gun this way probably had more to do with the fact that the distal portion of his index finger had been bitten off in a fight years before.

Fingerpoint shooting technique can be dangerous with small pocket pistols like this Seecamp LWS-32. The tip of the finger is exposed to muzzle blast at the very least.

The theory is that the handgun will automatically point at the target and enhance "instinctive" hit potential. Unfortunately, the theory does not translate well to reality. Ace law enforcement weapons trainer Tom Aveni published a calm, reasoned analysis of this technique in *The Firearms Instructor*, the respected journal of the International Association of Law Enforcement Firearms Instructors. He pointed out that when firing right handed, the index finger can bind the slide or block the ejection port of many auto pistols, and that the officer now has a very feeble two-fingered hold on the gun when the middle finger leaves the trigger. Since modern handguns are designed to point naturally with the index finger at the trigger, using the middle finger drops the muzzle so far that a shot "pointed" at the opponent's torso is more likely to hit at the opponent's feet. The technique is obviously too weak to allow effective weapon retention, and the "finger flange" device that is all but required would cause serious holstering problems.

Tactical high ready comes into its own when the searcher is moving upward, as shown. The pistol is a Ruger P90 .45.

All things considered, it's safe to say that the "point with the index finger, shoot with the middle finger" is impractical for the serious combat handgunner.

Position Sul

As the use of special tactical teams grew in domestic American law enforcement, it became increasingly apparent that when personnel were "stacked" one behind the other while making entry through narrow areas like doorways or preparing to do so, Officer A's gun muzzle could end up pointing at Officer B. Accidental discharges occurred with tragic results.

In lieu of this more commonly taught tactical ready position, some instructors and operators prefer...

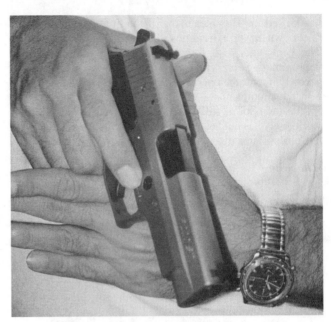

..."position sul," demonstrated here with a SIG P220 all-stainless .45.

Respected tactician Max Joseph's answer was a technique he called "Position Sul." In Portuguese, "sul" means "south," and the technique draws its name from the fact that the handgun's muzzle was pointed south, that is, straight down. This entailed drawing the gun in close to the front of the torso and bending the wrist of the shooting hand, while releasing the two-hand grasp.

This technique is also one answer to the question, "How do you do a 360-degree danger scan after firing without pointing your loaded gun at victims, innocent bystanders, and brother officers who might be present?"

I know of tactical teams that have adopted this technique. Though it has some obvious good points, it also brings some concerns with it. The gun is now low enough that it is out of the field of peripheral vision, particularly if tunnel vision

Respected defensive shooting instructor Andy Stanford demonstrates Position Sul, a concept he likes.

has kicked in. This means that if the gun muzzle points at one's own lower extremities, the operator may not notice. The bent wrist also forces the gun arm into something approximating a "chicken wing" arm-lock that could severely impair the operator's ability to protect the gun from a snatch attempt.

"Position Sul" is still a fairly new concept. The jury of real-world users has not yet come in with a definitive verdict on its usefulness. Time in the field will tell us how well it works.

The Scan

The wise shooting survivor, recognizing the internal danger of tunnel vision and the external danger of vicious criminals who travel in packs, wants to immediately scan his or her environment for additional danger once the first identified threat has been neutralized. This has led the more advanced instructors to teach lowering the gun after firing and scanning the area.

...as the officer quickly checks to his right, with gun still on the identified threat...

Ayoob demonstrates the post-shooting tactical scan. With the shooting over, gun de-cocked and finger removed from trigger guard, the gun stays on the identified threat, presumably downed in the snow, ...

All good, so far. Unfortunately, there are smart ways to do it and stupid ways to do it. Sometimes, the easiest way to make a good thing into a bad thing is to overdo the good thing. DO NOT SWING THE GUN ALONG WITH THE HEAD AS YOU SCAN! The statistics are sketchy on this, but the best information we have is that about 40 percent of gunfights involve multiple bad guys. Conversely, this means that *60 percent of gunfights involve only a single opponent.* Just because he's down doesn't mean he's out. He could be playing possum and waiting for an opportune moment in which your attention is diverted so he can pick up his gun and attempt to murder you a second time. An opportune moment like, oh, your swinging your gun off him to look for someone who isn't there.

...and glances back to make sure the downed suspect is not playing possum...

... followed by a quick check to officer's left...

...the officer re-scans to the right, this time looking behind him to his 6 o'clock...

... and back. The pistol is drawn slightly more into the shooter's body to make it less likely to turn off target as...

...and back...

... the scan is completed with final sweep to the left to six o'clock...

... and in a very short time, a 360-degree scan is completed and focus returns to downed identified threat, who has been monitored throughout the scan.

Suppose you have turned to look 90 degrees to one side to scan for criminal accomplices when, out of the corner of your eye, you see the first downed felon reach for his fallen weapon. You must now swing the gun back toward him. You'll have to slow down as it comes onto him or you'll swing

past. Or, you'll have to pull the gun into your chest, pivot, and then punch your gun out at him. Either of these things will take time…perhaps enough time for him to shoot you.

But suppose instead that you have been smart enough to *keep the gun trained on the downed suspect while you turned only your head to scan for accomplices.* Now all you have to do is get your finger back into the trigger guard and fire immediately. Try it on a safe, 180-degree firing range with an electronic timer and see for yourself. By keeping the gun trained on the identified threat, de-cocked if double action or on-safe if single-action, and of course with your finger removed from the trigger guard, you will be *much* faster if you have to engage the identified threat a second time.

But what if as you scan, you *do* see a second lethal threat? How much will it slow you down if the gun is pointed at the first bad guy 90 degrees away instead of at the new one you just spotted? The answer is, not much. You need to identify the threat, determine that deadly force is justifiable, and make the decision to shoot. While you're doing that, there will be time to bring the gun around 90 degrees and get it indexed.

DO NOT SCAN 180 DEGREES AND ASSUME THAT THE AREA HAS BEEN CLEARED. Nintey degrees left and 90 degrees right only clears half the circle. You still have to clear the most potentially lethal area, that which is 180 degrees behind you at 6 o'clock. Remember, the smartest predators will ambush you from behind.

Bring it all together and you get the following recommendation for performing the scan. When the initial threat goes down, analyze it for a moment and determine if it seems neutralized. Remove your trigger finger from the trigger guard, and de-cock or on-safe the gun, depending on its design. Take a quick look to your most exposed side. Now look back to the threat and make sure it's still neutral. Now you can check to 6 o'clock on the same side or to 3 or 9 o'clock on the side you haven't scanned yet. Now back to the initial threat to check it again. Finally, check whatever the last quadrant is that you have not visually scanned. During this procedure, it would be wise to be moving toward cover. You'll also find that as you scan toward your 6 o'clock in the last portions of the scan, the gun will stray less if you pull it closer to your body, as illustrated in the accompanying photos.

There is another reason not to perform the scan with the gun tracking along with the head and eyes. What you have trained yourself to do is what you most certainly WILL do when deadly danger has you in its grip. There is an excellent chance that the shooting scene will contain, or even be filled with, innocent bystanders. If you have performed the scan with your gun held on the downed, identified threat, those witnesses will perceive that "the person with the gun shot the suspect and then looked around to make sure we were all OK." However, if your gun has tracked with your eyes, they will perceive that "the person with the gun shot the suspect and then pointed the gun at all the rest of us, too!"

The scan is a life-saving technique. Armed conflict expert John Farnam reported the case of a South African police officer that shot and killed a terrorist. He was seen to scan left and right, and then lower his gun, apparently thinking himself safe at last. He was then shot in the back of the head and killed instantly by a second terrorist with an AK-47, who had been directly behind him and had gone unseen in the "half a circle scan" the brave officer had performed.

Yes, the scan is a good thing and you should practice it. But you should practice it *correctly,* because there is very definitely a right and a wrong way to do it.

CHAPTER TEN

BETTER TECHNIQUE = BETTER PERFORMANCE

Enhancing Grasp

Ethicists say that their discipline exists on two levels. There is simply "ethics," which can be a sterile and philosophical debate that often takes place in the proverbial ivory towers. Then there is "applied ethics." The latter, says Professor Preston Covey, head of the Center for Advancement of Applied Ethics at Carnegie-Mellon University, "is where the rubber meets the road."

With most handguns the author prefers the "wedge hold." The index finger of the support hand is wedged under the front of the trigger guard, camming the muzzle up and driving the grip tang more forcibly into the web of the hand. The V-shaped wedge of flesh and bone under the front of the guard also helps prevent lateral deviation of the gun muzzle due to a frisky trigger finger. Here, he demonstrates with a Glock 22.

In handgun shooting, particularly the kind that is done rapidly under stress, we have to do something similar. We need to make the transition from "shooting" to "applied shooting." Many long-standing rules of marksmanship go out the window when the adrenaline dump hits and the "fight or flight" response sends dexterity down the toilet and strength up through the roof.

As noted elsewhere in this book, the grasp of the firearm is where operator meets machine, and a key point where "the rubber meets the road." Let's review necessities for *combat* handgunning that might not be required for sport or recreational shooting.

The grasp **needs to work with one hand only,** in case the other hand is performing a critical survival task and

The rear of the butt of a baby Glock is ideally shaped to pull into the hollow of the palm. With the little finger tucked under the butt, if you don't use a Pearce grip extender, this grasp gives a surprisingly strong hold. Note the white fingernails, indicating desirable crush grip.

"can't make it to the appointment" for the two-hand hold that might have been the original plan.

The grasp also **needs to work two-handed,** for maximum life-saving efficiency, in case the circumstances evolving from the surprise that has called the combat handgun into play allow this to happen.

The grasp **needs to be strong enough to maintain control of the firearm even if the gun or hand are grasped or struck,** both predictable occurrences in the sort of situation that is the combat handgun's *raison d'etre.*

Master Grip Concept

Called the "master grip" by many instructors, a grasp of the gun that fulfills the above parameters is essential. Ideally, if the gun fits the user's hand, the following coordinates will all be achieved.

The trigger finger will have good leverage on the trigger. The web of the hand will be high up into the grip tang of the auto, or at the highest possible point on the backstrap of the revolver's grip-frame. The barrel of the gun will be in line with the long bones of the forearm.

Thumb-lock grip. The thumb of the support hand presses down on the median joint of the bent thumb of the firing hand, bonding both hands together. This grasp works particularly well with handguns producing jackhammer recoil, like this S&W J-frame Bodyguard in .357 Magnum.

Note "ripple of flesh" effect at the web of the hand with a high hold, reinforced by the wedge grasp of the support hand's index finger under the front of trigger guard. With a crush grip applied with both hands and the trigger finger at the distal joint contact, the shooter has maximum control of this GlockWorks custom Glock 17.

The hand should have firm enough a contact that the gun does not slip or move in the hand during recoil. No part of the hand(s) should be blocking essential functions of the handgun. No part of the hand(s) should be blocking the function of other parts of the hand(s).

While most of the last paragraph is self-explanatory, some of the last points need explanation for newer shooters. With a small gun and a large hand, if the grasping hand takes a natural "fist grasp" with the thumb curled down, the thumb may block the trigger finger's completion of the trigger pull. In larger hands, this can occur with the small J-frame revolvers or with the small Kahr pistols. The solution on the revolver is custom grips that extend backward from the grip-frame, which move the web of the shooter's hand back, lengthening the reach to the trigger and preventing "overtravel" of the trigger finger through the trigger guard. With the Kahr, the easiest solution is to go to a "high thumbs" grasp.

Obviously, we don't want to use the old-fashioned two-hand hold still seen on TV in which the thumb of the support hand crosses over the back of the firing hand. The hyperextension of the thumb in this direction weakens the grasp of the support hand, but this is the least of our concerns. With most auto pistols, this grasp puts the weak hand thumb directly behind the slide. This tends to result in a nasty laceration, could cause even worse physical damage than that, and also is likely to jam the gun at the worst possible moment. Even with a conventional revolver, this grip when taken hastily, or by someone with big thumbs and a smaller revolver than they are accustomed to, can block the hammer's rearward travel and prevent the gun from firing.

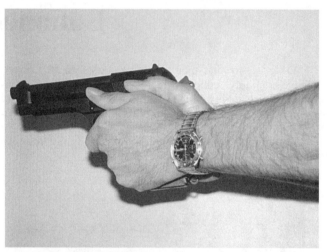

A "Straight thumbs" hold guarantees proper manipulation of the slide-mounted safety on this Beretta 92F, but one thumb will ride the slide stop and keep gun from locking open when empty.

As we shall see momentarily, sometimes compromises must be made. Let's say that you are a right-handed shooter who uses a Beretta 92F, a Smith & Wesson Model 4006, or a Ruger P90 or something similar. Each of these guns has a slide-mounted de-cocking lever that also serves as a safety catch. The lever will need to be in its "up" position, the length of the lever parallel with the length of the bore, for the pistol to fire when you need it to. Carrying the gun off-safe is not enough to guarantee that this will happen. We have documented cases where such a safety "went on" without the user's knowledge. This is not something the gun does by itself. It usually occurs if there is some sort of struggle for the gun, or the user accidentally hits the de-cocking lever while operating the slide, or the user has left the lever down while chambering a round and forgotten to raise it.

There are also those of us who intentionally carry such guns "lever down," on-safe, for handgun retention reasons. In either case, whether you carry off-safe or on, you want to either get that lever up as you draw or *verify* that it's up even if that's where you left it. This means a grasp in which the thumb of the firing hand is about 45 degrees upward, pointed straight toward the ejection port. The support hand thumb goes directly underneath it in a two-hand grasp. However, this hold often causes one thumb to ride on the slide stop and may prevent the pistol from locking its slide open when the magazine runs empty. This will vary from shooter to shooter and from gun to gun, depending on the

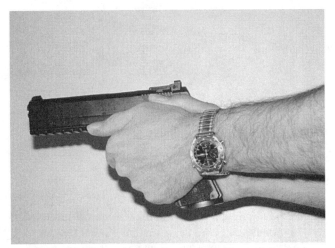

The Leatham-Enos hold is demonstrated on a Springfield Tactical Operator .45 auto. The support hand cants downward from the wrist, creating a strong lock. The thumb of the gun hand rides the safety as that of the support hand points downrange, aligning the hand with the radius bone of the forearm.

The author does his best 1911 shooting with both thumbs curled down in this "thumbprint over thumbnail" grasp that engenders maximum hand strength. The 1911 trigger guard is too short for him to take the wedge hold he prefers.

size and shape of pistol and of the hand. The author, for example, does not have this problem when shooting the S&W or Ruger, but invariably deactivates his own slide stop when taking this grasp on the Beretta pistol. Sometimes, the balance of competing harms and needs requires us to violate a lesser rule to more strictly enforce a more important one. In this case, it is less important to me to have the fastest of all possible reloads after I've fired 16 rounds of 9mm from my Beretta 92F, than it is for me to be certain that the first shot from that gun will be delivered as expeditiously as possible if needed in self-defense. The first shot is usually the most important, and the 17th is rarely the deciding factor.

This is one of three chapters in this book in which grasp is discussed, the others being "lost secrets of combat shooting" and "handgun fit." In those we explain in greater detail the importance of the barrel being in line with the forearm and the web of the hand high, and in the former we explain in detail the rationale of "crush grip" versus other concepts of strength of grasp.

A key element to finding a comfortable, effective hold for the individual combination of handgun and shooter is the placement of the thumbs. This is a good point at which to examine that issue in detail.

Thumb Position

Handgun coaches and marksmanship manuals often simply say or demonstrate, "hold your thumb(s) like this." It is disturbing that they often don't explain why. For the shooter to determine if a technique is right for the gun, the job, and the moment, he or she needs to understand the reasons for use of the technique: what its purpose is, whom it was developed for, and why it was developed. Let's apply this to thumb positions. We'll be focusing here on the "master grip," that is, on the primary hand's interface with the combat handgun.

Thumb Down. This is the way most people instinctively hold a gun, and there is much to be said for it. We're talking about a grasp in which the thumb is bent at the median joint

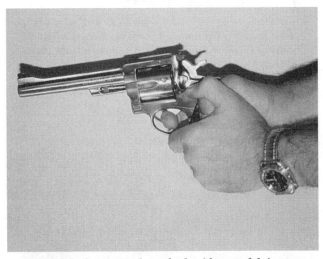

A thumb-lock grasp works perfectly with powerful sixguns like this Ruger .357 Magnum. If the thumb of the support hand crossed over the back of firing hand it would weaken the grasp, possibly block the revolver's hammer, and be in the way of an auto pistol's slide.

and the tip of the thumb is pointed toward the ground. It resembles a tightly curled fist. Most top revolver shooters use this grasp on their double-action wheelguns.

There is no stronger hold. The human hand evolved to work off its unique opposing thumb, and hyper-flexion of the thumb strengthens the hold. You can perform this simple test with one hand, without even putting this book down: Take your free hand, raise the thumb, and close the four fingers as tightly as you can. Mentally measure the strength you are applying. Now, still exerting maximum gripping force and still mentally measuring, *slowly close the thumb until its tip is pointed down.* You just felt a significant increase in strength as the hand closed.

An advantage to the thumb-down grip is that it puts a bar of flesh and bone, the thumb, in position to close what is otherwise an open channel on the side opposite the palm of the hand. If an opponent, one who knows what he's doing, attempts to disarm you, he will begin with a lateral strike to the gun to move it off his midline. If that strike is directed toward the open side of the hand, your gun could be knocked or torn loose from your grasp before you could react. With the thumb locked down, you have at least a fighting chance of keeping the gun in your grasp long enough to react and perform a handgun retention technique.

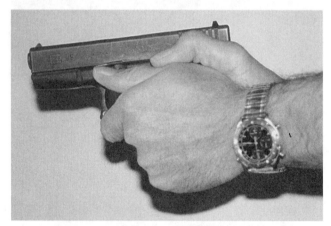

What feels most comfortable is not necessarily what you'll shoot best with. The author's hands are more comfortable with this Leatham-Enos type grasp, augmented with wedge hold on his 9mm Glock 19...

...but he shoots faster and straighter with his thumbs curled down, as shown here. The wedge hold works regardless of thumb position.

When the support hand comes in to assist, that hand's thumb has three options. It can simply hang out in space, a technique used by some to ensure that it doesn't block a part of their gun like the slide stop. While it's true that a thumb held in this fashion isn't getting in the way of anything, it is also true that it isn't doing anything positive to help you shoot faster and straighter. A second option is to lock the support hand's thumb at or behind the flexed joint of the primary hand's thumb. This works particularly well with revolvers, and frankly, it also works with most auto pistols. It is probably the single best "universal grasp" that is "friendly" to all manner of handguns. I call it the "thumb-lock grip" because

The thumbs are curled down with this Variant One HK USP pistol. If the thumb rides the USP's frame-mounted de-cocking lever, it can accidentally drive the lever down into de-cock position during a string of fire.

when the support hand's thumb presses down on the median joint of the flexed thumb on the shooting hand, it bonds the support hand to the firing hand. This prevents the hands from separating when there is really powerful recoil, as with a super-light .38 or with a .44 Magnum. Finally, the thumb of the support hand can come in with its thumbprint placed on the thumbnail of the firing hand. Now both hands are flexed and exerting maximum gripping strength.

Note that with some hands on some guns, the downward-pointing thumb can hit the magazine release button inadvertently. We have seen this on occasion with really huge hands on the 1911 pistol, and with average size male hands on the scaled down Colt .380 Government-style pistols.

Thumb Straight. This is the preferred technique of the target shooter. With the thumb pointing parallel to the barrel, the trigger finger will have its straightest and smoothest track to the rear. The difference is very subtle and very small, but master competitors take every edge they can get. It is also a fairly strong position, as it aligns the extended thumb with the long bones of the forearm. Japanese archers learned centuries ago to hold their bows with a similar grasp.

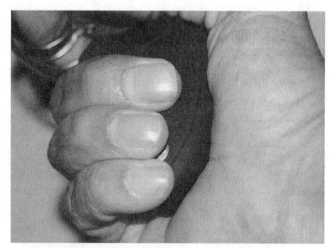

The pinky finger curls under the grip of a concealable, short-butt Taurus CIA. Though it can't help hold the gun directly, this finger's hyper-flexion adds strength to the other fingers that are wrapped around the stocks.

With a two-hand hold, the support hand's thumb is also straight. It tends to be forward of the firing hand's thumb, and parallel to it, perhaps a little below it. In the version of this grasp popularized years ago by combat match champions Rob Leatham and Brian Enos, the thumb of the firing hand thumb has little, if any contact, with the gun and rides atop the base joint of the support hand's thumb. Many shooters using 1911 pistols will leave the thumb of the shooting hand placed atop the manual safety lever.

Though not as strong a primary hold against a disarming attempt as the thumb downward master grip, this hold is much stronger in that regard than any of the high thumb positions. It is also very conducive to a grasp that evolved in IPSC shooting in which the support hand is canted slightly down from the wrist, so that the thumb is directly in line with the radius, the upper bone of the forearm. Some physiologists who have applied their skills to analysis of combat handgun technique insist that this gives the forward arm more strength with which to work.

Thumb 45 Degrees Upward. This is the grasp explained earlier in the chapter, and recommended for pistols with slide-mounted manual safety levers.

High Thumb. Characterized by a thumb that is in a high position with the median joint flexed and pointed upward, this

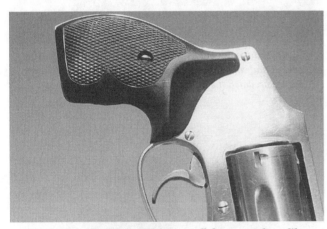

The master grip is important on small-frame revolvers like this S&W Centennial with Uncle Mike's Boot Grips…

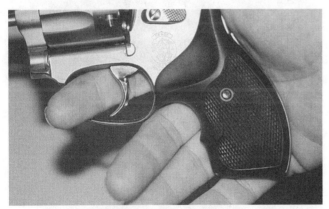

…as the web of hand goes all the way up to the top edge of the rear gripframe the curve of the backstrap will be pulled tight into the hollow of hand. Note that only two fingers will be able to grasp the stocks, and that there is "too much trigger finger" for the short trigger reach. So…

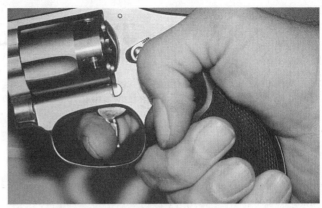

…the little finger is locked under and the index finger is cocked out slightly to the right so distal joint makes contact with the trigger. The thumb is curled down for strength, and is barely clear of the tip of the trigger finger in the rearward position. If the hand was any bigger, the thumb might have to be moved upward out of the way. Note that on "hammerless" style guns, the web of hand can ride higher than with conventional revolvers, proportionally lowering bore axis and giving the shooter more control.

hold is widely taught with the 1911 and similar pistols with frame-mounted safeties. While it does indeed depress the thumb safety, it tends to pull the web of the hand away from the 1911 pistol's grip safety. This can render the gun unable to fire at the worst possible time. Those who have taught this grasp have traditionally, for obvious reasons, also recommended that the grip safety be deactivated. However, as explained elsewhere in the book, it is a Herculean task to try to convince a jury that someone who would intentionally deactivate a safety mechanism on a deadly weapon is anything but reckless. This grasp also tends to apply thumb pressure to the slide, particularly when gloves are worn or when strength goes out of control in a fight-or-flight state, jamming the pistol. The prevalence of this grasp caused Pachmayr and others to develop a device called a slide shield that keeps the high thumb from binding the slide. Common sense tells us that any technique that requires a mechanical fix to shield your gun is probably a technique that could present problems in a life-threatening emergency. This writer cannot in good conscience, recommend this grasp.

Vertical Thumbs. This is a stylized technique that is a signature of certain schools. The thumbs are pointed straight up. We have seen slides retarded in this fashion, causing jams. As the earlier experiment with your open hand showed, this thumb position minimizes your hand's overall grasping strength. Try as we might, we have not been able to elicit a logical, bio-mechanical explanation of any advantage offered by this technique. All we hear is "high thumbs equal high scores." That's a slogan, not an explanation, and frankly it's a slogan not borne out in major competitions where speed and accuracy of fire are directly and fairly tested.

Summary

Fingerprints and palm prints are unique to the individual. Hand sizes and shapes as they interface with gun sizes and shapes are almost as much so. The shooter wants to spend lots of time experimenting with different grasps to see what works for *that* combination of user and hardware.

Two-Handed Stances

Virtually all credible experts agree that when it is possible, a two-handed grasp of the handgun will give the combat shooter more control, and thus more speed and accuracy. If one accepts that defensive shooting is a martial art, it is similar to other such arts in that practitioners love to argue over subtleties of style. In Korean martial arts, the debate might revolve around the circular blocks of *Tang Soo Do* versus the more linear blocks of *Tae Kwon Do*. Among combat handgunners, when the topic of stance comes up after the guns are locked away, it's more than a two-beer argument. Lay in at least a case before the discussion even opens.

Countless hours have been whiled away discussing the Isosceles stance versus the Weaver, with modified forms of each (usually the latter) often thrown in to spice up the discussion. This is rather like boxing fans debating the merits of the left jab versus the right cross versus the uppercut. The difference is, no knowledgeable boxing fan would recommend his favorite punch to the exclusion of all others, but an amazing number of shooters insist that their preferred shooting stance is so superior to every other stance in every respect, it is the *only* way to shoot.

The fact is, each stance became popular among knowledgeable people because it had significant strengths. By the

... while the more bladed Classic Weaver stance opens the armpit and some of the side to incoming fire. The Weaver stance predated the development of soft, wearable body armor.

The Isosceles stance, in squaring torso with an identified threat, maximizes the portions of the body protected by armor...

The classic Weaver Stance: Forward elbow down, both elbows bent, gun hand pushing, support hand pulling back.

same token, each stance has become less than first choice for some other knowledgeable people because it may have had significant weaknesses. A more sensible approach might be the one taken by boxers: an understanding that while every fighter will have a best punch, a one-punch fighter will not last long in the ring. There is a time and a place where each stance may come into its own and be the technique of choice, even if it is not the given shooter's particular favorite.

Is the shooter long-limbed or not? Does the shooter have limited range of movement? Does he or she wear body armor, or perhaps clothing that could restrict body mobility? Is the shooter muscular or slim? Are the shooter's dominant eye and dominant hand on the same side, or does "cross-dominance" exist? Any of these factors and more could determine the best stance for each individual shooter at a certain time in their lives.

Let's examine the three primary stances, warts and all, listing strengths and weaknesses.

Isosceles

This is perhaps the oldest two-handed pistol stance; this one involves thrusting both arms all the way forward until they are straight, forming an Isosceles triangle with the chest, which faces the target. Capt. William Fairbairn depicted it in the early 20th Century in his classic gunfight survival text "Shoot To Live," and Jeff Cooper at one time referred to the stance as the Fairbairn Isosceles.

Firearms instructor Simon Golub shows students how to begin in a ready position favored by competitive shooters and special forces operators…

… and quickly extend…

… to the Modern Isosceles stance, firing the whole way, if needed, with good accuracy.

The proper Isosceles stance: With the chest squared to the target, both arms are locked straight out, the upper body is very aggressively forward with the feet still farther apart, front-to-back as well as left-to-right.

Over the decades, this stance has gone through all manner of permutations. Done correctly, it is extremely powerful and has been used to win many championships shooting at high speed with powerful handguns. Done improperly, it may be the weakest of all shooting stances.

In the old days, when cops qualified with mild .38 Special wadcutters with insignificant recoil, they were taught to face the target squarely, standing straight up. If one Isosceles triangle (the arms) was good, coaches of the time seemed to be thinking, then two must be better: the officer was taught to spread the legs wide apart and often to lock them as well. Since there was now only precarious front-to-back balance, the legs being parallel, the outboard weight of the gun at the end of two fully extended arms tended to pull the shooter forward. To correct, shooters were taught to lean their shoulders back.

Various upper body shooting postures may be needed to adapt to certain positions when shooting from behind cover. Here, author finds the Isosceles works well from kneeling barricade position.

Balance was now completely gone. Even the .38 wadcutter would cause the gun's muzzle to rise significantly upon recoil. A more powerful gun could rock the shooter back on his heels with a single shot, and by the second or third round from a rapidly fired .44 Magnum, the officer might be tottering backwards. This sort of stance was to a proper Isosceles stance as Frankenstein's Monster was to humanity: a grotesque parody of the real thing.

A proper Isosceles stance, as taught in the StressFire (TM) shooting system, will see the chest squared to the target (as Dr. Walter Cannon, the first in-depth researcher of the fight or flight response, said the human body would do naturally in such a state), and the arms locked straight out to the target. However, the feet will be wide apart, not only side-to-side *but front to back,* and the head will come aggressively forward. Knees will be flexed; with the front leg's more so than the rear, but not to the exaggerated extent of the old, obsolete "FBI crouch." The head will be forward of the shoulders, and the shoulders forward of the hips.

Isosceles Advantages: 1) This is a very simple posture. We take the fight or flight stance defined by Dr. Cannon and simply put a handgun at the end of two arms that extend fully toward the target. Physiologists who have looked at

The Isosceles stance is the near unanimous choice of today's top professional shooters, such as Doug Koenig, shown here at the Mid-Winter National IDPA championships at S&W in 2001.

Isosceles shooting describe it as a simple gross motor skill, the kind easily accomplished under stress. 2) From Col. Rex Applegate to today's Bruce Siddle, trainers who look at these things scientifically find the Isosceles the most natural and logical two-hand hold for use under stress. 3) If the shooter is wearing body armor, this stance maximizes the armor's protective value as it squares the torso with the identified threat. 4) With the gun the maximum distance from head, the Isosceles minimizes ear damage if hearing protection cannot be worn. 5) It is ideal for night shooting. The Isosceles lines up the gun with the center of the shooter's head and body, and the head and body will align themselves instinctively in the direction of a suddenly perceived threat. 6) The Isosceles is ideally suited to pivoting toward the body's dominant hand side when feet are trapped in position and stepping is not possible.

Isosceles Disadvantages: 1) It works poorly if the shooter is off balance. 2) The stance may be impossible for those with elbow injuries, and difficult or impossible for those with inflamed elbow joints. 3) The gun bounces more than in a Weaver stance if the shooter fires when moving. 4) It is not compatible with tight, restrictive upper body garments such as tailored business suits, fastened motorcycle

Grandmaster Mark Mazzotta has won countless matches with the Isosceles stance.

Master shooter and instructor, and gunfight survivor, John Berletich prefers the Isosceles stance for all two-fisted handgunning. The pistol is Para-Ordnance LDA .45 auto.

jackets, or some types of cold weather gear. 5) It privides a limited range of pivot toward the non-dominant side of the body when the feet are trapped in position.

Cross-Dominant Correction: None. Since this stance brings the gun to the centerline of both the head and body, the left eye and the right eye align themselves naturally with equal ease no matter which is dominant. This is the easiest technique, by far, for the cross-dominant shooter.

Weaver Stance

In the 1950s in California, Col. Jeff Cooper began gunfight simulation contests originally called "Leatherslaps" as a research tool to determine the fastest, most accurate ways to return fire with handguns. It was thought originally that unsighted fire and one-handed shooting, being fastest, would rule. In the late 1950s a figure emerged to change that assumption forever. Jack Weaver was a deputy with the Los Angeles County Sheriff's Office. He brought his duty gun, a 6-inch Smith & Wesson K-38 revolver, to eye level for aiming and fired from a two-handed stance. He did both no matter what the distance...and he almost invariably got the center hits faster than the competition. Soon, his competitors realized that it wasn't just talent but superior technique that was at work.

The late John Plahn, an associate of Col. Cooper, was the one who really quantified Weaver's technique as more than just two-handed, eye-level shooting. He noticed that Weaver stood in a somewhat bladed stance, the strong side leg back to about 45 degrees, and that Jack bent both his arms sharply at the elbows. Weaver pulled back with his forward hand and pushed forward with his firing hand, with equal and opposite pressure.

Decades earlier, J.H. "Fitz" FitzGerald of Colt's had written a book on combat handgun shooting in which, as an alternate technique for use when one had time, he demonstrated the exact same technique, nuance for nuance. There is no reason to believe that Weaver copied him. Rather, Weaver appears to have re-invented the stance independently, and used it to great advantage. It was Col. Cooper who named the stance after Weaver and was almost single-

handedly responsible for promulgating it. During the 1980s, it was probably taught as the technique of choice by more police departments than any other, though by the 90s departments were tending to return to the Isosceles stance for a number of reasons.

Like the Isosceles, the Weaver is often interpreted incorrectly. If the body is too bladed, i.e., completely edgeways to the target, balance is lost. Great emphasis must be placed on a firm forward push of the gun hand and an equal and opposite rearward pull with the support hand. Without this dynamic, the bent arms lose force and not only is the gun's recoil exaggerated, but the frame can move so much that the slide "runs out of steam" and a cycling failure occurs, jamming the autoloader.

To avoid confusion with the many variations of "modified Weaver" stance, we'll refer here to the stance of Weaver and Cooper as the "Classic Weaver."

Classic Weaver Advantages: 1)Because the bent arms are foreshortened and do not extend as far, this Classic Weaver stance offers the shortest and therefore fastest path from holster to line of sight. 2) Because the gun is closer to the shooter's main body mass, it has less distance to move when the shooter must track multiple targets or moving targets, and is thus slightly faster in that regard. This is simple geometry based on the ARC principle (Axis, Radius, Circumference). 3) Because recoil is absorbed by the taut, bent arms acting as shock absorbers, this is the only two-handed stance that will survive an off-balance position in which the shooter's shoulders are leaning backward over the hips. 4) Because the gun is closer to the body and the elbows are tautly bent, that same shock absorption effect works from the ground up as well, making the Classic Weaver the most stable upper body position to use when firing while moving. 5) The Weaver's bent arms posture is much more comfortable for those with elbow injuries or ailments. 6) It is ideal for engaging to non-dominant side flank if the feet are not where they can quickly move. 7) Bringing the gun sights closer to the eyes, the Classic Weaver stance may work better for myopic shooters or with guns with small sights.

Look what's on Phil Goddard's gun arm. Tendonitis or other arm problems can make Classic Weaver the technique of choice...

... as it is for Phil.

... and with the Chapman stance...

Classic Weaver Disadvantages: 1) The Classic Weaver is not at its best with shooters who are light on muscle mass and tone in the arms. 2) With body armor, the somewhat bladed torso posture of the typical Weaver practitioner turns the vulnerable open portions of the vest toward the threat. 3) This stance is poorly suited for engaging to dominant-side flank if the feet cannot quickly step to a new position. 4) The gun is held closer to head than with other two-hand stances, increasing potential for ear damage from gunshot report when used in the field without hearing protection. 5) It is generally considered a complex psycho-motor skill by physiologists, and is more difficult to learn than the Isosceles.

Cross-Dominant Correction: Drop the head toward strong side, i.e., right cheek to right shoulder to align left eye with gun in the right master hand. The original Weaver stance usually proves to be the most difficult two-handed technique for the cross-dominant shooter.

SWAT cop and LFI instructor Larry Hickman demonstrates the correction for cross-dominance with a Classic Weaver stance...

... and with the Isosceles. The pistol is Beretta 92FS 9mm.

The Chapman stance, AKA Modified Weaver. The gun arm is locked with the shoulder forward; the bent forward arm pulls back tightly against gun arm. Note that feet are slightly farther apart and stance is slightly more aggressive.

"Modified Weaver": The Chapman Stance

Ray Chapman, a contemporary of Jeff Cooper, understood the advantages of the Weaver stance over the old-fashioned version of the Isosceles. A fan of strong shooting platforms, he did not like what he perceived to be the weakened firing mount that occurred when the elbow of the firing arm was bent, sometimes bent to the point where the wrist also unlocked. Chapman shot his way to the top of the heap with his own technique. The gun arm was locked at every joint, rigid behind the gun, and the forward arm was bent at the elbow and pulling the whole locked gun arm into the shoulder, as if pulling in tightly on a rifle stock.

Because the gun arm is locked, it can become a lever that jerks upward with accentuated recoil if the shoulders are at body center or tilting backward, the same dynamic that made the old-fashioned Isosceles a poor choice. Unfortunately, some who teach this stance did not get it direct from its developer and teach a rearward lean, which limits the level of speed their students can achieve with it. Chapman himself always emphasized that the body should be in a forward lean, with the shoulders forward of the hips at least slightly, to get maximum benefit from his shooting stance.

Chapman called his technique simply a modified Weaver stance. In the last quarter of the 20th Century, it had come into vogue to call almost every two-handed stance a "modified Weaver," and this became imprecise and confusing. Those who knew Chapman and saw and copied specifically what he was doing, called the posture "the Chapman stance." Some schools, ranging from Lethal Force Institute to Firearms Academy of Seattle, still use this term to distin-

guish the stance developed by Chapman from the myriad other "modified Weavers" that abound in the shooting field.

The Chapman stance can be seen in many ways as a bridge between the two more famous-name stances, the Classic Weaver and the Isosceles. On the dominant hand side we have the locked skeleto-muscular support structure of the Isosceles stance, and on the support hand side, we have dynamic tension, if not the truly isometric tension of the push/pull Classic Weaver. Thus, for many shooters this stance combines the best of both worlds without accepting the worst of either.

Chapman Stance Advantages: 1) This stance provides excellent commonality with long guns, as the gun arm func-

Seasoned competitor and daily gun carrier Bill Fish finds Chapman's stance works best for him. The pistol is a Glock.

tions like a rifle stock. 2) This posture is not particularly dependent on body shape or muscle tone/mass. 3.) It is better than the Weaver for those who wear body armor, since as the gun arm locks and the shoulder comes forward, the chest squares somewhat with the target.

Chapman Stance Disadvantages: 1) It does not give so much range of movement in pivot to the weak side as Weaver, nor to strong side as Isosceles. 2) The stance requires that shoulders be forward to work effectively, like Isosceles. 3) Not so effective for body armor wearers as Isosceles. Chapman himself taught police officers to shoot from Isosceles for this reason.

Veteran street cop, combat shooting champion, and LFI instructor Denny Reichard uses the Chapman stance by choice with his preferred weapon, the Smith & Wesson .44 Magnum loaded with full-power ammo.

Cross-Dominant Correction: Keep the head erect, bringing the jaw or chin to the shoulder or bicep. While the tilted-head position necessary to make this correction with the Classic Weaver is awkward and "buries" most of the weak eye's viewing scan, the Chapman correction keeps the full danger scan and merely moves it a few degrees to one side. Though easier than with Weaver, the cross-dominant correction with Chapman is still not so easy as with the Isosceles stance.

Notes On Terminology

Terminology in the world of the gun can be confusing, and once again "combat semantics" rears its ugly head. Shooting champion and master pistolsmith D.R. Middlebrooks has developed a stance in which the support arm is locked but the firing arm is bent, pushing against the locked gun arm. Some have called this a "reverse Chapman stance." The semantic correctness of this is debatable; it may appear that arms have swapped posture, but the dynamics are completely different.

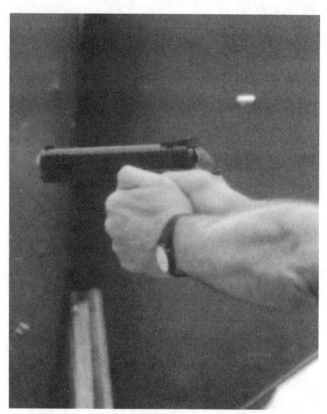

...and you can see the blur of the hammer falling and the bloom of flame at the muzzle from the second shot while the spent casing from the first shot is still only inches from the ejection port. The Isosceles stance gives many people the best control. Photos by Penny Maurer.

with it sufficiently to make it second nature, it may not be appropriate to call it any kind of an Isosceles stance.

Perhaps the most important point is this. Champions and gunfight survivors have used each of these stances alike. Each comes with a strong pedigree. Like the jab and the cross and the uppercut, there is a time and a place for each, and the competent fighter wants to know how to execute each of these techniques to perfection.

As Ayoob fires a "double tap" from an aggressive StressFire Isosceles stance on the way to winning an IDPA match, Penny Maurer's high-speed camera clicks. Look carefully at the area around the STI Trojan 9mm pistol...

A stance variously called "modern Isosceles" and "strong Isosceles" has become popular in IPSC circles. Both elbows are bent and a relaxed 40/60 percent pressure grasp is applied to the pistol. With elbows bent, the Isoscles triangle is broken into an uneven pentagonal shape. While this dexterity-intensive stance works in competition, and can certainly work in combat for someone who has practiced

The author feels a competent defensive shooter should be conversant with all three of the primary two-hand stances. Here, at right, Ayoob leads a class through an empty-hand refresher on the Chapman stance just before they fire for qualification.

The author demonstrates an aggressive StressFire version of the Isosceles with a Kimber .45 auto while doing a Bill Drill (6 shots, 2 seconds, 7 yards, from the holster) at the IDPA New England Regional Championships, 2000.

In the end, all those arguments over shooting stance may have been meaningless. For serious fighting, the ability to traverse from far weak side (favoring Weaver) to far strong side (favoring Isosceles) when you are caught on stairs or in tight spaces where you can't step into your favorite position has to be addressed. It really never should have been "Weaver versus Isosceles (versus Chapman stance)" at all. For the thinking practitioner of the combat handgun, it should be seen as knowing and being able to perform the true Weaver stance *and* the Isosceles stance *and* the Chapman stance.

One-Handed Stances

We all know that two-handed shooting is the most effective way to deliver fire with a combat handgun. Unfortunately, we also know that we won't always be able to use that method to return fire, so we have to have a Plan B in place. Plan B is a strong one-handed stance that gives you maximum delivery of accurate, rapid handgun fire under pressure.

Why can't we always do it from our strongest stance? It's one of those places where the rules of the range collide with

... is this .40 caliber Glock 22, mounted with an M3 Illuminator. Note that with the trigger finger manipulating the flashlight switch, it is kept safely off the trigger.

Firearms instructor Sam Young shows one reason one-handed shooting skills are important: you may have to use one hand to communicate while the other covers the danger zone. His home defense pistol...

the realities of the street. On the range, we normally know when we're going to fire and (we hope!) in what direction. Thus, we "address the target." That is, we get ourselves set to fire in a certain direction from a certain preferred stance, sometimes without even realizing we are doing it.

Unfortunately, attacks often come from unpredicted directions. A smart opponent will attack from the rear or the flank. As you spin to engage, one arm may reflexively go outward for balance as the other raises the gun. The subconscious, knowing that the support hand isn't going to reach its intended destination, sends its message to the trigger finger: "Open fire, *now!*"

Problems might arise because other situations besides the angle of attack. One hand could be pushing a victim out of the line of fire, or dragging a wounded partner, or clutching a communication device or a flashlight that's your only source of illumination in the darkness. There is also the possibility that the opponent has seized you by one arm, or has already wounded you there. Even those trained and practiced with two-handed shooting to the point where it constitutes 95 percent of their experience firing a handgun, may have to shoot one-handed when trouble strikes in the real world.

How often does that happen? Back in the 70s, I spent some time in New York City with the legendary Lt. Francis McGee, then head of NYPD's Firearms and Tactics Unit. I studied under him at the outdoor range facility at Rodman's Neck during the day, and picked his brains far into the night at his home, where I was staying. The SOP-9 study had by then been in place for several years. Standard Operating Procedure Number Nine, the intensive debriefing of every member of the service who fired his or her weapon anywhere but on the range, included the question, "Did you fire with one hand or with two?" The results thus far indicated that approximately half the shootings had caught the officers in such a position that they'd had to return fire one-handed.

Strong Stances

With half as many hands as we had to control the gun before, we have to get every ounce of hand strength out of the one we have left to fight with. If you don't care to shoot with the thumb curled down in two-handed postures, you might want to consider going to it now for added strength.

…with feet parallel, you flex your knees and drop your butt back in a mild version of a karate "horse stance"…

In the StressFire (TM) shooting system, if the opposite leg is forward you're in a reverse punch position…

… the single strongest stance is probably a forward punch posture, shown here…

...or making sure the thumb doesn't block the trigger finger with this small-handled Kahr K40 Covert pistol.

...and all three can be combined with the McMillan/ Chapman rotation of the pistol, which is especially suitable for cross dominant shooting. Note that in all cases the fist is drawn up to the pectoral muscle for added strength. A dummy Glock 19 is being used for photographer's safety.

What to do with the other arm? It needs to be out of the way where its mass, roughly 9 percent of body mass, won't pull the body to one side and take the gun off target. We teach that it be curled up tight to the side, palm up in a fist, the way the non-striking hand would be for a karate practitioner executing a reverse punch. This puts the hand about where it would be if it was holding a cell phone or police radio, or dragging a wounded partner. Turning the palm upwards and clenching the fist tightly creates a sympathetic tightening throughout the entire upper body's voluntary muscle structure, helping to tighten the firing hand still more. In fact, because human hands can manifest a phenomenon called interlimb response, the one hand won't reach full strength in grasp until the fingers of the opposite hand are sympathetically contracting.

Years ago, I hosted then-world champion Rob Leatham to teach an advanced combat competition course. Though Rob was a pioneer in shooting with the thumbs pointing toward the target in his own version of an Isosceles hold, he made a point of telling the advanced shooters to curl their thumbs down for added strength when they had to fire one-handed.

A locked-down thumb and a strong Shotokan Punch stance let the author easily control this powerful .357 SIG, Model P229.

The locked down thumb is important for one-handed shooting, and the author will sacrifice it only for something more important – in this case, disengaging the safety of this Ruger P90 .45...

It is interesting to look through a few decades of gun magazines and shooting manuals to see how the one-handed stance has evolved. In the old days, the shooter would stand erect, gun arm straight out, and free hand either hooked on the waist, tucked into a pocket, or on the hip or behind the back. Some would just let the arm hang free. And, if the camera captured the moment of the shot, the gun muzzle could be seen to be kicking skyward.

The institutionalization of IPSC in the mid-1970s brought some conformity to technique as the top shooters,

A lightweight, polymer-framed Ruger P97 is at the height of its recoil as Ayoob fires from 4 yards with .45 ball ammo.

known as the "super squad," generously shared their shooting tips with others. A hand flat on the belly got it out of the way and eliminated the "pendulum effect" of the loose arm swinging, but did nothing to actually enhance the firing hand's ability to do its job. The simultaneous development of the StressFire (TM) martial arts-based "punch" techniques, with the free hand now a fist, palm up, under the pectoral muscle, also emerged. These were widely copied.

With the upper body aggressively forward, and the head also forward (because "where the head goes, the body follows") shooters achieved much more powerful one-handed stances than those of the past. With one hand recoil was now controllable to the degree of the early version two-handed Weaver stance, and actually stronger than the old-fashioned version of the Isosceles. It was not, however, possible to make the one-handed posture stronger than the strongest, most efficient two-handed stances, and in all probability that will never prove possible.

Foot Position

The International Shooting Union (ISU) and practitioners of America's "Conventional Pistol" (i.e., bull's-eye) are taught to stand with their right foot forward if the pistol is in their right hand. This is because it applies no torque to the

spine, it balances the shooter well, and it extends the outboard weight of the upper limb directly over the weight-bearing lower limb.

Note that the rear leg is digging into ground, driving the upper body forward into the Colt 10mm during one-hand rapid fire. The recoil compensator on this Mark Morris gun helps, too!

Unfortunately, we can't always jump into our favorite position when attacked. The shooter needs to know how to fire effectively whether his strong foot is forward, or his weak-side foot is forward, or his feet are parallel. In the latter case, flexing at the knees and dropping the hips back will give a stable posture if the head and shoulders are forward.

LFI assistant instructor Cliff Ziegler demonstrates for students, keeping all hits in a tight chest group rapid-fire with his HK USP40 Compact.

In one-handed shooting, it is all the more important that the gun fits the hand. A Pearce grip extender for the little finger to grasp, and a locked down thumb help this shooter control the baby Glock.

If the weak side foot is forward, one can shoot from a well-balanced stance as if throwing what a karate stylist would call a reverse punch and a boxer, a right cross. The single strongest one-handed posture, however, will still be dominant hand forward/same side leg forward. This is the position a boxer would call a jab and a karate practitioner, a forward punch.

Turning the Gun

It has come into vogue in recent years to tilt the gun over to one side. Does this come under cinematic BS, or true secrets of the handgun ninja? Well, the answer is yes to both, depending how it's performed...

The technique goes back to the late 1950s. A young Marine pistol ace named Bill McMillan was shooting for the gold, but had one small problem: He was cross-dominant. He figured out that by adjusting the sights of his pistol, a cant of about 45 degrees inward aligned the sights dead on with the eye opposite his gun hand and still put the shots dead center. Soon he had moved to the head of the pack, winning the Gold Medal for the United States in the Pan-American Games circa 1960.

Tilting of the gun may happen naturally when emergencies require you to fire at awkward angles like this...

... or like this, as one California StressFire graduate had to when he came under fire from an ambusher with a rifle. The graduate won, killing his assailant.

Ray Chapman picked up on this trick and made it his technique of choice for one-handed work in practical handgun competition. With less precise accuracy required, the sights didn't need to be adjusted for the typical close range work. Chapman discovered that whichever side the shooter's dominant eye happened to be on, that slight turning of the wrist created a more propitious alignment of the skeleto-muscular support structure of the arm, resulting in a stronger hold. Chapman, it should be noted, always taught accuracy ahead of speed and always emphasized very strong shooting positions. Clint Smith, who later became head of the famous shooting school Thunder Ranch, has also taught the "McMillan rotation" for several years as the preferred one-handed technique.

Phil Goddard uses slight McMillan rotation when firing with the non-dominant hand only. The big .45 slugs from his Colt Combat Commander are staying in the "A" zone of the target.

Some find it works better for one hand than the other. At our school, we tell the students to feel free to "mix and match." Many end up preferring to shoot with the gun straight up on their dominant eye side, and in the McMillan/Chapman rotation when firing with their other hand. (Some shooters find that the rotation works in two-hand shooting

LFI student Joyce Fowler keeps them all in the A-zone with her .45 auto, while firing weak-hand-only using McMillan Tilt and StressFire Punch techniques. She went on to become multiple-time IDPA National Champion in the women's division.

as well. Larry Nichols, the nationally famous rangemaster and master police trainer from the Burbank (Cal.) PD, teaches this as technique of choice. Gila Hayes, another nationally known instructor, teaches it as a two-handed option for the cross-dominant shooter.)

The proper rotation is between 15 and 45 degrees. Less than that doesn't do much; more than that, and the arm is past the point of maximum strength. However, several years ago films exploiting urban violence began showing gang-bangers shooting with a strange hold in which the pistol was turned over 90 degrees. "Life imitates art," and soon this technique was being observed on the street, generally in the hands of the bad guys.

Firing from this awkward downed position, a shooter can't get body weight into the gun; the triceps muscle of the arm should be practiced in pulling this Glock 22 down from recoil.

Despite an injured elbow, Phil Goddard keeps every shot in a heart-size group with a straight-up hold and StressFire Punch technique, strong-hand-only.

Where did it come from? We may never know for sure. One theory is that a director or a technical advisor saw a security camera film of a felonious shooting in which the armed robber held his gun this way to reach over a counter and shoot a clerk who was trying to hide from him, and apparently decided that this was the new signature technique of the "gangstas." Another theory is that directors figured out that turning the pistol over allowed the menacing gun, and all of the actor's facial features, to be seen in the same frame by the camera. Who knows?

In any case, it is demonstrably a stupid way to shoot. The wrist has by this point run out of range of movement, and a person holding a handgun in this fashion can be disarmed with minimal effort. The recoil tracks the gun violently toward the weak hand side. This limits the ability to put multiple shots into the same stubborn aggressor, and it also probably accounts for some of the innocent bystanders hit by gang members who fire at one another this way.

The only time we've seen anything like this prove useful is for the person who is ducking to one side as they fire. As the body goes forward to the side, it will prove awkward to keep the sights upright, and it will be almost impossible to align them. In one California shooting, an officer trained in StressFire (TM) shooting came under fire from a suspect with an autoloading rifle as he bailed out the door of his patrol car. Raising his SIG P220, he saw the service pistol was turned over 90 degrees, but also that the sights were on the suspect. Remembering his instructor's admonition that if the sights were on target the shot would go true, he fired...and center-punched his attacker through the chest with a 230-grain .45 hollow-point, saving his own life.

Numerous "downed officer" positions, such as down laterally on the weak hand side, may make this position natural. However, vis-a-vis the body position, it *is* natural from here, since the shooter's arm is in its usual alignment with the torso.

Bottom Line

You want to practice with the one-handed techniques just as with the two-handed, to see which work best for you. Your brother may be a straight-up shooter and you may do your best with the McMillan tilt, or vice-versa. You won't know until you try them all and analyze your performance.

Be sure to spend lots of time practicing *weak-hand-only* shooting. This is a good reason to have an ambidextrous safety and/or decocking lever. History shows that because

A shooter's eye view as the thumb prepares to "wipe" a 1911's safety catch. One should always use the gun hand thumb to manipulate the safety, since often that's the only thumb that will be available to perform the task.

Using techniques recommended in this chapter, Ayoob is on his way to winning the revolver class at an IDPA match, sweeping an array of targets weak-hand-only with a Bob Lloyd-tuned S&W 4-inch Model 686.

humans look at what threatens them, and what threatens the armed criminal is the gun in the good person's hand, the good person's gun arm is disproportionately likely to draw fire and take a bullet. While a wound to the gun arm or hand may not leave you incapable of firing with that hand, there are no guarantees.

We also need to think ahead. We may not be disabled in a fight. We might simply break our dominant arm or wrist in a routine accident. This will be a lousy time to start learning how to defend ourselves and our families with a weak-hand-only option. It makes sense to start thinking right now about having an ambidextrous gun in a weak side holster from which we are familiar with drawing and firing using the non-dominant hand.

None of us seems to practice enough on one-handed shooting. When street results indicate that a good half of the time, that's exactly what we'll have to do, logic may be telling us to restructure our training priorities and schedule a whole lot more one-handed combat pistolcraft drills.

CHAPTER ELEVEN

AVOIDING MISTAKES

Gun Accidents

In the term "defensive weapon," the emphasis is normally on the first word. But as far as safety, the emphasis has to shift to the second. A weapon, by definition, can become a vehicle of unintended harm if handled or stored carelessly. We do not leave a can of lye open on the floor where the baby can reach it. We do not leave our car parked on a hill with the transmission set in Neutral. The firearm demands similar rules of common sense.

In the early 1990s, I was teaching a class being filmed by a crew doing a documentary on private ownership of firearms in the U.S. The topic had come around to home safety, and when I was done speaking, we opened it up for questions and answers. The person in charge of the documentary had noticed that my 9-year-old daughter was in the room, and he asked pointedly if I had taught her the safety rules I was propounding. I just said, "Why don't you ask her?"

They stuck the camera a few inches from my little girl's face and asked her about gun safety. With a perfect poise that approached nonchalance, Justine sweetly replied, "Treat every gun as if it is loaded. Never let it point at anything you aren't prepared to destroy. Never touch the trigger until you are going to fire, and always be sure of your target and what is behind it."

The film crew was dumbstruck. The father, on the other hand, had an ear-to-ear grin of pride. Justine had just recited the four primary rules of firearms safety as promulgated by one of the great leaders in the field, Col. Jeff Cooper.

Justine, like her older sister Cat, had grown up among firearms. Both her parents were licensed to carry, and one was required to at work. When they were tiny, guns were stored in such a way that they could not reach or activate them. Each began helping me clean guns at the age of 5. This de-mystified an object that the entertainment media had glorified as an instrument of power, and also de-glamorized it. They understood quickly how guns worked. An important benefit of this was that if they were ever in a playmate's house and the other child took his parents' gun out of the closet or nightstand, I wanted my kids to know how to "de-fang the snake" – how to unload the gun and/or lock up its firing mechanism.

Both began shooting at the age of 6 with .22s. Both had progressed to more powerful weapons by the age of 10 or 11. Neither ever gave their mother or me a minute's worry about firearms safety.

Loaded guns should not be left unsecured. They are vulnerable to burglars (who might turn them on innocent people sooner than you think, perhaps even on you or a family member who comes home unexpectedly and interrupts the burglary). They are vulnerable to certain members of the family, friends, and acquaintances who drop by unexpectedly and rummage about in other people's homes without permission. We always think of securing guns from children, but irresponsibility knows no age limit: the guns should be kept from *all* unauthorized hands. As the responsible owner, you are the one who determines who is authorized to touch the firearm.

Routine Handling

Every now and then you get something like a cartridge stuck in the chamber of an auto pistol. It will require you to forcibly manipulate the slide, maybe whack it with something, and you suddenly realize there's a live round that is stuck in there that can be fired from the gun. At such a moment, you'll want a safe direction in which to point the pistol. Accidental discharges have occurred during loading and particularly unloading. For all these reasons, think about something like a big bucket of sand in a corner of a kitchen. If a curious guest asks what it's doing there, you can honestly answer, "Fire safety."

All expert shooters can tell you that dry fire – going through the motions pulling the trigger of an unloaded gun – is an important route to shooting mastery. But we can all tell

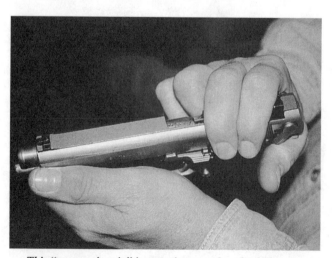

This "armorer's grip" is sometimes used to check the chamber of double-action autos. It gives more control when pulling slide back against a hammer that is being held down by a powerful mainspring.

This old method of chamber-checking a 1911 is dangerous since, at various points in the procedure, finger gets too close to loaded gun's muzzle and thumb gets too close to trigger...

...this method is better, but still brings hand uncomfortably close to business end...

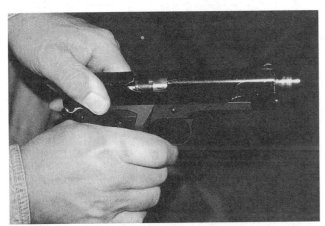

...and this, the slingshot technique, is the safest way of all.

This is one reason why basements have become favorite locations for shooting hobbyists' "gun rooms." I think it's a good idea for any armed citizen to own a bullet-resistant vest. I keep mine stored under the bed so I can throw it on any time the alarm goes off. Remember, the first definition of "alarm" is "a call to arms." Any situation for which I need a defensive firearm is a situation where a quickly donned vest would be comforting. And, more to the point at the moment, the bullet-resistant vest can always be set against a wall and used as the backstop for dry fire practice. It can always be set against the wall or on the floor when dealing with that pistol that had a round stuck in the chamber. It is simply one more safety net. How many things do we have in our homes that are designed to stop bullets? This is one.

Safe Manipulation

When you check the chamber of an auto pistol, don't do it from the front. If the hands slip, the strong recoil spring will slam forward hard enough to leave the muzzle of the loaded gun pointing at one or more of your fingers.

It's not just "on target, on trigger; off target, off trigger." That creates a subconscious mindset of putting the finger on the trigger as soon as you're taking a suspect at gunpoint, since the subconscious may believe that you are indeed on target. The rule is, *do not let the finger enter the trigger guard until the immediate intention to fire has been formulated and confirmed.*

Safety devices can fool you. They're just one more net in a layer of safety nets, and you never rely on just one. In the Midwest, a police officer wanted to show someone how the round in the chamber of his S&W 9mm would not fire if the magazine was removed. However, he maintained pressure on the trigger as he removed the magazine. This action bypassed the disconnector safety. He then put the palm of his hand in front of what he knew to be a still-loaded gun, and pulled the trigger. He shot the hell out of his own hand. Oddly enough, his response was to sue Smith & Wesson...sigh.

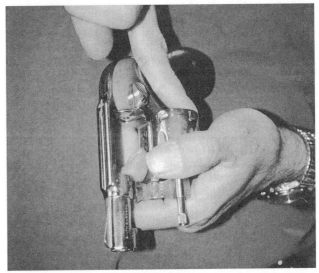

When checking to make sure the handgun is empty, get into the habit of checking by feel as well as sight. With a revolver, like this S&W Model 38 Bodyguard, press the index finger of the dominant hand into every empty chamber...

you stories of the day a live round somehow migrated into an empty firing chamber. This is why you should rigidly discipline yourself to dry fire only at something that could safely stop the most powerful bullet that might possibly emerge from that particular gun's muzzle.

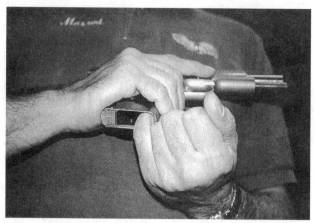

...with an auto pistol, use the little finger of the non-dominant hand to probe the magazine well...

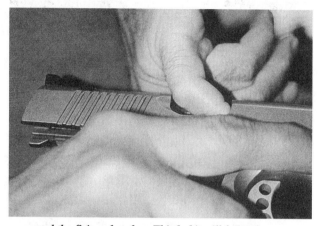

...and the firing chamber. This habit will fail-safe you when checking handguns in the dark or when there are distractions.

Do not lower the slide of a 1911 pistol while holding the trigger back. It is an archaic practice that will eventually lead to a slip and an accidental discharge. In the immortal words of John Dean, who was admittedly talking about something else at the time, "That information is no longer operative."

Do not carry the 1911 pistol with the hammer down, or at half cock, with a live round in the chamber. No matter what generation or style of manufacture, there is likely to be an unintended discharge if the hammer is struck, and there is a high likelihood of an accidental firing when cocking or lowering the hammer because of the awkwardness of the procedure. If you are not comfortable carrying it cocked and locked as it was designed to be, go to a double-action pistol or leave the 1911's chamber empty.

It is always safer to retract an auto pistol's slide with the "slingshot" rather than the "overhand" technique (see photos). With an overhand grasp, the arm wants to align itself in the direction in which it is applying force and, if your concentration slips for an instant, you can find the muzzle pointing at the elbow or at someone next to you. Similarly, avoid pulling the gun into your body for leverage as you work the slide. If it is too hard to pull back, use the heel of the free hand to cock the hammer. This will relieve mainspring pressure that is being exerted against the slide through the hammer, and allow the slide to be more easily retracted.

If the gun goes "poof" instead of "bang," *stop shooting!* An underloaded round has probably lodged a bullet in the barrel. Another shot behind it will lead to catastrophic pressures that can blow up the gun and cause serious injury.

A thickly packed stand-up pile of books or magazines makes a safe backstop for dry fire. Mark Maynard demonstrates with an S&W Model 686 revolver.

Never assume that someone else has cleared a gun of ammunition, even if he appears to do so. If I or any other professional hands you a gun we have just cleared, we *expect* you to double check it to confirm that it is unloaded. We may even be testing you. If you check what we just checked, no professional will be insulted; if you *don't,* we'll think you're an amateur.

When determining that a gun is unloaded, check by sight and feel. With the revolver, get into the habit of probing each empty chamber with the tip of your dominant hand index finger (usually the most sensitive of the 10 digits) until you feel the sharp-edged recess. With an auto pistol, lock it open and probe the magazine well and the firing chamber with the little finger of your non-dominant hand (usually the narrowest of the 10 digits). You may feel stupid doing this in clear light where you can plainly see that it is unloaded, but you are programming yourself for some high-stress dark and stormy night when you have to check a gun and can't see what's in it.

When you have set down an unloaded gun and left the room, or even turned your back on it, *check it again.* When an unloaded gun has left your line of sight, consider it contaminated.

When you remove a live cartridge from a semiautomatic pistol's firing chamber, don't eject it into your palm. This practice is a holdover from the old days of early military pistol designs with short ejectors. A long ejector, as found on today's 1911 pistols, most double action autos, and the Glock, can every now and then get into alignment with the primer, and if the primer is driven against it hard, it can fire the cartridge. This "open chamber detonation" will turn the shell casing into a hand grenade that spews brass fragments at high pressure into the palm of your hand, lacerating vulnerable nerves. We have seen cases of this that resulted in a reported 70 percent nerve damage to the afflicted area. Let the cartridge fall clear, keeping your face away from it. Always be wearing some sort of eye protection.

When dry firing, make sure there is no live ammunition anywhere in the same room. Never practice speed reloading

A "bullet-proof vest" has more safety uses than the obvious, as pointed out in this chapter.

and act out some homicidal rage by shooting it again and again. That's not how it works at all.

The reason shooting is such a good stress reliever is that, like sky-diving or rock climbing or SCUBA diving, *you have to concentrate on what you're doing to the point where all other BS is excluded from your mind. You must concentrate or you can get killed!* Our focus on safe shooting banishes our thoughts of job stress, family problems, or whether our team won the Super Bowl. If at any time we find ourselves on the line preoccupied with other, more compelling thoughts, it's

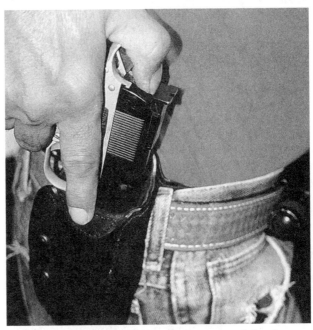

When holstering, keep the trigger finger extended so it can't foul the trigger, and the thumb on hammer. The thumb can catch a hammer that starts to move forward before a shot is fired, as with this Colt 10mm auto...

and trigger-pulling on the same night. When practicing reloading, use dummy ammunition or, better yet with an auto, weighted dummy magazines available from Dillon.

When cleaning the gun, make sure you're in a well-ventilated space, preferably outdoors. The carbon tetrachloride in some gun cleaning compounds can be toxic in cumulative doses. It is a good idea to wear latex or nitrile gloves while cleaning guns. This keeps lead and other toxins from getting into microscopic cuts on the hand. Wear an inexpensive gauze mask when cleaning. Remember, each time you pull that brush out of the barrel, you're putting tiny bits of lead into the same cubic yard of air you're about to inhale. Finally, always wear eye protection. In my experience, Gun Scrubber in the eyes is worse than pepper spray, and we know of one pistol champion who lost partial sight in one eye when the recoil spring cap of his pistol snapped free and hit his unprotected eye when he was taking the gun apart.

Gun Abuse/Substance Abuse

Common sense tells us that if we're going to get smashed at the New Year's Eve party, we should leave the gun at home. We also need to be certain about prescription medication. Any prescription with a warning label that says, "Do not operate dangerous equipment" can also be read as "don't go shooting while taking this medication." It is telling us that our concentration will be sufficiently impaired that we won't be at our best in maintaining our usual rigid care in firearms handling.

Similarly, if you are fatigued or distracted or angry, it is not a good time to be handling potentially lethal weapons. Anything that gets in the way of your concentration will get in the way of safe gun handling.

Things People Don't Think About

One reason shooting is such a great hobby is that it's a tremendously good stress-reliever. A lot of people don't understand how this works. They think that we go to the range, imagine our boss's face on the picture downrange,

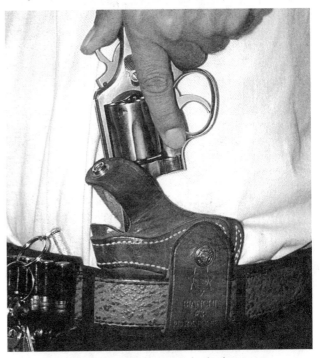

...or feel a double-action hammer rise in time to stop things before that hammer can fall and cause a discharge.

time to pack up and stop shooting for awhile, perhaps for the rest of the day. Not because we're going to have a psychotic break, but because we can't concentrate sufficiently on something that demands our complete attention. We do it this way for the same reason that we tell our teenage children not to drive when they're upset.

In defensive shooting, as in martial arts, the practitioner seeks to become so skillful that the techniques may be employed automatically without thinking about them when the proper stimulus comes. This is all to the good. However, we must walk a fine line when it comes to firearms safety. Automatic pilot is a fine thing, but it cannot be trusted exclusively. We must always strive for a "conscious competence" level when we're performing firearms safety tasks. We must think about what we are doing. If we have achieved the ideal Zen state of unconscious competence in firearms handling and do everything correctly without thinking about it, that's wonderful, but we need to double check once more at the conscious competence level to confirm the good job that we hope our unconscious competence carried out.

We need to be ruthlessly and honestly critical of ourselves. If we have what are currently called "anger management problems," we won't be ready to have immediate access to loaded firearms until those things are under control. If we sleepwalk, it may not be a good idea having guns available in the bedroom.

A good friend of mine is a world-class competitive shooter with a strong background in law enforcement. He is one of the most well adjusted human beings and family men I know. He also happens to be a very deep sleeper, and tends to be a bit groggy and disoriented for several seconds when suddenly awakened. Recognizing that, he has made a point of keeping his home defense pistol, a Browning 9mm semi-automatic, in a secured drawer across the bedroom. It is stored with the chamber empty. He knows that by the time he has gotten up, crossed the room, retrieved the gun, and chambered a round, he will be awake and clear-headed. This is the kind of self-analysis we all need to go through.

Layered Defense

The police officer on the street has layers of physical defenses. He is taught Verbal Judo (™), a crisis intervention skill. He is taught "soft" come-along holds and "hard" strikes with fist and forearm, with knee and foot. He carries pepper spray, and can resort, next, to his baton. He will have a handgun on the duty belt, and hopefully a shotgun and/or rifle in the patrol car if things get worse yet.

The citizen should have layered defenses in the home. Good locks in solid doors, secure windows, alarms, perhaps an intercom or even a closed-circuit TV at the door, perhaps professionally-trained protection dogs and, of course, firearms.

Gun safety also demands a layered series of defenses. We secure the guns from unauthorized hands. We are constantly aware of where any lethal weapon is and what its condition is. We check by sight and feel. Redundancy is the key. We want to create net after net after carefully deployed net to keep accidents from happening.

Let's close with a very insightful statement by an NRA Director and firearms instructor named Mike Baker. Says Mike, "Seemingly obsessive concern with firearms safety is the mark of the firearms professional."

The home defense gun should be only one of several layers of protection. Consider getting a good, properly trained dog...

...a good alarm system...

...and some kind of safe. Even the better hotel rooms, as shown here, have safes available for guests.

The Concealed Carry Faux Pas

"Sex and Violence: You can't enjoy the one if you don't survive the other."

Richard C. Davis, inventor of soft body armor, armed citizen, and gunfight survivor.

"I don't mind where people make love, so long as they don't do it in the street and frighten the horses."

Beatrice Tanner Campbell, arbiter of etiquette in days past.

Richard Davis and Beatrice Tanner Campbell aren't usually discussed in the same paragraph, but it's appropriate here. We lawfully carry guns because we want to stay alive to enjoy the good things in life. Because we are licensed to wear them in public, we do indeed "do it in the street," and therefore we must take all the more care not to "frighten the horses."

In most jurisdictions, concealment is not only authorized by the license, but also tacitly required. Rookie cops are known for the need to "flash," to just show someone that for the first time in their life, "they've got the power." Armed citizens are well advised to avoid that temptation. The mark of the professional is that few people know that they go about armed. Discretion is critical.

WRONG! A high reach with the hand on the holster side pulls up the jacket and flashes the gun, in this case an S&W .45 auto.

A spiritual descendant of Mrs. Campbell is Judith Martin, who writes the popular "Miss Manners" etiquette column for the newspapers. Some years ago she had a column that read something like this:

RIGHT! Discreetly holding down the hem of the jacket on the gun side, the pistol-packer makes the high reach with the opposite hand.

"Dear Miss Manners:

"My job requires me to carry a gun. Recently at a party, I sat down awkwardly on a couch and my gun fell to the floor in plain sight. Everyone stared and I was quite shaken. It was most embarrassing. What does one do in such a situation?"

(signed) "Armed and Confused"

The columnist's reply was similar to this:

"Dear Armed and Confused:

"You should have immediately picked up your firearm and secured it. You should have then self-effacingly stated, 'I'm terribly sorry. My job requires me to carry a gun. Don't worry, no one is in danger.' Then you should have made a graceful exit. And *then* you should have gone out immediately and purchased a holster that would not let your gun fall out. – Miss Manners"

Clearly, Judith Martin is one of us!

You want to avoid "flashing" the gun or allowing it to "print," that is, to become visible in outline under the concealing garments. If you carry in a pocket, use a pocket holster designed to break up the gun's distinctive outline.

Another option is to fold up a road map or pamphlet lengthwise, and put it in the pocket between the outer fabric and the gun. If you have a shallow pocket, this will also prevent someone standing in a waiting line behind you from glancing down and seeing the backstrap of the pistol peeking out of the opening of the pocket.

If you wear a shoulder holster, make sure the concealing garment is made of substantial fabric that the lines of the harness do not print. When you bend forward, use one hand or forearm to hold the garment closed on the holster side. Otherwise, a shoulder holster that is not secured to the belt may swing forward and become visible to someone on the side opposite the gun.

If you bend down to pick something up, do it like a back patient. Keep the spine and torso vertical, and bend at the knees. Bending at the waist causes a gun in a hip holster to print starkly.

Avoid middle of the back holsters. Anywhere else on your waistband, if the gun catches the hem of the garment and pulls it up revealingly, you'll quickly either feel it or notice it in peripheral vision. Neither will be true if the gun is in the small of your back. It may be completely exposed, and you'll be the only person within 300 yards who *doesn't* know that your gun is hanging out.

...however, leaving the gun exposed like this could "frighten the horses"...

The jacket covers the pistol, but let's say it's just too warm...

...so instead you shrug off the jacket while seated, like this...

It will be apparent in this book that the author is a believer in safety straps. That's partly so the gun won't be lost in a fall or foot pursuit or other strenuous activity. It's partly because if you're grappling with someone and his hands go around your waist, feel the gun, and begin tugging,

... and sort of puff it out around the holstered gun. You're comfortable. The gun is accessible but out of sight. Remember, however, to put your arms back into your sleeves before you stand up again!

you want to buy some "reactionary gap" time. It is also partly to avoid something as simple as sitting in a lattice-back chair and having your gun suddenly leave the holster.

I was once vacationing in Florida, legal to carry a gun, with a 1911 .45 auto, in an open-top, inside-the-waistband holster, under a loose sport shirt. I sat down in a beach chair next to a pool, adjusted the back of the chair up and settled myself. I heard a "clunk." I thought, *Clunk? Vas ist das Clunk?* I glanced down and saw a remarkably familiar combat custom .45 auto lying at poolside. So did a couple of other rather wide-eyed people. I scooped up the pistol and

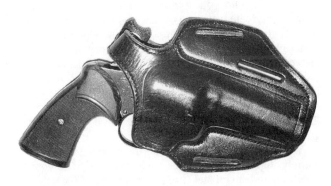

A good insurance policy against the gun coming out of the holster is a safety strap design. Here, an S&W Model 10 rides in a Strong Piece-Keeper...

...which uses a unique two-stage thumb-break that won't release by accident and is also likely to thwart an intentional gun-grab by unauthorized hands.

tucked it away, remarking to one concerned onlooker, "Sorry, I'm a cop, they make me carry this damn thing." Then, like the poor soul who wrote to Miss Manners, I beat a hasty retreat.

What had happened was that as I shifted my weight upward to settle in the chair, the butt of the pistol had become caught in the open latticework at the back of the chair. When I lowered myself, the movement in essence pulled the holster down and out from around the gun, which then toppled to the pavement.

This is also a good reason to carry a pistol that is "drop safe." It isn't enough to smugly say, "I don't intend to drop my gun." I didn't intend to, either. But if things we didn't intend to do never happened, we wouldn't have to carry guns in the first place. Out West, a lady with a cute little der-ringer in her purse dropped the bag accidentally. The pistol inside received the impact as the purse hit the floor and dis-charged, sending a bullet up out of the handbag and into the chest of a man standing nearby.

When you are reaching upward, particularly with a short jacket on, take care that the garment does not lift so much that it exposes the gun or even part of the holster. If the pis-tol is on your right hip, you might want to discreetly hold the hem of the jacket in place with your right hand as you reach with your left. If that will flash my spare magazine pouch, which some might find just as unsettling, this writer is of such an age that he can commandeer some passing youngster and say, "Excuse me, son, could you reach an item on that top shelf for an old man?"

If you have an ankle holster on, before you leave the house, sit down and see how much the pant's cuff rides up when you're seated. If the bottom of the holster becomes exposed, nature is telling you to pull your sock up on the *outside* of the holster, taking care that it does not come up over the edge of the holster mouth where it could snag a draw. Now, if the cuff lifts while you're sitting in a restaurant, it just looks like you have a baggy sock. You may get a summons from the Fashion Police, but the Gun Police will leave you alone.

When in restaurants, try to sit with your gun/holster side toward the wall. This will minimize chances of the gun being spotted as you get up.

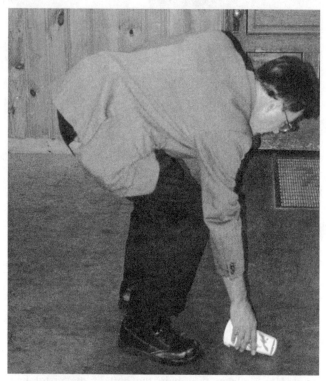

Bending at the waist causes a hip-holstered gun to "print." Keeping the torso vertical and squatting, "like a back patient," would be much less revealing.

If you are wearing a jacket and find yourself seated someplace unbearably hot, you can take off the jacket without flashing the gun. Simply sit down with the garment on, then shrug out of the sleeves and let the jacket sort of fluff up around your waist. Done with care, this will hide the gun. Now you'll be comfortable, and you won't become conspicuous by being the only person in the place wearing a jacket.

If you carry your firearm off-body in a purse or fake Daytimer (™) or whatever, *for Heaven's sake, don't get in the habit of setting it where you might get up and leave it unattended.* There are other countries where people have gone to jail for that, convicted of criminal negligence, if the abandoned weapon is stolen or found by a child. If the container is small enough, put it in your lap. If it's too big for your lap, put it on the seat *against* your hip. If you must, put it on the floor *against* your leg. Have it on the exiting side or between your feet. Yes, the exiting side is more accessible to the purse-snatcher, but ask yourself one question. How many times in your life has a thug snatched your purse or briefcase, compared to how many times in your life have you had to go back into a house or restaurant for a carry bag you inadvertently left behind? Between the feet is better, but on the exit side is acceptable too, because it's always where you can feel it and you can't slide out or get up without noticing it and reminding yourself to keep it with you.

Securing Guns In Vehicles

Do the neighbors and passers-by need to see you carrying guns out to your car for a day at the range? Dedicated gun bags, like the excellent Waller unit, look more like high quality gym bags or travel bags, and don't attract attention. The new generation fully enclosed golf club cases designed for air travel are ideal for transporting rifles and shotguns. If the case of ammo you put in the trunk looks like a plain cardboard box, no one is going to look twice.

We have a generation of "gun-free workplaces" where an armed citizen can be arrested for trespass after warning if they enter the office armed. Federal buildings such as post offices are normally considered to be off limits for gun carrying, even if you have a license to do so in public, and in many jurisdictions the same is true for courthouses, schools, and even places that sell alcohol. This means that if you're an armed citizen on a day off doing errands that include mailing a package, picking up a copy of a deed at the courthouse, and purchasing wine for a dinner party, you'll have to take your gun on and off at least three times during the trip.

You don't want to do it conspicuously. A frightened citizen who sees someone "doing something with a gun in a parked car" violates Mrs. Campbell's edict, "Don't frighten the horses." A thug who sees you put a pistol in the console knows that he can smash out a window with a rock and steal a pistol as soon as you're out of sight.

If you regularly carry a gun, it makes sense to get a small lock-box that easily opens by feel with combination push buttons, and bolt it to the floor or the transmission hump of your car, within reach of the driver's seat. This allows you to secure the gun as you approach your parking space, and carefully slip it back out and put it back on as you drive away. Why do this while you're in motion? Because most people won't be able to see you. (Take care about being observed by people in high-seated trucks, however.) You're much more likely to be noticed by a pedestrian who is walking by your parked car, since his natural visual angle is downward into your vehicle.

You might also want to slip the gun into a sturdy cloth shopper's bag (a fanny pack might become a target for a thief because it looks like it might contain a wallet) and lock it in your trunk when you go into the post office, then retrieve it into the passenger compartment when you return to your car.

While we're talking about guns and cars, it's not sound tactics to have gun-related decals or bumper stickers on your vehicle. Did you ever make a political decision and change your vote because you saw something on someone's bumper sticker? Probably not, and no one will vote for your gun rights because they saw your bumper sticker, either. However, those things put some cops on hyper-alert when they pull you over for having a taillight out. Your NRA bumper sticker may give some road-raging bozo the idea to call the police and say you threatened him with a gun. When the cops pull you over and find out you do indeed have a gun, you "fit the profile."

You also have to consider that the criminal element isn't entirely stupid. When they see a gun-related sign on your car, it tells them that you feel strongly about guns. That tells them you probably own several guns. They love to steal guns because firearms and prescription drugs are the only things they can steal from you that they can fence on the black market for more than their intrinsic value, instead of maybe a nickel on the dollar. Now they know that if they follow this car to its home, they can watch the house until people are gone, and then break in and steal guns. This is why the bumper sticker thing is just not wise. Show where your heart is on your rights to own firearms by working and contributing to gun owners' rights groups, instead. It'll do everyone, and the cause, and particularly you, a lot more good.

The Routine Traffic Stop

It can happen to any of us. We're driving along and suddenly the red, or blue, or red and blue lights start flashing in the rearview mirror. We're being pulled over! *And we're carrying a concealed gun!* What do we do?

Well, since we are law-abiding citizens and carrying legally, we pull over. Smoothly, steadily, turning on the signal as soon as we see those lights. At roadside, we park and turn off the ignition and engage the emergency flashers. At night, turn on the interior lights. Stay behind the wheel. If you get out and approach the officer unbidden, you not only indicate to him that there might be something inside the car that you don't want him to see, but your actions mimic the single most common pattern of ambush murder of police during traffic stops. Just stay in the car. Leave your hands relaxed in a high position on the steering wheel. Do not reach for license and registration in glove box or console or under the seat, either now or before coming to a stop. From a vehicle behind you, these movements mimic going for a weapon.

Remember Mrs. Campbell's advice. No cop gets through a police academy without horror stories of brother and sister officers murdered in traffic stops. The officer is carrying a gun and this is the *last* of Mrs. Campbell's horses that you want to frighten.

The officer will ask for license and registration. Make sure that when you open the glove box for the latter, there isn't a gun sitting there. If you have indeed left *la pistola* in the glove box, tell the officer, "I'm licensed to carry, and I have one in the glove box with my registration. How should we handle this?" It would be much better for the gun not to be in that location at all.

In some jurisdictions, when a permit is issued, there is a requirement that you identify yourself as armed any time you make contact with a police officer and are carrying. The easiest thing to do is carry the concealed handgun license next to the driver's license, and hand both to the officer together. Don't blurt something like, "I've got a gun!" It

sounds like a threatening statement. If you try to explain about the pistol and passing traffic obscures some of your words and the only thing the officer hears is "gun," your traffic stop can go downhill. Just hand over the CCW permit with the DL.

You'll want to do the same in jurisdictions where such identification may not be required by law, but where the Department of Motor Vehicles cross-references with issuing authorities on carry permits. In those jurisdictions – Washington state, for example, and many, if not most, parts of California at this writing – the officer will have been told by dispatch or will have seen on his mobile data terminal that you're someone who carries a gun. If you don't bring it up first, such action can seem to the officer as if you're hiding something from him. Again, hand over the CCW with the DL.

In jurisdictions where neither is the case, it's up to you. If I pull you over for a traffic stop in my community, and you are a law-abiding citizen who has been investigated, vetted, and licensed to carry a gun, it's none of my business. If I'm worried about it, I'll ask you if you have one, and will expect an honest answer at that time.

If at any point the officer asks you to please step out of the vehicle, things have changed. Either someone with a description similar to yours did a bad thing (which means you're going to be field interviewed and patted down until it's clear that "you ain't him"), or your operation was careless enough to give the officer probable cause to believe you're driving under the influence. This means there will be a roadside field sobriety test. In the typical Rohmberg test, arms will be going straight out to your sides, coats will be coming open, and this would be a very bad time to "flash."

So, if the officer asks you to step out, I would suggest you reply with exactly these words, if you haven't already handed over the CCW: "Certainly, Officer. However, I'm licensed to carry. I do have it on. Tell me what you want me to do." The cop will take it from there.

Now you're seeing why those of us who've been carrying for a long time understand a principle the courts call the "higher standard of care." It holds that we, of all people, should be smart enough not to make stupid mistakes with guns. This is why, among many other things, those of us who carry guns tend to rely more on the cruise control than the radar detector, and actually make an effort to drive at the speed limit, so we won't get pulled over in the first place.

Securing The Combat Handgun

Shooter A is a professional instructor in combat arms. He's on the road about half the time, usually alone. He keeps a pair of handcuffs in his suitcase and travels with a primary handgun and a backup weapon. When he goes to bed at night in a hotel room, one loaded pistol is in one of the shoes he plans to wear the next day, at bedside. The other is in the other shoe on the opposite side of the bed. He untucks the sheets and blankets at the bottom of the bed before turning in.

Rationale? He can reach the gun immediately if there's an intrusion. If he has to roll to the other side of the bed, he can reach a gun there too. If, like some of the victims he has

met over the years, he wakes up with the attacker on top of him in bed, there will be no tucked-in bedclothes to bind him like a straitjacket and he can roll the attacker off. If he has to leave the guns behind for any reason, he can lock them in the hard-shell case he keeps inside his regular suitcase, then use the handcuffs to secure the case to pipes under the bathroom sink.

The latter tactic is because research has taught him that many hotel burglars have suborned hotel staff and use their keys to enter rooms while guests are out. It's unlikely that these punks will have handcuff keys with them. If they break the pipes to get at the case, it will call immediate

The latest S&W revolvers come with both external (shown) and internal trigger locks. On this one, the case is lockable to boot.

attention to their activities. Hotel management will alert to what's going on, change locks and keys, and kill the golden goose.

Shooter B is a police officer with young children not yet at the age of responsibility. He is subject to call-out from off-duty status at any time. He has arrested and sent to jail some people who aren't too happy about it, and he feels that nothing less than an instantly accessible loaded handgun will keep him and his young family safe enough for his peace of mind.

The solution is a lock-box secured in his closet. When he comes home from work he is carrying his duty sidearm, a .45 auto, as an off-duty weapon. He simply leaves it on his person until he goes to bed. When that time comes, he goes to the lock box. The .45 goes in, and out of the box comes another gun that has reposed safely there all day. It is a Smith & Wesson .357 Combat Magnum revolver, loaded with 125-grain hollow-points and customized with a device called MagnaTrigger, which is not externally visible. When he turns in, he slips this gun under the bed where it's out of sight but he can reach it immediately. From his night-table drawer come two simple looking stainless steel rings. He puts one on the middle finger of each hand, and goes to sleep.

Here's how to use handcuffs to lock up a 1911 single-action auto. The hammer cannot come forward even if the trigger is pulled and the sear is tripped.

The rings have magnets attached to the palm side. There's one for each hand because he learned in police training that the dominant hand could become disabled in a fight and he might have to resort to his support hand. He is now the only one who can fire the MagnaTrigger gun, whose retrofitted mechanism blocks the internal rebound slide. At the bottom of the block is a piece of powerful cobalt samarium magnet. Only when a hand wearing a magnetic ring closes over the gun in a firing grasp will reverse polarity move the block out of the way and make the gun instantly "live." This device has been available and working well since 1975, and is currently available from Tarnhelm Supply, 431 High St., Boscawen, NH 03303. On the Web at www.tarnhelm.com. It can be applied only to a Smith & Wesson double-action revolver, K-frame or larger at this time.

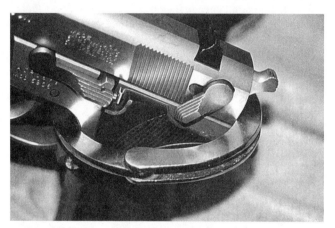

Handcuffs secure this double-action auto. The hammer of this S&W Model 5906 cannot rise, as the bracelet blocks it. The trigger cannot be drawn back enough to fire, again blocked by the bracelet.

Two very different people, and two very different approaches. Neither is likely to have a gun stolen. Neither is likely to have an unauthorized person handling their guns without their knowledge. Yet each is ready to instantaneously access a defensive handgun if there is a sudden, swift invasion of their domicile.

This writer has been a big fan of the MagnaTrigger concept since it came out in 1980. I no longer need it much, as my children are grown and have guns of their own. But with one child married already, I suspect it won't be long before the pitter-patter of grandchildren's feet calls the old MagnaTrigger gun out of mothballs. It is also useful for any time I want to have a gun in off-body carry instead of on my person. The gun is in the bag, but the rings are on me, and if anyone grabs the bag and runs, there's nothing they can do with the gun inside.

Why have you not heard about the MagnaTrigger from the mass media, in all their articles about gun control advocates calling for "smart guns"? Well, simply because those gun control advocates don't really want smart guns. They want no guns at all. Their strategy is to pass legislation requiring something that does not yet exist on the market: electronically controlled pistols. This will give them an avenue to ban "stupid guns" as dangerous, and then leave gun owners with nothing because the "smart guns" promised to replace them don't come through. If the public found out there actually was a smart gun that worked, the anti-gunners fear that people who don't buy guns now would buy these, and that would thwart their plans. The smart gun that works now is indeed the MagnaTrigger, hampered only by the fact that the technology has not yet been successfully translated to semiautomatic pistols.

Lock Boxes

The lock box, a small, rapid-access gun safe, has been a boon to armed citizens and off-duty police and security personnel. It leaves the gun as secure as if it was in a gun safe if the lock box is bolted to a floor or otherwise made so that it can't be just picked up and walked away with. I've personally had good luck with the Gun Vault brand, but there are several good units out there.

This old S&W Model 39 9mm auto is kept in a cut-out book. Note the warnings the owner has surrounded it with.

With the gun on your person, it is at once readily accessible to you and inaccessible to unauthorized hands. I wrote that more than 30 years ago in one of my first magazine articles. It was true then, and it is just as true now. Perhaps more so: armed home invasions seem to have become more frequent in certain areas.

There's another advantage to simply always being armed. You don't forget and leave your gun at home. I'll never forget one cop, the hero of one fatal gunfight a few years before, who told me, "I was on my own time, downtown, shopping. I heard the first gunshot go off, and my hand went to my hip, and there was nothing there because I had forgotten to put my gun on…" That particular event turned out all right, but I doubt that he ever made that mistake again. Educators call it "a reinforcement of the learning experience."

An ergonomic push button pattern and keyed over-ride are good features of the Gun Vault unit. This one is bolted to the transmission hump of an automobile. It is an ideal set-up for people who cannot bring their carry guns into certain buildings.

More lock boxes come out every year. Do yourself a favor and visit a gun shop with a wide selection, and try several demonstrator models. A combination dial will be difficult in dim light with shaking hands. You want push buttons, set well apart in ergonomic fashion, and one reason to try it in the shop is to make sure the unit you like fits your particular hands. Be sure to practice with it frequently. Remember that anything battery operated needs to have its batteries changed regularly. Get into the habit of changing the batteries in such a lock box when you change the batteries in your emergency flashlights and your smoke alarms: twice a year, when you change the clocks for Daylight Savings Time.

One Safe Place

No matter where your gun is stored, it is possible that a violent intrusion will happen so rapidly that you can't get to it in time. The one way to always be certain you can reach your gun is to always wear it. This doesn't mean you have to walk around the house with a Sam Browne belt, a high-capacity 9mm, and 45 rounds of ammo in pre-ban magazines. A snub-nose .38 in a side pocket will do nicely.

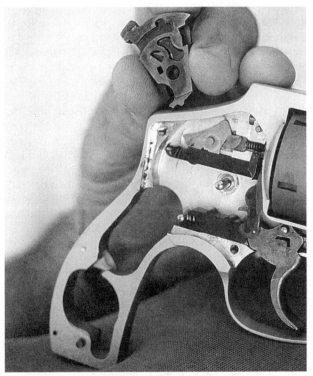

These are the operating parts of Smith & Wesson's internal gun lock, introduced in 2001.

Gun Locks and Trigger Locks

For decades in police work, it has been common practice to keep gun lockers at the entryways to each booking area or fingerprinting setup. We learned to slip our service weapon into the small locker, secure it, and pocket the key. Law enforcement quickly learned to put the guns in loaded, leave them loaded, take them out loaded, and re-holster them loaded.

An easily manipulated key operates the hammer lock on standard model Taurus revolvers. Note the keyway between hammer spur and frame.

Each time you load and unload, you're handling a live weapon, and that always creates an opening for an accidental discharge. There was always the possibility of an officer forgetting to reload and going back on patrol with an empty gun. This collective experience has proven that a loaded handgun in a lock box is as safe as safe can be.

I do not like the idea of trigger locks. If someone puts one on a loaded gun, the lock can jiggle against the trigger and cause an unintended discharge. There is no trigger lock that will keep the gun itself from being loaded. I simply don't trust that technology, and a lot of other long-time firearms professionals share that opinion.

If I have to lock up the gun without putting it in a container in which the firearm cannot be touched, I prefer something that locks the firing mechanism. First Taurus, and now Smith & Wesson, have begun producing their revolvers with integral locks. While some people oppose this concept on principle, I've so far seen nothing wrong with it mechanically. Neither the hammer-mounted lock of the Taurus nor the side plate-mounted integral flush lock on the S&W seem capable of "locking up" by themselves when you need them to fire, and I've hammered the heck out of these guns with hard-kicking ammo. We're talking full-power .454 Casull in the Taurus Raging Bull revolver and full-power .357 Magnum in the Smith & Wesson 340 PD, which weighs only 12 ounces. Similar technology exists now in some auto pistols.

One of my colleagues has speculated that if some of these guns are dropped into sand, the keyways will be blocked and the owners won't be able to make the lock work to "turn the gun on." Unless one is camping out of doors, I don't see too much problem with that. There's no reason for

a locked gun to be exposed anyway; it should be in a container if you're someplace where the gun must be secured.

The Handcuff Trick

Since long before this old guy pinned on a badge, cops have been securing their guns at home with their handcuffs. With the conventional double-action revolver, the bracelet goes between the rear of the trigger and the back of the trigger guard, and over the hammer. This at once blocks the rearward travel of the trigger and the rearward travel of the hammer, positively preventing firing. On a "hammerless" style revolver, the trigger is still blocked.

This is a double-action revolver secured with handcuffs. The hammer can't rise (and therefore can't fall), and the trigger can't be pulled far enough for discharge, because a handcuff bracelet blocks those parts on the S&W 686.

On a single-action such as the 1911 or the Hi-Power, the handcuff's bracelet is applied differently. On the 1911, which has a sliding trigger, it goes under the outside of the trigger guard at the juncture of the grip-frame, and over the back of the slide in a way that holds the hammer down if the chamber is empty, or back if the gun is cocked and locked and loaded. With the Browning, which has a freestanding trigger, it can be done just as on a revolver or if the gun is cocked and locked, the bracelet can be between the hammer and the slide while also blocking the trigger's travel toward the rear of the guard.

A wise police instructor, Peter Tarley, came up with the concept of unloading the Glock and then field stripping it. A practiced shooter familiar with the gun can quickly reassemble and then load it.

A double-action auto would be secured the same way, holding the hammer in the down position.

I don't see any way to effectively lock up the Glock pistol with handcuffs. What the Glock does lend itself to better than most other guns, is a home safety concept I first heard suggested by Peter Tarley, the world-class instructor who used to work for Glock. Simply unload the pistol, and field strip it. The Glock's barrel/slide assembly comes off *en bloc* as with many other guns, but unlike most others, there is no takedown lever that has to be manipulated a certain way during reassembly. When danger threatens, grab the barrel/slide assembly with your non-dominant hand, your frame assembly with your dominant hand, and put the two back together. Then holding the gun in the dominant hand, seize the loaded magazine, insert it, rack the slide, and you're holding a loaded Glock pistol. It's surprising how quickly this can be done. The old HK P9S, no longer produced, was one of the few other guns with which this trick works as well.

Remember, it's our gun. Power and responsibility must always be commensurate. When we need the power, we must accept – and live up to – the responsibility. In the end,

most of the time, you never needed the power, but you feel good about having fulfilled the responsibility.

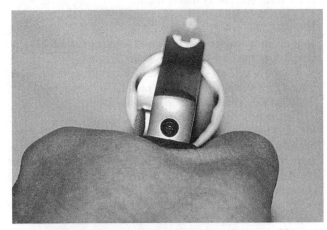

On Taurus' "hammerless" CIA revolver, the integral key lock is high on the backstrap of the grip-frame, just above the web of this shooter's hand.

Deadly Force Decision Errors

A book could be written about when private citizens may use lethal force in defense of self and others. In fact, it has been. I wrote it some time ago. The title is, *In the Gravest Extreme: The Role of the Firearm in Personal Protection.* Some kind people have called it the authoritative text on the topic, and it is available from Police Bookshelf, P.O. Box 122, Concord, NH 03302 or online at www.ayoob.com. There, I've done my part and warned you what you need to study.

With only a chapter for this, let's talk about avoiding some of the common mistakes typically made by well-intentioned good guys or gals when they righteously draw in self-defense. Until Lethal Force Institute was founded in 1981, there just wasn't any place a private citizen could go to be trained to the depth police are trained in the discipline the law calls judicious use of deadly force. For decades, there was nothing but either law school on the one end or macho talk around the cracker barrel at the gun shop on the other, and some pretty scary myths were widely distributed that some people take as gospel.

Stop shooting when the threat stops. He drew. You fired. He dropped his gun, turned, and staggered away. If you shoot him again now, it's no longer self-defense. You're looking at hard prison time. When the threat stops, the right to use deadly force stops with it.

Never plant a weapon on a man you've shot, or otherwise alter evidence. Trust me, it will be found. When it is, you lose the critical shield that the law calls the "mantle of innocence." If you altered the evidence, you're prima facie guilty of obstruction of justice. You've also showed the jury you're a lying SOB who covers your tracks to hide anything you figure might make you look bad. Do you think they're going to believe anything else you have to say if they found you planted fake evidence or otherwise misled them? Not hardly. Besides, some judges will allow the prosecutor to argue the theory that alteration of evidence can be seen as an indication of prior planning of a crime. Congratulations, you just turned justifiable homicide into premeditated murder.

Here the American Law Institute is filming a CLE-TV continuing legal education training film for attorneys. From left the panel includes the author, prosecutor Andy Yurick, defense lawyer Jeff Weiner, and Dick Nassberg of ALI, the moderator. The topic is defense of the justifiable shooting case.

Do not leave the scene of the shooting. There is a common law principle that says, "flight equals guilt." The argument is that a person who did the right thing would have stood his ground to explain himself to the authorities and the community, and only a guilty man would flee, to escape what he knew to be righteously deserved punishment. You don't want to fit the latter profile. But, there are times when it would make sense to leave the scene of a self-defense shooting. Perhaps there was no hope of getting emergency medical help there and you had to rush a wounded victim of the criminal to a hospital. Perhaps angry accomplices of the downed criminal were closing in to attack you. If the latter happens, as you leave you should shout at the top of your lungs, "Someone call the police and an ambulance! I'm going for the police and an ambulance!" History shows that some decent person who has heard you say that is likely to come forth and testify that it is true.

Then, head straight for police, ambulance, telephone, etc. If responding police interdict you en route, you want to be able to show that you were indeed heading for the PD, the hospital, or the nearest point of communication.

Carry a cell phone. This technology is to the private, armed citizen what the portable radio is to the police officer, a lifeline to survival and emergency assistance.

Be the first to call in. If you were a mugging victim who had to shoot an armed robber, ear-witnesses might have heard shouts and a pistol shot. They rush to their windows and see you with the smoking gun standing over the body of the deceased. They call in and say, "A man has murdered someone outside my home," and the stage is set. It's not a pretty stage. The criminal justice system is geared to the concept that the person who calls in and reports a crime, the complainant, is the victim, and the person they call to report is the perpetrator. If you don't win "the race to the telephone," you can end up being seen as the perpetrator who was reported in a criminal act of violence.

Most armed encounters don't end with shooting. Usually, when a criminal realizes he has attacked someone who has the power to kill him if his attack continues, he flees. This is the single most common pattern. The problem is, most citizens don't know what to do after they've driven off the mugger or attempted rapist. They just holster their gun and head for home.

But the mugger or rapist knows what to do. He doesn't appreciate this role reversal. He's going to ditch his weapon, make a phone call, and say, "A crazy person with a gun just tried to murder me! Here's his description…" And he describes you.

The cops catch up with you. You admit that you pulled the gun on the guy. "But he was going to rob/rape/murder me," you tell the responding officers. "He was going to hurt you so badly you had to pull a deadly weapon on him…and you didn't call us? Who do you think you're kidding? You're under arrest."

Remember: whoever calls in first is the victim/complainant. Whoever calls in second or doesn't call in at all becomes the criminal suspect by default. This happens with particular frequency these days in road rage situations. Why would the guy who tried to run you off the road call in and lie about what happened? For the same reason he tried to run you off the road! He's an out-of-control scumbag! Face it, they exist. That's why we have cops, and that's why you carry a gun.

Don't be standing there holding a gun when the police arrive. They've been called to the scene by a report describing "an armed man, there now." You do not want to look like "an armed man, there now." This is another reason that it is best to carry a holster of good quality and design that allows quick, one-handed re-holstering by feel.

If at all possible, have the gun already holstered before police arrive. Setting the gun down is not the best idea, for a number of reasons, some tactical and some evidentiary.

If you have to keep the suspect at gunpoint, and officers arrive and yell at you to drop the gun, do exactly what they say. *Drop the gun!* Make sure you're far enough away from the downed suspect that he can't reach it. Now you know yet another reason why professionals carry guns that are

"drop safe" and cannot discharge from impact when they hit the concrete.

Don't take it personally. The cops aren't mind readers. If it's any comfort to you, they'll do the same to me, even if I have my gun in one hand and badge in the other. If they don't know who I am, or even if they're local and can't recognize me in the dark, they don't know the badge is real. I'll be ordered to drop the gun too. Believe me, I will. I don't want to be killed in a mistaken identity shooting caused by my failure to comply with the lawful command of a police officer, and neither do you.

Don't become indignant with the police. They may treat you like a murder suspect. Well, guess what, you are one. The officers won't know different until this is all sorted out. If you start yelling and showing off or in any way resist, you "fit the profile" of the kind of out-of-control, violent person that juries like to see put away in prison where they won't harm innocent people.

Don't lie! At the scene you should establish that this man attacked you (or your family), and that you will sign a complaint against him. Point out witnesses and evidence that you know about before they disappear. Then, politely refuse to discuss the matter further until you have spoken with an attorney.

The time may come when you need to speak. A good lawyer who knows that the prosecutor is honest and reasonable may well advise you, some days after the shooting, that it is in your best interests to speak to investigators and DA's office personnel. If you choose to do so – and it often is a good idea – make sure the attorney is there with you, make sure you have the discussion videotaped by a professional court reporting service…*and don't lie about anything.*

If you don't know the answer to a question, say "I don't know." People feel during an interrogation that they're on the child side of a parent/child thing, and feel a compelling need to say something that will satisfy the questioner. Don't fall victim to that. If you don't know the answer, say, "I don't know."

Be completely honest with your attorney. He can't help you if he gets blindsided by something the other side knows that he or she doesn't.

If you think you fouled up in some small way, tell the attorney privately before police or prosecutors question you. You can't treat gangrenous tissue. If you ignore it and hope it will go away, it will spread and destroy a healthy limb or the entire organism. Gangrenous tissue must be amputated to save the rest. If you've done something wrong in some small detail, it's survivable. The jury may not like it that in a fear-filled moment you called the attacker a filthy name as you pulled the trigger, but they will understand. However, if you say you didn't and they later find out that you did, they won't believe anything else you have to say, and you're sunk. The jury can accept your not being perfect, but they'll never accept your lying to them.

Avoid discussing the shooting until it has been adjudicated. You drop into the neighborhood tavern for an after-work beer, a week subsequent to having been involved in a justifiable shooting. A friend asks you about it. You begin to speak, and some drunk says, "If I'd been you, I woulda' emptied the whole damn clip into that f---in' S.O.B.!" What do you want to bet that down at the end of the bar, there's a second drunk, who is going to remember this conversation as *you* saying, "I shoulda' emptied the whole damn clip into that f---in' SOB"?

It would be better if every person in the tavern could testify that they heard you say clearly, "Thanks for caring, but it was a very unpleasant experience and I would really rather not discuss it."

There is a possibility that you will be arrested after a self-defense shooting, and held in custody until things are sorted out. Overnight stays or all-weekend stays are not infrequent, and you might wind up in a common holding tank. Assorted unsavory people, some of whom will seem like decent folks, will approach you. You don't need me to tell you about the ones who will want things from you that you don't want to give. What we're concerned with at the moment is the friendly guy who asks you, "What happened, Buddy?"

Don't let the conversation start. There is an excellent chance that you've just been hit up by the resident snitch. He's worried about doing time and he'd sell his own mother for a good plea bargain. He has already snitched off all his criminal friends and has nothing left to bargain with. Tomorrow morning he's going to quietly ask to have a chat with a senior detective, somewhere private. He'll say, "You know that straight citizen type you brought in last night, who's gonna tell you he killed that guy in self-defense? Well, he told me he killed the guy 'cause he stiffed him on a dope deal. I'll testify to that, if you can just cut me a good deal on my little problem…"

It's his word against yours. If everyone else in the holding cell will testify, "Yeah, those guys were talkin' off in a corner by themselves for half, three-quarters of an hour," it will look as if his lies are the truth. It would be better if all those other people could remember you saying the same thing you would have said in the tavern: "Thanks for caring, but it was a very painful experience and I'd really rather not discuss it." Then step away and keep your distance. Stay solitary.

Having to use deadly force against another human being is never pleasant for a normal person. Even for law enforcement officers, whose training prepares them for it, it can be one of the most shattering line-of-duty events in a career that is constantly exposed to human tragedy.

But going through a trial and being wrongly accused will be a more soul-wrenching experience yet, and even more destructive (and far more expensive) to your loved ones. By avoiding the common mistakes mentioned above, you can save yourself and your family a great deal of grief.

I know this better than most people. I've been doing peer counseling with cops and armed citizens who've had to shoot people since 1981, when the famous post-shooting trauma psychologist, Dr. Walter Gorski, taught me in the discipline. Dr. Gorski and I have both seen people who gave up police work or gave up carrying a gun rather than face it.

If they couldn't face it, it's probably good that they got out in time, because the possession of a power you aren't fully prepared to command will get you into more trouble than it will get you out of. And not being able to face the aftermath could make you hesitate in a moment when only your immediate and decisive action could save innocent life.

But let me close by reminding you of one thing. Most of the people who know all these ramifications to their ugliest depths – Dr. Gorski, myself, and a great many others – still carry guns. It is a conscious and well-informed decision.

We would rather face the psychological trauma of killing a criminal, than the trauma of standing by helpless as he murdered an innocent victim. And we know enough not to make the above mistakes that would create unnecessary grief for ourselves, our loved ones, and others.

And so do you.

CHAPTER TWELVE

ACCESSORIZING

Responsible Customizing

Man has enhanced his weapons since he first stood erect and picked them up. Perhaps one caveman realized that a club with a wider end would have more momentum and hit harder then the untapered club used by the leader of tribe in the next valley. Sometimes the personalizing was just in the form of decoration to mark the weapon as this warrior's own and helped prevent theft. It also gave him more ego investment in the tool that might one day save his life.

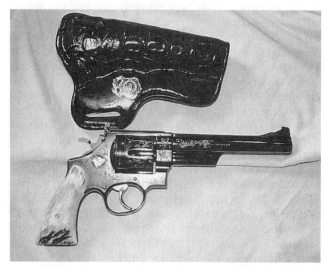

A "Barbecue Gun." This engraved, gold-inlaid S&W Model 629 also sports an action job by its owner, Detective Denny Reichard, and MeproLight night sights. Yes, he can control .44 Magnum recoil with those slim bone grips. You have to know Denny. The hand-tooled holster, with a miniature of the owner's shield, completes the ensemble.

The Author's Glock 17 has all "working mods," most from GlockWorks. Sights are Heinie Straight Eight with tritium. Pre-ban +2 magazine brings the fully loaded capacity to 20 rounds of 9mm Parabellum. InSights M3 light installs quickly on the frame and comes off almost as fast.

A couple of men I respect enormously, who've both "been there and done it", are known to possess what they call "barbecue guns." These are fancy, nay, *ornate* pistols that certainly work just fine, but most of the attention lavished upon them has been cosmetic rather than utilitarian. For one shooter it's an engraved and gold inlaid Colt .45 automatic with ivory grips. For the other, it's an engraved Smith & Wesson .44 Magnum with stag handles. My friends wear these guns to commemorate special occasions.

Pride of ownership is a good thing. Having your name or initials engraved on your gun makes it less desirable to a thief and easier to recover if stolen, though it impairs resale value. Today, most custom work done on handguns is more utilitarian than cosmetic.

That includes refinishing. While a gun with a new hardchrome finish may look better than before, it's also more impervious to the elements. Some finishes, like Robar's NP3, add an element of lubricity that make the gun work better.

White spots on an anodized blue S&W Model 3944 show where Rick Devoid has taken the sharp edges off. Such a job is cheap and the "user-friendliness" is huge. Devoid usually blends finish back as it was...

Action Jobs

In many cases, the most useful modification will be an "action job" that allows the trigger to be pulled more smoothly and cleanly. Remember, you don't need "light" so much as you need "smooth." That said, some guns that come with very heavy triggers – Colt DAO autos, the Kel-Tech P-11, and some others – can afford to lose a few pounds of pull weight.

In addition to double-action-only action slick and spurless hammer, Al Greco has installed a permanent trigger stop on the author's S&W Model 625 to reduce backlash.

What you don't want on any handgun that might actually be used to hold a human being at gunpoint is what a layman might call a "hair trigger." Most gunsmiths and forensic evidence technicians would define 4 pounds as an absolute minimum pull weight. Some go a little higher.

It never hurts to have the trigger's surface smoothed off, at the front and on the edges. Some may need the back edge of the trigger and the rear edge of the trigger guard smoothed as well. Certain shooters may benefit from having the inside bottom surface of a Glock's trigger guard taken down a little as well, if the size and shape of their fingers are such that the trigger finger drags on the inside of the guard.

Garrey Hindman at Ace Custom did the superb trigger work on this S&W 4506. The rear of the trigger guard and the trigger have been polished glass-smooth to match the internal action hone. The jewelling on the trigger and barrel are cosmetic, but nice touches.

Smooth triggers are also an important amenity for those who train seriously. We've found that after two or three days of intensive shooting on the range, a serrated trigger will often have produced a weeping blister.

You want smooth, not light. This Gunsite Custom S&W Airweight by Ted Yost is just as slick, and even more reliable, with a long mainspring (top) instead of the shorter, slightly lighter aftermarket replacement spring, below.

It is always a good idea for any revolver that is going to be kept or carried for self-defense to be rendered double-action-only. This eliminates the danger of both a hair trigger discharge if the gun is cocked, and the false allegation that such a thing happened when in fact it didn't. Grinding off the hammer spur isn't enough. The single-action cocking notch on the hammer (internal) needs to be removed by a competent and qualified gunsmith or armorer, or a new DAO hammer needs to be fitted.

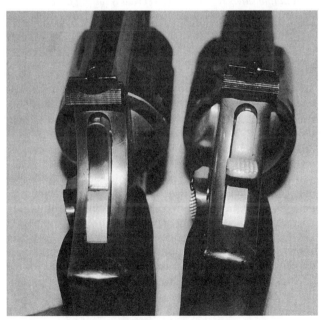

Right, a stock S&W Model 686; left, the same gun rendered double-action-only with the hammer spur removed. Reshaped and lighter, the hammer falls faster — better reliability in double-action shooting and slightly faster "lock time," i.e., a shorter interval between when the hammer begins to fall and when the shot goes off.

This seems less necessary on semiautomatic pistols. The more rearward placement of the hammer spur on an auto makes it more awkward to thumb-cock and, thus, less believable that someone would do so. A cocked auto pistol will also usually have a heavier trigger pull than a cocked double-action revolver. That said, fear of both accidents and false accusations of accidents have led a great many police departments, and more than a few citizens, to go with the double-action-only trigger concept on semiautomatic pistols as well as revolvers.

Safety Devices

A 1911 grip safety can dig and even lacerate the hand if it is not wide, edge-free, and smoothly polished. The thumb safeties of 1911 and P-35 type pistols are often too small, and rarely ambidextrous. An enlarged thumb safety lever makes that part more positive in use for many shooters, while the ambidextrous safety is desirable for any serious potential combatant and is of course a necessity for south-paws using such guns.

Most oversize magazine releases cause problems, but this useful one from GlockWorks is the exception. Author's Glock 17 also sports a Cominolli thumb safety.

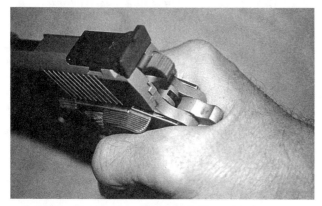

A thumb safety the size of a gas pedal is too big for carry, but some like it for competition. Adjustable sights can be argued either way. Springfield Armory, however, has already replaced the too narrow grip safety with a beavertail on current versions of this gun, their Trophy Match .45.

Excellent aftermarket parts of this type are available from Cylinder & Slide Shop, 800-448-1713; Ed Brown Products, 573-565-3261; and Wilson Custom, 870-545-3618, among many others. These three sources can usually retrofit the parts to your gun for you.

A thumb safety can be added to some guns that don't normally come that way. Joe Cominolli, at www.cominol-lio.com, can install one for your Glock, though at this writing he makes the unit for right-handed use only. Do you have a DAO S&W auto with a "slickslide" design? Rick Devoid, at www.tarnhelm.com, can install a dedicated, ambidextrous thumb safety on its slide for you. He's also the source for the one functional "smart gun" available at this writing, the Mag-naTrigger-modified S&W revolver, and finally, he can install a Murabito safety on any frame size S&W wheelgun to make the cylinder latch perform double duty as a thumb safety that works with a downward stroke like a 1911.

Removing or deactivating a safety device can get you into a world of trouble if you're ever accused of wrongdoing with a gun. A good lawyer won't have much trouble convincing a dozen laypersons that anyone who would deacti-vate the safety device on a lethal weapon had to be reckless. However, when you pay out of your pocket to enhance the safety devices on a firearm – to literally make it safer than it was when it left the factory – you can easily be shown to possess an unusually high degree of responsibility.

As a rule, any after-market "safety" that makes the gun go to the "fire" position faster and more positively when needed, will also make it go to the "on-safe" position faster and more positively, and it's hard to argue with that.

Reliability Packages

Some guns need an internal work-over before they achieve optimum function. For many years, this was true of the 1911 and the Browning P-35. For most of their history, they were military-specification pistols designed to work with mil-spec ammo. That is, full-metal-jacket round nose. Out of the box, they would feed hardball ammo, or Remington hollow-points that were jacketed up and over the tip to the same ogive as hardball, and that was about it. If you wanted them to run with more efficient, wider-mouth JHP bullets, you had to pay a gunsmith to "throat them out."

You want your defense gun work done by a master. Bill Laughridge, shown in the middle of his busy Cylinder & Slide Shop, fills the bill.

Both types of guns are now produced by a number of sources. Some companies still make "mil-spec" versions of the Colt and the Browning, of which the above remains true.

But there are many versions that now come from the box "factory throated" and ready to feed most anything you stuff in it. These include currently produced Colt and Browning brands, and also the Kimber, the Para-Ordnance, and the upper lines of Springfield Armory production.

Shown are two of the author's favorite "combat custom" Colt .45 autos. Top, is the LFI Special by Dave Lauck; below, is a "Workhorse" by D.R. Middlebrooks.

Your Beretta, Glock, HK, Kahr, Kel-Tec, Ruger, SIG, S&W, or Taurus auto as currently produced should not need a "reliability package." However, like some of the other models mentioned, they might benefit to a greater or lesser degree from having some of the sharp edges beveled at hand contact points. This is particularly true of the standard-line Smith & Wesson pistols. Any of them might also benefit from a good action hone, too.

Recoil Reduction Devices

The general consensus among defense-oriented combat shooters is that most recoil reduction devices pass the point of diminishing returns because they vent hot gases upward in a way that could strike the shooter in the face or eyes when shooting from a "speed rock" or "protected gun" position. That said, they also tame muzzle jump very effectively. Some people who carry guns simply don't have those close-to-the-body shooting positions in their repertoires and don't feel a loss in carrying a "compensated" gun.

For concealed carry, you don't want one of those humongous comps that hangs off the end of the gun and looks like a cross between a TV spy's "silencer" and Buck Rogers' ray gun. A good "Carry-Comp", as executed by Mark Morris in Washington State (www.morriscustom.com), will end up the same size as a Colt Government Model, but will feel almost recoil free. I have one in 10mm on which the comp works so efficiently, the gun all but recoils downward. When they're properly installed, you won't lose accuracy; my Morris 10mm CarryComp has won first place open-sight, big-

The author is partial to this Glock 23 for certain competitions. Modifications include…

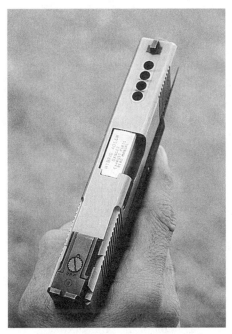

…Schuemann Hybrid-Porting, which radically reduces recoil, and BoMar sights, which enhance the capability of precision hits. Note the warning stamped on the chamber area of barrel, however.

bore awards for me at 100-yard NRA Hunter Pistol matches, shooting against Thompson/Center single shots and long-barreled Magnum hunting revolvers. It will just let you shoot a whole lot faster. This is the gun I was shooting when my daughter, Justine, and I won the speed-oriented match that

Combat pistol champ Marty Hayes has won awards with this Hybrid-ported Glock 22 in .40 S&W. He prefers...

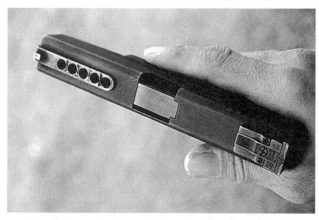

...this full-length sight radius, with Millett adjustable sights.

though the best gunsmiths can carefully balance a 1911's action to make it work with the reduced recoil that comes with the concept.

Seen in profile, Hybrid-Ported Glocks look like ordinary full-size (top) and compact .40s. The stainless Caspian slide on the bottom gun is easier to mill for adjustable sight installation than the super-hard Glock slide.

Beveled and Funneled Magazine Wells

When the 1911 single-stack pistol was *the* gun for serious combat shooters, a popular modification was beveling out the magazine well so a magazine would slip in more easily during loading or reloading. This worked, and has become a standard feature, on top-line 1911's by Colt, Kimber, Springfield Armory, etc. The guns with wider, double-stack magazines benefit less from this feature, since the

made us National Champion Parent/Child team in sub-junior (child age 13 and down) class at the first National Junior Handgun Championships. The ammunition was Triton's powerful Hi-Vel, spitting a 155-grain bullet at an honest 1,300 feet per second. With the CarryComp, the gun just sort of quivered as it went off.

With the exception of the brilliant Mag-na-Port concept pioneered by my old friend Larry Kelly, most recoil reduction jobs will magnify the blast of each shot, often to unpleasant levels. Mag-na-Port, I've found, works best on revolvers and long guns, and on autos with open-top slides like the Beretta, Glock Tactical/Practical, and Taurus. The factory-compensated Glocks work on a similar principle.

Hybrid-porting, developed by the brilliant Will Schuemann, gives dramatic recoil reduction with a series of big ports that go down the top of the barrel. The upside is great recoil reduction; downside is bright flash in front of the eyes in night shooting and significant velocity loss. This system seems to be at its best on the revolver and the Glock pistol,

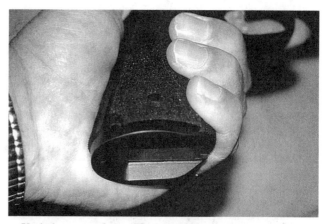

Variations on a theme. The extended, oversize magazine well on this Springfield TRP enhances reloading speed, but makes gun slightly less concealable and demands padded-bottom magazines for positive seating.

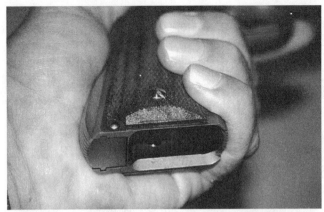

Merely beveling the frame without add-ons works quite well, as on this Springfield Trophy Match.

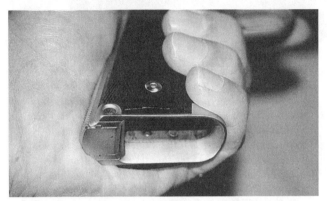

The most expensive option, and for some the best of all, is a swaged out magazine well, this one by Dave Lauck on a Colt.

tapered top of the magazine combines with the already large magazine well to create a funnel effect.

The cottage industry developed the concept into magazine chutes, which could either bolt onto the gun (requiring padded-bottom magazines, since the edges of the chutes extended below the pistol frames) or be swaged or welded into the gun butt by a good pistolsmith without lengthening the grip frame. For a single-stack magazine pistol in particular, this is an excellent idea. There is a distinct improvement in reloading speed even for experts, and those new to the gun will benefit even more.

Magazine chutes are now even made for the Glock, which probably doesn't need it. The bottom line of any modification is, if it doesn't hurt anything and it helps something, it's probably a good idea. Properly installed magazine chutes and beveled magazines fit that description. If they don't extend the length of the grip-frame, they have no disadvantages except cost. They definitely do make magazine changes easier all the way around.

Extended Slide Releases

As a rule, these are not a great idea. The slide releases of most standard pistols are adequate in size. Enlarging them can cause holster fit problems. There are also reliability issues. Oversize slide lock levers put extended weight on the part that levers it out of position and either keeps it from doing its job when the magazine runs dry, or more commonly, causes it to bounce up and lock the slide open prematurely while the pistol is cycling.

You shouldn't need an oversize slide release lever or magazine release button on most pistols; standard 1911 size parts do fine, as seen on this top-grade Springfield Armory pistol.

The single exception is probably the Glock pistol. Glock intentionally made the slide release a low-profile part, assuming that most shooters would jack the slide to reload the gun instead of the faster method of thumbing the lever. A slightly extended slide stop lever is available from Glock, originally developed for the target model guns, that will fit the concealed carry and duty models. The FBI has reportedly ordered it on all its duty Glocks. If you have trouble operating the standard lever, definitely retrofit with this one. It is a Glock part, so it doesn't void the warranty, and it works fine and has no disadvantages.

Checkered/Squared Trigger Guards

Some of the earlier practical shooting masters, such as Ray Chapman and Ross Seyfried, shot with the index fingers of their support hands wrapped around the front of the trigger guards of their Colt .45 autos. They had large hands and short guards and could get away with it. To make it work better, they checkered the front of the trigger guard and sometimes changed the guard to a more square shape.

For the overwhelming majority of shooters, having the support hand's index finger under the trigger guard will

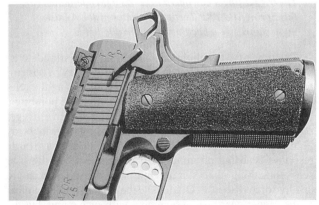

Well thought out "factory customizing" is seen on this Springfield Armory top-grade TRP (Tactical Response Pistol). Rugged adjustable night sights, easily manipulated ambidextrous thumb safety, "just right" street trigger, Barnhart Burner grips, checkered front-strap for a non-slip hold, and ergonomic beavertail grip safety with "speed bump" to allow activation in any reasonable firing grasp.

work better. If, however, the shooter insists on securing the weak hand finger on the guard, checkering will help reduce its natural tendency to slip off.

Flashlight Attachments

The HK USP began the trend of a dust cover (the front portion of the frame) molded or milled to accept a quickly attaching and detaching flashlight. HK had its own, called the UTL (Universal Tactical Light). Other companies quickly followed suit.

Glock, Springfield Armory, and a broad array of other brands have this option. The M-3 Illuminator by Insights Technologies works particularly well in this function.

If your pistol does not have an integral attachment rail, do not despair. SureFire makes a pistol-mounted flashlight that attaches to a standard 1911, Beretta, or other auto, with a part that replaces the slide stop. This is my personal favorite "gun flashlight"; it is naturally ergonomic, extremely bright, and ruggedly durable. I keep one on the pistol that I usually have at my bedside when at home. It is intended to be a dedicated unit, not a quickly attaching and detaching accessory.

The flashlight can be a lifesaver in more ways than one. We'll never know how many people who were shot when they reached in the dark for "something that looked like a gun" would be alive today if the person who shot them had been able to see that they were holding a harmless object. It wasn't the shooter's fault, but this technology would have saved those shooters much suffering, internal self-doubt, and lawsuits.

The trigger finger can operate the M3 light one-handed on this Springfield TRP Tactical Operator pistol. Adjustable night sights give a back-up option in dim light.

The powerful flashlight can also blind and intimidate an opponent. I've seen it happen in the field. However, remember that using your flashlight to search is like using the telescopic sight of your rifle to scan for game: you're pointing a loaded gun at anything you look at. I want a heavy trigger pull and/or an engaged safety on the weapon to which my light is attached. This will minimize the chance of a "startle response" causing an unintended discharge when the user sees something that startles him but doesn't warrant a deadly force response. Obviously, the finger should be clear of the trigger guard when searching with such a unit, but the heavy trigger and/or manual safety is one more redundant safety net to prevent tragedy.

Liability points

Few creatures can be more desperate than an attorney who has no case. Many people involved in law enforcement

have seen attorneys try to find negligence in after-market grips, colored or glow-in-the-dark gun sights, even the name of the gun. "Persuader" sounds more sinister than "Model 500," and "Cobra" sounds more violent and deadly than "Agent," even though in both cases it is essentially the same shotgun and revolver, respectively, under discussion.

Does this mean you shouldn't modify your gun, as some have suggested? This writer personally thinks that is going too far. Certainly, it would be a good idea to avoid a gun

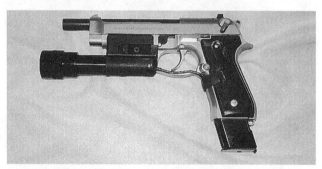

Looks spacey, works great. The author's bedside Beretta, a 92FS tuned by Bill Jarvis. A 6-inch Bar-Sto barrel gives pupil-of-the-eye accuracy at home defense distances, and added velocity that brings hot 9mm ammo up to otherwise unattainable ballistics. The extended barrel is Mag-na-Ported to reduce muzzle jump. Trijicon night sights allow precise shooting if the user chooses not to activate the powerful SureFire flashlight. The extended magazine creates a 21-shot pistol. The result is a high-capacity handgun with surgical accuracy that combines the recoil of a .380 with the power of a .357 Magnum and gives the user command of various light situations.

with a controversial name like "Pit Bull" or "Bonnie and Clyde," both of which have actually been used by American gunmakers. More important, however, is to avoid a "hair trigger" (lighter than 4 pounds) or a deactivated safety. Either can create the impression of a reckless gun owner.

There's nothing wrong with personalizing. This Seecamp .32 was special ordered with the author's initials as the serial number.

We've covered the innards and what might be called the superstructure of the handgun, but have not yet touched upon two critical points, the sights and the type and fit of the grips or stocks. That's because each is so important that they're worth their own chapters. We'll get to that immediately.

Combat Handgun Sights

The sights are your weapon's primary aiming tools. When a defense gun has to be employed, the sequence is something like this: Enemy fighter sighted, need to shoot confirmed…missiles locked on target…missiles launched…track target, prepare to launch more missiles if necessary.

The "missiles locked on target" part is accomplished by indexing the handgun, and that is best accomplished with the sights. But we must be able to see the sight under adverse conditions such as dim light, tunnel vision, and animal instinct screaming at us to focus on the threat when knowledge tells us to focus on the sights.

Sights on a combat handgun should be big, blocky, and easy to see under assorted light conditions. They should be rugged enough that they won't fall off the gun or be knocked out of alignment if the wearer falls on the holstered gun in a fight, or the gun bangs against a wall as the user ducks for cover, or if the gun is dropped on a hard surface in the course of a struggle.

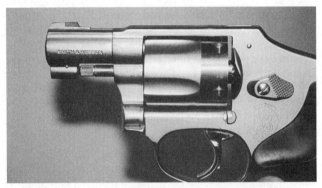

Master revolversmith Andy Cannon built up the front sight of this Model 940 S&W 9mm revolver for the author, and widened the rear sight proportionally. The improvement in "shootability" is dramatic.

The general rule of thumb is that fixed sights are more durable than adjustable sights. There are exceptions to that rule, however. We've seen fixed rear sights held in place in their dovetail by an Allen screw come loose and drift sideways or even fall off a pistol. The plastic fixed sights that come on some modern guns may be more likely to break than the most rugged steel adjustable sights. The latter include such time-proven units as the BoMar or the MMC adjustable night sight, which has large, shielding "ears" on either side, similar to the current S&W service auto adjustable sight design.

Night Sights

Tritium night sights go back to the Bar-Dot developed by Julio Santiago back in the 1970s. They have come a long way. Available in a multitude of shapes and colors, they not only aid in sighting on an identified target in the dark, but can help an officer find a gun that was dropped in the dark after he has won the struggle with the offender trying to take it. For those of us who travel a lot, waking up in the middle of the night in a dark, strange room is not conducive to finding your pistol. The glowing dots of the night sights, if the gun has been positioned with the sights toward the sleeping owner, are like airstrip landing lights that guide the legitimate user's eye and hand to the defensive weapon.

You can get three dots all the same color that line up horizontally, the type that works best for this writer. You can get one dot on top of the other; the configuration master pistolsmith and designer Dick Heinie dubbed the "Straight Eight" because it resembles a figure-8 in the dark. IWI pioneered an option now available from most other makers: one color front dot, a different color for the rear dots. If the front dot is the brighter color, the eye goes to it instinctively, and this concept also keeps the new shooter, or the one whose gun doesn't fit, from aligning the dots incorrectly and shooting way off to one side. Some, like officer survival expert Jim Horan, prefer just the single tritium dot on the front sight with no corresponding rear reference.

Eyesight varies hugely between different people. Any of these concepts can work. The best bet is to try them all and see which works best for you. This writer has found the three-dot system to be most visible to his particular eyes. It also works with the StressPoint Index concept mentioned in the point-shooting chapter. When the shooter sees an equilateral triangle of dots, the top one will be on the front sight, and the StressPoint Index is in place.

There are many brands. At one time, it was a choice of Trijicon and a few also-rans. Today, the quality has gone up

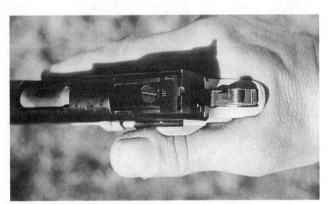

Because of the precise adjustments many consider these BoMar adjustable sights target equipment; but, they are extremely rugged and suitable for heavy duty.

The big rear notch of standard Beretta fixed sights…

...coupled with its proportionally large front sight, makes an easy combination for old or myopic eyes to see.

...and which is seen here in its multiple variations on Ring's brand dummy guns.

across the night sight industry, though I don't think anyone has yet exceeded Trijicon. I've been happy with the IWI night sights on my department-issue Ruger .45, with green up front and amber at the rear. I have no problem with the Meprolight sights on a pet Glock 22 that I carry often. Trijicons adorn my bedside Beretta, and a couple of my Glocks

Andy Stanford, who quantified the term "surgical speed shooting," is a big fan of the Ashley Express concept, which he demonstrates here...

and SIGs. I have Heinie Straight Eight sights on a Morris Custom Colt .45 and a Glock 17. They all work fine.

It has been said that you shouldn't need night sights, because if it's too dark to see your sights it's too dark to see your target. That's untrue for two reasons. First, the vagaries of artificial illumination and natural light and shadow are such that you might indeed be able to identify your opponent but not get a clear sight picture. Moreover, if the shape in the dark yells at you, "Die, infidel American!" and you see a muzzle flash, I think your target is identified and I for one would like for you to have the option of night sights.

Express Sights

Pioneered by my friend and student Ashley Emerson, whose company Ashley Outdoors is now in other hands and making these excellent sights under the title AO, the express sight with Ashley's copyrighted Big Dot makes a lot of sense for a lot of situations. The far-sighted person who can see to identify the threat just fine but can't see anything but a fuzzball at gun-sight distance is an ideal candidate for these. The rear is a shallow "v" with a white line down the middle, and the front sight is a humongous white (or glowing Tritium) circle. Put together, it looks like a big lollipop. Easy to see, fast to hit with in close. The express sight got its name because it has been used for well over a century on the powerful Express rifles hunters used for the biggest, most dangerous game at close range.

As noted earlier, it's subjective. This writer can't shoot worth a damn with express sights on a pistol at 25 yards. At very close range, though, they are slightly faster for me and tremendously faster and more accurate for those who can't see a regular sight picture. Definitely worth looking at, no pun intended.

Full- And Half-Ghost Rings

"Ghost ring" was Jeff Cooper's term for the 19th century deer hunter's trick of removing the sight disk from an aperture ("peep") sight and just looking through the big circle that held it to get a faster, coarser sight picture with his rifle. On a rifle or shotgun it turns out to be remarkably accurate, and Jeff did us all a favor in revitalizing the concept.

It has been tried on pistols with less success. Because the aperture is so much farther from the eye than it would be on

Police gun expert Gary Paul Johnston displays the "half ghost ring" sight he designed for Wayne Novak. The author feels this brilliant concept has not achieved the popularity it deserves.

Optical Sights

Conventional telescopic sights for handguns are too big for all-day-carry holstering, and because of their long eye relief generally too slow to aim with under combat conditions at combat distances. World champion Jerry Barnhart proved in the 1980s that the internal red dot sight was faster than any conventional iron sight. He proceeded to kick butt with it in matches until, in open class, red dot sights were all you saw.

a long gun, you don't get the same effect. It can be fast in close, and does give a big sight picture for those who can't focus on conventional sights, but there don't seem to be a lot of people who are terribly accurate with them. Some are, mind you, but not many. There are various brands available; for current options, check the advertising pages of *American Handgunner* magazine.

More useful to more people is a concept developed by gun expert Gary Paul Johnston and made a reality by Wayne Novak, master combat pistolsmith and designer of the famous, streamlined Novak fixed rear sight. The ghost ring is simply cut in half. A big, rectangular post front sight is now seen through a huge rear "u" notch. It is easy to line up even for myopic people with their corrective lenses off. I shot the one on Gary Paul's Novak Custom Browning when we were at a Winchester ammunition seminar together at Gunsite Ranch in Arizona, and was very favorably impressed with the combination of speed and accuracy it delivered. *Definitely* better than full ghost ring sights in this writer's opinion, but an apparently well-kept secret and, to my knowledge, available only through Novak's .45 Shop, 304-485-9525.

I once told William McMoore, designer of a fascinating work in progress called the Sceptre pistol that blends elements of the Glock and the 1911, that I thought the best "geezer sights" would be simply a square notch rear and a post front, but both absolutely huge. He tells me he has Ashley Emerson working on that very concept. Stay tuned.

The author's friend John Pride, gunfight survivor and many times National Police Handgun champion and Bianchi Cup winner, has a Tasco Pro-Point on the match gun he's wearing on his hip. But in his hand is a compact S&W auto with what may be the only practical concealed carry red dot optical sight at this writing...

...the extremely compact Tasco Optima...

"Geezer sights" Gunsmith/cop Denny Reichard "hogged out" the rear sight of this N-frame S&W for an aging shooter, and created a sight picture even fuzzy eyes can see.

...which fits on a pistol thus.

They are so fast and accurate because the unit's big screen gives a "head's up display" that is much more easily seen than the image in any telescopic sight when you're moving and shooting fast. The aiming dot and the target appear to be on the same visual plane, so the old problem of good focus on opponent or good focus on sights but not good focus on both is eliminated. U.S. military elite teams have gone to these in a big way. In Somalia in 1993, and much more so in the Afghanistan reprisal of 2001 and beyond, international news cameras caught countless images of these high-tech sights on American M-4 assault rifles.

The state of the art has improved enormously since the early days, but there are two problems. One is that they run on batteries, and anything that is battery-dependant can fail you at the worst possible time. The other is that most of them are too bulky to carry in a holster, particularly concealed.

There have been numerous attempts to make a small, practical, concealed carry internal dot sight. Only one, in my opinion, is worth looking at: the Optima 2000 from Tasco. Resembling a high, circular rear sight, it sits behind the ejection port on the slide of a semi-auto pistol, clear of the holster. It may not hide under a T-shirt well, but it can conceal under a sport jacket. To conserve battery life, it turns itself off in the dark and turns itself on when exposed to light. (Hmmm…could this be a problem in a very dark room?)

The concept isn't perfect, but Tasco sets it up so you can use the pistol's regular sights right through the lens of the Optima 2000, whether you can see the red dot or not. This protects against battery failure. If you have vision problems and are ready to try a high-tech solution, this is worth looking at. Unfortunately, Tasco has recently closed its doors. While Tasco products will remain available on the secondary market, there won't be anything new rolling off the production line. At this time no one can tell what this will do to prices.

Laser Sights

Because I didn't embrace the laser sight as the wave of the future I've been described in letters to gun magazine editors as an old Luddite who can't understand new technology. *Au contraire.* I merely pointed out that while the laser sometimes has intimidation effect, it sometimes doesn't, and may even provoke a homicidal response. I speak from experience.

This doesn't mean the laser has no tactical place in the defensive handgun world, it just means it has to be seen and used rationally. Says famous police combat instructor Marty Hayes, "Maybe the laser will intimidate the bad guy, and maybe it won't. But if there's even a chance it will, I want the laser on my side and my officers' side."

Personally, I don't think "intimidation factor" is anywhere near the top of the list of the laser sight's attributes. In a tactical setting, I think a laser-sighted pistol is the tool of choice for anyone working with a "body bunker," the bullet-resistant barrier that is carried like a shield. To aim through its Lexan viewing port with conventional sights, you have to bend your arm to an angle so weak that you risk gun malfunctions, and accentuated recoil slows down your rate of accurate fire. Keeping the wrist locked (and most of the arm behind the shield, another advantage), aiming with the projected laser dot, simply makes more sense and is safer for the officer. (Or the civilian: I also think the ballistic raid shield would be an extremely useful thing for an armed citizen to have in the bedroom closet in case of a home invasion.)

If both your arms are injured and you can't raise the gun, the laser dot gives you options. If you insist on using point-shooting techniques, the laser sight may indeed be the only thing that saves you. Marty Hayes' tests with students indicate that they handle night shooting problems distinctly better with laser sights than with regular night sights.

Certainly, there are downsides. The laser beam can track right back to you visually, giving your position away in the dark. This is made worse in fog or smoke, including gun smoke. A laser beam aimed through a window can be refracted, and the dot is no longer truly indicating where the gun is really pointed. If more than one of the good guys have lasers, it can be hard to tell whose dot is whose. If the bad guy is holding a hostage, you and your partner raise your guns, and one dot appears on the hostage's head and another on the criminal's, which one of you pulls the trigger?

In the end, all these problems can be solved by simply turning off the laser in dim light and fog, and trusting your regular gun sights when multiple dots are on multiple people or you have to shoot through glass. However, many instructors worry about shooters becoming "laser-dependent" and losing core skills. That, really, will depend on the students more than the instructors.

I feel the laser sight absolutely comes into its own as a firearms instructional aid. I use mine often to show students how easily a shot can be jerked off target by bad trigger control, or how accurately the students can shoot with their hands shaking violently. The demonstration can be done dry-fire in a classroom with a neutralized gun. In the students' own hands, the laser gives proof when they're jerking the trigger, and gives them instant positive feedback when they make a smooth stroke. In live fire in the dark, students can follow the laser dot's track and see graphically which techniques are working better for them in terms of recoil control.

Of the many laser sight options available, the most practical seem to be the modular ones that don't change the profile of the gun. At this writing, you're talking about two companies: Lasermax and Crimson Trace. Crimson Trace LaserGrips work particularly well in this regard. If you don't like them or don't need them, you can take them off. They are easily adjustable. On some models, the "finger in register on the frame" position can block the laser dot if you are shooting right-handed. The firm offers a pair on a dummy gun that is practical and economical for classroom training purposes.

The Lasermax unit replaces the recoil spring guide rod on Glock, SIG, Beretta, S&W, and 1911 pistols of that design, among others. This puts the light directly under the bore, an advantage. However, being at the "working end" of the pistol, the unit is also subjected to more heat and battering during firing than grip-mounted units. The Lasermax projects a pulsing dot, the Crimson Trace a solid one. The Crimson Trace best serves my own needs, but the Lasermax has also earned staunch supporters.

Fiber Optic

A fiber optic cylinder that gathers and focuses light and replaces your front sight can be a great aid in a fast, close pistol match done outdoors or in fading light. In the dark, it's useless – you want night sights for that – but for something like a bowling pin match, these things are ideal. There are also a number of people whose guns are likely to be used in lit conditions – shopkeepers, for example, given the

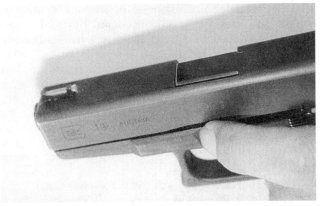

While they don't do much in the dark, these fiber-optic sights...

...can be a Godsend for aging or myopic eyes when there is any reasonable amount of ambient light for them to gather.

fact that most store robberies take place during business hours or just before or after closing, when the lights are still on – for whom such sights might be ideal. Accuracy is not so precise as the conventional post-in-notch sight picture, but speed can be awesome.

See the Proof

To determine what sights will be best for you for self-defense work, there is no substitute for getting out there and

shooting under different conditions. You have to find out for yourself what works best. Eyes are too individual for another person's suggestions to necessarily be the best for any one shooter. Once you've found something that works for you, check the other systems every few years. As we age, our eyes change, and a sighting system that just didn't work for you five years ago might be absolutely perfect for you now, and vice versa.

Making The Handgun Fit

Suppose you had to run a marathon, but they issued you the wrong running shoes. Three sizes too small, or three sizes too large. It's safe to say you won't perform your best, and if the mismatch in size is too grotesque, you may not be able to run at all. You might even get an injury trying.

you're too far back, you have poor leverage for steering and cannot operate the accelerator, clutch, or brake pedals efficiently.

A K-frame S&W is a perfect fit in the average adult male hand with (Hogue) grips that expose the backstrap. Note that the trigger finger is perfectly centered at the distal joint.

Different race: the stock car championships. You've got the most powerful, most maneuverable car on the track. Unfortunately, the driver's seat has been locked into position for someone a foot different from you in height. If you're too close to the wheel, you're hunched over it with a profoundly slowed ability to steer, and you can't reach the pedals without banging your knees on the steering column. If

Show and Go can go together. Hogue stocks on the author's Langdon Custom Beretta 92 fill the palm and feel great, while also looking great.

It's safe to say you're not going to win the race. In fact, the driver behind you in a less capable machine, but one that fits him perfectly, will soon leave you behind. And, if things get hairy and you can't manipulate the controls quickly and positively enough, you might go into the wall and be hurt or killed.

The police department doesn't issue every officer size 14 uniform shoes, nor does it lock the seat of every patrol car into position for a 6-foot, 7-inch lawman like Bill Jordan. Yet an amazing number of police departments issue the same size gun, often one that fits only larger hands, to all officers including the smallest. Then they seem surprised when many officers don't perform up to their potential.

As my teenager would say, "Well, *duh...*"

Fit of the equipment is critical to performance with the equipment. One advantage the private citizen has is that he or she doesn't have to trust his or her life to an issue firearm that's the wrong size. The "civilian" can go to the gun shop and buy something that fits properly. Now he or she is on the way to a maximum personal performance level.

As noted elsewhere in this book, the key dimension to fit is trigger reach. The index finger of the firing hand should be able to contact the trigger at the proper point while the barrel of the gun is in line with the long bones of the forearm. This will give the strongest combination of firm grip to control recoil in rapid fire, and maximum finger leverage for good trigger control at high speed.

The author won this Ruger Security Six more than a score of years ago at a regional championship. It has a Douglas barrel and action by Lou Ciamillo. Pachmayr Professional grips, cut only to the backstrap, give a perfect fit.

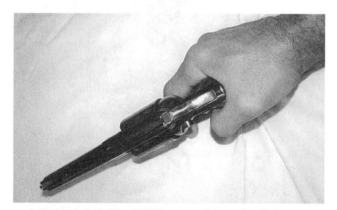

A Ruger Service Six .357 Magnum gives perfect fit for an average male hand with these Craig Spegel grips cut only to the backstrap of the grip-frame. Note that the barrel is in line with forearm, and the distal joint of the index finger is centered on the trigger.

Let's look at some examples of adapting guns to fit hands. The hands of the aforementioned Bill Jordan were huge, at least a digit longer in the fingers than those of the average man. Bill had to have his gloves custom made. Accordingly, the famous Jordan grips he designed for Steve Herrett had a big portion of wood added to the backstrap area, to push the web of his hand backward and give him "reaching room" to get his finger right to the joint on the trigger. The first time I picked up one of Bill's personal service revolvers, I felt like a little kid holding Daddy's gun. Bill, in turn, would have felt cramped using the smaller grips of my revolver.

The design factors are such that the revolver is much easier to adapt to different size hands than is the auto. This is particularly true of larger hands. Note how many big-handed men have put custom grips on tiny J-frame revolvers, grips that come rearward from the backstrap to increase their trigger reach. A petite female, conversely, will find that the J-frame fits her exactly when the web of her hand meets the backstrap. A female 5 feet 5 inches or shorter, with proportional hands, will usually lack about one digit's worth of finger length compared to the average adult male.

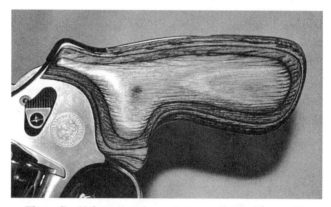

These slim N-frame revolver grips were designed by world record holder Jerry Miculek to give maximum reach to the trigger. They come standard on this S&W Performance Center Model 625 in .45 ACP.

The more research-oriented gun manufacturers have recognized this. Beretta figured out early on that their full-size Models 92 and 96 were big guns with long trigger reaches. They have offered their customers at least four hardware fixes for this. First came a shorter-reach trigger, which could be ret-

Here is a Beretta double-action 9mm in the hand of a 5-foot, 10-inch man...

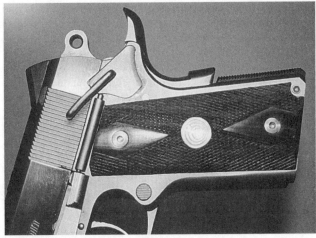

...and 5-foot woman. Note that she can barely reach the trigger.

This compact .45 caliber ParaOrdnance LDA Companion comes from the factory...

rofitted at the factory or by a factory-trained police armorer. Next came a special frame done for the Los Angeles County Sheriff's Department, which issues the Beretta 92 to deputies of all sizes. It had some material taken out of the frame at the upper backstrap area to get the web of the hand more "into" the gun and give the trigger finger greater reach.

Next came their Cougar series. Engineer types were most taken with the gun's rotary breech, but shooters and firearms instructors had far more appreciation for the altered frame dimension. The upper backstrap area was "niched out" to bring the hand more forward. Available in 9mm, .40 S&W, .357 SIG, and even .45 ACP, the Cougar was and is a much better fit for the small hand. Most recently, a redesigned 92/96 series pistol called the VerTek was introduced by Beretta. Essentially, it's the same gun with a light attachment rail up front and, much more importantly, a grip frame distinctly thinner in circumference. The shooter can not only get the trigger finger more forward, but can also get a stronger shooting hold with proportionally more of the grasping fingers in contact with the more svelte "handle."

Today's manufacturers pay more attention to "human engineering." This 9mm Ruger P95 is an extremely good fit in the average male hand.

Certain guns have had the almost mystical ability to feel good in hands of all sizes. The D-frame Colt revolver, typified by the Detective Special, is big enough for big hands yet small enough for small hands. In auto pistols, the classic examples are the Browning Hi-Power and the slim-grip M8 version of the HK P7.

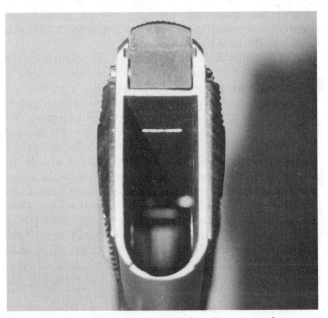

...with these slim-line grips. A slight enhancement for concealment, they can deliver huge enhancement of feel and control.

Walther pioneered the concept of an auto pistol with grip inserts that could adjust the size and circumference of the grasping circle. It was kept in the SW99 pistol, the collaboration between Smith & Wesson and Walther. This is a step forward.

Case In Point

The gun fit issue can be seen in microcosm by studying the history of the famous pistol that Colt introduced in 1911. In the early 20s, a study of how small arms had performed in the Great War determined that many soldiers felt the trigger of this pistol was too long to reach well. By the end of the decade, the military had created specifications for the 1911-A1. Among other changes, it had a much shorter trigger and a frame that was niched out just behind the trigger on each side. The intent was to enhance trigger reach, and that intent was dramatically fulfilled.

Before long, target shooters (who preferred to use the pad of their trigger finger, instead of the joint, for precise shooting) were having their personal guns retrofitted with longer triggers. Time went on. By the 1960s, the manufacturers' standard in place was that the "carry" Colt .45 auto, the Government Model or one of the Commander series, would have the short 1911-A1 trigger. In contrast, the Gold Cup target model would have a long, broad-surfaced trigger in what is known as the National Match configuration. This actually worked out pretty well for all concerned. Tastes changed as time wore on, and by the turn of the 21st century, most guns sold for carry had long triggers again. Progress is sometimes circular.

Let's say you have someone with truly huge hands. One of the regular competitors at the old Second Chance shoots was about 6 feet, 9 inches tall with proportional hands. He had a custom gunsmith build him a 1911 .45 auto with an incredibly long trigger, almost out to where the trigger guard is on a factory gun. The 'smith welded up a new trigger guard farther forward on the frame. This in turn, of course, demanded custom holsters, but the good-natured (and good-shooting) giant handgunner now had a 1911 that was literally made for his hand.

On the other end of the spectrum, the smartest female shooters and their coaches analyzed the situation too. In WWI, nutrition and prenatal care not being what they are today, the average adult male stood about 5 feet, 6 inches. The 1911-A1 trigger had in essence been engineered for hands proportional to that height, or smaller. The average adult female of today in this country stands about 5 feet, 5 inches. This means that the 1911-A1 pistol is *exactly the right size to fit most petite female hands* in terms of trigger reach. If the grip-frame is too long, the shorter Officer's size is readily available from Colt and other manufacturers. Thus, incongruous as it may sound, the big .45 auto – the gun of Mike Hammer and Sergeant Rock – is actually an excellent choice for the petite female hand. Privy to the 1920s study and 1911/1911-A1 metamorphosis and the reasons behind it, John Browning and Didionne Souave kept essentially the same trigger reach dimension as the 1911-A1 when they carefully crafted the Browning Hi-Power of 1935.

...while a petite woman has a proper grasp with the pad of the trigger finger in contact on the same gun.

This is why the Hi-Power fits so well in so many different hands, and why it is particularly appreciated by those with shorter fingers. Now, fast-forward again, to a modern pistol first produced in the 1990s, the Kahr. This gun is also particularly well configured for the small hand. It also points well. If you lay a Kahr over a Browning Hi-Power, you will see a remarkable similarity in shape. One of two things is clearly proven here: either Kahr designer Justin

The Browning Hi-Power, this one tuned by Novak, has the "magical" ability to fit well in the hand of the average man...

With the short 1911-A1 trigger on this Springfield Micro .45, the average adult male hand has perfect leverage with distal joint trigger finger placement...

...or a petite woman.

Moon did his homework and adapted the best of the Browning/Souave design to his own brainchild, or it is indeed true that great minds work in similar directions.

After-market Revolver Grips

In the occasional moment when there's nothing else to argue about, bored gun experts are known to debate whether those "handle thingies" are properly called "grips" or "stocks." For our purposes here, let's use the terms interchangeably.

Standard J-frame S&W grips give adequate trigger reach to the very short fingers of 5-foot-tall woman...

...but allow too much finger to get in the guard when the average adult male hand is applied...

...requiring that male shooter to "cock" the median knuckle of the trigger finger slightly outward to adjust.

Wooden grips, or synthetic grips that duplicate wood, tend to be smooth and unlikely to snag clothing. They conceal well. They also look good; there's a definite "pride of ownership" thing there. Custom grips with finger grooves and palm swells put you in mind of that hoary saying, "It feels like the handshake of an old friend." However, wooden grips do relatively little to absorb recoil. Smooth ones, especially without finger grooves, tend to shift in the hand when the gun kicks. The old, tiny grips that used to come with small revolvers, known to shooters as "splinter grips," made controlled shooting notoriously difficult. Checkering to secure the stocks to the palm helped some, but not much.

Composition stocks, known colloquially as "rubber grips," have long been a favorite of serious revolver shooters. The ones that cover the backstrap cushion recoil into the web of the hand like a recoil pad soaking up kick on a shotgun. Pachmayr led the market with their Decelerator brand by actually using, in the backstraps of the grip, the same shock-absorbing materials found in state-of-the-art recoil pads. Hogue offers a similar model.

This sort of stock tends to give the most comfortable shooting. Especially in the Hogue finger-grooved version, they allow much less slippage even when firing Magnum loads. The main revolver-makers have picked up on this, and so accoutered many of their double-action models at the factory. Smith & Wesson has used mostly Uncle Mike's and lately Hogue; Colt has used Hogue and Pachmayr; and Ruger has come up with its own in-house version made of what they call "live-feel" composite for their SP-101 hideout gun, their GP-100 service revolver, and some of their larger double-action Magnums. Taurus also uses in-house grips; particularly useful are the Ribber ™ style found on the .454 and .480 big boomers, and some of their "baby Magnums."

These big Trausch grips give maximum recoil control with the author's hard-kicking S&W lightweight Mountain Gun in .44 Magnum, but note that they also restrict trigger reach for double-action work.

From a practical standpoint, the only downside is that the tacky surface of some "rubber" grips adheres to jacket or shirt linings and causes the fabric to lift, revealing the guns. This doesn't happen with all such grips nor with all clothing.

Try before you buy, if possible. Finger-grooved grips don't fit all fingers. Women's police combat champion Sally Van Valzah of Georgia came up with a neat idea that was rediscovered a few years later by Lyn Bates, long time president of Armed Women Against Rape and Endangerment (AWARE). This is to simply remove the top flange, the one between the top two finger grooves. In that "average adult male hand" the industry always talks about, this leaves the middle finger and the ring finger with nothing in between, which is really no big deal. However, for a typical woman with slender fingers, all three of the grasping digits now wrap securely and fit well in the space of two male fingers. Most women who've tried this report improved feel and control.

Auto Pistol Grips

The auto pistol shooter seems less likely to need after-market grips than the revolver stalwart. Most semiautomatic designs, being more recent, have taken more account of human engineering factors. This makes them more likely to fit the shooter's hand as they come from the factory.

That's the good news. The bad news is if the gun doesn't fit to start, there's less you can do with it. A revolver's grip frame needs only hold the mainspring, and it lends itself to being reshaped, sometimes radically. The auto pistol's grip frame has to house the magazine *and* the mainspring, and the dimensions required for this limit your options as to reshaping.

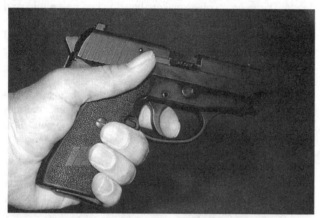

The very short trigger reach of this SIG P239 is one reason such a small gun seems so controllable in so many hands, even when chambered for the powerful .357 SIG cartridge like this specimen.

If a gun feels a little thin in your hand, Pachmayr or Hogue auto grips will fill the palm, and also give you a non-skid surface. However, a lot of us have found that the "rubber" grips slow the draw ever so slightly, because they're a little less forgiving of last-instant hand adjustment as the gun hand slides into position.

Sharply checkered wood or Micarta™ grip panels are more commonly seen. These come in a variety of styles. Many years ago, ace shooter and pistolsmith Mike Plaxco created the first slimline 1911 (for combat shooter John Sayle's lovely wife, Sally). Part of the job was taking metal off the front and back of the grip frame and tang, and part of it was creating the thinnest possible grip panels. This gives a dramatically improved reach to the trigger. Jeff Cooper pronounced it desirable not only for women but for most male shooters. Having that "average adult male hand," I can attest that a "slimline" job seems to give me a greater sense of control, and certainly more trigger reach. The last I heard, Plaxco is no longer doing gunsmithing, but the Gunsite custom shop does grip-slimming of the 1911 as a regular proce-

Slim-line grips are factory standard on the STI Trojan pistol, and allow the average length adult male finger to reach relatively long trigger with the distal joint.

dure. So does pistolsmith Dane Burns. For many shooters, just the slimmer grip panels will be enough, and these are advertised in the gun magazines from a variety of sources. Some makers offer slim-line .45 autos right off the gun factory production line. These include the Springfield Armory Micro .45 in a small hideout gun, the Para-Ordnance LDA Companion in a carry-size piece, and the STI Trojan in a full size Government Model.

On the other hand, some like a more substantial grip on a 1911, but may want something a little less tacky (in surface, and sometimes in looks) than neoprene. Makers such as Kim Ahrends (Custom Firearms, Box 203, Clarion, IA 50525) offers thicker 1911 panels that fill the palm with an exquisite feel, and pride of ownership is enhanced by finely finished exotic wood and superbly executed checkering.

Custom checkering has historically been part and parcel of handgun grip customizing. On a revolver, it's usually on the backstrap. Make sure, however, that you're comfortable with the grips you have now. If you go later to a grip design that covers the backstrap, hiding that fine workmanship you paid for will be like putting a drape over a Vermeer painting.

Auto pistols are more commonly checkered, usually on the front strap of the grip-frame and often on the back. We've found in training that the finer checkering gives all the slippage reduction you need, and doesn't chew your hands up during day after day of rapid-fire training with full power ammunition. Note that if you have checkering on both the frame and the grip panels, there can be so much traction that you wind up in the same situation as with wrap-around neoprene grips and have difficulty making last-instant adjustments. For this writer, the combination that has always worked best on an auto has been either checkered stocks and smooth front and backstraps, or checkered frame front and back and smooth grip panels. Remember, though, our hands are not all the same.

Another option is the Burner grip sold by Jerry Barnhart. The world champ crafted grip panels for 1911s, Berettas, and a few other guns with surfaces that feel like sandpaper. They give a rock-solid hold in the hand. I've worn them on a carry gun briefly and experienced no problems, but a friend who competes with the Beretta he carries says the Barnhart grips tend to eventually chew up coat linings. The surface is, after all, abrasive.

Jerry Barnhart's "Burner" grips, seen here on the Beretta Elite of multiple IDPA national champion Ernie Langdon.

Reshaping The Glock

The Glock pistol exhibits excellent human engineering and fits many hands perfectly as it comes out of its box. Some, however, want something bigger in their hand. They are customers for what have become known as "Glock Socks," rubber sleeves that fit on the grip rather like a piece of inner tube but with checkering, sometimes finger grooves, and always more class. Hogue, Pachmayr, and Uncle Mike's all offer suitable units. Some with smaller

If a factory produced "Glock sock" seems too expensive, you can make one like this out of bicycle inner tube.

hands agree with the great architect Mies van der Rohe that "less is more." For them, Robbie Barrkman pioneered the concept of filling the hollow back of the Glock grip frame with epoxy, then grinding the whole thing down. The Robar frame trim brings the web of the hand and the trigger finger forward. If you are among the one in 100 or fewer with hands so large the slide of the Glock contacts your hand as the pistol fires, he can also craft on an extended grip tang that will solve the problem. Dane Burns is another who has mastered the grip slimming and reshaping on the Glock. The addresses for Burns and Barrkman appear elsewhere in these pages.

The grip area of the handgun is the interface between the operator and the machine. A gun that fits is critical to good performance. You can get to where you can shoot very well with a gun that doesn't fit your hand. Hit with it, qualify with it, even win matches with it. But you will never achieve the personal best that you are capable of with a gun that does not fit you. The pinnacle of your ability to shoot fast and straight with a combat handgun will not be reached until you and that firearm fit together at the interface point as if you were made for one another.

CHAPTER THIRTEEN

BEYOND THE STEREOTYPES

Women And Combat Handguns

The public stereotype is that the gun is an icon of violence, that men are inherently violent, and that therefore women should be anti-gun. Like most stereotypes, this is flat-out wrong.

Why did a cluster of left-of-center political activists call that joke they started "the Million Mom March"? Probably because they knew from the start that they couldn't get a million *dads* to march in favor of banning guns. Guess what? It turned out they couldn't find a million moms, either. It wasn't even close. The Million Mom thing petered out as soon as it stopped being trendy. Perhaps the fact that at the end, the Misguided Moms were outnumbered at rallies by their opposite number, the Second Amendment Sisters, had something to do with it.

A society that expects women to be anti-gun is a society still mired in sexist stereotypes. It is a cruel irony that some

Terri Strayer, left, and Lieschen Gunter lecture an LFI class on concealed carry options for females.

If you look at it, the history of women's successful entry into male-dominated job markets was a history of using mechanical devices to make up for lack of upper body strength. Women didn't start off in construction as hod carriers, but at the hydraulically operated controls of tractors and backhoes. Similarly, women were able to function very well on police patrol because their batons and guns served as mechanical equalizers of strength..."force multipliers," as the current military terminology goes.

This is a Second Amendment Sisters Mothers' Day rally. It outdrew "Million Mom March" in same state in terms of attendance.

of the strongest opponents of gun owners' rights consider themselves part of the women's liberation movement. It is as if these speakers were saying, "You can have your own career, you can support yourself, you can become politically active. You can be financially and politically and emotionally independent...but you must always have a man around for protection, because you can't protect yourself to the extent a man could." What kind of enfranchisement is that? One book written by a noted feminist said that women should not own guns because the gun was the very icon of male violence, and each time a woman acquired one marked a symbolic triumph of male domination.

What a crock.

How many men do you know who can do this? LFI instructor Debbie Morris fires five 12-gauge Magnum rounds into a target in one second, flat, with her Benelli Super-90 shotgun. Those flying cigar-shaped objects are a trio of 3-inch Magnum spent shells simultaneously airborne.

Women's Strengths

It is true that most handguns and holsters were designed by men, for men. It is true that the average woman has less upper body strength than the average man. Yet it is the almost universal observation of handgun instructors that females learn the handgun faster than males.

Dexterity in action. Shooting southpaw, right-handed Gila May-Hayes pumps out a perfect qualification score with her 9mm Glock.

We can postulate several reasons for this. It is certainly true that firearms are dexterity intensive tools, and women tend to have greater fine motor dexterity than men. This is why women perform almost all the hand-assembly of the finest watches in Switzerland, and most of the precise hand checkering on expensive gunstocks like those of Ruger's top-line rifles and shotguns. Activities like knitting are considered so exclusively the domain of the delicate female hand that when a football player like Roosevelt Grier takes up knitting, it becomes national news.

There is also evidence that, given the same training and understanding of the situation, women can handle crisis better than men. In the past we have hooked up LFI students to sophisticated telemetry, and sometimes just taken their blood pressure and pulse, then sent them into a high-stress role-playing scenario. At the end of the exercises, we found that the women's vital signs did not increase so rapidly as the men's with what some would call "anxiety factors," and they would plateau sooner and at a lower level.

If a woman hasn't been brought up with the cultural predispositioning that tells her to faint when spoken to sharply or to jump onto a chair and scream when she sees a mouse, she has the internal wherewithal to handle stress and quite possibly, to do so better than her brothers.

Being more flexible (on the order of 30 percent more flexibility in the pelvic girdle alone), women can adapt better to awkward, expedient shooting positions or cramped zones of protective cover. The same factors that allow so many women to bend at the waist with their legs straight and put their palms to the floor, when so few of their brothers can do the same thing, allow this adaptation. Even standing the same height and weighing exactly the same, the female will have a lower center of gravity and, pound for pound, proportionally stronger legs.

Natural flexibility gives women better balance when firing from awkward cover positions. Jana-Pilar Gabarro demonstrates with her carry gun, a 9mm S&W Model 3913, during an IDPA match.

Many experts believe that women have greater powers of concentration than men, and longer attention spans. They are able to stay focused on a task longer. In a discipline that requires concentration, such as shooting, this is a distinct advantage.

Perhaps the most important factor is that women do not have a gender-based ego investment in gun handling. The motorcycle instructor, the karate sensei, and the firearms coach can all tell you the same thing: many males instinc-

Attorney Rebecca Rutter shows masterful control of full-power Colt .45 automatic.

Gila Hayes at instructor school with a perfect target fired during the revolver phase with a J-frame S&W .38. She outshot all the male instructors on the firing line.

tively resist being taught something with macho overtones by another man. The psychological process seems to be, "The teacher is the parent and the student is the child. But this thing is a manly thing. For me to accept that the teacher knows more than me about this is for me to accept that he is more of a man than I am. This I cannot do, so I must resist what I am being taught."

Female students are not burdened with this testosterone-filled baggage. Their attitude is generally more like, "I paid good money to learn how to do this, and it better work. What did he say to do? OK, I'll do it. Hey, it worked. OK, what's next?" There seems to be a much faster learning curve.

As the great female instructors have noted, women learn things differently than men. When women are asked to do something, they want to know why. Let's say that on two different sides of the city, a man and a woman, total strangers, are each about to buy their first firearm. I can about give you odds that when they go to the gun shop, the woman will spend more time asking the gun dealer how each specimen works. She will spend more time looking at lock-boxes and other safety devices. She will ask more questions in general, and she is more likely to seek formal training with her new gun. She tends to build at the foundation.

These are all good things.

The author congratulates Sally Bartoo, who led her LFI-I class with a perfect 300 qualification score, beating all the males including the SWAT cops.

Resources

In this book, we've taken care to address female needs in each chapter, including holster and gun selection, and gun fit. The stereotype that women should have cute, tiny little guns has been behind us for a long time. When I re-read the chapter on female shooters in one of my own early books, I am reminded of how far we have come.

Because of the pervasive cultural predispositioning that says guns are for boys and not for girls, a female often requires more soul-searching than a male before she arms herself. It is helpful for her to have access to positive female role models. Back in the 1980s, Lethal Force Institute was the first of the major training academies to offer special all-women's classes. We recognized that some of the students would likely be survivors of male violence, and that the presence of alpha males could detract from their learning experience. We tried as much as possible to have all-female training staffs.

In our regular "co-ed" classes for private citizens, which tend to average around 15% female enrollment, we find the women often outshoot most of the men. The big difference I noted in the all-women's classes was that the students were more enthusiastic, as if they felt free to be themselves and discuss their personal concerns.

Female shooters tend to learn the handgun quicker than males; this student has already exhibited perfect stance on first day of training.

It is always good to start with reading. Two books I recommend so strongly that I keep them in stock are Paxton Quigley's *Armed and Female*, and *Effective Defense: the Woman, the Plan, and the Gun* by Gila Hayes. Each of the authors is a woman who at one time had little use for firearms; indeed, Quigley began as an anti-gun activist. But, in each of their lives, they lost loved ones to hideous criminal violence that could only have been prevented by armed force. Each came on her own to the logical conclusion: when you are the smaller type of the species, when society itself calls you "the weaker sex," some sort of an equalizer is needed. Against the sort of force that produces death or great bodily harm, the only effective such equalizer is the firearm. Gila and Paxton make that more clear than I ever could.

The books do not duplicate themselves. *Armed and Female* is a manifesto for the empowered woman. It is a major in why a woman should be armed, and a strong minor in how to go about doing it responsibly. *Effective Defense* is better on the details of how to shoot, what hardware to select, and where to get training, and a strong minor in the philosophy and rationale of the armed woman. The two books thoroughly complement one another. They are available from Police Bookshelf at 800-624-9049.

Paxton is a moving and powerful speaker. Gila is one of the finest combat small arms instructors of either gender that I've had the pleasure to work with. Lyn Bates, former president of AWARE, is another powerful and inspirational spokesperson for the concept of the armed woman.

Consider treating a lady you care about to an excellent magazine called *Women and Guns*. Produced by the publishers of *Gun Week*, *W&G* has always been edited by women who carry guns. Gila, Lyn, and many other knowledgeable authors appear in every edition. Like the aforementioned books, this magazine reminds the public in general and women in particular that men have no hege-

The gun and other force multipliers were what allowed women to function effectively as police officers.

Penni Bachelor of the Pennsylvania chapter of Second Amendment Sisters addresses a rally for gun owners' civil rights.

mony over strength, and that no woman need sacrifice her femininity in any way when she seeks to not only own, but master, the defensive firearm. To order a subscription to *Women and Guns* call Second Amendment Foundation at their *Gun Week* publishing headquarters, 716-885-6408.

The Second Amendment Sisters, mentioned above, has state and local chapters. A visit to one of their meetings or rallies will do wonders to inform a woman who is thinking about picking up a gun. This group has also been extremely effective in neutralizing the bogus statistics that the now almost defunct "Million Mom March" group has been able to over-publicize and promulgate, and they've been extremely effective testifying at state legislatures against poorly conceived anti-gun and anti-self-protection legisla-tion. For more information, including a referral to your nearest state chapter, contact Second Amendment Sisters, Inc., 900 RR 620 S., Suite C101, PMB 228, Lakeway, TX 78734, toll free phone 877-271 6216.

Empowerment

It's not about "I can do your 'guy thing.' " It's about empowerment. Responsibility and power are commensu-rate. Responsibility without power is doomed to become helplessness, and power without responsibility can easily become tyranny. One responsibility of every adult is the ability to manage life-threatening crisis at a first responder level. That crisis might take the form of a fire, a car crash, someone choking on a piece of meat, or a violent assault. If we are going to be responsible for holding the line against these threats to life until the designated professionals get there to deal with it, we need wherewithal. This is why we have smoke alarms and fire extinguishers in our homes. This is why we learn first-aid. This is also why defensive fire-arms exist.

The arming of America's women is slowly breaking down the last bastion of the "Susie Housewife" mentality. It is nothing less than empowerment. It is the fulfillment of a final step to achieving full enfranchisement.

Minorities And Combat Handguns

The defensive handgun is a tool possessed primarily to protect oneself and others lawfully from violent criminal assault. Violent criminal assault is more likely to occur in high-crime neighborhoods. High-crime neighborhoods also tend to be low-income neighborhoods. Low-income neigh-borhoods tend to be peopled largely by minorities. Most crime victims share ethnicity with their assailants.

Therefore, one doesn't need a Masters Degree in socio-economics or criminology to figure out that the decent peo-ple who constitute the overwhelming majority of residents of minority neighborhoods are more likely than anyone else

to be victimized by violent criminals. This means that these are the people who most need firearms to protect themselves and their loved ones.

The stereotypes fed to the public by the media strike again. While a great many people from the rainbow of eth-nic backgrounds in high-risk areas do indeed acquire a fire-arm for self-defense, and are more likely than the average Joe Sixpack to need it for its intended purpose, they are less likely to seek training and skill with the gun.

Society has painted the gun as a symbol of the "white right," and the "gun culture" as a "whites-only" club. It has

An African-American officer tests his combat handgun skills at the Smith & Wesson Championships of 2002. Pistol is SIG P229 in 9mm.

This sort of prejudice has left a lot of the public believing that the gun world is racist. Ironically, the exact opposite is true, particularly in defensive handgun shooting sports such as IDPA and others. You don't see a lot of poor people or blue-collar workers at the golf club or at tennis matches. But if you go to a combat shoot (or a Second Amendment rally) you'll see a rainbow of ethnic backgrounds and religious backgrounds. You'll see male and female competing in the same arena. You'll see millionaires hanging out with laborers.

Perhaps a small part of it is the gun's history as an equalizer. A far more significant reason is that the combat handgun range is a meeting place of people with similar values…people who have looked at life, seen the same responsibilities, and come to the same conclusions. This is why the world of the combat handgun is perhaps the most egalitarian sphere in the galaxy of sports-related activities.

Kenneth V. Blanchard has written an excellent book titled *Black Man With A Gun*, available from the Second Amendment Foundation (425-454-7012). In it he details the single best philosophical argument I've seen for why every responsible, law-abiding member of the African-American community should not only own a gun, but join the NRA. He points out how members of the National Rifle Association welcomed him and other black people of his acquaintance with open arms, while a number of supposedly more liberal organizations were neither so forthcoming nor so honest.

Attempts to ban inexpensive small-caliber pistols such as this perfectly functional Raven .25 auto have had a strong negative impact on law-abiding citizens in lower income communities and disparate impact on minority citizens.

Ken Blanchard, ex-lawman and author of *Black Man With a Gun*, is one of our most persuasive voices for the black community's need to preserve their civil rights as gun owners. Here he addresses the annual Gun Rights Policy Conference hosted by Second Amendment Foundation and the Citizen's Committee for Right to Keep and Bear Arms.

been a long time since any of us have seen a mainstream newspaper publish a political cartoon that caricatured an African-American as Sambo or Stepin Fetchit, or a Jew as a hook-nosed Shylock, though there are many alive in this country who can remember when both images were commonly seen in such places. Even in the emotional turmoil that followed the atrocities of Sept. 11, 2001, we don't see cartoons that depict Arabs as snaggle-toothed vultures anymore. Yet, constantly, mainstream newspapers caricature American gun owners and NRA members as drooling troglodytes with Cro-Magnon foreheads. The depiction is invariably that of a white male.

Ken makes the point as well that the Dred Scott decision had to do with firearms. In the most shameful chapter in the history of the United States Supreme Court, that body ruled that the slave Dred Scott had no rights as a citizen, in part because if such a precedent were established, people of his race would be able to go armed.

The Dred Scott decision was not the last evidence that "gun control" in this country has been aimed largely at the black population. Prior to the Civil War, no citizen needed a permit to carry a loaded and concealed weapon in public. It was done as a matter of course, absolutely legal, and left to the citizen's discretion. The law merely forbade the practice to convicted felons and the mentally incapable. But in the

The Klan won't be riding in any time soon on this African-American citizen, testing his skills with his Colt .45 auto at an IDPA match in New Hampshire. Many laws restricting firearms ownership have been proven to be based in post-bellum racism.

Minority citizens, often at the greatest risk of becoming victims of violent crime, have a proportionally great need to own, and become skillful with, defensive firearms.

post-bellum years of Reconstruction, fearing the wrath of freed slaves no longer forbidden to own weapons, an ethnocentric white majority passed laws that would require a license to carry a gun in public. The plan was to make the sheriffs the issuing authority, and then be sure to elect only white males who would be sure to issue the permits only to other white males.

The strategy worked, with such frightening efficiency that it remains in force in many jurisdictions today. While more than 30 states have "shall-issue" laws that give equal rights in this respect to rich and poor, white and black, and male and female alike, there remain several states where the issue of the permits is discretionary. There are jurisdictions where "discretionary" is a code word that means, "We'll give you the permit if you're white, male, rich, and politically connected."

The motivation lay in economics as well as race. Industry and management had the clout to elect politicians, and they didn't want to empower labor to be able to shoot back at strikebreakers. The wish to "declaw" the working public is more clearly seen in Great Britain's history of gun control, beginning in the early part of the 20th century and escalating until, before the millennium, auto-loading rifles and all handguns had been confiscated by the British government.

Flash back to the present in the U.S.A. The same "divide and conquer" strategy is in play when anti-Second Amendment forces prey on the fears of minorities by painting gun owners as white racist. The gun club or pistol match as a "Caucasian only entity" has suffered from a self-fulfilling prophecy effect. We will never know how many people of color who wanted to get into organized combat pistol shooting decided not to, because they had been falsely led to believe that they would not be welcome.

Other sociological factors were at work as well. Poverty not only breeds crime, it leads to broken families. The matriarchal family is a strong tradition in lower income African-American communities. Mothers there know that criminal violence is the greatest danger their sons face. Strongly influential in their sons' lives, they aggressively warn their male progeny against drugs, gangs, and guns. Thus, the gun itself becomes psychologically demonized

along with the true causes of crime and danger. It is a big obstacle to hurdle when a law-abiding young black man comes to realize that he needs more than phrases like "just say no" to keep his loved ones safe in a dangerous place.

A number of African-American police recruits have had to overcome this deeply-instilled prejudice against firearms to qualify with their service guns when they became law enforcement officers.

Improving The Situation

Because there was an image in the black community that police were hostile to African-Americans, that group rarely applied to become law enforcement officers. The police community was able to improve that situation by aggressively recruiting for officers in the black community. It is time for the "gun culture" to do the same.

Ditto the Asian community, ditto the Latin community, ditto every "hyphenated-American" community. The egalitarianism of the "gun culture" is a well-kept secret that needs to be told. Gun clubs, shooting associations, and gun owners' civil rights groups need to be more active in recruiting minority members. We need to be arranging firearms safety training programs, affordably or at no charge, in the inner city and in other ethnic enclaves.

It is here that decent citizens are most at risk. It is here we find the people who need to exercise this freedom the most…and a huge, untapped resource to help us defend that freedom, for the sake of us all. Not only our generation, but also those to come…a topic we'll go to next.

Young People And Combat Handguns

In February of 2002 in South Bend, Indiana, a man held a box-cutter to a widow's throat and demanded her valuables, including her late husband's weapons collection. A convicted armed robber and self-confessed drug dealer, the 27-year-old intruder meant business. The woman, Mrs. Sue Gay, thought she was going to be killed.

But Mrs. Gay's grandson ran upstairs and obtained a loaded .45 caliber pistol. He rushed back down and confronted the man, who tried to use the grandmother as a human shield. However, the petite hostage proved to be too small to hide behind. Seeing an opening and fearing for his grandmother's life, the grandson fired one shot.

The criminal turned and ran out the door. Mrs. Gay rushed forward and slammed it shut behind him and called 911. When police arrived, they found the career criminal outside, bleeding from a .45 caliber gunshot wound of the chest. He died in the emergency room.

This little guy is still in elementary school, but he turned in a strong performance with a Smith & Wesson K-22 at the National Junior Handgun Championships.

Mrs. Gay told South Bend Tribune reporter Owen O'Brien of her rescue by her grandson. "He hit the bottom of the stairs with the .45 and stood (in a) ready stance with the gun…one shot and he got him. He's my little hero."

The boy who fired the rescue shot was 11 years old.

The youngster had lost his father to a heart attack three years before. Prior to his death, however, the conscientious father had taught the boy shooting skills and gun safety. "Before his dad died, they'd go target shooting. He knows they're not toys and not something to mess with," the grandmother confirmed.

St. Joseph County prosecutor Chris Toth almost immediately ruled the shooting justifiable. "The young man reasonably believed his mother and himself to be in danger of dying. It was clear to us this was a justifiable homicide," the prosecutor told reporters.

This little one is learning that parents Heidi and Jeff Williams will reward her for her responsible behavior in adult-oriented theaters.

The killing of a human being was "an unfortunate burden for an 11-year-old to have on him," the prosecutor said, and surely all of us can agree with that. At the same time, there is no question that having his grandmother murdered before his eyes as he stood helpless would have been much more traumatic.

As we look over the lists of righteous armed citizen shootings that have been compiled for decades by the National Rifle Association, we see things like this cropping up, albeit infrequently. We mention elsewhere in this book the case of a much younger boy who saved his mother, who was being beaten to death by an adult male psycho. A .25 caliber bullet fired by the child from an inexpensive Raven pistol into the attacker's brain preserved his mom's life. In another incident, a boy only slightly older than the one in South Bend was home in bed when a stalker broke into the family home. Obsessed with the woman the boy's father had brought into the home, the stalker had come to commit murder, and did. He killed the woman and the boy's older brother, and shot and gravely wounded the father, leaving him for dead. As the mass murderer entered the young man's room to complete what he thought was the extermination of the family, there was one thing he didn't know.

The dad had trusted the youngster to have a handgun of his own in his room. By the time the stalker entered, the kid had been able to arm himself with his Ruger Single-Six .22 sporting revolver. A moment later the rampage ended as the murderer fell to the floor with one of the boy's small caliber bullets in his brain. The youth and his father survived.

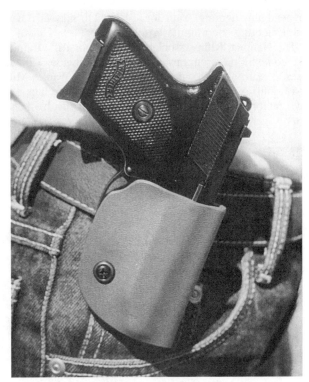

Gun expert Andy Kemp bought this combination – a Walther TP-22 pistol and Ky-Tac holster – to teach his little girls safe gun handling. Gun and holster were proportional. His oldest was winning IDPA awards with a Glock 19 in 9mm by age 11.

We don't like to think of it, but any of our children could be caught alone in a terrible situation. We tell them what to do (drop and roll) if their clothing catches fire. We put them through "drown-proofing" programs when they're little. This is simply another emergency that could befall a child for whom we are responsible when we aren't there to physically protect them.

It doesn't always involve an adult human predator. Some years ago, a pack of vicious dogs attacked a little girl playing in her yard. Her older brother, an early adolescent, grabbed a .22 rifle and used it to excellent effect, saving his sister's life.

The author watches as Samantha Kemp coolly and precisely perforates a target with her dad's Glock 19.

A few years ago in California, a girl in her early teens was in charge of her younger siblings when an adult male, who could be described as a homicidal maniac, burst into the home, armed with a pitchfork. She ran for her father's guns, which she knew how to use, but they were locked up and inaccessible to her. She managed to escape to a neighbor's house, begging for a gun; the adult neighbor refused the weapon and kept her with him, but called the police. When officers arrived the maniac attacked them, and they shot him dead. They entered the home to discover that he had already murdered the other children. Their grandmother has since publicly stated her conviction that, had the older child been able to access a gun, she could have saved the lives of the little ones.

Perspectives

When the U.S. was more rural than urban, children were taught firearms safety and marksmanship as a matter of course. When they were little boys, Alvin York and Audie Murphy were sent into the woods, alone, with a .22 rifle and a few cartridges, and expected to bring home meat for the family table. They lived up to these responsibilities, and the skills they learned served them well when they had to defend their country, in WWI and WWII respectively. Each earned the Congressional Medal of Honor. Each was preserved, thanks to his shooting skills, to return home to his family.

An LFI-III graduate supervises a youngster with an adult-size Beretta 92 9mm. Note that the coach's folded hands show body language of confidence, but this responsible adult is in position to reach instantly and correct things should there be a lapse of safety.

This book is not suggesting that young children be taught "gunfighting." What is suggested is that children be taught firearms safety, and safety protocols for every other potentially dangerous "adults-only" object in the adult-oriented world that surrounds them.

We know that the Eddie Eagle firearms safety program for younger children has been a huge success. Few people realize that it evolved from a program developed by Florida firefighters to prevent injury to children who came upon blasting caps or other explosives that had been left unattended. A Spokane firefighter who was also a firearms instructor, Robert Smith, learned of the program and suggested to the NRA that they develop something similar for children who find themselves in the presence of a firearm not supervised by an adult.

The program teaches children to memorize a four-step protocol. "Stop! Don't touch! Leave the area! Tell an adult!"

The parents of this little boy don't know that his shooting coach is a psychologist and an accomplished combat handgunner; as they watch from beyond camera range, they only know that their son is in safe hands.

The entertainment media has made the gun in general and the handgun in particular an emblem of heroism and power. Child psychologists tell us that because children are little and weak and dependent, they crave strength and freedom. They seek responsibility and power, the cornerstones of adulthood, and the gun becomes an embodiment of both. Bill Watterson for many years wrote a fabulously successful comic strip called "Calvin and Hobbes," about a 6-year-old boy with an active fantasy life that revolved around his stuffed tiger. Watterson's work, like Mark Twain's, was multi-dimensional, simple humor on one level but biting social satire on another. In one telling cartoon, Calvin describes to Hobbes what adulthood should be: "Women should all wear tight clothing," he tells his toy tiger, "and men should all carry powerful handguns."

Satire is a reflection of social values, and here, Bill Watterson had it nailed. Calvin constantly imagined himself a private eye with a .38 or a .45, or "Spaceman Spiff," armed with a deadly ray gun. This is precisely the effect that TV and movie depictions have on our nation's youth. It makes a real gun almost irresistible to touch.

What is a parent or guardian to do? The father of the little boy in South Bend had it right. Outdoor sportsmen say, "When you take your child hunting, you won't have to go hunting for your child." When a parent or other trusted adult takes a child to the range and teaches her or him to shoot, the curiosity about guns aroused by the media is satisfied, and channeled safely and appropriately.

Your state's department of Fish and Game or Wildlife has responsibility for Hunter Safety Programs. You can phone them for a list of courses and instructors near you. This in turn will lead you to a list of gun clubs in your area. Your local gun shop (though probably not the clerk at the firearms counter of the Big Box discount store) can also guide you to gun clubs and firearms learning opportunities near you.

At this writing, the Boy Scouts of America still endorse optional firearms safety programs and offer merit badges for riflery, though there is no provision within the current BSA

for handgun shooting. Your local 4-H Club may also have youth shooting opportunities available.

The National Rifle Association has Junior Rifle training and competition programs available nationwide. Contact them to learn about local programs at 11350 Waples Mills Road, Fairfax, VA 22030. Some of the hosting clubs also have junior shooter programs available that involve handguns.

Firearms instructor Jeff Williams coaches a youngster with a full-size SIG P226 9mm. In a few minutes, the boy will "fly solo" under watchful guidance.

The National Junior Handgun Championship was created at the famous Second Chance Shoot in 1997. John Maxwell, already coaching his son Cody successfully toward a spot in Olympic shooting, led the study team. Tom Sheppardson of Michigan, a middle school administrator, and this writer joined him. Sheppardson, with access to extensive research in physical education for young people, determined that the best breaking point between child and young adult would be age 13. Because the Second Chance format of bowling pin shooting requires powerful guns, we wanted to make sure that youngsters with growing and forming bones didn't damage themselves by absorbing too much recoil from powerful sidearms. Age 14-17 was set for Junior class, and age 13 and down for Sub-Junior. The kids in the Junior class

Taking your kids shooting exposes them to wonderful people. Justine Ayoob was 13 in this photo when she listened carefully to the advice of famed grandmaster shooter Ken Tapp.

shot the same target array with the same type of handguns as the adults, while the younger ones had a "five-pin tipover" event with the pins set at the back of the tables so they could shoot lighter-kicking .38s, 9mms, and even .22s.

The first National Junior Handgun Championships, sponsored by Richard Davis at Second Chance in 1998, was resoundingly successful. Unfortunately, after that year the Second Chance Shoot went on hiatus and another venue was sought. Steve and Clare Dixon hosted it the following year in Iowa, using the same format. That venue was suspended also, and the event went into hibernation until the Pioneer Sportsmen Club, Inc. in Dunbarton, NH, took it over and, with the support of the Second Amendment Foundation, scheduled a match for the summer of 2002. The format was changed to all .22 caliber handguns, and the course of fire was made a mix of bull's-eye shooting, a Steel Challenge event, and an NRA Hunter Pistol stage of fire. Sub-Juniors could shoot two-handed throughout, while Juniors would have to shoot the bull's-eye stage in the traditional one-handed fashion. Information is available through Pioneer Sportsmen, Inc., P.O. Box 403, Concord, NH 03302.

Tool Of Parenting

This writer can honestly say that he has found the gun to be nothing less than a tool of parenting. My kids started shooting at 6. My older daughter won her first pistol match against adult males at 11, and she was 19 when she won High Woman at the National Tactical Invitational at Gunsite. She beat not only a very strong field of highly accomplished adult female *pistoleras,* but most of the male SWAT cops, etc., as well. My younger daughter was 11 when she shot her first match, a side event at a national tournament, and at 13 carried her dad to National Champion Parent/Child Handgun Team in Sub-Junior class in 1998.

The awards were the least of it. Throughout the years of their growing up, their handgun owning and shooting privileges gave their mother and I one more way to show them the path to adulthood. As young women in a world dominated by adult men, they learned that if they developed their skills and understood the rules, they could beat grown-up men at their own game on a level playing field. They learned that when they were given power, commensurate responsibility would be expected of them, and when they lived up to that responsibility, they would be given more power, and so on...a microcosm of adult life path.

Each grew up comfortable in adult company, not intimidated by those who for the moment had more power than they, and learning how to give respect without obeisance. Each earned academic honors that both parents were proud of, but more importantly, each grew up to be a natural protector, someone to whom their peers would come when in trouble.

Understanding of when to use force was something else they absorbed. When the younger was about 10, she switched from karate to aikido because she had learned that in the latter art, she could spar against adults instead of children. When she had been a *karate-ka,* her father had watched from the back of the dojo with heart in mouth as she sparred against young men three years older than she

and head and shoulders taller. She never lost. In one such encounter, she evaded a vicious punch to the head and countered with a roundhouse kick delivered so hard that it emptied the air from the boy's lungs temporarily and dropped him, heavy protective gear notwithstanding. A few years later, attacked for real by a mentally ill young man much stronger than she, who was trying to smash her in the head with a bottle, she coolly performed the exact same maneuver, saving herself and dropping her attacker in a gasping heap.

The older daughter had taken comfortably to the gun, and was issued a concealed carry permit at the unusually early age of 18. A little over a year later, she was targeted by two adult males as she came from the sidewalk up the steps of her house. Realizing that she could not get her key in the door before the first fast-running attacker would be upon her, she spun to face them and went for the Smith & Wesson Model 3913 9mm she carried in her waistband. The would-be rapists turned and fled. I suspect they were less intimidated by the small, silver-colored pistol than by the body language and facial expression of the resolute young woman who so swiftly and expertly drew it.

Parent As Teacher

Just as the teacher is a surrogate parent for much of a child's day, the parent is also a teacher for much of the rest of the time. Before the baby bird leaves the nest, it must be taught to take care of itself.

Whether or not a given parent wants their child to possess firearms even when they grow up, the fact remains that some 40 percent to 50 percent of American homes contain guns. Unless we keep our children from ever visiting a friend's home, we cannot guarantee that they won't be exposed to guns. But knowledge is power, and there is no safety in ignorance.

A child who knows how to make a firearm safe is a child who is not endangered by the mere presence of one. There is no set age at which to introduce a child to firearms; only the parent can gauge the development of the necessary responsibility. I have been hunting in the field with little kids whom I trusted behind me holding loaded guns, and I have been in the presence of adults who are still not ready for the responsibility. One good barometer is watching how the child handles pets. If they keep feeding and brushing the puppy even when the newness has worn off, it's a positive sign.

The "gun culture" is an aging one. Opponents of the civil right of firearms ownership have used the same techniques of "manufactured social undesirability" that worked to reduce cigarette smoking, to demonize interest in legitimate firearms ownership among the young. It is working. We of this generation need to remain tirelessly politically active if we are to pass on to our successors the right to own weapons to protect oneself and one's family. Concomitantly, we must work to educate the young to appreciate this right, and to protect and cherish it as we do, or it will be lost forever.

John Maxwell said it best, simply and starkly: "The children are the future."

CHAPTER FOURTEEN

PARTING WORDS

As I was putting the foregoing chapters together, I leafed through the first edition of *Combat Handgunnery* written by Jack Lewis and Jack Mitchell in 1983. I remembered how much I had enjoyed reading it when it came out. Their incisive commentary has stood the test of time.

There were a few pictures of me in it. It's good to be reminded that there was a time when I didn't have a potbelly and only had one chin and nothing had gone gray yet. But that sort of thing reminds us all of how much can happen in 20 years.

The input of physiologists and kinesiologists into both the shooting sports and scientific firearms training has brought things forward in quantum leaps. Technology has evolved, but technique has evolved more. It's not about more high-tech "space guns." The shooters of today, using stock guns of a kind available a score of years ago, are shooting faster and straighter than the champions of two decades ago did with tricked-out specialty target guns.

It's not about the gun so much as it is about the shooter. It's not even about the shooter so much as it's about consistent application of proven tactics and techniques.

Get experience beforehand in shooting from awkward, "downed" positions.

Make it a plan to get behind cover before the shooting starts.

There's simply too much to put into any one book. Things have to be prioritized. Some of the topics of previous editions – malfunction clearing, for example, and night shooting – had to be left on the cutting room floor when we ran out of space in this edition. It was more important to nail down advances in shooting technique, how to pick the most suitable tools for the task, and how to avoid doing the wrong thing in an increasingly complex tactical environment. In any case, malfunction clearing and night shooting have been covered very well in past editions.

In the very short space that remains, let's talk about priorities. Training is always a better investment than equipment. Software in your brain is always with you, and there's only so much hardware you can carry. And there are places

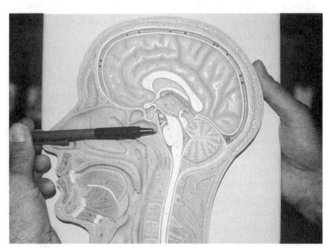

Marksmanship is important. The pen of an LFI consulting physician shows how small the target is for a hit in the part of the brain that will collapse an opponent without him pulling his trigger even reflexively.

where you can't carry this kind of hardware at all. I take at least a week of training a year for myself, and would recommend the same regimen to you. I can recommend without reservation schools like Chuck Taylor's ASAA, Chapman Academy, the Critical Reaction Training Center near Milwaukee, John Farnam's DTI, Firearms Academy of Seattle, Front Sight, Gunsite, the Midwest Training Group, Clint Smith's Thunder Ranch, and more. You're also welcome to inquire about my own school, Lethal Force Institute, at PO Box 122, Concord, NH 03302 or on the Web at www.ayoob.com.

A thumb-break holster buys you more time…

The author seconds the advice about awareness on this "tombstone."

Remember that awareness and alertness are more important than combat tactics, because they can keep you out of combat to begin with. Tactics are more important than marksmanship, because they can often keep you out of danger without you having to fire a shot. Skill with your safety equipment, including your weapons, is more important than what type of weapon you have. With all those things accomplished, your choice of equipment is one of the few things

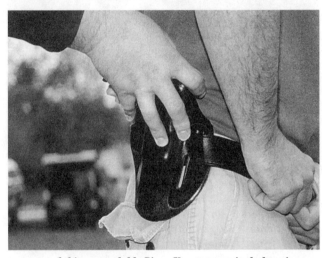

… and this concealable Piece-Keeper security holster is even more snatch-resistant, and only slightly slower on the draw.

you can work out before the fight, so it makes sense to have the best quality gear of a kind ideally suited for your predictable threat situation.

Don't just drill on drawing and firing. Drill on movement. Make the use of cover a high priority. Take a class in

Think about handgun retention. An open-top holster does nothing to protect this Ruger .45, which is fortunately on safe…

Underlying all this hi-tech kit is a Second Chance Ultima ballistic vest. Any situation where you want a defense gun is a situation where you want body armor.

handgun retention, the art and science of defeating a disarming attempt. Learn to shoot from downed positions and with either hand. Learn from the cops: More than 2,500 officers at this writing have been saved by the concealed body armor that armed citizen Rich Davis invented in the early 1970s. As Kevlar Survivors' Club member #1946 and Second Chance Save #682, I can tell you that the stuff works. If your local dealers won't sell it to law-abiding private citizens, look up the LFI Web site, but be prepared to show proof of a clean criminal record.

If you need to carry a gun, you probably need to carry two. Invest in a backup gun if you're licensed to carry. Backups have saved countless police officers, and could have saved countless more if those slain officers had had recourse to a second weapon.

"If you need a gun," said street-wise commentator Phil Engeldrum, "you probably need two." NAA Guardian .380, left, and Kahr MK40 are both popular backup pistols.

Make sure your loved ones and your regular companions know what the plan is going to be if this particular kind of danger strikes. That "fight or flight" thing is really "fight, flight, or freeze." The ones who freeze are the ones who don't have a plan. If you have something in your mind that says, "Given stimulus A, I *will* carry out response A,"

you've made the best possible investment in survival. You want to share the same concept with people you care about, who might be with you when a crisis strikes.

Your plans should include what your partners are going to do. These Lake County, Mont., deputies prepare for the day they may have to drag a wounded brother to safety under fire.

Thanks for taking the time to read this book. The plan is to update this book on a fairly regular basis. I don't know who's going to write the next one...but I'm going to do everything I can to make sure I'm around to read it.

Good luck. Stay safe.

Massad Ayoob
Concord, NH USA
March, 2002

- **The right to self-defense neither begins nor ends at a state border.**

- **A law-abiding citizen does not suffer a character change by crossing a state line.**

- **An "unalienable right" is not determined by geographical bundaries.**

- **A patchwork of state laws regarding the carrying of firearms can make criminals out of honest folks, especially those who frequently must travel the states to earn a living.**

- **Using data for all 3,054 U.S. counties from 1977 to 1994, University of Chicago Prof. John Lott finds that for each additional year a concealed handgun law is in effect the murder rate declines by 3%, robberies by over 2%, and the rape rate by 2%.**

In spite of the truth of these statements and the fact that nearly half of all Americans live in states that allow a law-abiding citizen to carry a firearm concealed for personal protection, it has not been commonplace that these same citizens could carry their firearm across states lines. NRA-ILA is working to pass right-to-carry reciprocity laws granting permit holders the ability to carry their firearms legally while visiting or traveling beyond their home state.

In order to assist NRA Members in determining which states recognize their permits, NRA-ILA has created this guide. **This guide is not to be considered as legal advice or a restatement of the law. It is important to remember that state carry laws vary considerably. Be sure to check with state and local authorities outside your home state for a complete listing of restrictions on carrying concealed in that state.** Many states restrict carrying in bars, restaurants (where alcohol is served), establishments where packaged alcohol is sold, schools, colleges, universities, churches, parks, sporting events, correctional facilities, courthouses, federal and state government offices/buildings, banks, airport terminals, police stations, polling places, any posted private property restricting the carrying of concealed firearms, etc. In addition to state restrictions, federal law prohibits carrying on military bases, in national parks and the sterile area of airports. National Forests usually follow laws of the state wherein the forest is located.

NOTE: Vermont does not issue permits, but allows carrying of concealed firearms if there is no intent to commit a crime. Vermont residents traveling to other states must first obtain a non-resident permit from that state—if available—prior to carrying concealed.

•• Last Revised 12/2000 ••

NRA - RIGHT-TO-CARRY RECIPROCITY GUIDE

Alabama

Right-to-Carry Law Type
Right-to-Carry

Issuing Authority:
County Sheriff
These states also recognize your permit:
Idaho, Indiana, Michigan, Utah, Vermont, Wyoming
Contact agency for non-resident permits if granted:
Permits not granted.
www.legislature.state.al.us/codeofalabama/1975/coatoc.htm

Alaska

Right-to-Carry Law Type
Right-to-Carry

Issuing Authority:
State Trooper
These states also recognize your permit:
Idaho, Indiana, Michigan, Montana, Texas, Vermont, Wyoming
Contact agency for non-resident permits if granted:
Permits not granted.
www.dps.state.ak.us/ast/achp/

Arizona

Right-to-Carry Law Type
Right-to-Carry

Issuing Authority:
Department of Public Safety
These states also recognize your permit:
Arkansas, Idaho, Indiana, Kentucky, Michigan, Montana, Texas, Utah, Vermont, Wyoming
Contact agency for non-resident permits if granted:
Permits not granted.
www.dps.state.az.us/ccw/welcome.htm

Arkansas

Right-to-Carry Law Type
Right-to-Carry

Issuing Authority:
State Police
These states also recognize your permit:
Arizona, Florida, Idaho, Indiana, Kentucky, Michigan, Montana, Oklahoma, South Carolina, Tennessee, Texas, Utah, Vermont, Wyoming
Contact agency for non-resident permits if granted:
Permits not granted.
www.state.ar.us/asp/handgun.html

California

Right-to-Carry Law Type
Limited Issue

Issuing Authority:
County Sheriff
These states also recognize your permit:
Idaho, Indiana, Michigan, Montana, Vermont, Wyoming
Contact agency for non-resident permits if granted:
Permits not granted.
caag.state.ca.us/firearms/

Colorado

Right-to-Carry Law Type
Limited Issue

Issuing Authority:
Chief of Police/County Sheriff
These states also recognize your permit:
Idaho, Indiana, Michigan, Montana, Vermont, Wyoming
Contact agency for non-resident permits if granted:
Permits not granted.
www.state.co.us/gov_dir/cdps/firearms.htm

Connecticut

Right-to-Carry Law Type
Right-to-Carry

Issuing Authority:
Commissioner of State Police
These states also recognize your permit:
Idaho, Indiana, Michigan, Montana, Utah, Vermont, Wyoming
Contact agency for non-resident permits if granted:
State Police Special Licensing Division; (860) 685-8290
www.bfpe.state.ct.us/

Delaware

Right-to-Carry Law Type
Limited Issue

Issuing Authority:
Prothonotary of Superior Court
These states also recognize your permit:
Idaho, Indiana, Michigan, Vermont, Wyoming
Contact agency for non-resident permits if granted:
Permits not granted.
www.lexislawpublishing.com/resources/

Florida

Right-to-Carry Law Type
Right-to-Carry

Issuing Authority:
Department of State
These states also recognize your permit:
Arkansas, Georgia, Idaho, Indiana, Kentucky, Louisiana, Michigan, Mississippi, Montana, New Hampshire, North Dakota, Tennessee, Texas, Utah, Vermont, Wyoming
Contact agency for non-resident permits if granted:
Dept. of State, Division of Licensing; (904) 488-5381
licweb.dos.state.fl.us/weapons/index

Georgia

Right-to-Carry Law Type
Right-to-Carry

Issuing Authority:
County Probate Judge
These states also recognize your permit:
Florida, Idaho, Indiana, Kentucky, Michigan, Montana, New Hampshire, Tennessee, Vermont, Wyoming
Contact agency for non-resident permits if granted:
Permits not granted.
www.ganet.or/cgi-bin/pub/ocode/ocresearch?number=16-11-128

Hawaii

Right-to-Carry Law Type
Limited Issue

Issuing Authority:
Chief of Police
These states also recognize your permit:
Idaho, Indiana, Michigan, Vermont, Wyoming
Contact agency for non-resident permits if granted:
Permits not granted.
www.capitol.hawaii.gov/site1/docs/docs.asp?press1=docs

Idaho

Right-to-Carry Law Type
Right-to-Carry

Issuing Authority:
County Sheriff
These states also recognize your permit:
Florida, Georgia, Indiana, Kentucky, Michigan, Montana, Vermont, Wyoming
Contact agency for non-resident permits if granted:
Any Sheriffs' Department
www3./state.id.us/newidst?sctid=180330002.k

Illinois

Right-to-Carry Law Type
None

Issuing Authority:
n/a
These states also recognize your permit:

Contact agency for non-resident permits if granted:
Permits not granted.
www.legis.state.il.us/ilcs/ch720act5articles/ch720act5sub34.htm

Indiana

Right-to-Carry Law Type
Right-to-Carry

Issuing Authority:
Chief Law Enforcement Officer of Municipality
These states also recognize your permit:
Florida, Georgia, Idaho, Kentucky, Michigan, Montana, Vermont, Wyoming
Contact agency for non-resident permits if granted:
Permits not granted.
www.ai.org/legislative/ic/code/title35/ar47/ch2.htm

Iowa

Right-to-Carry Law Type
Limited Issue

Issuing Authority:
(resident) Sheriff (non-resident) Commissioner of Public Safety
These states also recognize your permit:
Idaho, Indiana, Michigan, Montana, Vermont, Wyoming
Contact agency for non-resident permits if granted:
Commissioner of Public Safety; (515) 281-7610
www.state.ia.us/government/dps/asd/wp/index.htm

Kansas

Right-to-Carry Law Type
None

Issuing Authority:
n/a
These states also recognize your permit:

Contact agency for non-resident permits if granted:
Permits not granted.
www.ink.org/public/legislative/statutes/statutes.cgi

Kentucky

Right-to-Carry Law Type
Right-to-Carry

Issuing Authority:
State Police
These states also recognize your permit:
Arizona, Arkansas, Florida, Georgia, Idaho, Indiana, Louisiana, Michigan, Mississippi, Montana, Tennessee, Texas, Utah, West Virginia, Vermont, Wyoming
Contact agency for non-resident permits if granted:
Permits not granted.
www.state.ky.us/agencies/ksp/ccdw/ccdfr.htm

Louisiana

Right-to-Carry Law Type
Right-to-Carry

Issuing Authority:
Deputy Secretary of the Department of Public Safety & Corrections.
These states also recognize your permit:
Florida, Idaho, Indiana, Kentucky, Michigan, Montana, Tennessee, Texas, Utah, Vermont, Wyoming
Contact agency for non-resident permits if granted:
Permits not granted.
www.dps.state.la.us/lsp/chips.html

Maine

Right-to-Carry Law Type
Right-to-Carry

Issuing Authority:
County Sheriff/Chief of Police
These states also recognize your permit:
Idaho, Indiana, Michigan, Vermont, Wyoming
Contact agency for non-resident permits if granted:
Chief of State Police; (207) 624-8775
janus.state.me.us/legis/ros/meconlaw.htm

Maryland

Right-to-Carry Law Type
Limited Issue

Issuing Authority:
Superintendent of State Police
These states also recognize your permit:
Idaho, Indiana, Michigan, Montana, Vermont, Wyoming
Contact agency for non-resident permits if granted:
Permits not granted.
www.inform.umd.edu/ums+state/md_resources/mdsp/license.htm

Massachusetts

Right-to-Carry Law Type
Limited Issue

Issuing Authority:
Chief of Police
These states also recognize your permit:
Idaho, Indiana, Michigan, Montana, Utah, Vermont, Wyoming
Contact agency for non-resident permits if granted:
Permits not granted.
www.state.ma.us/msp/firearms/index.htm

Michigan

Right-to-Carry Law Type
Limited Issue

Issuing Authority:
County Gun Board/Sheriff
These states also recognize your permit:
Florida, Georgia, Idaho, Indiana, Kentucky, Montana, Vermont, Wyoming
Contact agency for non-resident permits if granted:
Permits not granted.
www.msp.state.mi.us/reports/ccw/ccwtoc.htm

Minnesota

Right-to-Carry Law Type
Limited Issue

Issuing Authority:
Chief of Police/County Sheriff
These states also recognize your permit:
Idaho, Indiana, Michigan, Montana, Vermont, Wyoming
Contact agency for non-resident permits if granted:
Permits not granted.
www.revisor.leg.state.mn.us/

Mississippi

Right-to-Carry Law Type
Right-to-Carry

Issuing Authority:
Department of Public Safety
These states also recognize your permit:
Florida, Idaho, Indiana, Kentucky, Michigan, Montana, Tennessee, Vermont, Wyoming
Contact agency for non-resident permits if granted:
Permits not granted.
www.mscode.com/free/statutes/45/009/0101.htm

Missouri

Right-to-Carry Law Type
None

Issuing Authority:
n/a
These states also recognize your permit:

Contact agency for non-resident permits if granted:
Permits not granted.
www.moga.state.mo.us/statutes/c500-599/5710030.htm

Montana

Right-to-Carry Law Type
Right-to-Carry

Issuing Authority:
County Sheriff
These states also recognize your permit:
Florida, Idaho, Indiana, Michigan, North Dakota, Vermont, Wyoming
Contact agency for non-resident permits if granted:
Permits not granted.
www.doj.state.mt.us/ls/weaponslist.htm

Nebraska

Right-to-Carry Law Type
None

Issuing Authority:
n/a
These states also recognize your permit:

Contact agency for non-resident permits if granted:
Permits not granted.
www.unicam.state.ne.us/statutes.htm

Nevada

Right-to-Carry Law Type
Right-to-Carry

Issuing Authority:
County Sheriff
These states also recognize your permit:
Idaho, Indiana, Michigan, Montana, Utah, Vermont, Wyoming
Contact agency for non-resident permits if granted:
Permits not granted.
www.leg.state.nv.us/law1.htm

New Hampshire

Right-to-Carry Law Type
Right-to-Carry

Issuing Authority:
Selectman/Mayor or Chief of Police
These states also recognize your permit:
Florida, Georgia, Idaho, Indiana, Kentucky, Michigan, North Dakota, Vermont, Wyoming
Contact agency for non-resident permits if granted:
Director of State Police; (603) 271-3575
199.192.9.6/rsa/12/159-6-d.htm

New Jersey

Right-to-Carry Law Type
Limited Issue

Issuing Authority:
Chief of Police/Superintendent of State Police
These states also recognize your permit:
Idaho, Indiana, Michigan, Montana, Vermont, Wyoming
Contact agency for non-resident permits if granted:
Superintendent of State Police; (609) 882-2000 ext. 2664
www.njleg.state.nj.us/html.statutes.htm

New Mexico

Right-to-Carry Law Type
None

Issuing Authority:
n/a
These states also recognize your permit:

Contact agency for non-resident permits if granted:
Permits not granted.
www.dps.nm.org/faq/concealcarry.htm

New York

Right-to-Carry Law Type
Limited Issue

Issuing Authority:
Varies by county
These states also recognize your permit:
Idaho, Indiana, Michigan, Montana, Vermont, Wyoming
Contact agency for non-resident permits if granted:
Permits not granted.
leginfo.state.ny.us:82/index1.html

North Carolina

Right-to-Carry Law Type
Right-to-Carry

Issuing Authority:
County Sheriff
These states also recognize your permit:
Idaho, Indiana, Michigan, Montana, Utah, Vermont, Wyoming
Contact agency for non-resident permits if granted:
Permits not granted.
www.jus.state.nc.us/ncja/guns.htm

North Dakota

Right-to-Carry Law Type
Right-to-Carry

Issuing Authority:
Chief of the Bureau of Criminal Investigation
These states also recognize your permit:
Florida, Idaho, Indiana, Michigan, Montana, Vermont, Wyoming
Contact agency for non-resident permits if granted:
Permits not granted.
expedition.bismarck.ag.state.nd.us/ndag/manuals/weapons.html

Ohio

Right-to-Carry Law Type
None

Issuing Authority:
n/a
These states also recognize your permit:

Contact agency for non-resident permits if granted:
Permits not granted.
orc.avv.com

Oklahoma

Right-to-Carry Law Type
Right-to-Carry

Issuing Authority:
State Bureau of Investigation
These states also recognize your permit:
Arkansas, Idaho, Indiana, Michigan, Montana, Texas, Utah, Vermont, Wyoming
Contact agency for non-resident permits if granted:
Permits not granted.
www.osbi.state.ok.us/sda/sda.html

Oregon

Right-to-Carry Law Type
Right-to-Carry

Issuing Authority:
County Sheriff
These states also recognize your permit:
Idaho, Indiana, Michigan, Montana, Utah, Vermont, Wyoming
Contact agency for non-resident permits if granted:
Permits not granted.
www.leg.state.or.us/ors/166.html

Pennsylvania

Right-to-Carry Law Type
Right-to-Carry

Issuing Authority:
County Sheriff
These states also recognize your permit:
Idaho, Indiana, Michigan, Montana, Vermont, Wyoming
Contact agency for non-resident permits if granted:
Any Sheriff's Department
www.pacode.com

Rhode Island

Right-to-Carry Law Type
Limited Issue

Issuing Authority:
Attorney General
These states also recognize your permit:
Idaho, Indiana, Michigan, Vermont, Wyoming
Contact agency for non-resident permits if granted:
Attorney General by mail only (no phone calls) send self-addressed stamped envelope to: Dept. of Attorney General 150 South Main Street Providence, RI 02903 Attn: Bureau of Criminal Identification
www.rilin.state.ri.us/statutes/title11/11-47/s00014.htm

South Carolina

Right-to-Carry Law Type
Right-to-Carry

Issuing Authority:
S.C. Law Enforcement Division
These states also recognize your permit:
Arkansas, Idaho, Indiana, Michigan, Montana, Tennessee, Utah, Vermont, Wyoming
Contact agency for non-resident permits if granted:
Permits not granted.
www.lpitr.state.sc.us/code/statmast.htm

NRA - RIGHT-TO-CARRY RECIPROCITY GUIDE

South Dakota
Right-to-Carry Law Type
Right-to-Carry

Issuing Authority:
Chief of Police/County Sheriff
These states also recognize your permit:
Idaho, Indiana, Michigan, Vermont, Wyoming
Contact agency for non-resident permits if granted:
Permits not granted.
legis.state.sd.us/statutes/index.cfm

Tennessee
Right-to-Carry Law Type
Right-to-Carry

Issuing Authority:
Department of Public Safety
These states also recognize your permit:
Arkansas, Florida, Idaho, Indiana, Kentucky, Louisiana,
Michigan, Mississippi, Montana, South Carolina, Texas, Utah,
Virginia, Vermont, Wyoming
Contact agency for non-resident permits if granted:
Permits not granted.
www.state.tn.us/safety/handguns.html

Texas
Right-to-Carry Law Type
Right-to-Carry

Issuing Authority:
Department of Public Safety
These states also recognize your permit:
Alaska, Arizona, Arkansas, Idaho, Indiana, Louisiana, Michigan,
Montana, Oklahoma, Tennessee, Utah, Vermont, Wyoming
Contact agency for non-resident permits if granted:
Permits granted by DPS to qualified non-residents from states
with no concealed carry permit system. Call (800) 224-5744 or
(512) 424-7293.
www.txdps.state.tx.us./administration/crime_records/chl/chlsin
dex.htm

Utah
Right-to-Carry Law Type
Right-to-Carry

Issuing Authority:
Department of Public Safety
These states also recognize your permit:
Arizona, Arkansas, Idaho, Indiana, Michigan, Montana,
Oklahoma, South Carolina, Vermont, Wyoming
Contact agency for non-resident permits if granted:
Department of Public Safety; (801) 965-4484
www.le.state.ut.us/ÿ7Ecode/title 76/htm/76-oco45.htm

Vermont
Right-to-Carry Law Type
Right-to-Carry

Issuing Authority:
Vermont allows concealed carry without a permit and issues no
official permit.
These states also recognize your permit:
N/A
Contact agency for non-resident permits if granted:
No permit required.
www.leg.state.vt.us/statutes/title13/chap085.htm

Virginia
Right-to-Carry Law Type
Right-to-Carry

Issuing Authority:
Clerk of Circuit Court
These states also recognize your permit:
Idaho, Indiana, Michigan, Montana, Tennessee, West Virginia,
Vermont, Wyoming
Contact agency for non-resident permits if granted:
Permits not granted.
www.vsp.state.va.us/basrcwp.html

Washington
Right-to-Carry Law Type
Right-to-Carry

Issuing Authority:
Chief of Police/Sheriff
These states also recognize your permit:
Idaho, Indiana, Michigan, Montana, Vermont, Wyoming
Contact agency for non-resident permits if granted:
Any Sheriff's Department
www.leg.wa.gov/wsladm/rcw.htm

West Virginia
Right-to-Carry Law Type
Right-to-Carry

Issuing Authority:
Sheriff
These states also recognize your permit:
Idaho, Indiana, Kentucky, Michigan, Montana, Virginia,
Vermont, Wyoming
Contact agency for non-resident permits if granted:
Permits not granted.
www.wvstatepolice.com/legal/legal.shtml

Wisconsin
Right-to-Carry Law Type
None

Issuing Authority:
n/a
These states also recognize your permit:

Contact agency for non-resident permits if granted:
Permits not granted.
www.legis.state.wi.us/rsb/stats.html

Wyoming
Right-to-Carry Law Type
Right-to-Carry

Issuing Authority:
Attorney General
These states also recognize your permit:
Florida, Idaho, Indiana, Kentucky, Michigan, Mississippi,
Montana, North Dakota, Oklahoma, South Carolina, Vermont
Contact agency for non-resident permits if granted:
Permits not granted.
www.state.wy.us/~ag/dci/cw.html

ARMS ASSOCIATIONS

UNITED STATES

ALABAMA
Alabama Gun Collectors Assn.
Secretary, P.O. Box 70965, Tuscaloosa, AL 35407

ALASKA
Alaska Gun Collectors Assn., Inc.
C.W. Floyd, Pres., 5240 Little Tree, Anchorage, AK 99507

ARIZONA
Arizona Arms Assn.
Don DeBusk, President, 4837 Bryce Ave., Glendale, AZ 85301

CALIFORNIA
California Cartridge Collectors Assn.
Rick Montgomery, 1729 Christina, Stockton, CA 95204/209-463-7216 evs.
California Waterfowl Assn.
4630 Northgate Blvd., #150, Sacramento, CA 95834
Greater Calif. Arms & Collectors Assn.
Donald L. Bullock, 8291 Carburton St., Long Beach, CA 90808-3302
Los Angeles Gun Ctg. Collectors Assn.
F.H. Ruffra, 20810 Amie Ave., Apt. #9, Torrance, CA 90503
Stock Gun Players Assn.
6038 Appian Way, Long Beach, CA, 90803

COLORADO
Colorado Gun Collectors Assn.
L.E.(Bud) Greenwald, 2553 S. Quitman St., Denver, CO 80219/303-935-3850
Rocky Mountain Cartridge Collectors Assn.
John Roth, P.O. Box 757, Conifer, CO 80433

CONNECTICUT
Ye Connecticut Gun Guild, Inc.
Dick Fraser, P.O. Box 425, Windsor, CT 06095

FLORIDA
Unified Sportsmen of Florida
P.O. Box 6565, Tallahassee, FL 32314

GEORGIA
Georgia Arms Collectors Assn., Inc.
Michael Kindberg, President, P.O. Box 277, Alpharetta, GA 30239-0277

ILLINOIS
Illinois State Rifle Assn.
P.O. Box 637, Chatsworth, IL 60921
Mississippi Valley Gun & Cartridge Coll. Assn.
Bob Filbert, P.O. Box 61, Port Byron, IL 61275/309-523-2593
Sauk Trail Gun Collectors
Gordell M. Matson, P.O. Box 1113, Milan, IL 61264
Wabash Valley Gun Collectors Assn., Inc.
Roger L. Dorsett, 2601 Willow Rd., Urbana, IL 61801/217-384-7302

INDIANA
Indiana State Rifle & Pistol Assn.
Thos. Glancy, P.O. Box 552, Chesterton, IN 46304
Southern Indiana Gun Collectors Assn., Inc.
Sheila McClary, 309 W. Monroe St., Boonville, IN 47601/812-897-3742

IOWA
Beaver Creek Plainsmen Inc.
Steve Murphy, Secy., P.O. Box 298, Bondurant, IA 50035
Central States Gun Collectors Assn.
Dennis Greischar, Box 841, Mason City, IA 50402-0841

KANSAS
Kansas Cartridge Collectors Assn.
Bob Linder, Box 84, Plainville, KS 67663

KENTUCKY
Kentuckiana Arms Collectors Assn.
Charles Billips, President, Box 1776, Louisville, KY 40201
Kentucky Gun Collectors Assn., Inc.
Ruth Johnson, Box 64, Owensboro, KY 42302/502-729-4197

LOUISIANA
Washitaw River Renegades
Sandra Rushing, P.O. Box 256, Main St., Grayson, LA 71435

MARYLAND
Baltimore Antique Arms Assn.
Mr. Cillo, 1034 Main St., Darlington, MD 21304

MASSACHUSETTS
Bay Colony Weapons Collectors, Inc.
John Brandt, Box 111, Hingham, MA 02043
Massachusetts Arms Collectors
Bruce E. Skinner, P.O. Box 31, No. Carver, MA 02355/508-866-5259

MICHIGAN
Association for the Study and Research of .22 Caliber Rimfire Cartridges
George Kass, 4512 Nakoma Dr., Okemos, MI 48864

MINNESOTA
Sioux Empire Cartridge Collectors Assn.
Bob Cameron, 14597 Glendale Ave. SE, Prior Lake, MN 55372

MISSISSIPPI
Mississippi Gun Collectors Assn.
Jack E. Swinney, P.O. Box 16323, Hattiesburg, MS 39402

MISSOURI
Greater St. Louis Cartridge Collectors Assn.
Don MacChesney, 634 Scottsdale Rd., Kirkwood, MO 63122-1109
Mineral Belt Gun Collectors Assn.
D.F. Saunders, 1110 Cleveland Ave., Monett, MO 65708
Missouri Valley Arms Collectors Assn., Inc.
L.P Brammer II, Membership Secy., P.O. Box 33033, Kansas City, MO 64114

MONTANA
Montana Arms Collectors Assn.
Dean E. Yearout, Sr., Exec. Secy., 1516 21st Ave. S., Great Falls, MT 59405
Weapons Collectors Society of Montana
R.G. Schipf, Ex. Secy., 3100 Bancroft St., Missoula, MT 59801/406-728-2995

NEBRASKA
Nebraska Cartridge Collectors Club
Gary Muckel, P.O. Box 84442, Lincoln, NE 68501

NEW HAMPSHIRE
New Hampshire Arms Collectors, Inc.
James Stamatelos, Secy., P.O. Box 5, Cambridge, MA 02139

NEW JERSEY
Englishtown Benchrest Shooters Assn.
Michael Toth, 64 Cooke Ave., Carteret, NJ 07008
Jersey Shore Antique Arms Collectors
Joe Sisia, P.O. Box 100, Bayville, NJ 08721-0100
New Jersey Arms Collectors Club, Inc.
Angus Laidlaw, Vice President, 230 Valley Rd., Montclair, NJ 07042/201-746-0939; e-mail: acclaidlaw@juno.com

NEW YORK
Iroquois Arms Collectors Assn.
Bonnie Robinson, Show Secy., P.O. Box 142, Ransomville, NY 14131/716-791-4096
Mid-State Arms Coll. & Shooters Club
Jack Ackerman, 24 S. Mountain Terr., Binghamton, NY 13903

NORTH CAROLINA
North Carolina Gun Collectors Assn.
Jerry Ledford, 3231-7th St. Dr. NE, Hickory, NC 28601

OHIO
Ohio Gun Collectors Assn.
P.O. Box 9007, Maumee, OH 43537-9007/419-897-0861; Fax:419-897-0860
Shotshell Historical and Collectors Society
Madeline Bruemmer, 3886 Dawley Rd., Ravenna, OH 44266
The Stark Gun Collectors, Inc.
William I. Gann, 5666 Waynesburg Dr., Waynesburg, OH 44688

OREGON
Oregon Arms Collectors Assn., Inc.
Phil Bailey, P.O. Box 13000-A, Portland, OR 97213-0017/503-281-6864; off.:503-281-0918
Oregon Cartridge Collectors Assn.
Boyd Northrup, P.O. Box 285, Rhododendron, OR 97049

PENNSYLVANIA
Presque Isle Gun Collectors Assn.
James Welch, 156 E. 37 St., Erie, PA 16504

SOUTH CAROLINA
Belton Gun Club, Inc.
Attn. Secretary, P.O. Box 126, Belton, SC 29627/864-369-6767

Gun Owners of South Carolina
Membership Div.: William Strozier, Secretary, P.O. Box 70, Johns Island, SC 29457-0070/803-762-3240; Fax:803-795-0711; e-mail:76053.222@compuserve.com

SOUTH DAKOTA
Dakota Territory Gun Coll. Assn., Inc.
Curt Carter, Castlewood, SD 57223

TENNESSEE
Smoky Mountain Gun Coll. Assn., Inc.
Hugh W. Yabro, President, P.O. Box 23225, Knoxville, TN 37933

Tennessee Gun Collectors Assn., Inc.
M.H. Parks, 3556 Pleasant Valley Rd., Nashville, TN 37204-3419

TEXAS
Houston Gun Collectors Assn., Inc.
P.O. Box 741429, Houston, TX 77274-1429
Texas Gun Collectors Assn.
Bob Eder, Pres., P.O. Box 12067, El Paso, TX 79913/915-584-8183
Texas State Rifle Assn.
1131 Rockingham Dr., Suite 101, Richardson, TX 75080-4326

VIRGINIA
Virginia Gun Collectors Assn., Inc.
Addison Hurst, Secy., 38802 Charlestown Height, Waterford, VA 20197/540-882-3543

WASHINGTON
Association of Cartridge Collectors on the Pacific Northwest
Robert Jardin, 14214 Meadowlark Drive KPN, Gig Harbor, WA 98329
Washington Arms Collectors, Inc.
Joyce Boss, P.O. Box 389, Renton, WA, 98057-0389/206-255-8410

WISCONSIN
Great Lakes Arms Collectors Assn., Inc.
Edward C. Warnke, 2913 Woodridge Lane, Waukesha, WI 53188
Wisconsin Gun Collectors Assn., Inc.
Lulita Zellmer, P.O. Box 181, Sussex, WI 53089

WYOMING
Wyoming Weapons Collectors
P.O. Box 284, Laramie, WY 82073/307-745-4652 or 745-9530

NATIONAL ORGANIZATIONS

Amateur Trapshooting Assn.
David D. Bopp, Exec. Director, 601 W. National Rd., Vandalia, OH 45377/937-898-4638; Fax:937-898-5472
American Airgun Field Target Assn.
5911 Cherokee Ave., Tampa, FL 33604
American Coon Hunters Assn.
Opal Johnston, P.O. Cadet, Route 1, Box 492, Old Mines, MO 63630
American Custom Gunmakers Guild
Jan Billeb, Exec. Director, 22 Vista View Drive, Cody, WY 82414-9606 (307) 587-4297 (phone/fax). Email: acgg@acgg.org Website: www.acgg.org
American Defense Preparedness Assn.
Two Colonial Place, 2101 Wilson Blvd., Suite 400, Arlington, VA 22201-3061
American Paintball League
P.O. Box 3561, Johnson City, TN 37602/800-541-9169
American Pistolsmiths Guild
Alex B. Hamilton, Pres., 1449 Blue Crest Lane, San Antonio, TX 78232/210-494-3063
American Police Pistol & Rifle Assn.
3801 Biscayne Blvd., Miami, FL 33137

American Single Shot Rifle Assn.
Charles Kriegel, Secy., 1346C Whispering Woods Drive, West Carrollton OH 45449/937-866-9064. Website: www.assra.com
American Society of Arms Collectors
George E. Weatherly, P.O. Box 2567, Waxahachie, TX 75165
American Tactical Shooting Assn.(A.T.S.A.)
c/o Skip Gochenour, 2600 N. Third St., Harrisburg, PA 17110/717-233-0402; Fax:717-233-5340
Association of Firearm and Tool Mark Examiners
Lannie G. Emanuel, Secy., Southwest Institute of Forensic Sciences, P.O. Box 35728, Dallas, TX 75235/214-920-5979; Fax:214-920-5928; Membership Secy., Ann D. Jones, VA Div. of Forensic Science, P.O. Box 999, Richmond, VA 23208/804-786-4706; Fax:804-371-8328
Boone & Crockett Club
250 Station Dr., Missoula, MT 59801-2753
Browning Collectors Assn.
Secretary:Scherrie L. Brennac, 2749 Keith Dr., Villa Ridge, MO 63089/314-742-0571
The Cast Bullet Assn., Inc.
Ralland J. Fortier, Editor, 4103 Foxcraft Dr., Traverse City, MI 49684
Citizens Committee for the Right to Keep and Bear Arms
Natl. Hq., Liberty Park, 12500 NE Tenth Pl., Bellevue, WA 98005
Colt Collectors Assn.
25000 Highland Way, Los Gatos, CA 95030/408-353-2658.
Ducks Unlimited, Inc.
Natl. Headquarters, One Waterfowl Way, Memphis, TN 38120/901-758-3937
Fifty Caliber Shooters Assn.
PO Box 111, Monroe UT 84754-0111
Firearms Coalition/Neal Knox Associates
Box 6537, Silver Spring, MD 20906/301-871-3006
Firearms Engravers Guild of America
Rex C. Pedersen, Secy., 511 N. Rath Ave., Lundington, MI 49431/616-845-7695(Phone and Fax)
Foundation for North American Wild Sheep
720 Allen Ave., Cody, WY 82414-3402/web site: http://iigi.com/os/non/fnaws/fnaws.htm; e-mail: fnaws@wyoming.com
Freedom Arms Collectors Assn.
P.O. Box 160302, Miami, FL 33116-0302
Garand Collectors Assn.
P.O. Box 181, Richmond, KY 40475
Glock Shooting Sports Foundation
PO Box 309, Smyrna GA 30081 770-432-1202 Website: www.gssfonline.com
Golden Eagle Collectors Assn. (G.E.C.A.)
Chris Showler, 11144 Slate Creek Rd., Grass Valley, CA 95945
Gun Owners of America
8001 Forbes Place, Suite 102, Springfield, VA 22151/703-321-8585

ARMS ASSOCIATIONS

Handgun Hunters International
J.D. Jones, Director, P.O. Box 357 MAG, Bloomingdale, OH 43910

Harrington & Richardson Gun Coll. Assn.
George L. Cardet, 330 S.W. 27th Ave., Suite 603, Miami, FL 33135

High Standard Collectors' Assn.
John J. Stimson, Jr., Pres., 540 W. 92nd St., Indianapolis, IN 46260 Website: www.highstandard.org

Hopkins & Allen Arms & Memorabilia Society (HAAMS)
P.O. Box 187, 1309 Pamela Circle, Delphos, OH 45833

International Ammunition Association, Inc.
C.R. Punnett, Secy., 8 Hillock Lane, Chadds Ford, PA 19317/610-358-1285;Fax:610-3 58-1560

International Benchrest Shooters
Joan Borden, RR1, Box 250BB, Springville, PA 18844/717-965-2366

International Blackpowder Hunting Assn.
P.O. Box 1180, Glenrock, WY 82637/307-436-9817

IHMSA (Intl. Handgun Metallic Silhouette Assn.)
PO Box 368, Burlington, IA 52601 Website: www.ihmsa.org

International Society of Mauser Arms Collectors
Michael Kindberg, Pres., P.O. Box 277, Alpharetta, GA 30239-0277

Jews for the Preservation of Firearms Ownership (JPFO) 501(c)(3)
2872 S. Wentworth Ave., Milwaukee, WI 53207/414-769-0760; Fax:414-483-8435

The Mannlicher Collectors Assn.
Membership Office: P.O. Box1249, The Dalles, Oregon 97058

Marlin Firearms Collectors Assn., Ltd.
Dick Paterson, Secy., 407 Lincoln Bldg., 44 Main St., Champaign, IL 61820

Merwin Hulbert Association,
2503 Kentwood Ct., High Point, NC 27265

Miniature Arms Collectors/Makers Society, Ltd.
Ralph Koebbeman, Pres., 4910 Kilburn Ave., Rockford, IL 61101/815-964-2569

M1 Carbine Collectors Assn. (M1-CCA)
623 Apaloosa Ln., Gardnerville, NV 89410-7840

National Association of Buckskinners (NAB)
Territorial Dispatch—1800s Historical Publication, 4701 Marion St., Suite 324, Livestock Exchange Bldg., Denver, CO 80216/303-297-9671

The National Association of Derringer Collectors
P.O. Box 20572, San Jose, CA 95160

National Assn. of Federally Licensed Firearms Dealers
Andrew Molchan, 2455 E. Sunrise, Ft. Lauderdale, FL 33304

National Association to Keep and Bear Arms
P.O. Box 78336, Seattle, WA 98178

National Automatic Pistol Collectors Assn.
Tom Knox, P.O. Box 15738, Tower Grove Station, St. Louis, MO 63163

National Bench Rest Shooters Assn., Inc.
Pat Ferrell, 2835 Guilford Lane, Oklahoma City, OK 73120-4404/405-842-9585; Fax: 405-842-9575

National Muzzle Loading Rifle Assn.
Box 67, Friendship, IN 47021 / 812-667-5131. Website: www.nmlra@nmlra.org

National Professional Paintball League (NPPL)
540 Main St., Mount Kisco, NY 10549/914-241-7400

National Reloading Manufacturers Assn.
One Centerpointe Dr., Suite 300, Lake Oswego, OR 97035

National Rifle Assn. of America
11250 Waples Mill Rd., Fairfax, VA 22030 / 703-267-1000. Website: www.nra.org

National Shooting Sports Foundation, Inc.
Robert T. Delfay, President, Flintlock Ridge Office Center, 11 Mile Hill Rd., Newtown, CT 06470-2359/203-426-1320; FAX: 203-426-1087

National Skeet Shooting Assn.
Dan Snyuder, Director, 5931 Roft Road, San Antonio, TX 78253-9261/800-877-5338. Website: nssa-nsca.com

National Sporting Clays Association
Ann Myers, Director, 5931 Roft Road, San Antonio, TX 78253-9261/800-877-5338. Website: nssa-nsca.com

National Wild Turkey Federation, Inc.
P.O. Box 530, 770 Augusta Rd., Edgefield, SC 29824

North American Hunting Club
P.O. Box 3401, Minnetonka, MN 55343/612-936-9333; Fax: 612-936-9755

North American Paintball Referees Association (NAPRA)
584 Cestaric Dr., Milpitas, CA 95035

North-South Skirmish Assn., Inc.
Stevan F. Meserve, Exec. Secretary, 507 N. Brighton Court, Sterling, VA 20164-3919

Old West Shooter's Association
712 James Street, Hazel TX 76020 817-444-2049

Remington Society of America
Gordon Fosburg, Secretary, 11900 North Brinton Road, Lake, MI 48623

Rocky Mountain Elk Foundation
P.O. Box 8249, Missoula, MT 59807-8249/406-523-4500;Fax: 406-523-4581 Website: www.rmef.org

Ruger Collector's Assn., Inc.
P.O. Box 240, Greens Farms, CT 06434

Safari Club International
4800 W. Gates Pass Rd., Tucson, AZ 85745/520-620-1220

Sako Collectors Assn., Inc.
Jim Lutes, 202 N. Locust, Whitewater, KS 67154

Second Amendment Foundation
James Madison Building, 12500 NE 10th Pl., Bellevue, WA 98005

Single Action Shooting Society (SASS)
23255-A La Palma Avenue, Yorba Linda, CA 92887/714-694-1800; FAX: 714-694-1815/email: sasseot@aol.com Website: www.sassnet.com

Smith & Wesson Collectors Assn.
Cally Pletl, Admin. Asst.,PO Box 444, Afton, NY 13730

The Society of American Bayonet Collectors
P.O. Box 234, East Islip, NY 11730-0234

Southern California Schuetzen Society
Dean Lillard, 34657 Ave. E., Yucaipa, CA 92399

Sporting Arms and Ammunition Manufacturers' Institute (SAAMI)
Flintlock Ridge Office Center, 11 Mile Hill Rd., Newtown, CT 06470-2359/203-426-4358; FAX: 203-426-1087

Sporting Clays of America (SCA)
Ron L. Blosser, Pres., 9257 Buckeye Rd., Sugar Grove, OH 43155-9632/614-746-8334; Fax: 614-746-8605

Steel Challenge
23234 Via Barra, Valencia CA 91355 Website: www.steelchallenge.com

The Thompson/Center Assn.
Joe Wright, President, Box 792, Northboro, MA 01532/508-845-6960

U.S. Practical Shooting Assn./IPSC
Dave Thomas, P.O. Box 811, Sedro Woolley, WA 98284/360-855-2245 Website: www.uspsa.org

U.S. Revolver Assn.
Brian J. Barer, 40 Larchmont Ave., Taunton, MA 02780/508-824-4836

U.S.A. Shooting
U.S. Olympic Shooting Center, One Olympic Plaza, Colorado Springs, CO 80909/719-578-4670. Website: wwwusashooting.org

The Varmint Hunters Assn., Inc.
Box 759, Pierre, SD 57501/Member Services 800-528-4868

Weatherby Collectors Assn., Inc.
P.O. Box 478, Pacific, MO 63069 Website: www.weatherbycollectors.com Email: WCAsecretary@aol.com

The Wildcatters
P.O. Box 170, Greenville, WI 54942

Winchester Arms Collectors Assn.
P.O. Box 230, Brownsboro, TX 75756/903-852-4027

The Women's Shooting Sports Foundation (WSSF)
4620 Edison Avenue, Ste. C, Colorado Springs, CO 80915/719-638-1299; FAX: 719-638-1271/email: wssf@worldnet.att.net

ARGENTINA

Asociacion Argentina de Coleccionistas de Armes y Municiones
Castilla de Correos No. 28, Succursal I B, 1401 Buenos Aires, Republica Argentina

AUSTRALIA

Antique & Historical Arms Collectors of Australia
P.O. Box 5654, GCMC Queensland 9726, Australia

The Arms Collector's Guild of Queensland Inc.
Ian Skennerton, P.O. Box 433, Ashmore City 4214, Queensland, Australia

Australian Cartridge Collectors Assn., Inc.
Bob Bennett, 126 Landscape Dr., E. Doncaster 3109, Victoria, Australia

Sporting Shooters Assn. of Australia, Inc.
P.O. Box 2066, Kent Town, SA 5071, Australia

CANADA

ALBERTA

Canadian Historical Arms Society
P.O. Box 901, Edmonton, Alb., Canada T5J 2L8

National Firearms Assn.
Natl. Hq: P.O. Box 1779, Edmonton, Alb., Canada T5J 2P1

BRITISH COLUMBIA

The Historical Arms Collectors of B.C. (Canada)
Harry Moon, Pres., P.O. Box 50117, South Slope RPO, Burnaby, BC V5J 5G3, Canada/604-438-0950; Fax:604-277-3646

ONTARIO

Association of Canadian Cartridge Collectors
Monica Wright, RR 1, Millgrove, ON, LOR IVO, Canada

Tri-County Antique Arms Fair
P.O. Box 122, RR #1, North Lancaster, Ont., Canada K0C 1Z0

EUROPE

BELGIUM

European Cartridge Research Assn.
Graham Irving, 21 Rue Schaltin, 4900 Spa, Belgium/32.87.77.43.40; Fax:32.87.77.27.51

CZECHOSLOVAKIA

Spolecnost Pro Studium Naboju (Czech Cartridge Research Assn.)
JUDr. Jaroslav Bubak, Pod Homolko 1439, 26601 Beroun 2, Czech Republic

DENMARK

Aquila Dansk Jagtpatron Historic Forening (Danish Historical Cartridge Collectors Club)
Steen Elgaard Møller, Ulriksdalsvej 7, 4840 Nr. Alslev, Denmark 10045-53846218;Fax:00455384 6209

ENGLAND

Arms and Armour Society
Hon. Secretary A. Dove, P.O. Box 10232, London, 5W19 2ZD, England

Dutch Paintball Federation
Aceville Publ., Castle House 97 High Street, Colchester, Essex CO1 1TH, England/011-44-206-564840

European Paintball Sports Foundation
c/o Aceville Publ., Castle House 97 High St., Colchester, Essex, CO1 1TH, England

Historical Breechloading Smallarms Assn.
D.J. Penn M.A., Secy., P.O. Box 12778, London SE1 6BX, England. Journal and newsletter are $23 a yr., including airmail.

National Rifle Assn.
(Great Britain) Bisley Camp, Brookwood, Woking Surrey GU24 OPB, England/01483.797777; Fax: 014730686275

United Kingdom Cartridge Club
Ian Southgate, 20 Millfield, Elmley Castle, Nr. Pershore, Worcestershire, WR10 3HR, England

FRANCE

STAC-Western Co.
3 Ave. Paul Doumer (N.311); 78360 Montesson, France/01.30.53-43-65; Fax: 01.30.53.19.10

GERMANY

Bund Deutscher Sportschützen e.v. (BDS)
Borsigallee 10, 53125 Bonn 1, Germany

Deutscher Schützenbund
Lahnstrasse 120, 65195 Wiesbaden, Germany

SPAIN

Asociacion Espanola de Colleccionistas de Cartuchos (A.E.C.C.)
Secretary: Apdo. Correos No. 1086, 2880-Alcala de Henares (Madrid), Spain. President: Apdo. Correos No. 682, 50080 Zaragoza, Spain

SWEDEN

Scandinavian Ammunition Research Assn.
c/o Morten Stoen, Annerudstubben 3, N-1383 Asker, Norway

NEW ZEALAND

New Zealand Cartridge Collectors Club
Terry Castle, 70 Tiraumea Dr., Pakuranga, Auckland, New Zealand

New Zealand Deerstalkers Assn.
P.O. Box 6514 TE ARO, Wellington, New Zealand

SOUTH AFRICA

Historical Firearms Soc. of South Africa
P.O. Box 145, 7725 Newlands, Republic of South Africa

Republic of South Africa Cartridge Collectors Assn.
Arno Klee, 20 Eugene St., Malanshof Randburg, Gauteng 2194, Republic of South Africa

S.A.A.C.A. (Southern Africa Arms and Ammunition Assn.)
Gauteng office: P.O. Box 7597, Weltevreden Park, 1715, Republic of South Africa/011-679-1151; Fax: 011-679-1131; e-mail: saaaca@iafrica.com. Kwa-Zulu Natal office: P.O. Box 4065, Northway, Kwazulu-Natal 4065, Republic of South Africa

SAGA (S.A. Gunowners' Assn.)
P.O. Box 35203, Northway, Kwazulu-Natal 4065, Republic of South Africa

PERIODICAL PUBLICATIONS

AAFTA News (M)

5911 Cherokee Ave., Tampa, FL 33604. Official newsletter of the American Airgun Field Target Assn.

Action Pursuit Games Magazine (M)

CFW Enterprises, Inc., 4201 W. Vanowen Pl., Burbank, CA 91505 818-845-2656. $4.99 single copy U.S., $5.50 Canada. Editor: Dan Reeves. World's leading magazine of paintball sports.

Air Gunner Magazine

4 The Courtyard, Denmark St., Wokingham, Berkshire RG11 2AZ, England/011-44-734-771677. $U.S. $44 for 1 yr. Leading monthly airgun magazine in U.K.

Airgun Ads

Box 33, Hamilton, MT 59840/406-363-3805; Fax: 406-363-4117. $35 1 yr. (for first mailing; $20 for second mailing; $35 for Canada and foreign orders.) Monthly tabloid with extensive For Sale and Wanted airgun listings.

The Airgun Letter

Gapp, Inc., 4614 Woodland Rd., Ellicott City, MD 21042-6329/410-730-5496; Fax: 410-730-9544; e-mail: staff@airgnltr.net; http://www.airgunletter.com. $21 U.S., $24 Canada, $27 Mexico and $33 other foreign orders, 1 yr. Monthly newsletter for airgun users and collectors.

Airgun World

4 The Courtyard, Denmark St., Wokingham, Berkshire RG40 2AZ, England/011-44-734-771677. Call for subscription rates. Oldest monthly airgun magazine in the U.K., now a sister publication to Air Gunner.

Alaska Magazine

Morris Communications, 735 Broad Street, Augusta, GA 30901/706-722-6060. Hunting, Fishing and Life on the Last Frontier articles of Alaska and western Canada.

American Firearms Industry

Nat'l. Assn. of Federally Licensed Firearms Dealers, 2455 E. Sunrise Blvd., Suite 916, Ft. Lauderdale, FL 33304. $35.00 yr. For firearms retailers, distributors and manufacturers.

American Guardian

NRA, 11250 Waples Mill Rd., Fairfax, VA 22030. Publications division. $15.00 1 yr. Magazine features personal protection; home-self-defense; family recreation shooting; women's issues; etc.

American Gunsmith

Belvoir Publications, Inc., 75 Holly Hill Lane, Greenwich, CT 06836-2626/203-661-6111. $49.00 (12 issues). Technical journal of firearms repair and maintenance.

American Handgunner*

Publisher's Development Corp., 591 Camino de la Reina, Suite 200, San Diego, CA 92108/800-537-3006 $16.95 yr. Articles for handgun enthusiasts, competitors, police and hunters.

American Hunter (M)

National Rifle Assn., 11250 Waples Mill Rd., Fairfax, VA 22030 (Same address for both.) Publications Div. $35.00 yr. Wide scope of hunting articles.

American Rifleman (M)

National Rifle Assn., 11250 Waples Mill Rd., Fairfax, VA 22030 (Same address for both). Publications Div. $35.00 yr. Firearms articles of all kinds.

American Survival Guide

McMullen Angus Publishing, Inc., 774 S. Placentia Ave., Placentia, CA 92670-6846. 12 issues $19.95/714-572-2255; FAX: 714-572-1864.

Armes & Tir*

c/o FABECO, 38, rue de Trévise 75009 Paris, France. Articles for hunters, collectors, and shooters. French text.

Arms Collecting (Q)

Museum Restoration Service, P.O. Box 70, Alexandria Bay, NY 13607-0070. $22.00 yr.; $62.00 3 yrs.; $112.00 5 yrs.

Australian Shooter (formerly Australian Shooters Journal)

Sporting Shooters' Assn. of Australia, Inc., P.O. Box 2066, Kent Town SA 5071, Australia. $60.00 yr. locally; $65.00 yr. overseas surface mail. Hunting and shooting articles.

The Backwoodsman Magazine

P.O. Box 627, Westcliffe, CO 81252. $16.00 for 6 issues per yr.; $30.00 for 2 yrs.; sample copy $2.75. Subjects include muzzle-loading, woodslore, primitive survival, trapping, homesteading, blackpowder cartridge guns, 19th century how-to.

Black Powder Cartridge News (Q)

SPG, Inc., P.O. Box 761, Livingston, MT 59047/Phone/Fax: 406-222-8416. $17 yr. (4 issues) ($6 extra 1st class mailing). For the blackpowder cartridge enthusiast.

Blackpowder Hunting (M)

Intl. Blackpowder Hunting Assn., P.O. Box 1180Z, Glenrock, WY 82637/307-436-9817. $20.00 1 yr., $36.00 2 yrs. How-to and where-to features by experts on hunting; shooting; ballistics; traditional and modern blackpowder rifles, shotguns, pistols and cartridges.

Black Powder Times

P.O. Box 234, Lake Stevens, WA 98258. $20.00 yr.; add $5 per year for Canada, $10 per year other foreign. Tabloid newspaper for blackpowder activities; test reports.

Blade Magazine

Krause Publications, 700 East State St., Iola, WI 54990-0001. $25.98 for 12 issues. Foreign price (including Canada-Mexico) $50.00. A magazine for all enthusiasts of handmade, factory and antique knives.

Caliber

GFI-Verlag, Theodor-Heuss Ring 62, 50668 K"ln, Germany. For hunters, target shooters and reloaders.

The Caller (Q) (M)

National Wild Turkey Federation, P.O. Box 530, Edgefield, SC 29824. Tabloid newspaper for members; 4 issues per yr. (membership fee $25.00)

Cartridge Journal (M)

Robert Mellichamp, 907 Shirkmere, Houston, TX 77008/713-869-0558. Dues $12 for U.S. and Canadian members (includes the newsletter); 6 issues.

The Cast Bullet*(M)

Official journal of The Cast Bullet Assn. Director of Membership, 203 E. 2nd St., Muscatine, IA 52761. Annual membership dues $14, includes 6 issues.

COLTELLI, che Passione (Q)

Casella postale N.519, 20101 Milano, Italy/Fax:02-48402857. $15 1 yr., $27 2 yrs. Covers all types of knives—collecting, combat, historical. Italian text.

Combat Handguns*

Harris Publications, Inc., 1115 Broadway, New York, NY 10010.

Deer & Deer Hunting Magazine

Krause Publications, 700 E. State St., Iola, WI 54990-0001. $19.95 yr. (9 issues). For the serious deer hunter. Website: www.krause.com

The Derringer Peanut (M)

The National Association of Derringer Collectors, P.O. Box 20572, San Jose, CA 95160. A newsletter dedicated to developing the best derringer information. Write for details.

Deutsches Waffen Journal

Journal-Verlag Schwend GmbH, Postfach 100340, D-74503 Schwäbisch Hall, Germany/0791-404-500; FAX:0791-404-505 and 404-424. DM102 p. yr. (interior); DM125.30 (abroad), postage included. Antique and modern arms and equipment. German text.

Double Gun Journal

P.O. Box 550, East Jordan, MI 49727/800-447-1658. $35 for 4 issues.

Ducks Unlimited, Inc. (M)

1 Waterfowl Way, Memphis, TN 38120

The Engraver (M) (Q)

P.O. Box 4365, Estes Park, CO 80517/970-586-2388; Fax: 970-586-0394. Mike Dubber, editor. The journal of firearms engraving.

PERIODICAL PUBLICATIONS

The Field

King's Reach Tower, Stamford St., London SE1 9LS England. £36.40 U.K. 1 yr.; 49.90 (overseas, surface mail) yr.; £82.00 (overseas, air mail) yr. Hunting and shooting articles, and all country sports.

Field & Stream

Time4 Media, Two Park Ave., New York, NY 10016/212-779-5000. Monthly shooting column. Articles on hunting and fishing.

Field Tests

Belvoir Publications, Inc., 75 Holly Hill Lane; P.O. Box 2626, Greenwich, CT 06836-2626/203-661-6111; 800-829-3361 (subscription line). U.S. & Canada $29 1 yr., $58 2 yrs.; all other countries $45 1 yr., $90 2 yrs. (air).

Fur-Fish-Game

A.R. Harding Pub. Co., 2878 E. Main St., Columbus, OH 43209. $15.95 yr. Practical guidance regarding trapping, fishing and hunting.

The Gottlieb-Tartaro Report

Second Amendment Foundation, James Madison Bldg., 12500 NE 10th Pl., Bellevue, WA 98005/206-454-7012;Fax:206-451-3959. $30 for 12 issues. An insiders guide for gun owners.

Gray's Sporting Journal

Gray's Sporting Journal, P.O. Box 1207, Augusta, GA 30903. $36.95 per yr. for 6 issues. Hunting and fishing journals. Expeditions and Guides Book (Annual Travel Guide).

Gun List†

700 E. State St., Iola, WI 54990. $36.98 yr. (26 issues); $65.98 2 yrs. (52 issues). Indexed market publication for firearms collectors and active shooters; guns, supplies and services. Website: www.krause.com

Gun News Digest (Q)

Second Amendment Fdn., P.O. Box 488, Station C, Buffalo, NY 14209/716-885-6408;Fax:716-884-4471. $10 U.S.; $20 foreign.

The Gun Report

World Wide Gun Report, Inc., Box 38, Aledo, IL 61231-0038. $33.00 yr. For the antique and collectable gun dealer and collector.

Gunmaker (M) (Q)

ACGG, P.O. Box 812, Burlington, IA 52601-0812. The journal of custom gunmaking.

The Gunrunner

Div. of Kexco Publ. Co. Ltd., Box 565G, Lethbridge, Alb., Canada T1J 3Z4. $23.00 yr., sample $2.00. Monthly newspaper, listing everything from antiques to artillery.

Gun Show Calendar (Q)

700 E. State St., Iola, WI 54990. $14.95 yr. (4 issues). Gun shows listed; chronologically and by state. Website: www.krause.com

Gun Tests

11 Commerce Blvd., Palm Coast, FL 32142. The consumer resource for the serious shooter. Write for information.

Gun Trade News

Bruce Publishing Ltd., P.O. Box 82, Wantage, Ozon OX12 7A8, England/44-1-235-771770; Fax: 44-1-235-771848. Britain's only "trade only" magazine exclusive to the gun trade.

Gun Week†

Second Amendment Foundation, P.O. Box 488, Station C, Buffalo, NY 14209. $35.00 yr. U.S. and possessions; $45.00 yr. other countries. Tabloid paper on guns, hunting, shooting and collecting (36 issues).

Gun World

Y-Visionary Publishing, LP 265 South Anita Drive, Ste. 120, Orange, CA 92868. $21.97 yr.; $34.97 2 yrs. For the hunting, reloading and shooting enthusiast.

Guns & Ammo

Primedia, 6420 Wilshire Blvd., Los Angeles, CA 90048/213-782-2780. $23.94 yr. Guns, shooting, and technical articles.

Guns

Publishers Development Corporation, P.O. Box 85201, San Diego, CA 92138/800-537-3006. $19.95 yr. In-depth articles on a wide range of guns, shooting equipment and related accessories for gun collectors, hunters and shooters.

Guns Review

Ravenhill Publishing Co. Ltd., Box 35, Standard House, Bonhill St., London EC 2A 4DA, England. £20.00 sterling (approx. U.S. $38 USA & Canada) yr. For collectors and shooters.

H.A.C.S. Newsletter (M)

Harry Moon, Pres., P.O. Box 50117, South Slope RPO, Burnaby BC, V5J 5G3, Canada/604-438-0950; Fax:604-277-3646. $25 p. yr. U.S. and Canada. Official newsletter of The Historical Arms Collectors of B.C. (Canada).

Handgunner*

Richard A.J. Munday, Seychelles house, Brightlingsen, Essex CO7 ONN, England/012063-305201. £18.00 (sterling).

Handguns

Primedia, 6420 Wilshire Blvd., Los Angeles, CA 90048/323-782-2868. $23/94 yr. For the handgunning and shooting enthusiast.

Handloader*

Wolfe Publishing Co., 2626 Stearman Road, Ste. A, Prescott, AZ 86301/520-445-7810;Fax:520-778-5124. $22.00 yr. The journal of ammunition reloading.

INSIGHTS*

NRA, 11250 Waples Mill Rd., Fairfax, VA 22030. Editor, John E. Robbins. $15.00 yr., which includes NRA junior membership; $10.00 for adult subscriptions (12 issues). Plenty of details for the young hunter and target shooter; emphasizes gun safety, marksmanship training, hunting skills.

International Arms & Militaria Collector (Q)

Arms & Militaria Press, P.O. Box 80, Labrador, Qld. 4215, Australia. A$39.50 yr. (U.S. & Canada), 2 yrs. A$77.50; A$37.50 (others), 1 yr., 2 yrs. $73.50 all air express mail; surface mail is less. Editor: Ian D. Skennerton.

International Shooting Sport*/UIT Journal

International Shooting Union (UIT), Bavariaring 21, D-80336 Munich, Germany. Europe: (Deutsche Mark) DM44.00 yr., 2 yrs. DM83.00; outside Europe: DM50.00 yr., 2 yrs. DM95.00 (air mail postage included.) For international sport shooting.

Internationales Waffen-Magazin

Habegger-Verlag Zürich, Postfach 9230, CH-8036 Zürich, Switzerland. SF 105.00 (approx. U.S. $73.00) surface mail for 10 issues. Modern and antique arms, self-defense. German text; English summary of contents.

The Journal of the Arms & Armour Society (M)

A. Dove, P.O. Box 10232, London, SW19 2ZD England. £15.00 surface mail; £20.00 airmail sterling only yr. Articles for the historian and collector.

Journal of the Historical Breechloading Smallarms Assn.

Published annually. P.O. Box 12778, London, SE1 6XB, England. $21.00 yr. Articles for the collector plus mailings of short articles on specific arms, reprints, newsletters, etc.

Knife World

Knife World Publications, P.O. Box 3395, Knoxville, TN 37927. $15.00 yr.; $25.00 2 yrs. Published monthly for knife enthusiasts and collectors. Articles on custom and factory knives; other knife-related interests, monthly column on knife identification, military knives.

Man At Arms*

P.O. Box 460, Lincoln, RI 02865. $27.00 yr., $52.00 2 yrs. plus $8.00 for foreign subscribers. The N.R.A. magazine of arms collecting-investing, with excellent articles for the collector of antique arms and militaria.

The Mannlicher Collector (Q)(M)

Mannlicher Collectors Assn., Inc., P.O. Box 7144, Salem Oregon 97303. $20/ yr. subscription included in membership.

MAN/MAGNUM

S.A. Man (Pty) Ltd., P.O. Box 35204, Northway, Durban 4065, Republic of South Africa. SA Rand 200.00 for 12 issues. Africa's only publication on hunting, shooting, firearms, bushcraft, knives, etc.

The Marlin Collector (M)

R.W. Paterson, 407 Lincoln Bldg., 44 Main St., Champaign, IL 61820.

Muzzle Blasts (M)

National Muzzle Loading Rifle Assn., P.O. Box 67, Friendship, IN 47021/812-667-5131. $35.00 yr. annual membership. For the blackpowder shooter.

Muzzleloader Magazine*

Scurlock Publishing Co., Inc., Dept. Gun, Route 5, Box 347-M, Texarkana, TX 75501. $18.00 U.S.; $22.50 U.S./yr. for foreign subscribers. The publication for blackpowder shooters.

National Defense (M)*

American Defense Preparedness Assn., Two Colonial Place, Suite 400, 2101 Wilson Blvd., Arlington, VA 22201-3061/703-522-1820; FAX: 703-522-1885. $35.00 yr. Articles on both military and civil defense field, including weapons, materials technology, management.

National Knife Magazine (M)

Natl. Knife Coll. Assn., 7201 Shallowford Rd., P.O. Box 21070, Chattanooga, TN 37424-0070. Membership $35 yr.; $65.00 International yr.

National Rifle Assn. Journal (British) (Q)

Natl. Rifle Assn. (BR.), Bisley Camp, Brookwood, Woking, Surrey, England. GU24, OPB. £24.00 Sterling including postage.

National Wildlife*

Natl. Wildlife Fed., 1400 16th St. NW, Washington, DC 20036, $16.00 yr. (6 issues); International Wildlife, 6 issues, $16.00 yr. Both, $22.00 yr., includes all membership benefits. Write attn.: Membership Services Dept., for more information.

New Zealand GUNS*

Waitekauri Publishing, P.O. 45, Waikino 3060, New Zealand. $NZ90.00 (6 issues) yr. Covers the hunting and firearms scene in New Zealand.

New Zealand Wildlife (Q)

New Zealand Deerstalkers Assoc., Inc., P.O. Box 6514, Wellington, N.Z. $30.00 (N.Z.). Hunting, shooting and firearms/game research articles.

North American Hunter* (M)

P.O. Box 3401, Minnetonka, MN 55343/612-936-9333; e-mail: huntingclub@pclink.com. $18.00 yr. (7 issues). Articles on all types of North American hunting.

Outdoor Life

Time4 Media, Two Park Ave., New York, NY 10016. $16.95/yr. Extensive coverage of hunting and shooting. Shooting column by Jim Carmichel.

La Passion des Courteaux (Q)

Phenix Editions, 25 rue Mademoiselle, 75015 Paris, France. French text.

Paintball Games International Magazine

Aceville Publications, Castle House, 97 High St., Colchester, Essex, England CO1 1TH/011-44-206-564840. Write for subscription rates. Leading magazine in the U.K. covering competitive paintball activities.

Paintball News

PBN Publishing, P.O. Box 1608, 24 Henniker St., Hillsboro, NH 03244/603-464-6080. $35 U.S. 1 yr. Bi-weekly. Newspaper covering the sport of paintball, new product reviews and industry features.

Paintball Sports (Q)

Paintball Publications, Inc., 540 Main St., Mount Kisco, NY 10549/941-241-7400. $24.75 U.S. 1 yr., $32.75 foreign. Covering the competitive paintball scene.

Performance Shooter

Belvoir Publications, Inc., 75 Holly Hill Lane, Greenwich, CT 06836-2626/203-661-6111. $45.00 yr. (12 issues). Techniques and technology for improved rifle and pistol accuracy.

Petersen's HUNTING Magazine

Primedia, 6420 Wilshire Blvd., Los Angeles, CA 90048. $19.94 yr.; Canada $29.34 yr.; foreign countries $29.94 yr. Hunting articles for all game; test reports.

P.I. Magazine

America's Private Investigation Journal, 755 Bronx Dr., Toledo, OH 43609. Chuck Klein, firearms editor with column about handguns.

Pirsch

BLV Verlagsgesellschaft mbH, Postfach 400320, 80703 Munich, Germany/089-12704-0;Fax:089-12705-3 54. German text.

Point Blank

Citizens Committee for the Right to Keep and Bear Arms (sent to contributors), Liberty Park, 12500 NE 10th Pl., Bellevue, WA 98005

POINTBLANK (M)

Natl. Firearms Assn., Box 4384 Stn. C, Calgary, AB T2T 5N2, Canada. Official publication of the NFA.

The Police Marksman*

6000 E. Shirley Lane, Montgomery, AL 36117. $17.95 yr. For law enforcement personnel.

Police Times (M)

3801 Biscayne Blvd., Miami, FL 33137/305-573-0070.

Popular Mechanics

Hearst Corp., 224 W. 57th St., New York, NY 10019. Firearms, camping, outdoor oriented articles.

Precision Shooting

Precision Shooting, Inc., 222 McKee St., Manchester, CT 06040. $37.00 yr. U.S. Journal of the International Benchrest Shooters, and target shooting in general. Also considerable coverage of varmint shooting, as well as big bore, small bore, schuetzen, lead bullet, wildcats and precision reloading.

Rifle*

Wolfe Publishing Co., 2626 Stearman Road, Ste. A, Prescott, AZ 86301/520-445-7810; Fax: 520-778-5124. $19.00 yr. The sporting firearms journal.

Rifle's Hunting Annual

Wolfe Publishing Co., 2626 Stearman Road, Ste. A, Prescott, AZ 86301/520-445-7810; Fax: 520-778-5124. $4.99 Annual. Dedicated to the finest pursuit of the hunt.

Rod & Rifle Magazine

Lithographic Serv. Ltd., P.O. Box 38-138, Wellington, New Zealand. $50.00 yr. (6 issues). Hunting, shooting and fishing articles.

Safari* (M)

Safari Magazine, 4800 W. Gates Pass Rd., Tucson, AZ 85745/602-620-1220. $55.00 (6 times). The journal of big game hunting, published by Safari Club International. Also publish Safari Times, a monthly newspaper, included in price of $55.00 national membership.

Second Amendment Reporter

Second Amendment Foundation, James Madison Bldg., 12500 NE 10th Pl., Bellevue, WA 98005. $15.00 yr. (non-contributors).

Shoot! Magazine*

Shoot! Magazine Corp., 1770 West State Stret PMB 340, Boise ID 83702/208-368-9920; Fax: 208-338-8428. Website: www.shootmagazine.com $32.95 (6 times/yr.). Articles of interest to the cowboy action shooter, or others interested the Western-era firearms and ammunition.

Shooter's News

23146 Lorain Rd., Box 349, North Olmsted, OH 44070/216-979-5258;Fax:216-979-5259. $29 U.S. 1 yr., $54 2 yrs.; $52 foreign surface. A journal dedicated to precision riflery.

PERIODICAL PUBLICATIONS

Shooting Industry

Publisher's Dev. Corp., 591 Camino de la Reina, Suite 200, San Diego, CA 92108. $50.00 yr. To the trade. $25.00.

Shooting Sports USA

National Rifle Assn. of America, 11250 Waples Mill Road, Fairfax, VA 22030. Annual subscriptions for NRA members are $5 for classified shooters and $10 for non-classified shooters. Non-NRA member subscriptions are $15. Covering events, techniques and personalities in competitive shooting.

Shooting Sportsman*

P.O. Box 11282, Des Moines, IA 50340/800-666-4955 (for subscriptions). Editorial: P.O. Box 1357, Camden, ME 04843. $19.95 for six issues. The magazine of wingshooting and fine guns.

The Shooting Times & Country Magazine (England)†

IPC Magazines Ltd., King's Reach Tower, Stamford St, 1 London SE1 9LS, England/0171-261-6180;Fax:0171-261-7179. £65 (approx. $98.00) yr.; £79 yr. overseas (52 issues). Game shooting, wild fowling, hunting, game fishing and firearms articles. Britain's best selling field sports magazine.

Shooting Times

Primedia, 2 News Plaza, P.O. Box 1790, Peoria, IL 61656/309-682-6626. $16.97 yr. Guns, shooting, reloading; articles on every gun activity.

The Shotgun News‡

Primedia, 2 News Plaza, P.O. Box 1790, Peoria, IL 61656/800-495-8362. $28.95 yr.; foreign subscription call for rates. Sample copy $4.00. Gun ads of all kinds.

SHOT Business

National Shooting Sports Foundation, Flintlock Ridge Office Center, 11 Mile Hill Rd., Newtown, CT 06470-2359/203-426-1320; FAX: 203-426-1087. For the shooting, hunting and outdoor trade retailer.

Shotgun Sports

P.O. Box 6810, Auburn, CA 95604/916-889-2220; FAX:916-889-9106. $31.00 yr. Trapshooting how-to's, shotshell reloading, shotgun patterning, shotgun tests and evaluations, Sporting Clays action, waterfowl/upland hunting. Call 1-800-676-8920 for a free sample copy.

The Single Shot Exhange Magazine

PO box 1055, York SC 29745/803-628-5326 phone/fax. $31.50/yr., monthly. Articles of interest to the blackpowder cartridge shooter and antique arms collector.

Single Shot Rifle Journal* (M)

Editor John Campbell, PO Box 595, Bloomfield Hills, MI 48303/248-458-8415. Email: jcampbel@dmbb.com Annual dues $35 for 6 issues. Journal of the American Single Shot Rifle Assn.

The Sixgunner (M)

Handgun Hunters International, P.O. Box 357, MAG, Bloomingdale, OH 43910

The Skeet Shooting Review

National Skeet Shooting Assn., 5931 Roft Rd., San Antonio, TX 78253. $20.00 yr. (Assn. membership includes mag.) Competition results, personality profiles of top Skeet shooters, how-to articles, technical, reloading information.

Soldier of Fortune

Subscription Dept., P.O. Box 348, Mt. Morris, IL 61054. $29.95 yr.; $39.95 Canada; $50.95 foreign.

Sporting Clays Magazine

Patch Communications, 5211 South Washington Ave., Titusville, FL 32780/407-268-5010; FAX: 407-267-7216. $29.95 yr. (12 issues). Official publication of the National Sporting Clays Association.

Sporting Goods Business

Miller Freeman, Inc., One Penn Plaza, 10th Fl., New York, NY 10119-0004. Trade journal.

Sporting Goods Dealer

Two Park Ave., New York, NY 10016. $100.00 yr. Sporting goods trade journal.

Sporting Gun

Bretton Court, Bretton, Peterborough PE3 8DZ, England. £27.00 (approx. U.S. $36.00), airmail £35.50 yr. For the game and clay enthusiasts.

The Squirrel Hunter

P.O. Box 368, Chireno, TX 75937. $14.00 yr. Articles about squirrel hunting.

Stott's Creek Calendar

Stott's Creek Printers, 2526 S 475 W, Morgantown, IN 46160/317-878-5489. 1 yr (3 issues) $11.50; 2 yrs. (6 issues) $20.00. Lists all gun shows everywhere in convenient calendar form; call for information.

Super Outdoors

2695 Aiken Road, Shelbyville, KY 40065/502-722-9463; 800-404-6064; Fax: 502-722-8093. Mark Edwards, publisher. Contact for details.

TACARMI

Via E. De Amicis, 25; 20123 Milano, Italy. $100.00 yr. approx. Antique and modern guns. (Italian text.)

Territorial Dispatch—1800s Historical Publication (M)

National Assn. of Buckskinners, 4701 Marion St., Suite 324, Livestock Exchange Bldg., Denver, CO 80216. Michael A. Nester & Barbara Wyckoff, editors. 303-297-9671.

Trap & Field

1000 Waterway Blvd., Indianapolis, IN 46202. $25.00 yr. Official publ. Amateur Trapshooting Assn. Scores, averages, trapshooting articles.

Turkey Call* (M)

Natl. Wild Turkey Federation, Inc., P.O. Box 530, Edgefield, SC 29824. $25.00 with membership (6 issues per yr.)

Turkey & Turkey Hunting*

Krause Publications, 700 E. State St., Iola, WI 54990-0001. $13.95 (6 issue p. yr.). Magazine with leading-edge articles on all aspects of wild turkey behavior, biology and the successful ways to hunt better with that info. Learn the proper techniques to calling, the right equipment, and more.

The Accurate Rifle

Precisions Shooting, Inc., 222 Mckee Street, Manchester CT 06040. $37 yr. Dedicated to the rifle accuracy enthusiast.

The U.S. Handgunner* (M)

U.S. Revolver Assn., 40 Larchmont Ave., Taunton, MA 02780. $10.00 yr. General handgun and competition articles. Bi-monthly sent to members.

U.S. Airgun Magazine

P.O. Box 2021, Benton, AR 72018/800-247-4867; Fax: 501-316-8549. 10 issues a yr. Cover the sport from hunting, 10-meter, field target and collecting. Write for details.

The Varmint Hunter Magazine (Q)

The Varmint Hunters Assn., Box 759, Pierre, SD 57501/800-528-4868. $24.00 yr.

Waffenmarkt-Intern

GFI-Verlag, Theodor-Heuss Ring 62, 50668 K"ln, Germany. Only for gunsmiths, licensed firearms dealers and their suppliers in Germany, Austria and Switzerland.

Wild Sheep (M) (Q)

Foundation for North American Wild Sheep, 720 Allen Ave., Cody, WY 82414. Website: http://iigi.com/os/non/fnaws/fnaws.htm; e-mail: fnaws@wyoming.com. Official journal of the foundation.

Wisconsin Outdoor Journal

Krause Publications, 700 E. State St., Iola, WI 54990-0001. $17.97 yr. (8 issues). For Wisconsin's avid hunters and fishermen, with features from all over that state with regional reports, legislative updates, etc. Website: www.krause.com

Women & Guns

P.O. Box 488, Sta. C, Buffalo, NY 14209. $24.00 yr. U.S.; $72.00 foreign (12 issues). Only magazine edited by and for women gun owners.

World War II*

Cowles History Group, 741 Miller Dr. SE, Suite D-2, Leesburg, VA 20175-8920. Annual subscriptions $19.95 U.S.; $25.95 Canada; 43.95 foreign. The title says it— WWII; good articles, ads, etc.

*Published bi-monthly
† Published weekly
‡Published three times per month. All others are published monthly.

THE ARMS LIBRARY

FOR COLLECTOR ◆ HUNTER ◆ SHOOTER ◆ OUTDOORSMAN

IMPORTANT NOTICE TO BOOK BUYERS

Books listed here may be bought from Ray Riling Arms Books Co., 6844 Gorsten St., P.O. Box 18925, Philadelphia, PA 19119, Phone 215/438-2456; FAX: 215-438-5395. E-Mail: sales@rayrilingarmsbooks.com. Joe Riling is the researcher and compiler of "The Arms Library" and a seller of gun books for over 32 years. The Riling stock includes books classic and modern, many hard-to-find items, and many not obtainable elsewhere. These pages list a portion of the current stock. They offer prompt, complete service, with delayed shipments occurring only on out-of-print or out-of-stock books.

Visit our web site at **www.rayrilingarmsbooks.com** and order all of your favorite titles on line from our secure site.

NOTICE FOR ALL CUSTOMERS: Remittance in U.S. funds must accompany all orders. For your convenience we now accept VISA, Master-Card & American Express. For shipments in the U.S. add $7.00 for the 1st book and $2.00 for each additional book for postage and insurance. Minimum order $10.00. International Orders add $13.00 for the 1st book and $5.00 for each additional book. All International orders are shipped at the buyer's risk unless an additional $5 for insurance is included. USPS does not offer insurance to all countries unless shipped Air-Mail please e-mail or call for pricing.

Payments in excess of order or for "Backorders" are credited or fully refunded at request. Books "As-Ordered" are not returnable except by permission and a handling charge on these of 10% or $2.00 per book which ever is greater is deducted from refund or credit. Only Pennsylvania customers must include current sales tax.

A full variety of arms books also available from Rutgers Book Center, 127 Raritan Ave., Highland Park, NJ 08904/908-545-4344; FAX: 908-545-6686 or I.D.S.A. Books, 1324 Stratford Drive, Piqua, OH 45356/937-773-4203; FAX: 937-778-1922.

BALLISTICS AND HANDLOADING

ABC's of Reloading, 6th Edition, by C. Rodney James and the editors of Handloader's Digest, DBI Books, a division of Krause Publications, Iola, WI, 1997. 288 pp., illus. Paper covers. $21.95
The definitive guide to every facet of cartridge and shotshell reloading.

Accurate Arms Loading Guide Number 2, by Accurate Arms. McEwen, TN: Accurate Arms Company, Inc., 2000. Paper Covers. $18.95
Includes new data on smokeless powders XMR4064 and XMP5744 as well as a special section on Cowboy Action Shooting. The new manual includes 50 new pages of data. An appendix includes nominal rotor charge weights, bullet diameters.

The American Cartridge, by Charles Suydam, Borden Publishing Co. Alhambra, CA, 1986. 184 pp., illus. $24.95
An illustrated study of the rimfire cartridge in the United States.

Ammo and Ballistics, by Robert W. Forker, Safari Press, Inc., Huntington Beach, CA., 1999. 252 pp., illustrated. Paper covers. $18.95
Ballistic data on 125 calibers and 1,400 loads out to 500 yards.

Ammunition: Grenades and Projectile Munitions, by Ian V. Hogg, Stackpole Books, Mechanicsburg, PA, 1998. 144 pp., illus. $22.95
Concise guide to modern ammunition. International coverage with detailed specifications and illustrations.

Barnes Reloading Manual #2, Barnes Bullets, American Fork, UT, 1999. 668 pp., illus. $24.95
Features data and trajectories on the new weight X, XBT and Solids in calibers from .22 to .50 BMG.

Big Bore Rifles And Cartridges, Wolfe Publishing Co., Prescott, AZ, 1991. Paper covers. $26.00
This book covers cartridges from 8mm to .600 Nitro with loading tables.

Black Powder Guide, 2nd Edition, by George C. Nonte, Jr., Stoeger Publishing Co., So. Hackensack, NJ, 1991. 288 pp., illus. Paper covers. $14.95
How-to instructions for selection, repair and maintenance of muzzleloaders, making your own bullets, restoring and refinishing, shooting techniques.

Blackpowder Loading Manual, 3rd Edition, by Sam Fadala, DBI Books, a division of Krause Publications, Iola, WI, 1995. 368 pp., illus. Paper covers. $20.95
Revised and expanded edition of this landmark blackpowder loading book. Covers hundreds of loads for most of the popular blackpowder rifles, handguns and shotguns.

Cartridges of the World, 9th Edition, by Frank Barnes, Krause Publications, Iola, WI, 2000. 512 pp., illus. Paper covers. $27.95
Completely revised edition of the general purpose reference work for which collectors, police, scientists and laymen reach first for answers to cartridge identification questions.

Cartridge Reloading Tools of the Past, by R.H. Chamberlain and Tom Quigley, Tom Quigley, Castle Rock, WA, 1998. 167 pp., illustrated. Paper covers. $25.00
A detailed treatment of the extensive Winchester and Ideal line of handloading tools and bullet molds, plus Remington, Marlin, Ballard, Browning, Maynard, and many others.

Cast Bullets for the Black Powder Rifle, by Paul A. Matthews, Wolfe Publishing Co., Prescott, AZ, 1996. 133 pp., illus. Paper covers. $22.50
The tools and techniques used to make your cast bullet shooting a success.

Complete Blackpowder Handbook, 3rd Edition, by Sam Fadala, DBI Books, a division of Krause Publications, Iola, WI, 1997. 400 pp., illus. Paper covers. $21.95
Expanded and completely rewritten edition of the definitive book on the subject of blackpowder.

Complete Reloading Guide, by Robert & John Traister, Stoeger Publishing Co., Wayne, NJ, 1997. 608 pp., illus. Paper covers. $34.95
Perhaps the finest, most comprehensive work ever published on the subject of reloading.

Complete Reloading Manual, One Book / One Caliber. California: Load Books USA, 2000. $7.95 Each
Containing unabridged information from U. S. Bullet and Powder Makers. With thousands of proven and tested loads, plus dozens of various bullet designs and different powders. Spiral bound. Available in all Calibers.

Early Loading Tools & Bullet Molds, Pioneer Press, 1988. 88 pages, illustrated. Softcover. $7.50

THE ARMS LIBRARY

European Sporting Cartridges: Volume 1, by Brad Dixon, Seattle, WA: Armory Publications, 1997. 1st edition. 250 pp., Illus. $60.00

Photographs and drawings of over 550 centerfire cartridge case types in 1,300 illustrations produced in Germany and Austria from 1875-1995.

European Sporting Cartridges: Volume 2, by Brad Dixon, Seattle, WA: Armory Publications, 2000. 1st edition. 240 pages. $60.00

An illustrated history of centerfire hunting and target cartridges produced in Czechoslovakia, Switzerland, Norway, Sweden, Finland, Russia, Italy, Denmark, Belguim from 1875 to 1998. Adds 50 specimens to volume 1, Germany-Austria. Also, illustrates 40 small arms magazine experiments during the late 19th Century, and includes the English-Language export ammunition catalogue of Kovo (Povaszke Strojarne), Prague, Czeck. from the 1930's.

Game Loads and Practical Ballistics for the American Hunter, by Bob Hagel, Wolfe Publishing Co., Prescott, AZ, 1992. 310 pp., illus. $27.90

Hagel's knowledge gained as a hunter, guide and gun enthusiast is gathered in this informative text.

German 7.9MM Military Ammunition 1888-1945, by Daniel Kent, Ann Arbor, MI: Kent, 1990. 153 pp., plus appendix. illus., b&w photos. $35.00

Handbook for Shooters and Reloaders, by P.O. Ackley, Salt Lake City, UT, 1998, (Vol. I), 567 pp., illus. Includes a separate exterior ballistics chart. $21.95
(Vol. II), a new printing with specific new material. 495 pp., illus. $20.95

Handgun Muzzle Flash Tests: How Police Cartridges Compare, by Robert Olsen, Paladin Press, Boulder, CO.Fully illustrated. 133 pages. Softcover. $20.00

Tests dozens of pistols and revolvers for the brightness of muzzle flash, a critical factor in the safety of law enforcement personnel.

Handgun Stopping Power; The Definitive Study, by Marshall & Sandow. Boulder, CO: Paladin Press, 1992. 240 pages. $45.00

Offers accurate predictions of the stopping power of specific loads in calibers from .380 Auto to .45 ACP, as well as such specialty rounds as the Glaser Safety Slug, Federal Hydra-Shok, MagSafe, etc. This is the definitive methodology for predicting the stopping power of handgun loads, the first to take into account what really happens when a bullet meets a man.

Handloader's Digest, 17th Edition, edited by Bob Bell. DBI Books, a division of Krause Publications, Iola, WI, 1997. 480 pp., illustrated. Paper covers. $27.95

Top writers in the field contribute helpful information on techniques and components. Greatly expanded and fully indexed catalog of all currently available tools, accessories and components for metallic, blackpowder cartridge, shotgun reloading and swaging.

Handloader's Manual of Cartridge Conversions, by John J. Donnelly, Stoeger Publishing Co., So. Hackensack, NJ, 1986. Unpaginated. $39.95

From 14 Jones to 70-150 Winchester in English and American cartridges, and from 4.85 U.K. to 15.2x28R Gevelot in metric cartridges. Over 900 cartridges described in detail.

Hatcher's Notebook, by S. Julian Hatcher, Stackpole Books, Harrisburg, PA, 1992. 488 pp., illus. $39.95

A reference work for shooters, gunsmiths, ballisticians, historians, hunters and collectors.

History and Development of Small Arms Ammunition; Volume 2 Centerfire: Primitive, and Martial Long Arms.

by George A. Hoyem. Oceanside, CA: Armory Publications, 1991. 303 pages, illustrated. $60.00

Covers the blackpowder military centerfire rifle, carbine, machine gun and volley gun ammunition used in 28 nations and dominions, together with the firearms that chambered them.

History and Development of Small Arms Ammunition; Volume 4, American Military Rifle Cartridges. Oceanside, CA: Armory Publications, 1998. 244pp., illus. $60.00

Carries on what Vol. 2 began with American military rifle cartridges. Now the sporting rifle cartridges are at last organized by their originators-235 individual case types designed by eight makers of single shot rifles and four of magazine rifles from .50-140 Winchester Express to .22-15-60 Stevens. plus experimentals from .70-150 to .32-80. American Civil War enthusiasts and European collectors will find over 150 primitives in Appendix A to add to those in Volumes One and Two. There are 16 pages in full color of 54 box labels for Sharps, Remington and Ballard cartridges. There are large photographs with descriptions of 15 Maynard, Sharps, Winchester, Browning, Freund, Remington-Hepburn, Farrow and other single shot rifles, some of them rare one of a kind specimens.

Hodgdon Powder Data Manual #27, Hodgdon Powder Co., Shawnee Mission, KS, 1999. 800 pp. $27.95

Reloading data for rifle and pistol loads.

Hodgdon Shotshell Data Manual, Hodgdon Powder Co., Shawnee Mission, KS, 1999. 208 pp. $19.95

Contains hundreds of loads for lead shot, buck shot, slugs, bismuth shot and steel shot plus articles on ballistics, patterning, special reloads and much more.

Home Guide to Cartridge Conversions, by Maj. George C. Nonte Jr., The Gun Room Press, Highland Park, NJ, 1976. 404 pp., illus. $24.95

Revised and updated version of Nonte's definitive work on the alteration of cartridge cases for use in guns for which they were not intended.

Hornady Handbook of Cartridge Reloading, 5th Edition, Vol. I and II, Edited by Larry Steadman, Hornady Mfg. Co., Grand Island, NE, 2000., illus. $49.95

2 Volumes; Volume 1, 773 pp.; Volume 2, 717 pp. New edition of this famous reloading handbook covers rifle and handgun reloading data and ballistic tables.
Latest loads, ballistic information, etc.

How-To's for the Black Powder Cartridge Rifle Shooter, by Paul A. Matthews, Wolfe Publishing Co., Prescott, AZ, 1995. 45 pp. Paper covers. $22.50

Covers lube recipes, good bore cleaners and over-powder wads. Tips include compressing powder charges, combating wind resistance, improving ignition and much more.

The Illustrated Reference of Cartridge Dimensions, edited by Dave Scovill, Wolfe Publishing Co., Prescott, AZ, 1994. 343 pp., illus. Paper covers. $19.00

A comprehensive volume with over 300 cartridges. Standard and metric dimensions have been taken from SAAMI drawings and/or fired cartridges.

Kynock, by Dale J. Hedlund, Armory Publications, Seattle, WA, 2000. 130 pages, illus. 9" x 12" with four color dust jacket. $59.95

A comprehensive review of Kynoch shotgun cartridges covering over 50 brand names and case types, and over 250 Kynoch shotgun cartridge headstamps. Additional information on Kynoch metallic ammunition including the identity of the mysterious .434 Seelun.

THE ARMS LIBRARY

Lee Modern Reloading, by Richard Lee, 350 pp. of charts and data and 85 illustrations. 512 pp. $24.95

Bullet casting, lubricating and author's formula for calculating proper charges for cast bullets. Includes virtually all current load data published by the powder suppliers. Exclusive source of volume measured loads.

Loading the Black Powder Rifle Cartridge, by Paul A Matthews, Wolfe Publishing Co., Prescott, AZ, 1993. 121 pp., illus. Paper covers. $22.50

Author Matthews brings the blackpowder cartridge shooter valuable information on the basics, including cartridge care, lubes and moulds, powder charges and developing and testing loads in his usual authoritative style.

Loading the Peacemaker—Colt's Model P, by Dave Scovill, Wolfe Publishing Co., Prescott, AZ, 1996. 227 pp., illus. $24.95

A comprehensive work about the history, maintenance and repair of the most famous revolver ever made, including the most extensive load data ever published.

Lyman Cast Bullet Handbook, 3rd Edition, edited by C. Kenneth Ramage, Lyman Publications, Middlefield, CT, 1980. 416 pp., illus. Paper covers. $19.95

Information on more than 5000 tested cast bullet loads and 19 pages of trajectory and wind drift tables for cast bullets.

Lyman Black Powder Handbook, edited by C. Kenneth Ramage, Lyman Products for Shooters, Middlefield, CT, 1975. 239 pp., illus. Paper covers. $14.95

Comprehensive load information for the modern blackpowder shooter.

Lyman Pistol & Revolver Handbook, 2nd Edition, edited by Thomas J. Griffin, Lyman Products Co., Middlefield, CT, 1996. 287 pp., illus. Paper covers. $18.95

The most up-to-date loading data available including the hottest new calibers, like 40 S&W, 9x21, 9mm Makarov, 9x25 Dillon and 454 Casull.

Lyman Reloading Handbook No. 47, edited by Edward A. Matunas, Lyman Publications, Middlefield, CT, 1992. 480 pp., illus. Paper covers. $24.95

A comprehensive reloading manual complete with "How to Reload" information. Expanded data section with all the newest rifle and pistol calibers.

Lyman Shotshell Handbook, 4th Edition, edited by Edward A. Matunas, Lyman Products Co., Middlefield, CT, 1996. 330 pp., illus. Paper covers. $24.95

Has 9000 loads for rifle and handgun, slugs and buckshot, plus feature articles and a full color I.D. section.

Lyman's Guide to Big Game Cartridges & Rifles, by Edward Matunas, Lyman Publishing Corporation, Middlefield, CT, 1994. 287 pp., illus. Paper covers. $17.95

A selection guide to cartridges and rifles for big game— antelope to elephant.

Making Loading Dies and Bullet Molds, by Harold Hoffman, H & P Publishing, San Angelo, TX, 1993. 230 pp., illus. Paper covers. $24.95

A good book for learning tool and die making.

Metallic Cartridge Reloading, 3rd Edition, by M.L. McPherson, DBI Books, a division of Krause Publications, Iola, WI., 1996. 352 pp., illus. Paper covers. $21.95

A true reloading manual with over 10,000 loads for all popular metallic cartridges and a wealth of invaluable technical data provided by a recognized expert.

Military Rifle and Machine Gun Cartridges, by Jean Huon, Alexandria, VA: Ironside International, 1995. 1st edition. 378 pages, over 1,000 photos. $34.95

Superb reference text.

Modern Combat Ammunition, by Duncan Long, Paladin Press, Boulder, CO, 1997, soft cover, photos, illus., 216 pp. $34.00

Now, Paladin's leading weapons author presents his exhaustive evaluation of the stopping power of modern rifle, pistol, shotgun and machine gun rounds based on actual case studies of shooting incidents. He looks at the hot new cartridges that promise to dominate well into the next century .40 S&W, 10mm auto, sub-sonic 9mm's - as well as the trusted standbys. Find out how to make your own exotic tracers, fléchette and sabot rounds, caseless ammo and fragmenting bullets.

Modern Exterior Ballistics, by Robert L. McCoy, Schiffer Publishing Co., Atglen, PA, 1999. 128 pp. $95.00

Advanced students of exterior ballistics and flight dynamics will find this comprehensive textbook on the subject a useful addition to their libraries.

Modern Handloading, by Maj. Geo. C. Nonte, Winchester Press, Piscataway, NJ, 1972. 416 pp., illus. $15.00

Covers all aspects of metallic and shotshell ammunition loading, plus more loads than any book in print.

Modern Reloading, by Richard Lee, Inland Press, 1996. 510 pp., illus. $24.98

The how-to's of rifle, pistol and shotgun reloading plus load data for rifle and pistol calibers.

Modern Sporting Rifle Cartridges, by Wayne van Zwoll, Stoeger Publishing Co., Wayne, NJ, 1998. 310 pp., illustrated. Paper covers. $21.95

Illustrated with hundreds of photos and backed up by dozens of tables and schematic drawings, this four-part book tells the story of how rifle bullets and cartridges were developed and, in some cases, discarded.

Modern Practical Ballistics, by Art Pejsa, Pejsa Ballistics, Minneapolis, MN, 1990. 150 pp., illus. $29.95

Covers all aspects of ballistics and new, simplified methods. Clear examples illustrate new, easy but very accurate formulas.

Mr. Single Shot's Cartridge Handbook, by Frank de Haas, Mark de Haas, Orange City, IA, 1996. 116 pp., illus. Paper covers. $21.50

This book covers most of the cartridges, both commercial and wildcat, that the author has known and used.

Nick Harvey's Practical Reloading Manual, by Nick Harvey, Australian Print Group, Maryborough, Victoria, Australia, 1995. 235 pp., illus. Paper covers. $24.95

Contains data for rifle and handgun including many popular wildcat and improved cartridges. Tools, powders, components and techniques for assembling optimum reloads with particular application to North America.

Nosler Reloading Manual #4, edited by Gail Root, Nosler Bullets, Inc., Bend, OR, 1996. 516 pp., illus. $26.99

Combines information on their Ballistic Tip, Partition and Handgun bullets with traditional powders and new powders never before used, plus trajectory information from 100 to 500 yards.

The Paper Jacket, by Paul Matthews, Wolfe Publishing Co., Prescott, AZ, 1991. Paper covers. $13.50

Up-to-date and accurate information about paper-patched bullets.

Reloading Tools, Sights and Telescopes for S/S Rifles, by Gerald O. Kelver, Brighton, CO, 1982. 163 pp., illus. Softcover. $15.00

A listing of most of the famous makers of reloading tools, sights and telescopes with a brief description of the products they manufactured.

Reloading for Shotgunners, 4th Edition, by Kurt D. Fackler and M.L. McPherson, DBI Books, a division of

Krause Publications, Iola, WI, 1997. 320 pp., illus. Paper covers. $19.95

Expanded reloading tables with over 11,000 loads. Bushing charts for every major press and component maker. All new presentation on all aspects of shotshell reloading by two of the top experts in the field.

The Rimfire Cartridge in the United States and Canada, Illustrated history of rimfire cartridges, manufacturers, and the products made from 1857-1984. by John L. Barber, Thomas Publications, Gettysburg, PA 2000. 1st edition. Profusely illustrated. 221 pages. $50.00

The author has written an encyclopedia of rimfire cartridges from the .22 to the massive 1.00 in. Gatling. Fourteen chapters, six appendices and an excellent bibliography make up a reference volume that all cartridge collectors should aquire.

Sierra 50th Anniversary, 4th Edition Rifle Manual, edited by Ken Ramage, Sierra Bullets, Santa Fe Springs, CA, 1997. 800 pp., illus. $26.99

New cartridge introductions, etc.

Sierra 50th Anniversary, 4th Edition Handgun Manual, edited by Ken Ramage, Sierra Bullets, Santa Fe, CA, 1997. 700 pp., illus. $21.99

Histories, reloading recommendations, bullets, powders and sections on the reloading process, etc.

Sixgun Cartridges and Loads, by Elmer Keith, The Gun Room Press, Highland Park, NJ, 1986. 151 pp., illus. $24.95

A manual covering the selection, uses and loading of the most suitable and popular revolver cartridges. Originally published in 1936. Reprint.

Speer Reloading Manual No. 13, edited by members of the Speer research staff, Omark Industries, Lewiston, ID, 1999. 621 pp., illustrated. $24.95

With thirteen new sections containing the latest technical information and reloading trends for both novice and expert in this latest edition. More than 9,300 loads are listed, including new propellant powders from Accurate Arms, Alliant, Hodgdon and Vihtavuori.

Street Stoppers, The Latest Handgun Stopping Power Street Results, by Marshall & Lanow. Boulder, CO, Paladin Press, 1996. 374 pages, illus. Softcover. $42.95

Street Stoppers is the long-awaited sequel to Handgun Stopping Power. It provides the latest results of real-life shootings in all of the major handgun calibers, plus more than 25 thought-provoking chapters that are vital to anyone interested in firearms, would ballistics, and combat shooting. This book also covers the street results of the hottest new caliber to hit the shooting world in years, the .40 Smith & Wesson. Updated street results of the latest exotic ammunition including Remington Golden Saber and CCI-Speer Gold Dot, plus the venerable offerings from MagSafe, Glaser, Cor-Bon and others. A fascinating look at the development of Hydra-Shok ammunition is included.

Understanding Ballistics, Revised 2nd Edition by Robert A. Rinker, Mulberry House Publishing Co., Corydon, IN, 2000. 430 pp., illus Paper covers. New, Revised and Expanded. 2nd Edition. $24.95

Explains basic to advanced firearm ballistics in understandable terms.

Why Not Load Your Own?, by Col. T. Whelen, Gun Room Press, Highland Park, NJ 1996, 4th ed., rev. 237 pp., illus. $20.00

A basic reference on handloading, describing each step, materials and equipment. Includes loads for popular cartridges.

Wildcat Cartridges Volumes 1 & 2 Combination, by the editors of Handloaders magazine, Wolfe Publishing Co., Prescott, AZ, 1997. 350 pp., illus. Paper covers. $39.95

A profile of the most popular information on wildcat cartridges that appeared in the Handloader magazine.

GENERAL

Action Shooting: Cowboy Style, by John Taffin, Krause Publications, Iola, WI, 1999. 320 pp., illustrated. $39.95.

Details on the guns and ammunition. Explanations of the rules used for many events. The essential cowboy wardrobe.

Advanced Muzzleloader's Guide, by Toby Bridges, Stoeger Publishing Co., So. Hackensack, NJ, 1985. 256 pp., illus. Paper covers. $14.95.

The complete guide to muzzle-loading rifles, pistols and shotguns—flintlock and percussion.

Aids to Musketry for Officers & NCOs, by Capt. B.J. Friend, Excalibur Publications, Latham, NY, 1996. 40 pp., illus. Paper covers. $7.95.

A facsimile edition of a pre-WWI British manual filled with useful information for training the common soldier.

Air Gun Digest, 3rd Edition, by J.I. Galan, DBI Books, a division of Krause Publications, Iola, WI, 1995. 258 pp., illus. Paper covers. $19.95

Everything from A to Z on air gun history, trends and technology.

American and Imported Arms, Ammunition and Shooting Accessories, Catalog No. 18 of the Shooter's Bible, Stoeger, Inc., reprinted by Fayette Arsenal, Fayetteville, NC, 1988. 142 pp., illus. Paper covers. $10.95.

A facsimile reprint of the 1932 Stoeger's Shooter's Bible.

America's Great Gunmakers, by Wayne van Zwoll, Stoeger Publishing Co., So. Hackensack, NJ, 1992. 288 pp., illus. Paper covers. $16.95.

This book traces in great detail the evolution of guns and ammunition in America and the men who formed the companies that produced them.

Ammunition: Small Arms, Grenades and Projected Munitions, by Ian V. Hogg, Greenhill Books, London, England, 1998. 144 pp., illustrated. $22.95.

The best concise guide to modern ammunition. Wide-ranging and international coverage. Detailed specifications and illustrations.

Armed and Female, by Paxton Quigley, E.P. Dutton, New York, NY, 1989. 237 pp., illus. $16.95.

The first complete book on one of the hottest subjects in the media today, the arming of the American woman.

Arming the Glorious Cause: Weapons of the Second War for Independence, by James B. Whisker, Daniel D. Hartzler and Larry W. Yantz, R & R Books, Livonia, NY, 1998. 175 pp., illustrated. $45.00.

A photographic study of Confederate weapons.

Arms and Armour in Antiquity and the Middle Ages, by Charles Boutell, Stackpole Books, Mechanicsburg, PA, 1996. 352 pp., illus. $22.95.

Detailed descriptions of arms and armor, the development of tactics and the outcome of specific battles.

Arms & Armor in the Art Institute of Chicago, by Walter J. Karcheski, Jr., Bulfinch Press, Boston, MA, 1995. 128 pp., illus. $35.00.

Now, for the first time, the Art Institute of Chicago's arms and armor collection is presented in the visual delight of 103 color illustrations.

THE ARMS LIBRARY

Arms for the Nation: Springfield Longarms, edited by David C. Clark, Scott A. Duff, Export, PA, 1994. 73 pp., illus. Paper covers. $9.95.

A brief history of the Springfield Armory and the arms made there.

Arsenal of Freedom, The Springfield Armory, 1890-1948: A Year-by-Year Account Drawn from Official Records, compiled and edited by Lt. Col. William S. Brophy, USAR Ret., Andrew Mowbray, Inc., Lincoln, RI, 1991. 400 pp., illus. Soft covers. $29.95.

A "must buy" for all students of American military weapons, equipment and accoutrements.

Assault Pistols, Rifles and Submachine Guns, by Duncan Long, Paladin Press, Boulder, CO, 1997, 8 1/2 x 11, soft cover, photos, illus. 152 pp. $21.95

This book offers up-to-date, practical information on how to operate and field-strip modern military, police and civilian combat weapons. Covers new developments and trends such as the use of fiber optics, liquid-recoil systems and lessening of barrel length are covered. Troubleshooting procedures, ballistic tables and a list of manufacturers and distributors are also included.

Assault Weapons, 5th Edition, The Gun Digest Book of, edited by Jack Lewis and David E. Steele, DBI Books, a division of Krause Publications, Iola, WI, 2000. 256 pp., illustrated. Paper covers. $21.95.

This is the latest word on true assault weaponry in use today by international military and law enforcement organizations.

The Belgian Rattlesnake: The Lewis Automatic Machine Gun, by William M. Easterly, Collector Grade Publications, Inc., Cobourg, Ont. Canada, 1998. 542 pp., illus. $79.95.

A social and technical biography of the Lewis automatic machine gun and its inventors.

The Big Guns: Civil War Siege, Seacoast, and Naval Cannon, by Edwin Olmstead, Wayne E. Stark and Spencer C. Tucker, Museum Restoration Service, Bloomfield, Ontario, Canada, 1997. 360 pp., illus. $80.00.

This book is designed to identify and record the heavy guns available to both sides during the Civil War.

Blackpowder Loading Manual, 3rd Edition, by Sam Fadala, DBI Books, a division of Krause Publications, Iola, WI, 1995. 368 pp., illus. Paper covers. $20.95.

Revised and expanded edition of this landmark blackpowder loading book. Covers hundreds of loads for most of the popular blackpowder rifles, handguns and shotguns.

Bolt Action Rifles, 3rd Edition, by Frank de Haas, DBI Books, a division of Krause Publications, Iola, WI, 1995. 528 pp., illus. Paper covers. $24.95.

A revised edition of the most definitive work on all major bolt-action rifle designs.

The Book of the Crossbow, by Sir Ralph Payne-Gallwey, Dover Publications, Mineola, NY, 1996. 416 pp., illus. Paper covers. $14.95.

Unabridged republication of the scarce 1907 London edition of the book on one of the most devastating hand weapons of the Middle Ages.

Bows and Arrows of the Native Americans, by Jim Hamm, Lyons & Burford Publishers, New York, NY, 1991. 156 pp., illus. $19.95.

A complete step-by-step guide to wooden bows, sinew-backed bows, composite bows, strings, arrows and quivers.

British Small Arms of World War 2, by Ian D. Skennerton, I.D.S.A. Books, Piqua, OH, 1988. 110 pp., 37 illus. $25.00.

"Carbine," the Story of David Marshall Williams, by Ross E. Beard, Jr. Phillips Publications, Williamstown, NJ, 1999. 225 pp., illus. $29.95.

The story of the firearms genius, David Marshall "Carbine" Williams. From prison to the pinnacles of fame, the tale of this North Carolinian is inspiring. The author details many of Williams' firearms inventions and developments.

Combat Handgunnery, 4th Edition, The Gun Digest Book of, by Chuck Taylor, DBI Books, a division of Krause Publications, Iola, WI, 1997. 256 pp., illus. Paper covers. $18.95.

This edition looks at real world combat handgunnery from three different perspectives—military, police and civilian.

The Complete Blackpowder Handbook, 3rd Edition, by Sam Fadala, DBI Books, a division of Krause Publications, Iola, WI, 1997. 400 pp., illus. Paper covers. $21.95.

Expanded and completely rewritten edition of the definitive book on the subject of blackpowder.

The Complete Guide to Game Care and Cookery, 3rd Edition, by Sam Fadala, DBI Books, a division of Krause Publications, Iola, WI, 1994. 320 pp., illus. Paper covers. $18.95.

Over 500 photos illustrating the care of wild game in the field and at home with a separate recipe section providing over 400 tested recipes.

The Complete .50-caliber Sniper Course, by Dean Michaelis, Paladin Press, Boulder, CO, 2000. 576 pp, illustrated, $60.00

The history from German Mauser T-Gewehr of World War 1 to the Soviet PTRD and beyond. Includes the author's Program of Instruction for Special Operations Hard-Target Interdiction Course.

Complete Guide to Guns & Shooting, by John Malloy, DBI Books, a division of Krause Publications, Iola, WI, 1995. 256 pp., illus. Paper covers. $18.95.

What every shooter and gun owner should know about firearms, ammunition, shooting techniques, safety, collecting and much more.

Cowboy Action Shooting, by Charly Gullett, Wolfe Publishing Co., Prescott, AZ, 1995. 400 pp., illus. Paper covers. $24.50.

The fast growing of the shooting sports is comprehensively covered in this text—the guns, loads, tactics and the fun and flavor of this Old West era competition.

Crossbows, edited by Roger Combs, DBI Books, a division of Krause Publications, Iola, WI, 1986. 192 pp., illus. Paper covers. $15.95.

Complete, up-to-date coverage of the hottest bow going—and the most controversial.

Custom Firearms Engraving, by Tom Turpin, Krause Publications, Iola, WI, 1999. 208 pp., illustrated. $49.95.

Provides a broad and comprehensive look at the world of firearms engraving. The exquisite styles of more than 75 master engravers are shown on beautiful examples of handguns, rifles, shotguns, and other firearms, as well as knives.

Dead On, by Tony Noblitt and Warren Gabrilska, Paladin Press, Boulder, CO, 1998. 176 pp., illustrated. Paper covers. $22.00

The long-range marksman's guide to extreme accuracy.

Death from Above: The German FG42 Paratrooper Rifle, by Thomas B. Dugelby and R. Blake Stevens, Collector Grade Publications, Toronto, Canada, 1990. 147 pp., illus. $39.95.

The first comprehensive study of all seven models of the FG42.

THE ARMS LIBRARY

Early American Flintlocks, by Daniel D. Hartzler and James B. Whisker, Bedford Valley Press, Bedford, PA 2000. 192 pp., Illustrated.

Covers early Colonial Guns, New England Guns, Pennsylvania Guns and Souther Guns.

Encyclopedia of Modern Firearms, Vol. 1, compiled and publ. by Bob Brownell, Montezuma, IA, 1959. 1057 pp. plus index, illus. $70.00. Dist. By Bob Brownell, Montezuma, IA 50171.

Massive accumulation of basic information of nearly all modern arms pertaining to "parts and assembly." Replete with arms photographs, exploded drawings, manufacturers' lists of parts, etc.

Encyclopedia of Native American Bows, Arrows and Quivers, by Steve Allely and Jim Hamm, The Lyons Press, N.Y., 1999. 160 pp., illustrated. $29.95.

A landmark book for anyone interested in archery history, or Native Americans.

The Exercise of Armes, by Jacob de Gheyn, edited and with an introduction by Bas Kist, Dover Publications, Inc., Mineola, NY, 1999. 144 pp., illustrated. Paper covers. $12.95.

Republications of all 117 engravings from the 1607 classic military manual. A meticulously accurate portrait of uniforms and weapons of the 17th century Netherlands.

Exploded Long Gun Drawings, The Gun Digest Book of, edited by Harold A. Murtz, DBI Books, a division of Krause Publications, Iola, WI, 512 pp., illus. Paper covers. $20.95.

Containing almost 500 rifle and shotgun exploded drawings.

Fighting Iron; A Metals Handbook for Arms Collectors, by Art Gogan, Mowbray Publishers, Inc., Lincoln, RI, 1999. 176 pp., illustrated. $28.00.

A guide that is easy to use, explains things in simple English and covers all of the different historical periods that we are interested in.

The Fighting Submachine Gun, Machine Pistol, and Shotgun, a Hands-On Evaluation, by Timothy J. Mullin, Paladin Press, Boulder, CO, 1999. 224 pp., illustrated. Paper covers. $35.00.

An invaluable reference for military, police and civilian shooters who may someday need to know how a specific weapon actually performs when the targets are shooting back and the margin of errors is measured in lives lost.

Fireworks: A Gunsight Anthology, by Jeff Cooper, Paladin Press, Boulder, CO, 1998. 192 pp., illus. Paper cover. $27.00

A collection of wild, hilarious, shocking and always meaningful tales from the remarkable life of an American firearms legend.

Frank Pachmayr: The Story of America's Master Gunsmith and his Guns, by John Lachuk, Safari Press, Huntington Beach, CA, 1996. 254 pp., illus. First edition, limited, signed and slipcased. $85.00; Second printing trade edition. $50.00.

The colorful and historically significant biography of Frank A. Pachmayr, America's own gunsmith emeritus.

From a Stranger's Doorstep to the Kremlin Gate, by Mikhail Kalashnikov, Ironside International Publishers, Inc., Alexandria, VA, 1999. 460 pp., illustrated. $34.95.

A biography of the most influential rifle designer of the 20th century. His AK-47 assault rifle has become the most widely used (and copied) assault rifle of this century.

The Frontier Rifleman, by H.B. LaCrosse Jr., Pioneer Press, Union City, TN, 1989. 183 pp., illus. Soft covers. $17.50.

The Frontier rifleman's clothing and equipment during the era of the American Revolution, 1760-1800.

The Gatling Gun: 19th Century Machine Gun to 21st Century Vulcan, by Joseph Berk, Paladin Press, Boulder, CO, 1991. 136 pp., illus. $34.95.

Here is the fascinating on-going story of a truly timeless weapon, from its beginnings during the Civil War to its current role as a state-of-the-art modern combat system.

German Artillery of World War Two, by Ian V. Hogg, Stackpole Books, Mechanicsburg, PA, 1997. 304 pp., illus. $44.95.

Complete details of German artillery use in WWII.

Grand Old Lady of No Man's Land: The Vickers Machine Gun, by Dolf L. Goldsmith, Collector Grade Publications, Cobourg, Canada, 1994. 600 pp., illus. $79.95.

Goldsmith brings his years of experience as a U.S. Army armourer, machine gun collector and shooter to bear on the Vickers, in a book sure to become a classic in its field.

The Grenade Recognition Manual, Volume 1, U.S. Grenades & Accessories, by Darryl W. Lynn, Service Publications, Ottawa, Canada, 1998. 112 pp., illus. Paper covers. $29.95.

This new book examines the hand grenades of the United States beginning with the hand grenades of the U.S. Civil War and continues through to the present.

The Grenade Recognition Manual, Vol. 2, British and Commonwealth Grenades and Accessories, by Darryl W. Lynn, Printed by the Author, Ottawa, Canada, 2001. 201 pp., illustrated with over 200 photos and drawings. Paper covers. $29.95.

Covers British, Australian, and Canadian Grenades. It has the complete British Numbered series, most of the L series as well as the Australian and Canadian grenades in use. Also covers Launchers, fuzes and lighters, launching cartridges, fillings, and markings.

Gun Digest Treasury, 7th Edition, edited by Harold A. Murtz, DBI Books, a division of Krause Publications, Iola, WI, 1994. 320 pp., illus. Paper covers. $17.95.

A collection of some of the most interesting articles which have appeared in Gun Digest over its first 45 years.

Gun Digest 2002, 56th Edition, edited by Ken Ramage, DBI Books a division of Krause Publications, Iola, WI, 2001. 544 pp., illustrated. Paper covers. $24.95.

This all new 56th edition continues the editorial excellence, quality, content and comprehensive cataloguing that firearms enthusiasts have come to know and expect. The most read gun book in the world for the last half century.

Gun Engraving, by C. Austyn, Safari Press Publication, Huntington Beach, CA, 1998. 128 pp., plus 24 pages of color photos. $50.00.

A well-illustrated book on fine English and European gun engravers. Includes a fantastic pictorial section that lists types of engravings and prices.

Gun Notes, Volume 1, by Elmer Keith, Safari Press, Huntington Beach, CA, 1995. 219 pp., illustrated Limited Edition, Slipcased. $75.00

A collection of Elmer Keith's most interesting columns and feature stories that appeared in "Guns & Ammo" magazine from 1961 to the late 1970's.

Gun Notes, Volume 2, by Elmer Keith, Safari Press, Huntington Beach, CA, 1997. 292 pp., illus. Limited 1st edition, numbered and signed by Keith's son. Slipcased. $75.00. Trade edition. $35.00.

Covers articles from Keith's monthly column in "Guns & Ammo" magazine during the period from 1971 through Keith's passing in 1982.

Gun Talk, edited by Dave Moreton, Winchester Press, Piscataway, NJ, 1973. 256 pp., illus. $9.95.

A treasury of original writing by the top gun writers and editors in America. Practical advice about every aspect of the shooting sports.

The Gun That Made the Twenties Roar, by Wm. J. Helmer, rev. and enlarged by George C. Nonte, Jr., The Gun Room Press, Highland Park, NJ, 1977. Over 300 pp., illus. $24.95.

Historical account of John T. Thompson and his invention, the infamous "Tommy Gun."

Gun Trader's Guide, 23rd Edition, published by Stoeger Publishing Co., Wayne, NJ, 1999. 592 pp., illus. Paper covers. $23.95.

Complete specifications and current prices for used guns. Prices of over 5,000 handguns, rifles and shotguns both foreign and domestic.

Gun Writers of Yesteryear, compiled by James Foral, Wolfe Publishing Co., Prescott, AZ, 1993. 449 pp. $35.00.

Here, from the pre-American rifleman days of 1898-1920, are collected some 80 articles by 34 writers from eight magazines.

The Gunfighter, Man or Myth? by Joseph G. Rosa, Oklahoma Press, Norman, OK, 1969. 229 pp., illus. (including weapons). Paper covers. $14.95.

A well-documented work on gunfights and gunfighters of the West and elsewhere. Great treat for all gunfighter buffs.

Gunfitting: The Quest for Perfection, by Michael Yardley, Safari Press, Huntington Beach, CA, 1995. 128 pp., illus. $24.95.

The author, a very experienced shooting instructor, examines gun stocks and gunfitting in depth.

Guns Illustrated 2002, 3rd Edition, edited by Ken Ramage, DBI Books a division of Krause Publications, Iola, WI, 1999. 352 pp., illustrated. Paper covers. $22.95.

Highly informative, technical articles on a wide range of shooting topics by some of the top writers in the industry. A catalog section lists more than 3,000 firearms currently manufactured in or imported to the U.S.

Guns & Shooting: A Selected Bibliography, by Ray Riling, Ray Riling Arms Books Co., Phila., PA, 1982. 434 pp., illus. Limited, numbered edition. $75.

A limited edition of this superb bibliographical work, the only modern listing of books devoted to guns and shooting.

Guns, Bullets, and Gunfighters, by Jim Cirillo, Paladin Press, Boulder, CO, 1996. 119 pp., illus. Paper covers. $16.00.

Lessons and tales from a modern-day gunfighter.

Guns, Loads, and Hunting Tips, by Bob Hagel, Wolfe Publishing Co., Prescott, AZ, 1986. 509 pp., illus. $19.95.

A large hardcover book packed with shooting, hunting and handloading wisdom.

Handgun Digest, 3rd Edition, edited by Chris Christian, DBI Books, a division of Krause Publications, Iola, WI, 1995. 256 pp., illus. Paper covers. $18.95.

Full coverage of all aspects of handguns and handgunning from a highly readable and knowledgeable author.

Hidden in Plain Sight, "A Practical Guide to Concealed Handgun Carry" (Revised 2nd Edition), by Trey Blood-worth and Mike Raley, Paladin Press, Boulder, CO, 1997, 5 1/2 x 8 1/2, softcover, photos, 176 pp. $20.00

Concerned with how to comfortably, discreetly and safely exercise the privileges granted by a CCW permit? This invaluable guide offers the latest advice on what to look for when choosing a CCW, how to dress for comfortable, effective concealed carry, traditional and more unconventional carry modes, accessory holsters, customized clothing and accessories, accessibility data based on draw-time comparisons and new holsters on the market. Includes 40 new manufacturer listings.

HK Assault Rifle Systems, by Duncan Long, Paladin Press, Boulder, CO, 1995. 110 pp., illus. Paper covers. $27.95.

The little known history behind this fascinating family of weapons tracing its beginnings from the ashes of World War Two to the present time.

The Hunter's Table, by Terry Libby/Recipes of Chef Richard Blondin, Countrysport Press, Selma, AL, 1999. 230 pp. $30.00.

The Countrysport book of wild game guisine.

I Remember Skeeter, compiled by Sally Jim Skelton, Wolfe Publishing Co., Prescott, AZ, 1998. 401 pp., illus. Paper covers. $19.95.

A collection of some of the beloved storyteller's famous works interspersed with anecdotes and tales from the people who knew best.

In The Line of Fire, "A Working Cop's Guide to Pistol Craft", by Michael E. Conti, Paladin Press, Boulder, CO, 1997, soft cover, photos, illus., 184 pp. $30.00

As a working cop, you want to end your patrol in the same condition you began: alive and uninjured. Improve your odds by reading and mastering the information in this book on pistol selection, stopping power, combat reloading, stoppages, carrying devices, stances, grips and Conti's "secrets" to accurate shooting.

Joe Rychertinik Reflects on Guns, Hunting, and Days Gone By, by Joe Rychertinik, Precision Shooting, Inc., Manchester, CT, 1999. 281 pp., illustrated. Paper covers. $16.95.

Thirty articles by a master story-teller.

Kill or Get Killed, by Col. Rex Applegate, Paladin Press, Boulder, CO, 1996. 400 pp., illus. $39.95.

The best and longest-selling book on close combat in history.

Larrey: Surgeon to Napoleon's Imperial Guard, by Robert G. Richardson, Quiller Press, London, 2000. 269 pp., illus. B & W photos, maps and drawings. $23.95

Not a book for the squeamish, but one full of interest, splendidly researched, bringing both the character of the Napoleonic wars and Larrey himself vividly to life. Authenticity of detail is preserved throughout.

The Long-Range War: Sniping in Vietnam, by Peter R. Senich, Paladin Press, Boulder, CO, 1994. 280 pp., illus. $49.95.

The most complete report on Vietnam-era sniping ever documented.

Manual for H&R Reising Submachine Gun and Semi-Auto Rifle, edited by George P. Dillman, Desert Publications, El Dorado, AZ, 1994. 81 pp., illus. Paper covers. $12.95.

A reprint of the Harrington & Richardson 1943 factory manual and the rare military manual on the H&R submachine gun and semi-auto rifle.

The Manufacture of Gunflints, by Sydney B.J. Skertchly, facsimile reprint with new introduction by Seymour de

THE ARMS LIBRARY

Lotbiniere, Museum Restoration Service, Ontario, Canada, 1984. 90 pp., illus. $24.50.

Limited edition reprinting of the very scarce London edition of 1879.

Master Tips, by J. Winokur, Potshot Press, Pacific Palisades, CA, 1985. 96 pp., illus. Paper covers. $11.95.

Basics of practical shooting.

The Military and Police Sniper, by Mike R. Lau, Precision Shooting, Inc., Manchester, CT, 1998. 352 pp., illustrated. Paper covers. $44.95.

Advanced precision shooting for combat and law enforcement.

Military Rifle & Machine Gun Cartridges, by Jean Huon, Paladin Press, Boulder, CO, 1990. 392 pp., illus. $34.95.

Describes the primary types of military cartridges and their principal loadings, as well as their characteristics, origin and use.

Military Small Arms of the 20th Century, 7th Edition, by Ian V. Hogg and John Weeks, DBI Books, a division of Krause Publications, Iola, WI, 2000. 416 pp., illustrated. Paper covers. $24.95.

Cover small arms of 46 countries. Over 800 photographs and illustrations.

Modern Custom Guns, Walnut, Steel, and Uncommon Artistry, by Tom Turpin, Krause Publications, Iola, WI, 1997. 206 pp., illus. $49.95.

From exquisite engraving to breathtaking exotic woods, the mystique of today's custom guns is expertly detailed in word and awe-inspiring color photos of rifles, shotguns and handguns.

Modern Guns Identification & Values, 13th Edition, by Russell & Steve Quertermous, Collector Books, Paducah, KY, 1999. 516 pp., illus. Paper covers. $12.95.

A standard reference for over 20 years. Over 1,800 illustrations of over 2,500 models with their current values.

Modern Law Enforcement Weapons & Tactics, 2nd Edition, by Tom Ferguson, DBI Books, a division of Krause Publications, Iola, WI, 1991. 256 pp., illus. Paper covers. $18.95.

An in-depth look at the weapons and equipment used by law enforcement agencies of today.

Modern Machine Guns, by John Walter, Stackpole Books, Inc. Mechanicsburg, PA, 2000. 144 pp., with 146 illustrations. $22.95.

A compact and authoritative guide to post-war machine-guns. A gun-by-gun directory identifying individual variants and types including detailed evaluations and technical data.

Modern Sporting Guns, by Christopher Austyn, Safari Press, Huntington Beach, CA, 1994. 128 pp., illus. $40.00.

A discussion of the "best" English guns; round action, over-and-under, boxlocks, hammer guns, bolt action and double rifles as well as accessories.

The More Complete Cannoneer, by M.C. Switlik, Museum & Collectors Specialties Co., Monroe, MI, 1990. 199 pp., illus. $19.95.

Compiled agreeably to the regulations for the U.S. War Department, 1861, and containing current observations on the use of antique cannons.

The MP-40 Machine Gun, Desert Publications, El Dorado, AZ, 1995. 32 pp., illus. Paper covers. $11.95.

A reprint of the hard-to-find operating and maintenance manual for one of the most famous machine guns of World War II.

Naval Percussion Locks and Primers, by Lt. J. A. Dahlgren, Museum Restoration Service, Bloomfield, Canada, 1996. 140 pp., illus. $35.00

First published as an Ordnance Memoranda in 1853, this is the finest existing study of percussion locks and primers origin and development.

The Official Soviet AKM Manual, translated by Maj. James F. Gebhardt (Ret.), Paladin Press, Boulder, CO, 1999. 120 pp., illustrated. Paper covers. $18.00.

This official military manual, available in English for the first time, was originally published by the Soviet Ministry of Defence. Covers the history, function, maintenance, assembly and disassembly, etc. of the 7.62mm AKM assault rifle.

The One-Round War: U.S.M.C. Scout-Snipers in Vietnam, by Peter Senich, Paladin Press, Boulder, CO, 1996. 384 pp., illus. Paper covers $59.95.

Sniping in Vietnam focusing specifically on the Marine Corps program.

Pin Shooting: A Complete Guide, by Mitchell A. Ota, Wolfe Publishing Co., Prescott, AZ, 1992. 145 pp., illus. Paper covers. $14.95.

Traces the sport from its humble origins to today's thoroughly enjoyable social event, including the mammoth eight-day Second Chance Pin Shoot in Michigan.

Powder and Ball Small Arms, by Martin Pegler, Windrow & Greene Publishing, London, 1998. 128 pp., illustrated with 200 color photos. $39.95.

Part of the new "Live Firing Classic Weapons" series. Full-color photos of experienced shooters dressed in authentic costumes handling, loading and firing historic weapons.

Principles of Personal Defense, by Jeff Cooper, Paladin Press, Boulder, CO, 1999. 56 pp., illustrated. Paper covers. $14.00.

This revised edition of Jeff Cooper's classic on personal defense offers great new illustrations and a new preface while retaining the timeliness theory of individual defense behavior presented in the original book.

E.C. Prudhomme, Master Gun Engraver, A Retrospective Exhibition: 1946-1973, intro. by John T. Amber, The R. W. Norton Art Gallery, Shreveport, LA, 1973. 32 pp., illus. Paper covers. $9.95.

Examples of master gun engravings by Jack Prudhomme.

The Quotable Hunter, edited by Jay Cassell and Peter Fiduccia, The lyons Press, N.Y., 1999. 224 pp., illustrated. $20.00.

This collection of more than three hundred memorable quotes from hunters through the ages captures the essence of the sport, with all its joys idiosyncrasies, and challenges.

A Rifleman Went to War, by H. W. McBride, Lancer Militaria, Mt. Ida, AR, 1987. 398 pp., illus. $29.95.

The classic account of practical marksmanship on the battlefields of World War I.

Sharpshooting for Sport and War, by W.W. Greener, Wolfe Publishing Co., Prescott, AZ, 1995. 192 pp., illus. $30.00.

This classic reprint explores the *first* expanding bullet; service rifles; shooting positions; trajectories; recoil; external ballistics; and other valuable information.

The Shooter's Bible 2002, No. 93, edited by William S. Jarrett, Stoeger Publishing Co., Wayne, NJ, 2001. 576 pp., illustrated. Paper covers. $23.95.

Over 3,000 firearms currently offered by major American and foreign gunmakers. Represented are handguns, rifles, shotguns and black powder arms with complete specifications and retail prices.

THE ARMS LIBRARY

Shooting To Live, by Capt. W. E. Fairbairn & Capt. E. A. Sykes, Paladin Press, Boulder, CO, 1997, 4 1/2 x 7, soft cover, illus., 112 pp. $14.00

Shooting to Live is the product of Fairbairn's and Sykes' practical experience with the handgun. Hundreds of incidents provided the basis for the first true book on life-or-death shootouts with the pistol. Shooting to Live teaches all concepts, considerations and applications of combat pistol craft.

Shooting Sixguns of the Old West, by Mike Venturino, MLV Enterprises, Livingston, MT, 1997. 221 pp., illus. Paper covers. $26.50.

A comprehensive look at the guns of the early West: Colts, Smith & Wesson and Remingtons, plus blackpowder and reloading specs.

Sniper Training, FM 23-10, Reprint of the U.S. Army field manual of August, 1994, Paladin Press, Boulder, CO, 1995. 352pp., illus. Paper covers. $30.00

The most up-to-date U.S. military sniping information and doctrine.

Sniping in France, by Major H. Hesketh-Prichard, Lancer Militaria, Mt. Ida, AR, 1993. 224 pp., illus. $24.95.

The author was a well-known British adventurer and big game hunter. He was called upon in the early days of "The Great War" to develop a program to offset an initial German advantage in sniping. How the British forces came to overcome this advantage.

Special Warfare: Special Weapons, by Kevin Dockery, Emperor's Press, Chicago, IL, 1997. 192 pp., illus. $29.95.

The arms and equipment of the UDT and SEALS from 1943 to the present.

Sporting Collectibles, by Dr. Stephen R. Irwin, Stoeger Publishing Co., Wayne, NJ, 1997. 256 pp., illus. Paper covers. $19.95.

A must book for serious collectors and admirers of sporting collectibles.

The Sporting Craftsmen: A Complete Guide to Contemporary Makers of Custom-Built Sporting Equipment, by Art Carter, Countrysport Press, Traverse City, MI, 1994. 240 pp., illus. $35.00.

Profiles leading makers of centerfire rifles; muzzleloading rifles; bamboo fly rods; fly reels; flies; waterfowl calls; decoys; handmade knives; and traditional longbows and recurves.

Sporting Rifle Takedown & Reassembly Guide, 2nd Edition, by J.B. Wood, DBI Books, a division of Krause Publications, Iola, WI, 1997. 480 pp., illus. $19.95.

An updated edition of the reference guide for anyone who wants to properly care for their sporting rifle. (Available September 1997)

2001 Standard Catalog of Firearms, the Collector's Price & Reference Guide, 11th Edition, by Ned Schwing, Krause Publications, Iola, WI, 2000. 1,248 pp., illus. Paper covers. $32.95.

Packed with more than 80,000 real world prices with more than 5,000 photos. Easy to use master index listing every firearm model.

The Street Smart Gun Book, by John Farnam, Police Bookshelf, Concord, NH, 1986. 45 pp., illus. Paper covers. $11.95.

Weapon selection, defensive shooting techniques, and gunfight-winning tactics from one of the world's leading authorities.

Stress Fire, Vol. 1: Stress Fighting for Police, by Massad Ayoob, Police Bookshelf, Concord, NH, 1984. 149 pp., illus. Paper covers. $9.95.

Gunfighting for police, advanced tactics and techniques.

Survival Guns, by Mel Tappan, Desert Publications, El Dorado, AZ, 1993. 456 pp., illus. Paper covers. $21.95.

Discusses in a frank and forthright manner which handguns, rifles and shotguns to buy for personal defense and securing food, and the ones to avoid.

The Tactical Advantage, by Gabriel Suarez, Paladin Press, Boulder, CO, 1998. 216 pp., illustrated. Paper covers. $22.00.

Learn combat tactics that have been tested in the world's toughest schools.

Tactical Marksman, by Dave M. Lauch, Paladin Press, Boulder, CO, 1996. 165 pp., illus. Paper covers. $35.00.

A complete training manual for police and practical shooters.

Thompson Guns 1921-1945, Anubis Press, Houston, TX, 1980. 215 pp., illus. Paper covers. $15.95.

Facsimile reprinting of five complete manuals on the Thompson submachine gun.

To Ride, Shoot Straight, and Speak the Truth, by Jeff Cooper, Paladin Press, Boulder, CO, 1997, 5 1/2 x 8 1/2, soft-cover, illus., 384 pp. $32.00

Combat mind-set, proper sighting, tactical residential architecture, nuclear war - these are some of the many subjects explored by Jeff Cooper in this illustrated anthology. The author discusses various arms, fighting skills and the importance of knowing how to defend oneself, and one's honor, in our rapidly changing world.

Trailriders Guide to Cowboy Action Shooting, by James W. Barnard, Pioneer Press, Union City, TN, 1998. 134 pp., plus 91 photos, drawings and charts. Paper covers. $24.95.

Covers the complete spectrum of this shooting discipline, from how to dress to authentic leather goods, which guns are legal, calibers, loads and ballistics.

The Ultimate Sniper, by Major John L. Plaster, Paladin Press, Boulder, CO, 1994. 464 pp., illus. Paper covers. $42.95.

An advanced training manual for military and police snipers.

Unrepentant Sinner, by Col. Charles Askins, Paladin Press, Boulder, CO, 2000. 322 pp., illustrated. $29.95.

The autobiography of Colonel Charles Askins.

U.S. Marine Corp Rifle and Pistol Marksmanship, 1935, reprinting of a government publication, Lancer Militaria, Mt. Ida, AR, 1991. 99 pp., illus. Paper covers. $11.95.

The old corps method of precision shooting.

U.S. Marine Corps Scout/Sniper Training Manual, Lancer Militaria, Mt. Ida, AR, 1989. Soft covers. $19.95.

Reprint of the original sniper training manual used by the Marksmanship Training Unit of the Marine Corps Development and Education Command in Quantico, Virginia.

U.S. Marine Corps Scout-Sniper, World War II and Korea, by Peter R. Senich, Paladin Press, Boulder, CO, 1994. 236 pp., illus. $44.95.

The most thorough and accurate account ever printed on the training, equipment and combat experiences of the U.S. Marine Corps Scout-Snipers.

U.S. Marine Corps Sniping, Lancer Militaria, Mt. Ida, AR, 1989. Irregular pagination. Soft covers. $17.95.

A reprint of the official Marine Corps FMFM1-3B.

Weapons of the Waffen-SS, by Bruce Quarrie, Sterling Publishing Co., Inc., 1991. 168 pp., illus. $24.95.

An in-depth look at the weapons that made Hitler's Waffen-SS the fearsome fighting machine it was.

THE ARMS LIBRARY

Weatherby: The Man, The Gun, The Legend, by Grits and Tom Gresham, Cane River Publishing Co., Natchitoches, LA, 1992. 290 pp., illus. $24.95.

A fascinating look at the life of the man who changed the course of firearms development in America.

The Winchester Era, by David Madis, Art & Reference House, Brownsville, TX, 1984. 100 pp., illus. $19.95.

Story of the Winchester company, management, employees, etc.

Winchester Repeating Arms Company by Herbert Houze, Krause Publications, Iola, WI. 512 pp., illus. $50.00.

With British Snipers to the Reich, by Capt. C. Shore, Lander Militaria, Mt. Ida, AR, 1988. 420 pp., illus. $29.95.

One of the greatest books ever written on the art of combat sniping.

The World's Machine Pistols and Submachine Guns - Vol. 2a 1964 to 1980, by Nelson & Musgrave, Ironside International, Alexandria, VA, 2000. 673 pages, illustrated. $59.95

Containing data, history and photographs of over 200 weapons. With a special section covering shoulder stocked automatic pistols, 100 additional photos.

The World's Submachine Guns - Vol. 1 1918 to 1963, by Nelson & Musgrave, Ironside International, Alexandria, VA, 2001. 673 pages, illustrated. $59.95.

A revised edition covering much new material that has come to light since the book was originally printed in 1963.

The World's Sniping Rifles, by Ian V. Hogg, Paladin Press, Boulder, CO, 1998. 144 pp., illustrated. $22.95.

A detailed manual with descriptions and illustrations of more than 50 high-precision rifles from 14 countries and a complete analysis of sights and systems.

GUNSMITHING

Accurizing the Factory Rifle, by M.L. McPhereson, Precision Shooting, Inc., Manchester, CT, 1999. 335 pp., illustrated. Paper covers. $44.95.

A long-awaiting book, which bridges the gap between the rudimentary (mounting sling swivels, scope blocks and that general level of accomplishment) and the advanced (precision chambering, barrel fluting, and that general level of accomplishment) books that are currently available today.

Advanced Rebarreling of the Sporting Rifle, by Willis H. Fowler, Jr., Willis H. Fowler, Jr., Anchorage, AK, 1994. 127 pp., illus. Paper covers. $32.50.

A manual outlining a superior method of fitting barrels and doing chamber work on the sporting rifle.

The Art of Engraving, by James B. Meek, F. Brownell & Son, Montezuma, IA, 1973. 196 pp., illus. $38.95.

A complete, authoritative, imaginative and detailed study in training for gun engraving. The first book of its kind—and a great one.

Artistry in Arms, The R. W. Norton Gallery, Shreveport, LA, 1970. 42 pp., illus. Paper covers. $9.95.

The art of gunsmithing and engraving.

Barrels & Actions, by Harold Hoffman, H&P Publishers, San Angelo, TX, 1990. 309 pp., illus. Spiral bound. $29.95.

A manual on barrel making.

Black Powder Hobby Gunsmithing, by Sam Fadala and Dale Storey, DBI Books, a division of Krause Publications, Iola, WI., 1994. 256 pp., illus. Paper covers. $18.95.

A how-to guide for gunsmithing blackpowder pistols, rifles and shotguns from two men at the top of their respective fields.

Checkering and Carving of Gun Stocks, by Monte Kennedy, Stackpole Books, Harrisburg, PA, 1962. 175 pp., illus. $39.95.

Revised, enlarged cloth-bound edition of a much sought-after, dependable work.

The Complete Metal Finishing Book, by Harold Hoffman, H&P Publishers, San Angelo, TX, 1992. 364 pp., illus. Paper covers. $29.95.

Instructions for the different metal finishing operations that the normal craftsman or shop will use. Primarily firearm related.

Exploded Handgun Drawings, The Gun Digest Book of, edited by Harold A. Murtz, DBI Books, a division of Krause Publications, Iola, WI. 1992. 512 pp., illus. Paper covers. $20.95.

Exploded or isometric drawings for 494 of the most popular handguns.

Exploded Long Gun Drawings, The Gun Digest Book of, edited by Harold A. Murtz, DBI Books, a division of Krause Publications, Iola, WI. 512 pp., illus. Paper covers. $20.95.

Containing almost 500 rifle and shotgun exploded drawings. An invaluable aid to both professionals and hobbyists.

The Finishing of Gun Stocks, by Harold Hoffman, H&P Publishers, San Angelo, TX, 1994. 98 pp., illus. Paper covers. $17.95.

Covers different types of finishing methods and finishes.

Firearms Assembly/Disassembly, Part I: Automatic Pistols, 2nd Revised Edition, The Gun Digest Book of, by J.B. Wood, DBI Books, a division of Krause Publications, Iola, WI, 1999. 480 pp., illus. Paper covers. $24.95.

Covers 58 popular autoloading pistols plus nearly 200 variants of those models integrated into the text and completely cross-referenced in the index.

Firearms Assembly/Disassembly Part II: Revolvers, Revised Edition, The Gun Digest Book of, by J.B. Wood, DBI Books, a division of Krause Publications, Iola, WI, 1990. 480 pp., illus. Paper covers. $19.95.

Covers 49 popular revolvers plus 130 variants. The most comprehensive and professional presentation available to either hobbyist or gunsmith.

Firearms Assembly/Disassembly Part III: Rimfire Rifles, Revised Edition, The Gun Digest Book of, by J. B. Wood, DBI Books, a division of Krause Publications, Iola, WI., 1994. 480 pp., illus. Paper covers. $19.95.

Greatly expanded edition covering 65 popular rimfire rifles plus over 100 variants all completely cross-referenced in the index.

Firearms Assembly/Disassembly Part IV: Centerfire Rifles, Revised Edition, The Gun Digest Book of, by J.B. Wood, DBI Books, a division of Krause Publications, Iola, WI, 1991. 480 pp., illus. Paper covers. $19.95.

Covers 54 popular centerfire rifles plus 300 variants. The most comprehensive and professional presentation available to either hobbyist or gunsmith.

Firearms Assembly/Disassembly, Part V: Shotguns, Revised Edition, The Gun Digest Book of, by J.B. Wood, DBI Books, a division of Krause Publications, Iola, WI, 1992. 480 pp., illus. Paper covers. $19.95.

Covers 46 popular shotguns plus over 250 variants with step-by-step instructions on how to dismantle and reassemble each. The most comprehensive and professional presentation available to either hobbyist or gunsmith.

Firearms Assembly/Disassembly Part VI: Law Enforcement Weapons, The Gun Digest Book of, by J.B. Wood,

DBI Books, a division of Krause Publications, Iola, WI, 1981. 288 pp., illus. Paper covers. $16.95.

Step-by-step instructions on how to completely dismantle and reassemble the most commonly used firearms found in law enforcement arsenals.

Firearms Assembly 3: The NRA Guide to Rifle and Shotguns, NRA Books, Wash., DC, 1980. 264 pp., illus. Paper covers. $13.95.

Text and illustrations explaining the takedown of 125 rifles and shotguns, domestic and foreign.

Firearms Assembly 4: The NRA Guide to Pistols and Revolvers, NRA Books, Wash., DC, 1980. 253 pp., illus. Paper covers. $13.95.

Text and illustrations explaining the takedown of 124 pistol and revolver models, domestic and foreign.

Firearms Bluing and Browning, By R.H. Angier, Stackpole Books, Harrisburg, PA. 151 pp., illus. $19.95.

A world master gunsmith reveals his secrets of building, repairing and renewing a gun, quite literally, lock, stock and barrel. A useful, concise text on chemical coloring methods for the gunsmith and mechanic.

Firearms Disassembly—With Exploded Views, by John A. Karns & John E. Traister, Stoeger Publishing Co., S. Hackensack, NJ, 1995. 320 pp., illus. Paper covers. $19.95.

Provides the do's and don'ts of firearms disassembly. Enables owners and gunsmiths to disassemble firearms in a professional manner.

Guns and Gunmaking Tools of Southern Appalachia, by John Rice Irwin, Schiffer Publishing Ltd., 1983. 118 pp., illus. Paper covers. $9.95.

The story of the Kentucky rifle.

Gunsmithing: Pistols & Revolvers, by Patrick Sweeney, DBI Books, a division of Krause Publications, Iola, WI, 1998. 352 pp., illus. Paper covers. $24.95.

Do-it-Yourself projects, diagnosis and repair for pistols and revolvers.

Gunsmithing: Rifles, by Patrick Sweeney, Krause Publications, Iola, WI, 1999. 352 pp., illustrated. Paper covers. $24.95.

Tips for lever-action rifles. Building a custom Ruger 10/22. Building a better hunting rifle.

Gunsmithing Tips and Projects, a collection of the best articles from the *Handloader* and *Rifle* magazines, by various authors, Wolfe Publishing Co., Prescott, AZ, 1992. 443 pp., illus. Paper covers. $25.00.

Includes such subjects as shop, stocks, actions, tuning, triggers, barrels, customizing, etc.

Gunsmith Kinks, by F.R. (Bob) Brownell, F. Brownell & Son, Montezuma, IA, 1st ed., 1969. 496 pp., well illus. $22.98.

A widely useful accumulation of shop kinks, short cuts, techniques and pertinent comments by practicing gunsmiths from all over the world.

Gunsmith Kinks 2, by Bob Brownell, F. Brownell & Son, Publishers, Montezuma, IA, 1983. 496 pp., illus. $22.95.

A collection of gunsmithing knowledge, shop kinks, new and old techniques, shortcuts and general know-how straight from those who do them best—the gunsmiths.

Gunsmith Kinks 3, edited by Frank Brownell, Brownells Inc., Montezuma, IA, 1993. 504 pp., illus. $24.95.

Tricks, knacks and "kinks" by professional gunsmiths and gun tinkerers. Hundreds of valuable ideas are given in this volume.

Gunsmith Kinks 4, edited by Frank Brownell, Brownells Inc., Montezuma, IA, 2001. 564 pp., illus. $27.75

332 detailed illustrations. 560+ pages with 706 separate subject headings and over 5000 cross-indexed entries. An incredible gold mine of information.

Gunsmithing, by Roy F. Dunlap, Stackpole Books, Harrisburg, PA, 1990. 742 pp., illus. $34.95.

A manual of firearm design, construction, alteration and remodeling. For amateur and professional gunsmiths and users of modern firearms.

Gunsmithing at Home: Lock, Stock and Barrel, by John Traister, Stoeger Publishing Co., Wayne, NJ, 1997. 320 pp., illus. Paper covers. $19.95.

A complete step-by-step fully illustrated guide to the art of gunsmithing.

The Gunsmith's Manual, by J.P. Stelle and Wm. B. Harrison, The Gun Room Press, Highland Park, NJ, 1982. 376 pp., illus. $19.95.

For the gunsmith in all branches of the trade.

Home Gunsmithing the Colt Single Action Revolvers, by Loren W. Smith, Ray Riling Arms Books, Co., Phila., PA, 2001. 119 pp., illus. $29.95.

Affords the Colt Single Action owner detailed, pertinent information on the operating and servicing of this famous and historic handgun.

How to Convert Military Rifles, Williams Gun Sight Co., Davision, MI, new and enlarged seventh edition, 1997. 76 pp., illus. Paper covers. $13.95.

This latest edition updated the changes that have occured over the past thirty years. Tips, instructions and illustratons on how to convert popular military rifles as the Enfield, Mauser 96 nad SKS just to name a few are presented.

Mauser M98 & M96, by R.A. Walsh, Wolfe Publishing Co., Prescott, AR, 1998. 123 pp., illustrated. Paper covers. $32.50.

How to build your own favorite custom Mauser rifle from two of the best bolt action rifle designs ever produced—the military Mauser Model 1898 and Model 1896 bolt rifles.

Mr. Single Shot's Gunsmithing-Idea-Book, by Frank de Haas, Mark de Haas, Orange City, IA, 1996. 168 pp., illus. Paper covers. $21.50.

Offers easy to follow, step-by-step instructions for a wide variety of gunsmithing procedures all reinforced by plenty of photos.

Pistolsmithing, by George C. Nonte, Jr., Stackpole Books, Harrisburg, PA, 1974. 560 pp., illus. $34.95.

A single source reference to handgun maintenance, repair, and modification at home, unequaled in value.

Practical Gunsmithing, by the editors of American Gunsmith, DBI Books, a division of Krause Publications, Iola, WI, 1996. 256 pp., illus. Paper covers. $19.95.

A book intended primarily for home gunsmithing, but one that will be extremely helpful to professionals as well.

Professional Stockmaking, by D. Wesbrook, Wolfe Publishing Co., Prescott AZ, 1995. 308 pp., illus. $54.00.

A step-by-step how-to with complete photographic support for every detail of the art of working wood into riflestocks.

Recreating the American Longrifle, by William Buchele, et al, George Shumway Publisher, York, Pa, 5th edition, 1999. 175 pp., illustrated. $40.00.

Includes full size plans for building a Kentucky rifle.

THE ARMS LIBRARY

Riflesmithing, The Gun Digest Book of, by Jack Mitchell, DBI Books, a division of Krause Publications, Iola, WI, 1982. 256 pp., illus. Paper covers. $16.95.

The art and science of rifle gunsmithing. Covers tools, techniques, designs, finishing wood and metal, custom alterations.

Shotgun Gunsmithing, The Gun Digest Book of, by Ralph Walker, DBI Books, a division of Krause Publications, Iola, WI, 1983. 256 pp., illus. Paper covers. $16.95.

The principles and practices of repairing, individualizing and accurizing modern shotguns by one of the world's premier shotgun gunsmiths.

Sporting Rifle Take Down & Reassembly Guide, 2nd Edition, by J.B. Wood, Krause Publications, Iola, WI, 1997. 480 pp., illus. Paper covers. $19.95.

Hunters and shooting enthusiasts must have this reference featuring 52 of the most popular and widely used sporting centerfire and rimfire rifles.

The Story of Pope's Barrels, by Ray M. Smith, R&R Books, Livonia, NY, 1993. 203 pp., illus. $39.00.

A reissue of a 1960 book whose author knew Pope personally. It will be of special interest to Schuetzen rifle fans, since Pope's greatest days were at the height of the Schuetzen-era before WWI.

Survival Gunsmithing, by J.B. Wood, Desert Publications, Cornville, AZ, 1986. 92 pp., illus. Paper covers. $11.95.

A guide to repair and maintenance of the most popular rifles, shotguns and handguns.

The Tactical 1911, by Dave Lauck, Paladin Press, Boulder, CO, 1998. 137 pp., illus. Paper covers. $20.00.

Here is the only book you will ever need to teach you how to select, modify, employ and maintain your Colt.

HANDGUNS

Advanced Master Handgunning, by Charles Stephens, Paladin Press, Boulder, CO., 1994. 72 pp., illus. Paper covers. $14.00.

Secrets and surefire techniques for winning handgun competitions.

American Beauty: The Prewar Colt National Match Government Model Pistol, by Timothy Mullin, Collector Grade Publications, Canada, 1999. 72 pp., 69 illus. $34.95

69 illustrations, 20 in full color photos of factory engraved guns and other authenticated upgrades, including rare 'double-carved' ivory grips.

Axis Pistols: WORLD WAR TWO 50 YEARS COMMEMORATIVE ISSUE, by Jan C. Stills, Walsworth Publishing, 1989. 360 pages, illus. $59.95

The Ayoob Files: The Book, by Massad Ayoob, Police Bookshelf, Concord, NH, 1995. 223 pp., illus. Paper covers. $14.95.

The best of Massad Ayoob's acclaimed series in American Handgunner magazine.

Big Bore Sixguns, by John Taffin, Krause Publications, Iola, WI, 1997. 336 pp., illus. $39.95.

The author takes aim on the entire range of big bores from .357 Magnums to .500 Maximums, single actions and cap-and-ball sixguns to custom touches for big bores..

The Browning High Power Automatic Pistol (Expanded Edition), by Blake R. Stevens, Collector Grade Publications, Canada, 1996. 310 pages, with 313 illus. $49.95

An in-depth chronicle of seventy years of High Power history, from John M Browning's original 16-shot prototypes to the present. Profusely illustrated with rare original photos and drawings from the FN Archive to describe virtually every sporting and military version of the High Power. The numerous modifications made to the basic design over the years are, for the first time, accurately arranged in chronological order, thus permitting the dating of any High Power to within a few years of its production. Full details on the WWII Canadian-made Inglis Browning High Power pistol. The Expanded Edition contains 30 new pages on the interesting Argentine full-auto High Power, the latest FN 'MK3' and BDA9 pistols, plus FN's revolutionary P90 5.7x28mm Personal Defence Weapon, and more!

Browning Hi-Power Pistols, Desert Publications, Cornville, AZ, 1982. 20 pp., illus. Paper covers. $11.95.

Covers all facets of the various military and civilian models of the Browning Hi-Power pistol.

Canadian Military Handguns 1855-1985, by Clive M. Law, Museum Restoration Service, Bloomfield, Ont. Canada, 1994. 130pp., illus. $40.00.

A long-awaited and important history for arms historians and pistol collectors.

The Colt .45 Auto Pistol, compiled from U.S. War Dept. Technical Manuals, and reprinted by Desert Publications, Cornville, AZ, 1978. 80 pp., illus. Paper covers. $11.95.

Covers every facet of this famous pistol from mechanical training, manual of arms, disassembly, repair and replacement of parts.

Colt Automatic Pistols, by Donald B. Bady, Pioneer Press, Union City, TN, 1999. 368 pp., illustrated. Softcover. $19.95.

A revised and enlarged edition of a key work on a fascinating subject. Complete information on every Colt automatic pistol.

Combat Handgunnery, 4th Edition, by Chuck Taylor, DBI Books, a division of Krause Publications, Iola, WI, 1997. 256 pp., illus. Paper covers. $18.95.

This all-new edition looks at real world combat handgunnery from three different perspectives—military, police and civilian. Available, October, 1996.

Combat Revolvers, by Duncan Long, Paladin Press, Boulder, CO, 1999, 8 1/2 x 11, soft cover, 115 photos, 152 pp. $21.95

This is an uncompromising look at modern combat revolvers. All the major foreign and domestic guns are covered: the Colt Python, S&W Model 29, Ruger GP 100 and hundreds more. Know the gun that you may one day stake your life on.

The Complete Book of Combat Handgunning, by Chuck Taylor, Desert Publications, Cornville, AZ, 1982. 168 pp., illus. Paper covers. $20.00.

Covers virtually every aspect of combat handgunning.

Complete Guide to Compact Handguns, by Gene Gangarosa, Jr., Stoeger Publishing Co., Wayne, NJ, 1997. 228 pp., illus. Paper covers. $22.95.

Includes hundreds of compact firearms, along with text results conducted by the author.

Complete Guide to Service Handguns, by Gene Gangarosa, Jr., Stoeger Publishing Co., Wayne, NJ, 1998. 320 pp., illus. Paper covers. $22.95.

The author explores the revolvers and pistols that are used around the globe by military, law enforcement and civilians.

The Custom Government Model Pistol, by Layne Simpson, Wolfe Publishing Co., Prescott, AZ, 1994. 639 pp., illus. Paper covers. $24.50.

The book about one of the world's greatest firearms and the things pistolsmiths do to make it even greater.

THE ARMS LIBRARY

The CZ-75 Family: The Ultimate Combat Handgun, by J.M. Ramos, Paladin Press, Boulder, CO, 1990. 100 pp., illus. Soft covers. $25.00.

An in-depth discussion of the early-and-late model CZ-75s, as well as the many newest additions to the Czech pistol family.

Encyclopedia of Pistols & Revolvers, by A.E. Hartnik, Knickerbocker Press, New York, NY, 1997. 272 pp., illus. $19.95.

A comprehensive encyclopedia specially written for collectors and owners of pistols and revolvers.

Experiments of a Handgunner, by Walter Roper, Wolfe Publishing Co., Prescott, AZ, 1989. 202 pp., illus. $37.00.

A limited edition reprint. A listing of experiments with functioning parts of handguns, with targets, stocks, rests, handloading, etc.

The Farnam Method of Defensive Handgunning, by John S. Farnam, Police Bookshelf, 1999. 191 pp., illus. Paper covers. $25.00

A book intended to not only educate the new shooter, but also to serve as a guide and textbook for his and his instructor's training courses.

Fast and Fancy Revolver Shooting, by Ed. McGivern, Anniversary Edition, Winchester Press, Piscataway, NJ, 1984. 484 pp., illus. $18.95.

A fascinating volume, packed with handgun lore and solid information by the acknowledged dean of revolver shooters.

.45 ACP Super Guns, by J.M. Ramos, Paladin Press, Boulder, CO, 1991. 144 pp., illus. Paper covers. $24.00.

Modified .45 automatic pistols for competition, hunting and personal defense.

The .45, The Gun Digest Book of, by Dean A. Grennell, DBI Books, a division of Krause Publications, Iola, WI, 1989. 256 pp., illus. Paper covers. $17.95.

Definitive work on one of America's favorite calibers.

Glock: The New Wave in Combat Handguns, by Peter Alan Kasler, Paladin Press, Boulder, CO, 1993. 304 pp., illus. $27.00.

Kasler debunks the myths that surround what is the most innovative handgun to be introduced in some time.

Glock's Handguns, by Duncan Long, Desert Publications, El Dorado, AR, 1996. 180 pp., illus. Paper covers. $18.95.

An outstanding volume on one of the world's newest and most successful firearms of the century.

Hand Cannons: The World's Most Powerful Handguns, by Duncan Long, Paladin Press, Boulder, CO, 1995. 208 pp., illus. Paper covers. $22.00.

Long describes and evaluates each powerful gun according to their features.

The Handgun, by Geoffrey Boothroyd, Safari Press, Inc., Huntington Beach, CA, 1999. 566 pp., illustrated. $50.00.

A very detailed history of the handgun. Now revised and a completely new chapter written to take account of developments since the 1970 edition.

Handguns 2002, 13th Edition, edited by Ken Ramage, DBI Books a division of Krause Publications, Iola, WI, 1999. 352 pp., illustrated. Paper covers. $22.95.

Top writers in the handgun industry give you a complete report on new handgun developments, testfire reports on the newest introductions and previews on what's ahead.

Handgun Digest, 3rd Edition, edited by Chris Christian, DBI Books, a division of Krause Publications, Iola, WI, 1995. 256 pp., illus. Paper covers. $18.95.

Full coverage of all aspects of handguns and handgunning from a highly readable and knowledgeable author.

Handgun Reloading, The Gun Digest Book of, by Dean A. Grennell and Wiley M. Clapp, DBI Books, a division of Krause Publications, Iola, WI, 1987. 256 pp., illus. Paper covers. $16.95.

Detailed discussions of all aspects of reloading for handguns, from basic to complex. New loading data.

Handgun Stopping Power "The Definitive Study", by Evan P. Marshall & Edwin J. Sanow, Paladin Press, Boulder, CO, 1997, soft cover, photos, 240 pp. $45.00

Dramatic first-hand accounts of the results of handgun rounds fired into criminals by cops, storeowners, cabbies and others are the heart and soul of this long-awaited book. This is the definitive methodology for predicting the stopping power of handgun loads, the first to take into account what really happens when a bullet meets a man.

Heckler & Koch's Handguns, by Duncan Long, Desert Publications, El Dorado, AR, 1996. 142 pp., illus. Paper covers. $19.95.

Traces the history and the evolution of H&K's pistols from the company's beginning at the end of WWII to the present.

Hidden in Plain Sight, by Trey Bloodworth & Mike Raley, Professional Press, Chapel Hill, NC, 1995. Paper covers. $19.95.

A practical guide to concealed handgun carry.

High Standard Automatic Pistols 1932-1950, by Charles E. Petty, The Gunroom Press, Highland Park, NJ, 1989. 124 pp., illus. $19.95.

A definitive source of information for the collector of High Standard arms.

Hi-Standard Pistols and Revolvers, 1951-1984, by James Spacek, James Spacek, Chesire, CT, 1998. 128 pp., illustrated. Paper covers. $12.50.

Technical details, marketing features and instruction/parts manual of every model High Standard pistol and revolver made between 1951 and 1984. Most accurate serial number information available.

The Hi-Standard Pistol Guide, by Burr Leyson, Duckett's Sporting Books, Tempe AZ, 1995. 128 pp., illus. Paper covers. $22.00.

Complete information on selection, care and repair, ammunition, parts, and accessories.

How to Become a Master Handgunner: The Mechanics of X-Count Shooting, by Charles Stephens, Paladin Press, Boulder, CO, 1993. 64 pp., illus. Paper covers. $14.00.

Offers a simple formula for success to the handgunner who strives to master the technique of shooting accurately.

Hunting for Handgunners, by Larry Kelly and J.D. Jones, DBI Books, a division of Krause Publications, Iola, WI, 1990. 256 pp., illus. Paper covers. $16.95.

Covers the entire spectrum of hunting with handguns in an amusing, easy-flowing manner that combines entertainment with solid information.

Illustrated Encyclopedia of Handguns, by A.B. Zhuk, Stackpole Books, Mechanicsburg, PA, 1994. 256 pp., illus. Cloth cover, $49.95

Identifies more than 2,000 military and commercial pistols and revolvers with details of more than 100 popular handgun cartridges.

The Inglis Diamond: The Canadian High Power Pistol, by Clive M. Law, Collector Grade Publications, Canada, 2001. 312 pp., illustrated. $49.95

This definitive work on Canada's first and indeed only mass produced handgun, in production for a very brief span of time and consequently made in relatively few numbers, the venerable Inglis-made Browning High Power covers the

THE ARMS LIBRARY

pistol's initial history, the story of Chinese and British adoption, use post-war by Holland, Australia, Greece, Belgium, New Zealand, Peru, Brasil and other countries. All new information on the famous light-weights and the Inglis Diamond variations. Completely researched through official archives in a dozen countries. Many of the bewildering variety of markings have never been satisfactorily explained until now. Also included are many photos of holsters and accessories.

Instinct Combat Shooting, by Chuck Klein, The Goose Creek, IN, 1989. 49 pp., illus. Paper covers. $12.00.

Defensive handgunning for police.

Know Your Czechoslovakian Pistols, by R.J. Berger, Blacksmith Corp., Chino Valley, AZ, 1989. 96 pp., illus. Soft covers. $12.95.

A comprehensive reference which presents the fascinating story of Czech pistols.

Know Your 45 Auto Pistols—Models 1911 & A1, by E.J. Hoffschmidt, Blacksmith Corp., Southport, CT, 1974. 58 pp., illus. Paper covers. $12.95.

A concise history of the gun with a wide variety of types and copies.

Know Your Walther P38 Pistols, by E.J. Hoffschmidt, Blacksmith Corp., Southport, CT, 1974. 77 pp., illus. Paper covers. $12.95.

Covers the Walther models Armee, M.P., H.P., P.38—history and variations.

Know Your Walther PP & PPK Pistols, by E.J. Hoffschmidt, Blacksmith Corp., Southport, CT, 1975. 87 pp., illus. Paper covers. $12.95.

A concise history of the guns with a guide to the variety and types.

La Connaissance du Luger, Tome 1, by Gerard Henrotin, H & L Publishing, Belguim, 1996. 144 pages, illustrated. $45.00.

(The Knowledge of Luger, Volume 1, translated.) B&W and Color photo's. French text.

The Luger Handbook, by Aarron Davis, Krause Publications, Iola, WI, 1997. 112 pp., illus. Paper covers. $9.95.

Now you can identify any of the legendary Luger variations using a simple decision tree. Each model and variation includes pricing information, proof marks and detailed attributes in a handy, user-friendly format. Plus, it's fully indexed. Instantly identify that Luger!

Lugers of Ralph Shattuck, by Ralph Shattuck, Peoria, AZ, 2000. 49 pages, illus. Hardcover. $29.95.

49 pages, illustrated with maps and full color photos of here to now never before shown photos of some of the rarest lugers ever. Written by one of the world's renowned collectors. A MUST have book for any Luger collector.

Lugers at Random (Revised Format Edition), by Charles Kenyon, Jr., Handgun Press, Glenview, IL, 2000. 420 pp., illus. $59.95.

A new printing of this classic, comprehensive reference for all Luger collectors.

The Luger Story, by John Walter, Stackpole Books, Mechanicsburg, PA, 2001. 256 pp., illus. Paper Covers. $29.95.

The standard history of the world's most famous handgun.

The Mauser Self-Loading Pistol, by Belford & Dunlap, Borden Publ. Co., Alhambra, CA. Over 200 pp., 300 illus., large format. $29.95.

The long-awaited book on the "Broom Handles," covering their inception in 1894 to the end of production. Complete and in detail: pocket pistols, Chinese and Spanish copies, etc.

9mm Handguns, 2nd Edition, The Gun Digest Book of, edited by Steve Comus, DBI Books, a division of Krause Publications, Iola, WI, 1993. 256 pp., illus. Paper covers. $18.95.

Covers the 9mm cartridge and the guns that have been made for it in greater depth than any other work available.

9mm Parabellum; The History & Development of the World's 9mm Pistols & Ammunition, by Klaus-Peter Konig and Martin Hugo, Schiffer Publishing Ltd., Atglen, PA, 1993. 304 pp., illus. $39.95.

Detailed history of 9mm weapons from Belguim, Italy, Germany, Israel, France, USA, Czechoslovakia, Hungary, Poland, Brazil, Finland and Spain.

The Official 9mm Markarov Pistol Manual, translated into English by Major James Gebhardt, U.S. Army (Ret.), Desert Publications, El Dorado, AR, 1996. 84 pp., illus. Paper covers. $12.95.

The information found in this book will be of enormous benefit and interest to the owner or a prospective owner of one of these pistols.

The Official Soviet 7.62mm Handgun Manual, by Translation by Maj. James F. Gebhardt Ret.), Paladin Press, Boulder, CO, 1997, soft cover, illus., 104 pp. $20.00

This Soviet military manual, now available in English for the first time, covers instructions for use and maintenance of two side arms, the Nagant 7.62mm revolver, used by the Russian tsarist armed forces and later the Soviet armed forces, and the Tokarev7.62mm semi-auto pistol, which replaced the Nagant.

P-38 Automatic Pistol, by Gene Gangarosa, Jr., Stoeger Publishing Co., S. Hackensack, NJ, 1993. 272 pp., illus. Paper covers. $16.95

This book traces the origins and development of the P-38, including the momentous political forces of the World War II era that caused its near demise and, later, its rebirth.

The P-38 Pistol: The Walther Pistols, 1930-1945. Volume 1. by Warren Buxton, Ucross Books, Los Alamos, MN 1999. $68.50

A limited run reprint of this scarce and sought-after work on the P-38 Pistol. 328 pp. with 160 illustrations.

The P-38 Pistol: The Contract Pistols, 1940-1945. Volume 2. by Warren Buxton, Ucross Books, Los Alamos, MN 1999. 256 pp. with 237 illustrations. $68.50

The P-38 Pistol: Postwar Distributions, 1945-1990. Volume 3. by Warren Buxton, Ucross Books, Los Alamos, MN 1999. $68.50

Plus an addendum to Volumes 1 & 2. 272 pp. with 342 illustrations.

PARABELLUM - A Technical History of Swiss Lugers, by V. Bobba, Italy.1998. 224pp, profuse color photos, large format. $100.00.

The is the most beautifully illustrated and well-documented book on the Swiss Lugers yet produced. This splendidly produced book features magnificent images while giving an incredible amount of detail on the Swiss Luger. In-depth coverage of key issues include: the production process, pistol accessories, charts with serial numbers, production figures, variations, markings, patent drawings, etc. Covers the Swiss Luger story from 1894 when the first Bergmann-Schmeisser models were tested till the commercial model 1965. Shows every imaginable production variation in amazing detail and full color! A must for all Luger collectors. This work has been produced in an extremely attractive package using quality materials throughout and housed in a protective slipcase.

Pistols and Revolvers, by Jean-Noel Mouret, Barns and Noble, Rockleigh, N.J., 1999. 141 pp., illustrated. $12.98.

Here in glorious display is the master guidebook to flintlocks, minatures, the Sig P-210 limited edition, the Springfield

THE ARMS LIBRARY

Trophy Master with Aimpoint 5000 telescopic sight, every major classic and contemporary handgun, complete with their technical data.

Report of Board on Tests of Revolvers and Automatic Pistols, From the Annual Report of the Chief of Ordnance, 1907. Reprinted by J.C. Tillinghast, Marlow, NH, 1969. 34 pp., 7 plates, paper covers. $9.95.

A comparison of handguns, including Luger, Savage, Colt, Webley-Fosbery and other makes.

Ruger Automatic Pistols and Single Action Revolvers, by Hugo A. Lueders, edited by Don Findley, Blacksmith Corp., Chino Valley, AZ, 1993. 79 pp., illus. Paper covers. $14.95.

The definitive work on Ruger automatic pistols and single action revolvers.

The Ruger "P" Family of Handguns, by Duncan Long, Desert Publications, El Dorado, AZ, 1993. 128 pp., illus. Paper covers. $14.95.

A full-fledged documentary on a remarkable series of Sturm Ruger handguns.

The Ruger .22 Automatic Pistol, Standard/Mark I/Mark II Series, by Duncan Long, Paladin Press, Boulder, CO, 1989. 168 pp., illus. Paper covers. $16.00.

The definitive book about the pistol that has served more than 1 million owners so well.

The Semiautomatic Pistols in Police Service and Self Defense, by Massad Ayoob, Police Bookshelf, Concord, NH, 1990. 25 pp., illus. Soft covers. $9.95.

First quantitative, documented look at actual police experience with 9mm and 45 police service automatics.

The Sharpshooter—How to Stand and Shoot Handgun Metallic Silhouettes, by Charles Stephens, Yucca Tree Press, Las Cruces, NM, 1993. 86 pp., illus. Paper covers. $10.00.

A narration of some of the author's early experiences in silhouette shooting, plus how-to information.

Shooting Colt Single Actions, by Mike Venturino, Livingston, MT, 1997. 205 pp., illus. Paper covers. $25.00

A definitive work on the famous Colt SAA and the ammunition it shoots.

Sig/Sauer Handguns, by Duncan Long, Desert Publications, El Dorado, AZ, 1995. 150 pp., illus. Paper covers. $16.95.

The history of Sig/Sauer handguns, including Sig, Sig-Hammerli and Sig/Sauer variants.

Sixgun Cartridges and Loads, by Elmer Keith, reprint edition by The Gun Room Press, Highland Park, NJ, 1984. 151 pp., illus. $24.95.

A manual covering the selection, use and loading of the most suitable and popular revolver cartridges.

Sixguns, by Elmer Keith, Wolfe Publishing Company, Prescott, AZ, 1992. 336 pp. Paper covers. $29.95. Hardcover $35.00

The history, selection, repair, care, loading, and use of this historic frontiersman's friend—the one-hand firearm.

Smith & Wesson's Automatics, by Larry Combs, Desert Publications, El Dorado, AZ, 1994. 143 pp., illus. Paper covers. $19.95.

A must for every S&W auto owner or prospective owner.

Spanish Handguns: The History of Spanish Pistols and Revolvers, by Gene Gangarosa, Jr., Stoeger Publishing Co., Accokeek, MD, 2001. 320 pp., illustrated. B & W photos. Paper covers. $21.95

Street Stoppers: The Latest Handgun Stopping Power Street Results, by Evan P. Marshall & Edwin J. Sandow, Paladin Press, Boulder, CO, 1997. 392 pp., illus. Paper covers. $42.95.

Compilation of the results of real-life shooting incidents involving every major handgun caliber.

The Tactical 1911, by Dave Lauck, Paladin Press, Boulder, CO, 1999. 152 pp., illustrated. Paper covers. $22.00.

The cop's and SWAT operator's guide to employment and maintenance.

The Tactical Pistol, by Gabriel Suarez with a foreword by Jeff Cooper, Paladin Press, Boulder, CO, 1996. 216 pp., illus. Paper covers. $25.00.

Advanced gunfighting concepts and techniques.

The Thompson/Center Contender Pistol, by Charles Tephens, Paladin Press, Boulder, CO, 1997. 58 pp., illus. Paper covers. $14.00.

How to tune and time, load and shoot accurately with the Contender pistol.

The .380 Enfield No. 2 Revolver, by Mark Stamps and Ian Skennerton, I.D.S.A. Books, Piqua, OH, 1993. 124 pp., 80 illus. Paper covers. $19.95.

The Truth About Handguns, by Duane Thomas, Paladin Press, Boulder, CO, 1997. 136 pp., illus. Paper covers. $18.00.

Exploding the myths, hype, and misinformation about handguns.

Walther Pistols: Models 1 Through P99, Factory Variations and Copies, by Dieter H. Marschall, Ucross Books, Los Alamos, NM. 2000. 140 pages, with 140 b & w illustrations, index. Paper Covers. $19.95.

This is the English translation, revised and updated, of the highly successful and widely acclaimed German language edition. This book provides the collector with a reference guide and overview of the entire line of the Walther military, police, and self-defense pistols from the very first to the very latest. Models 1-9, PP, PPK, MP, AP, HP, P.38, P1, P4, P38K, P5, P88, P99 and the Manurhin models. Variations, where issued, serial ranges, calibers, marks, proofs, logos, and design aspects in an astonishing quantity and variety are crammed into this very well researched and highly regarded work.

U.S. Handguns of World War 2, The Secondary Pistols and Revolvers, by Charles W. Pate, Mowbray Publishers, Lincoln, RI, 1997. 368 pp., illus. $39.00.

This indispensable new book covers all of the American military handguns of W.W.2 except for the M1911A1.

RIFLES

The Accurate Rifle, by Warren Page, Claymore Publishing, Ohio, 1997. 254 pages, illustrated. Revised edition. Paper Covers. $17.95

Provides hunters & shooter alike with detailed practical information on the whole range of subjects affecting rifle accuracy, he explains techniques in ammo, sights & shooting methods. With a 1996 equipment update from Dave Brennan.

The Accurate Varmint Rifle, by Boyd Mace, Precision Shooting, Inc., Whitehall, NY, 1991. 184 pp., illus. $15.00

A long overdue and long needed work on what factors go into the selection of components for and the subsequent assembly of...the accurate varmint rifle.

The AK-47 Assault Rifle, Desert Publications, Cornville, AZ, 1981. 150 pp., illus. Paper covers. $13.95

Complete and practical technical information on the only weapon in history to be produced in an estimated 30,000,000 units.

THE ARMS LIBRARY

American Hunting Rifles: Their Application in the Field for Practical Shooting, by Craig Boddington, Safari Press, Huntington Beach, CA, 1996. 446 pp., illus. First edition, limited, signed and slipcased. $85.00. Second printing trade edition. $35.00

Covers all the hunting rifles and calibers that are needed for North America's diverse game.

The AR-15/M16, A Practical Guide, by Duncan Long. Paladin Press, Boulder, CO, 1985. 168 pp., illus. Paper covers. $22.00

The definitive book on the rifle that has been the inspiration for so many modern assault rifles.

The Art of Shooting With the Rifle, by Col. Sir H. St. John Halford, Excalibur Publications, Latham, NY, 1996. 96 pp., illus. Paper covers. $12.95

A facsimile edition of the 1888 book by a respected rifleman providing a wealth of detailed information.

The Art of the Rifle, by Jeff Cooper, Paladin Press, Boulder, CO, 1997. 104 pp., illus. $29.95

Everything you need to know about the rifle whether you use it for security, meat or target shooting.

Australian Military Rifles & Bayonets, 200 Years of, by Ian Skennerton, I.D.S.A. Books, Piqua, OH, 1988. 124 pp., 198 illus. Paper covers. $19.50

Australian Service Machine Guns, 100 Years of, by Ian Skennerton, I.D.S.A. Books, Piqua, OH, 1989. 122 pp., 150 illus. Paper covers. $19.50

The Big Game Rifle, by Jack O'Connor, Safari Press, Huntington Beach, CA, 1994. 370 pp., illus. $37.50

An outstanding description of every detail of construction, purpose and use of the big game rifle.

Big Game Rifles and Cartridges, by Elmer Keith, reprint edition by The Gun Room Press, Highland Park, NJ, 1984. 161 pp., illus. $17.95

Reprint of Elmer Keith's first book, a most original and accurate work on big game rifles and cartridges.

Black Magic: The Ultra Accurate AR-15, by John Feamster, Precision Shooting, Manchester, CT, 1998. 300 pp., illustrated. $29.95

The author has compiled his experiences pushing the accuracy envelope of the AR-15 to its maximum potential. A wealth of advice on AR-15 loads, modifications and accessories for everything from NRA Highpower and Service Rifle competitions to benchrest and varmint shooting.

The Black Rifle, M16 Retrospective, R. Blake Stevens and Edward C. Ezell, Collector Grade Publications, Toronto, Canada, 1987. 400 pp., illus. $59.50

The complete story of the M16 rifle and its development.

Bolt Action Rifles, 3rd Edition, by Frank de Haas, DBI Books, a division of Krause Publications, Iola, WI, 1995. 528 pp., illus. Paper covers. $24.95

A revised edition of the most definitive work on all major bolt-action rifle designs.

The Book of the Garand, by Maj. Gen. J.S. Hatcher, The Gun Room Press, Highland Park, NJ, 1977. 292 pp., illus. $26.95

A new printing of the standard reference work on the U.S. Army M1 rifle.

The Book of the Twenty-Two: The All American Caliber, by Sam Fadala, Stoeger Publishing Co., So. Hackensack, NJ, 1989. 288 pp., illus. Soft covers. $16.95

The All American Caliber from BB caps up to the powerful 226 Barnes. It's about ammo history, plinking, target shooting, and the quest for the one-hole group.

British Military Martini, Treatise on the, Vol. 1, by B.A. Temple and Ian Skennerton, I.D.S.A. Books, Piqua, OH, 1983. 256 pp., 114 illus. $40.00

British Military Martini, Treatise on the, Vol. 2, by B.A. Temple and Ian Skennerton, I.D.S.A. Books, Piqua, OH, 1989. 213 pp., 135 illus. $40.00

British .22RF Training Rifles, by Dennis Lewis and Robert Washburn, Excaliber Publications, Latham, NY, 1993. 64 pp., illus. Paper covers. $10.95

The story of Britain's training rifles from the early Aiming Tube models to the post-WWII trainers.

Classic Sporting Rifles, by Christopher Austyn, Safari Press, Huntington Beach, CA, 1997. 128 pp., illus. $50.00

As the head of the gun department at Christie's Auction House the author examines the "best" rifles built over the last 150 years.

The Complete AR15/M16 Sourcebook, by Duncan Long, Paladin Press, Boulder, CO, 1993. 232 pp., illus. Paper covers. $35.00

The latest development of the AR15/M16 and the many spin-offs now available, selective-fire conversion systems for the 1990s, the vast selection of new accessories.

The Competitive AR15: The Mouse That Roared, by Glenn Zediker, Zediker Publishing, Oxford, MS, 1999. 286 pp., illustrated. Paper covers. $29.95

A thorough and detailed study of the newest precision rifle sensation.

Complete Book of U.S. Sniping, by Peter R. Senich, Paladin Press, Boulder, CO, 1997, 8 1/2 x 11, hardcover, photos, 288 pp. $52.95

Trace American sniping materiel from its infancy to today's sophisticated systems with this volume, compiled from Senich's early books, Limited War Sniping and The Pictorial History of U.S. Sniping. Almost 400 photos, plus information gleaned from official documents and military archives, pack this informative work.

Complete Guide To The M1 Garand and The M1 Carbine, by Bruce Canfield, Andrew Mowbray, Inc., Lincoln, RI, 1999. 296 pp., illustrated. $39.50

Covers all of the manufacturers of components, parts, variations and markings. Learn which parts are proper for which guns. The total story behind these guns, from their invention through WWII, Korea, Vietnam and beyond! 300+ photos show you features, markings, overall views and action shots. Thirty-three tables and charts give instant reference to serial numbers, markings, dates of issue and proper configurations. Special sections on Sniper guns, National Match Rifles, exotic variations, and more!

The Complete M1 Garand, by Jim Thompson, Paladin Press, Boulder, CO, 1998. 160 pp., illustrated. Paper cover. $25.00

A guide for the shooter and collector, heavily illustrated.

Exploded Long Gun Drawings, The Gun Digest Book of, edited by Harold A. Murtz, DBI Books, a division of Krause Publications, Iola, WI, 512 pp., illus. Paper covers. $20.95

Containing almost 500 rifle and shotgun exploded drawings. An invaluable aid to both professionals and hobbyists.

The FAL Rifle, by R. Blake Stevens and Jean van Rutten, Collector Grade Publications, Cobourg, Canada, 1993. 848 pp., illus. $129.95

Originally published in three volumes, this classic edition covers North American, UK and Commonwealth and the metric FAL's.

THE ARMS LIBRARY

The Fighting Rifle, by Chuck Taylor, Paladin Press, Boulder, CO, 1983. 184 pp., illus. Paper covers. $25.00

The difference between assault and battle rifles and auto and light machine guns.

Firearms Assembly/Disassembly Part III: Rimfire Rifles, Revised Edition, The Gun Digest Book of, by J. B. Wood, DBI Books, a division of Krause Publications, Iola, WI., 1994. 480 pp., illus. Paper covers. $19.95

Covers 65 popular rimfires plus over 100 variants, all cross-referenced in the index.

Firearms Assembly/Disassembly Part IV: Centerfire Rifles, Revised Edition, The Gun Digest Book of, by J.B. Wood, DBI Books, a division of Krause Publications, Iola, WI, 1991. 480 pp., illus. Paper covers. $19.95

Covers 54 popular centerfire rifles plus 300 variants. The most comprehensive and professional presentation available to either hobbyist or gunsmith.

The FN-FAL Rifle, et al, by Duncan Long, Delta Press, El Dorado, AR, 1998. 148 pp., illustrated. Paper covers. $18.95

A comprehensive study of one of the classic assault weapons of all times. Detailed descriptions of the basic models plus the myriad of variants that evolved as a result of its universal acceptance.

Forty Years with the .45-70, second edition, revised and expanded, by Paul A. Matthews, Wolfe Publishing Co., Prescott, AZ, 1997. 184 pp., illus. Paper covers. $14.95

This book is pure gun lore-lore of the .45-70. It not only contains a history of the cartridge, but also years of the author's personal experiences.

F.N.-F.A.L. Auto Rifles, Desert Publications, Cornville, AZ, 1981. 130 pp., illus. Paper covers. $16.95

A definitive study of one of the free world's finest combat rifles.

German Sniper 1914-1945, by Peter R. Senich, Paladin Press, Boulder, CO, 1997 8 1/2 x 11, hardcover, photos, 468 pp. $69.95

The complete story of Germany's sniping arms development through both World Wars. Presents more than 600 photos of Mauser 98's, Selbstladegewehr 41s and 43s, optical sights by Goerz, Zeiss, etc., plus German snipers in action. An exceptional hardcover collector's edition for serious military historians everywhere.

Hints and Advice on Rifle-Shooting, by Private R. McVittie with new introductory material by W.S. Curtis, W.S. Curtis Publishers, Ltd., Clwyd, England, 1993. 32 pp. Paper covers. $10.00

A reprint of the original 1886 London edition.

How-To's for the Black Powder Cartridge Rifle Shooter, by Paul A. Matthews, Wolfe Publishing Co., Prescott, AZ, 1996. 136 pp., illus. Paper covers. $22.50

Practices and procedures used in the reloading and shooting of blackpowder cartridges.

Hunting with the .22, by C.S. Landis, R&R Books, Livonia, NY, 1995. 429 pp., illus. $35.00

A reprinting of the classical work on .22 rifles.

The Hunting Rifle, by Townsend Whelen, Wolfe Publishing Co., Prescott, Arizona, 1984. 463 pp., illustrated. $24.95

A thoroughly dependable coverage on the materiel and marksmanhip with relation to the sportsman's rifle for big game.

Illustrated Handbook of Rifle Shooting, by A.L. Russell, Museum Restoration Service, Alexandria Bay, NY, 1992. 194 pp., illus. $24.50

A new printing of the 1869 edition by one of the leading military marksman of the day.

Know Your M1 Garand, by E. J. Hoffschmidt, Blacksmith Corp., Southport, CT, 1975, 84 pp., illus. Paper covers. $15.95

Facts about America's most famous infantry weapon. Covers test and experimental models, Japanese and Italian copies, National Match models.

Know Your Ruger 10/22 Carbine, by William E. Workman, Blacksmith Corp., Chino Valley, AZ, 1991. 96 pp., illus. Paper covers. $12.95

The story and facts about the most popular 22 autoloader ever made.

The Lee Enfield No. 1 Rifles, by Alan M. Petrillo, Excaliber Publications, Latham, NY, 1992. 64 pp., illus. Paper covers. $10.95

Highlights the SMLE rifles from the Mark 1-VI.

The Lee Enfield Number 4 Rifles, by Alan M. Petrillo, Excalibur Publications, Latham, NY, 1992. 64 pp., illus. Paper covers. $10.95

A pocket-sized, bare-bones reference devoted entirely to the .303 World War II and Korean War vintage service rifle.

Legendary Sporting Rifles, by Sam Fadala, Stoeger Publishing Co., So. Hackensack, NJ, 1992. 288 pp., illus. Paper covers. $16.95

Covers a vast span of time and technology beginning with the Kentucky Long-rifle.

The Li'l M1 .30 Cal. Carbine, by Duncan Long, Desert Publications, El Dorado, AZ, 1995. 203 pp., illus. Paper covers. $14.95

Traces the history of this little giant from its original creation.

Make It Accurate: Get the Maximum Performance from Your Hunting Rifle, by Craig Boddington, Safari Press Publications, Huntington Beach, CA, 1999. 224 pp., illustrated. $24.95

Tips on how to select the rifle, cartridge, and scope best suited to your needs. A must-have for any hunter who wants to improve his shot.

Mauser Smallbore Sporting, Target and Training Rifles, by Jon Speed, Collector Grade Publications, Inc., Cobourg, Ont., Canada, 1998. 372 pp., illustrated. $67.50

The history of all the smallbore sporting, target and training rifles produced by the legendary Mauser-Werke of Obendorf am Neckar.

Mauser: Original-Oberndorf Sporting Rifles, by Jon Speed, Collector Grade Publications, Inc., Cobourg, Ont., Canada, 1997. 508 pp., illustrated. $89.95

The most exhaustive study ever published of the design origins and manufacturing history of the original Oberndorf Mauser Sporter.

M14/M14A1 Rifles and Rifle Markmanship, Desert Publications, El Dorado, AZ, 1995. 236 pp., illus. Paper covers. $18.95

Contains a detailed description of the M14 and M14A1 rifles and their general characteristics, procedures for disassembly and assembly, operating and functioning of the rifles, etc.

The M14 Owner's Guide and Match Conditioning Instructions, by Scott A. Duff and John M. Miller, Scott A. Duff Publications, Export, PA, 1996. 180 pp., illus. Paper covers. $19.95

Traces the history and development from the T44 through the adoption and production of the M14 rifle.

The M-14 Rifle, facsimile reprint of FM 23-8, Desert Publications, Cornville, AZ, 50 pp., illus. Paper $11.95

Well illustrated and informative reprint covering the M-14 and M-14E2.

THE ARMS LIBRARY

The M14-Type Rifle: A Shooter's and Collector's Guide, by Joe Poyer, North Cape Publications, Tustin, CA, 1997. 82 pp., illus. Paper covers. $18.95

Covers the history and development, commercial copies, cleaning and maintenance instructions, and targeting and shooting.

The M16/AR15 Rifle, by Joe Poyer, North Cape Publications, Tustin, CA, 1998. 150 pp., illustrated. Paper covers. $19.95

From its inception as the first American assault battle rifle to the firing lines of the National Matches, the M16/AR15 rifle in all its various models and guises has made a significant impact on the American rifleman.

Military Bolt Action Rifles, 1841-1918, by Donald B. Webster, Museum Restoration Service, Alexander Bay, NY, 1993. 150 pp., illus. $34.50

A photographic survey of the principal rifles and carbines of the European and Asiatic powers of the last half of the 19th century and the first years of the 20th century.

The Mini-14, by Duncan Long, Paladin Press, Boulder, CO, 1987. 120 pp., illus. Paper covers. $17.00

History of the Mini-14, the factory-produced models, specifications, accessories, suppliers, and much more.

Mr. Single Shot's Book of Rifle Plans, by Frank de Haas, Mark de Haas, Orange City, IA, 1996. 85 pp., illus. Paper covers. $22.50

Contains complete and detailed drawings, plans and instructions on how to build four different and unique breech-loading single shot rifles of the author's own proven design.

M1 Carbine Owner's Manual, M1, M2 & M3 .30 Caliber Carbines, Firepower Publications, Cornville, AZ, 1984. 102 pp., illus. Paper covers. $16.95

The complete book for the owner of an M1 Carbine.

The M1 Garand Serial Numbers & Data Sheets, by Scott A. Duff, Scott A. Duff, Export, PA, 1995. 101 pp. Paper covers. $11.95

This pocket reference book includes serial number tables and data sheets on the Springfield Armory, Gas Trap Rifles, Gas Port Rifles, Winchester Repeating Arms, International Harvester and H&R Arms Co. and more.

The M1 Garand: Post World War, by Scott A. Duff, Scott A. Duff, Export, PA, 1990. 139 pp., illus. Soft covers. $19.95

A detailed account of the activities at Springfield Armory through this period. International Harvester, H&R, Korean War production and quantities delivered. Serial numbers.

The M1 Garand: World War 2, by Scott A. Duff, Scott A. Duff, Export, PA, 1993. 210 pp., illus. Paper covers. $39.95

The most comprehensive study available to the collector and historian on the M1 Garand of World War II.

Modern Sniper Rifles, by Duncan Long, Paladin Press, Boulder, CO, 1997, 8 1/2 x 11, soft cover, photos, illus., 120 pp. $20.00

Noted weapons expert Duncan Long describes the .22 LR, single-shot, bolt-action, semiautomatic and large-caliber rifles that can be used for sniping purposes, including the U.S. M21, Ruger Mini-14, AUG and HK-94SG1. These and other models are evaluated on the basis of their features, accuracy, reliability and handiness in the field. The author also looks at the best scopes, ammunition and accessories.

More Single Shot Rifles and Actions, by Frank de Haas, Mark de Haas, Orange City, IA, 1996. 146 pp., illus. Paper covers. $22.50

Covers 45 different single shot rifles. Includes the history plus photos, drawings and personal comments.

The Muzzle-Loading Rifle...Then and Now, by Walter M. Cline, National Muzzle Loading Rifle Association, Friendship, IN, 1991. 161 pp., illus. $32.00

This extensive compilation of the muzzleloading rifle exhibits accumulative preserved data concerning the development of the "hallowed old arms of the Southern highlands."

The No. 4 (T) Sniper Rifle: An Armourer's Perspective, by Peter Laidler with Ian Skennerton, I.D.S.A. Books, Piqua, OH, 1993. 125 pp., 75 illus. Paper covers. $19.95

Notes on Rifle-Shooting, by Henry William Heaton, reprinted with a new introduction by W.S. Curtis, W.S. Curtis Publishers, Ltd., Clwyd, England, 1993. 89 pp. $19.95

A reprint of the 1864 London edition. Captain Heaton was one of the great rifle shots from the earliest days of the Volunteer Movement.

The Official SKS Manual, Translation by Major James F. Gebhardt (Ret.), Paladin Press, Boulder, CO, 1997. 96 pp., illus. Paper covers. $16.00

This Soviet military manual covering the widely distributed SKS is now available in English.

The Pennsylvania Rifle, by Samuel E. Dyke, Sutter House, Lititz, PA, 1975. 61 pp., illus. Paper covers. $10.00

History and development, from the hunting rifle of the Germans who settled the area. Contains a full listing of all known Lancaster, PA, gunsmiths from 1729 through 1815.

Police Rifles, by Richard Fairburn, Paladin Press, Boulder, CO, 1994. 248 pp., illus. Paper covers. $35.00

Selecting the right rifle for street patrol and special tactical situations.

The Poor Man's Sniper Rifle, by D. Boone, Paladin Press, Boulder, CO, 1995. 152 pp., illus. Paper covers. $18.95

Here is a complete plan for converting readily available surplus military rifles to high-performance sniper weapons.

A Potpourri of Single Shot Rifles and Actions, by Frank de Haas, Mark de Haas, Ridgeway, MO, 1993. 153 pp., illus. Paper covers. $22.50

The author's 6th book on non-bolt-action single shots. Covers more than 40 single-shot rifles in historical and technical detail.

Precision Shooting with the M1 Garand, by Roy Baumgardner, Precision Shooting, Inc., Manchester, CT, 1999. 142 pp., illustrated. Paper covers. $12.95

Starts off with the ever popular ten-article series on accurinzing the M1 that originally appeared in Precision Shooting in the 1993-95 era. There follows nine more Baumgardner authored articles on the M1 Garand and finally a 1999 updating chapter.

Purdey Gun and Rifle Makers: The Definitive History, by Donald Dallas, Quiller Press, London, 2000. 245 pp., illus. Color throughout. $100.00

A limited edition of 3,000 copies. Signed and Numbered. With a PURDEY book plate.

The Remington 700, by John F. Lacy, Taylor Publishing Co., Dallas, TX, 1990. 208 pp., illus. $44.95

Covers the different models, limited editions, chamberings, proofmarks, serial numbers, military models, and much more.

The Revolving Rifles, by Edsall James, Pioneer Press, Union City, TN, 1975. 23 pp., illus. Paper covers. $5.00

Valuable information on revolving cylinder rifles, from the earliest matchlock forms to the latest models of Colt and Remington.

Rifle Guide, by Sam Fadala, Stoeger Publishing Co., S. Hackensack, NJ, 1993. 288 pp., illus. Paper covers. $16.95

This comprehensive, fact-filled book beckons to both the seasoned rifleman as well as the novice shooter.

THE ARMS LIBRARY

The Rifle: Its Development for Big-Game Hunting, by S.R. Truesdell, Safari Press, Huntington Beach, CA, 1992. 274 pp., illus. $35.00

The full story of the development of the big-game rifle from 1834-1946.

Riflesmithing, The Gun Digest Book of, by Jack Mitchell, DBI Books, a division of Krause Publications, Iola, WI, 1982. 256 pp., illus. Paper covers. $16.95

Covers tools, techniques, designs, finishing wood and metal, custom alterations.

Rifles of the World, 2nd Edition, edited by John Walter, DBI Books, a division of Krause Publications, Iola, WI, 1998. 384 pp., illus. $24.95

The definitive guide to the world's centerfire and rimfire rifles.

Ned H. Roberts and the Schuetzen Rifle, edited by Gerald O. Kelver, Brighton, CO, 1982. 99 pp., illus. $13.95

A compilation of the writings of Major Ned H. Roberts which appeared in various gun magazines.

Schuetzen Rifles, History and Loading, by Gerald O. Kelver, Gerald O. Kelver, Publisher, Brighton, CO, 1972. Illus. $13.95

Reference work on these rifles, their bullets, loading, telescopic sights, accuracy, etc. A limited, numbered ed.

Shooting the Blackpowder Cartridge Rifle, by Paul A. Matthews, Wolfe Publishing Co., Prescott, AZ, 1994. 129 pp., illus. Paper covers. $22.50

A general discourse on shooting the blackpowder cartridge rifle and the procedure required to make a particular rifle perform.

Shooting Lever Guns of the Old West, by Mike Venturino, MLV Enterprises, Livingston, MT, 1999. 300 pp., illustrated. Paper covers. $27.95

Shooting the lever action type repeating rifles of our American west.

Single Shot Rifles and Actions, by Frank de Haas, Orange City, IA, 1990. 352 pp., illus. Soft covers. $27.00

The definitive book on over 60 single shot rifles and actions.

Sixty Years of Rifles, by Paul A. Matthews, Wolfe Publishing Co., Prescott, AZ, 1991. 224 pp., illus. $19.50

About rifles and the author's experience and love affair with shooting and hunting.

S.L.R.—Australia's F.N. F.A.L. by Ian Skennerton and David Balmer, I.D.S.A. Books, Piqua, OH, 1989. 124 pp., 100 illus. Paper covers. $19.50

Small Arms Identification Series, No. 2—.303 Rifle, No. 4 Marks I, & I*, Marks 1/2, 1/3 & 2, by Ian Skennerton, I.D.S.A. Books, Piqua, OH, 1994. 48 pp. $9.50

Small Arms Identification Series, No. 3—9mm Austen Mk I & 9mm Owen Mk I Sub-Machine Guns, by Ian Skennerton, I.D.S.A. Books, Piqua, OH, 1994. 48 pp. $9.50

Small Arms Identification Series, No. 4—.303 Rifle, No. 5 Mk I, by Ian Skennerton, I.D.S.A. Books, Piqua, OH, 1994. 48 pp. $9.50

Small Arms Identification Series, No. 5—.303-in. Bren Light Machine Gun, by Ian Skennerton, I.D.S.A. Books, Piqua, OH, 1994. 48 pp. $9.50

Small Arms Series, No. 1 DeLisle's Commando Carbine, by Ian Skennerton, I.D.S.A. Books, Piqua, OH, 1981. 32 pp., 24 illus. $9.00

Small Arms Identification Series, No. 1—.303 Rifle, No. 1 S.M.L.E. Marks III and III*, by Ian Skennerton, I.D.S.A. Books, Piqua, OH, 1981. 48 pp. $9.50

Sporting Rifle Takedown & Reassembly Guide, 2nd Edition, by J.B. Wood, DBI Books, a division of Krause Publications, Iola, WI, 1997. 480 pp., illus. $19.95

An updated edition of the reference guide for anyone who wants to properly care for their sporting rifle. (Available September 1997)

The Springfield Rifle M1903, M1903A1, M1903A3, M1903A4, Desert Publications, Cornville, AZ, 1982. 100 pp., illus. Paper covers. $12.00

Covers every aspect of disassembly and assembly, inspection, repair and maintenance.

Still More Single Shot Rifles, by James J. Grant, Pioneer Press, Union City, TN, 1995. 211 pp., illus. $29.95

This is Volume Four in a series of Single-Shot Rifles by America's foremost authority. It gives more in-depth information on those single-shot rifles which were presented in the first three books.

The Sturm, Ruger 10/22 Rifle and .44 Magnum Carbine, by Duncan Long, Paladin Press, Boulder, CO, 1988. 108 pp., illus. Paper covers. $15.00

An in-depth look at both weapons detailing the elegant simplicity of the Ruger design. Offers specifications, troubleshooting procedures and ammunition recommendations.

The Tactical Rifle, by Gabriel Suarez, Paladin Press, Boulder, CO, 1999. 264 pp., illustrated. Paper covers. $25.00

The precision tool for urban police operations.

Target Rifle in Australia, by J.E. Corcoran, R&R, Livonia, NY, 1996. 160 pp., illus. $40.00

A most interesting study of the evolution of these rifles from 1860 - 1900. British rifles from the percussion period through the early smokeless era are discussed.

To the Dreams of Youth: The .22 Caliber Single Shot Winchester Rifle, by Herbert Houze, Krause Publications, Iola, WI, 1993. 192 pp., illus. $34.95

A thoroughly researched history of the 22-caliber Winchester single shot rifle, including interesting photographs.

The Ultimate in Rifle Accuracy, by Glenn Newick, Stoeger Publishing Co., Wayne, N.J., 1999. 205 pp., illustrated. Paper covers. $11.95

This handbook contains the information you need to extract the best performance from your rifle.

U.S. Marine Corps AR15/M16 A2 Manual, reprinted by Desert Publications, El Dorado, AZ, 1993. 262 pp., illus. Paper covers. $16.95

A reprint of TM05538C-23&P/2, August, 1987. The A-2 manual for the Colt AR15/M16.

U.S. Rifle M14—From John Garand to the M21, by R. Blake Stevens, Collector Grade Publications, Inc., Toronto, Canada, revised second edition, 1991. 350 pp., illus. $49.50

A classic, in-depth examination of the development, manufacture and fielding of the last wood-and-metal ("lock, stock, and barrel") battle rifle to be issued to U.S. troops.

War Baby!: The U.S. Caliber 30 Carbine, Volume I, by Larry Ruth, Collector Grade Publications, Toronto, Canada, 1992. 512 pp., illus. $69.95

Volume 1 of the in-depth story of the phenomenally popular U.S. caliber 30 carbine. Concentrates on design and production of the military 30 carbine during World War II.

THE ARMS LIBRARY

War Baby Comes Home: The U.S. Caliber 30 Carbine, Volume 2, by Larry Ruth, Collector Grade Publications, Toronto, Canada, 1993. 386 pp., illus. $49.95

The triumphant competion of Larry Ruth's two-volume in-depth series on the most popular U.S. military small arm in history.

The Winchester Model 52, Perfection in Design, by Herbert G. Houze, Krause Publications, Iola, WI, 1997. 192 pp., illus. $34.95

This book covers the complete story of this technically superior gun.

The Winchester Model 94: The First 100 Years, by Robert C. Renneberg, Krause Publications, Iola, WI, 1991. 208 pp., illus. $34.95

Covers the design and evolution from the early years up to today.

Winchester Slide-Action Rifles, Volume I: Model 1890 and Model 1906 by Ned Schwing, Krause Publications, Iola, WI. 352 pp., illus. $39.95

Traces the history through word and picture in this chronolgy of the Model 1890 and 1906.

Winchester Slide-Action Rifles, Volume II: Model 61 & Model 62 by Ned Schwing, Krause Publications, Iola, WI. 256 pp., illus. $34.95

Historical look complete with markings, stampings and engraving.

SHOTGUNS

Advanced Combat Shotgun: The Stress Fire Concept, by Massad Ayoob, Police Bookshelf, Concord, NH, 1993. 197 pp., illus. Paper covers. $9.95

Advanced combat shotgun fighting for police.

Best Guns, by Michael McIntosh, Countrysport Press, Selma, AL, 1999, revised edition. 418 pp. $39.00

Combines the best shotguns ever made in America with information on British and Continental makers.

The Better Shot, by Ken Davies, Quiller Press, London, England, 1992. 136 pp., illus. $39.95

Step-by-step shotgun technique with Holland and Holland.

The Big Shots; Edwardian Shooting Parties, by Jonathan Ruffer, Quiller Press, London, England, 1997 160pp. B & W illus. $24.95

A book about Edwardian shooting parties, now a former pastime and enjoyed by the selected few, who recall the hunting of pheasants. Foreword by HRH The Prince of Wales.

The British Shotgun, Volume 1, 1850-1870, by I.M. Crudington and D.J. Baker, Barrie & Jenkins, London, England, 1979. 256 pp., illus. $65.00

An attempt to trace, as accurately as is now possible, the evolution of the shotgun during its formative years in Great Britain.

Boothroyd on British Shotguns, by Geoffrey Boothroyd, Sand Lake Press, Amity, OR, 1996. 221 pp., illus. plus a 32 page reproduction of the 1914 Webley & Scott catalog. A limited, numbered edition. $34.95

Based on articles by the author that appeared in the British Publication *Shooting Times & Country Magazine*.

Boss & Co. Builders of the Best Guns Only, by Donald Dallas, Quiller Press, London, 1995. 262 pp., illustrated. $79.95

Large four colour plates, b/w photos, bibliography. The definitive history authorized by Boss & Co.

The British Over-and-Under Shotgun, by Geoffrey and Susan Boothroyd, Sand Lake Press, Amity, OR, 1996. 137 pp., illus. $34.95

Historical outline of the development of the O/U shotgun with individual chapters devoted to the twenty-two British makers.

The Browning Superposed: John M. Browning's Last Legacy, by Ned Schwing, Krause Publications, Iola, WI, 1996. 496 pp., illus. $49.95

An exclusive story of the man, the company and the best-selling over-and-under shotgun in North America.

Clay Target Handbook, by Jerry Meyer, Lyons & Buford, Publisher, New York, NY, 1993. 182 pp., illus. $22.95

Contains in-depth, how-to-do-it information on trap, skeet, sporting clays, international trap, international skeet and clay target games played around the country.

Clay Target Shooting, by Paul Bentley, A&C Black, London, England, 1987. 144 pp., illus. $25.00

Practical book on clay target shooting written by a very successful international competitor, providing valuable professional advice and instruction for shooters of all disciplines.

Cogswell & Harrison; Two Centuries of Gunmaking, by G. Cooley & J. Newton, Safari Press, Long Beach, CA, 2000. 128pp, 30 color photos, 100 b&w photos. $39.95

The authors have gathered a wealth of fascinating historical and technical material that will make the book indispensable, not only to many thousands of "Coggie" owners worldwide, but also to anyone interested in the general history of British gunmaking.

A Collector's Guide to United States Combat Shotguns, by Bruce N. Canfield, Andrew Mowbray Inc., Publishers, Lincoln, RI, 1993. 184 pp., illus. Paper covers. $24.00

Full coverage of the combat shotgun, from the earliest examples to the Gulf War and beyond.

Combat Shotgun and Submachine Gun, "A Special Weapons Analysis" by Chuck Taylor, Paladin Press, Boulder, CO, 1997, soft cover, photos, 176 pp. $25.00

From one of America's top shooting instructors comes an analysis of two controversial, misunderstood and misemployed small arms. Hundreds of photos detail field-testing of both, basic and advanced training drills, tactical rules, gun accessories and modifications. Loading procedures, carrying and fighting positions and malfunction clearance drills are included to promote weapon effectiveness.

Cradock on Shotguns, by Chris Cradock, Banford Press, London, England, 1989. 200 pp., illus. $45.00

A definitive work on the shotgun by a British expert on shotguns.

The Defensive Shotgun, by Louis Awerbuck, S.W.A.T. Publications, Cornville, AZ, 1989. 77 pp., illus. Soft covers. $14.95

Cuts through the myths concerning the shotgun and its attendant ballistic effects.

The Double Shotgun, by Don Zutz, Winchester Press, Piscataway, NJ, 1985. 304 pp., illus. $22.95

Revised, updated, expanded edition of the history and development of the world's classic sporting firearms.

The Ducks Unlimited Guide to Shotgunning, by Don Zutz, Willow Creek Press, Minocqua, WI, 2000. 166 pg. Illustrated. $24.50

This book covers everything from the grand old guns of yesterday to todays best shotguns and loads, from the basic shotgun fit and function to expert advice on ballistics, chocks, and shooting techniques.

THE ARMS LIBRARY

Finding the Extra Target, by Coach John R. Linn & Stephen A. Blumenthal, Shotgun Sports, Inc., Auburn, CA, 1989. 126 pp., illus. Paper covers. $14.95

The ultimate training guide for all the clay target sports.

Fine Gunmaking: Double Shotguns, by Steven Dodd Hughes, Krause Publications Iola, WI, 1998. 167 pp., illustrated. $34.95

An in-depth look at the creation of fine shotguns.

Firearms Assembly/Disassembly, Part V: Shotguns, Revised Edition, The Gun Digest Book of, by J.B. Wood, DBI Books, a division of Krause Publications, Iola, WI, 1992. 480 pp., illus. Paper covers. $19.95

Covers 46 popular shotguns plus over 250 variants. The most comprehensive and professional presentation available to either hobbyist or gunsmith.

A.H. Fox "The Finest Gun in the World", revised and enlarged edition, by Michael McIntosh, Countrysport, Inc., New Albany, OH, 1995. 408 pp., illus. $49.00

The first detailed history of one of America's finest shotguns.

Game Shooting, by Robert Churchill, Countrysport Press, Selma, AL, 1998. 258 pp., illus. $30.00

The basis for every shotgun instructional technique devised and the foundation for all wingshooting and the game of sporting clays.

The Golden Age of Shotgunning, by Bob Hinman, Wolfe Publishing Co., Inc., Prescott, AZ, 1982. $22.50

A valuable history of the late 1800s detailing that fabulous period of development in shotguns, shotshells and shotgunning.

The Greener Story, by Graham Greener, Safari Press, Long Beach, CA, 2000. 231pp, color and b&w illustrations. $69.95

The history of the Greener Gunmakers and their guns

Grand Old Shotguns, by Don Zutz, Shotgun Sports Magazine, Auburn, CA, 1995. 136 pp., illus. Paper covers. $19.95

A study of the great smoothbores, their history and how and why they were discontinued. Find out the most sought-after and which were the best shooters.

Gun Digest Book of Sporting Clays, 2nd Edition, edited by Harold A. Murtz, Krause Publications, Iola, WI, 1999. 256 pp., illus. Paper covers. $21.95

A concise Gun Digest book that covers guns, ammo, chokes, targets and course layouts so you'll stay a step ahead.

The Gun Review Book, by Michael McIntosh, Countrysport Press, Selman, AL, 1999. Paper covers. $19.95

Compiled here for the first time are McIntosh's popular gun reviews from *Shooting Sportsman; The Magazine of Wingshooting* and *Fine Shotguns*. The author traces the history of gunmakes, then examines, analyzes, and critique the fine shotguns of England, Continental Europe and the United States.

Hartman on Skeet, by Barney Hartman, Stackpole Books, Harrisburg, PA, 1973. 143 pp., illus. $19.95

A definitive book on Skeet shooting by a pro.

The Heyday of the Shotgun, by David Baker, Safari Press, Inc., Huntington Beach, CA, 2000. 160 pp., illustrated. $39.95

The art of the gunmaker at the turn of the last century when British craftsmen brought forth the finest guns ever made.

The Italian Gun, by Steve Smith & Laurie Morrow, wilderness Adventures, Gallatin Gateway, MT, 1997. 325 pp., illus. $49.95

The first book ever written entirely in English for American enthusiasts who own, aspire to own, or simply admire Italian guns.

The Ithaca Featherlight Repeater; the Best Gun Going, by Walter C. Snyder, Southern Pines, NC, 1998. 300 pp., illus. $89.95.

Describes the complete history of each model of the legendary Ithaca Model 37 and Model 87 Repeaters from their conception in 1930 throught 1997.

The Ithaca Gun Company from the Beginning, by Walter C. Snyder, Cook & Uline Publishing Co., Southern Pines, NC, 2nd Edition, 1999. 384 pp., illustrated in color and black and white. $90.00

The entire family of Ithaca Gun Company products is described along with new historical information and the serial number/date of manufacturing listing has been improved.

L.C. Smith Shotguns, by Lt. Col. William S. Brophy, The Gun Room Press, Highland Park, NJ, 1979. 244 pp., illus. $35.00

The first work on this very important American gun and manufacturing company.

The Little Trapshooting Book, by Frank Little, Shotgun Sports Magazine, Auburn, CA, 1994. 168 pp., illus. Paper covers. $19.95

Packed with know-how from one of the greatest trapshooters of all time.

Lock, Stock, and Barrel, by C. Adams & R. Braden, Safari Press, Huntington Beach, CA, 1996. 254 pp., illus. $24.95

The process of making a best grade English gun from a lump of steel and a walnut tree trunk to the ultimate product plus practical advise on consistent field shooting with a double gun.

Mental Training for the Shotgun Sports, by Michael J. Keyes, Shotgun Sports, Auburn, CA, 1996. 160 pp., illus. Paper covers. $24.95

The most comprehensive book ever published on what it takes to shoot winning scores at trap, Skeet and Sporting Clays.

The Model 12, 1912-1964, by Dave Riffle, Dave Riffle, Ft. Meyers, FL, 1995. 274 pp., illus. $49.95

The story of the greatest hammerless repeating shotgun ever built.

More Shotguns and Shooting, by Michael McIntosh, Countrysport Books, Selma, AL, 1998. 256 pp., illustrated. $30.00

From specifics of shotguns to shooting your way out of a slump, it's McIntosh at his best.

Mossberg: More Gun for the Money, by Victor & Cheryl Havlin, Blue Book Publications, Minneapolis, MN, 1995. 204 pages, illustrated. $24.95

The History of O.F. Mossberg & Sons, Inc.

Mossberg's Shotguns, by Duncan Long, Delta Press, El Dorado, AR, 2000. 120 pp., illustrated. $24.95

This book contains a brief history of the company and it's founder, full coverage of the pump and semiautomatic shotguns, rare products and a care and maintenance section.

The Mysteries of Shotgun Patterns, by George G. Oberfell and Charles E. Thompson, Oklahoma State University Press, Stillwater, OK, 1982. 164 pp., illus. Paper covers. $25.00

Shotgun ballistics for the hunter in non-technical language.

The Parker Gun, by Larry Baer, Gun Room Press, Highland Park, NJ, 1993. 195 pages, illustrated with B & W and Color photos. $35.00

Covers in detail, production of all models on this classic gun. Many fine specimens from great collections are illustrated.

THE ARMS LIBRARY

Parker Guns "The Old Reliable", by Ed Muderiak, Safari Press, Inc., Huntington Beach, CA, 1997. 325 pp., illus. $40.00

A look at the small beginnings, the golden years, and the ultimate decline of the most famous of all American shotgun manufacturers.

The Parker Story; Volumes 1 & 2, by Bill Mullins, "etal". The Double Gun Journal, East Jordan, MI, 2000. 1,025 pages of text and 1,500 color and monochrome illustrations. Hardbound in a gold-embossed cover. $295.00

The most complete and attractive "last word" on America's preeminent double gun maker. Includes tables showing the number of guns made by gauge, barrel length and special features for each grade.

Positive Shooting, by Michael Yardley, Safari Press, Huntington Beach, CA, 1995. 160 pp., illus. $30.00

This book will provide the shooter with a sound foundation from which to develop an effective, personal technique that can dramatically improve shooting performance.

Purdey Gun and Rifle Makers: The Definitive History, by Donald Dallas, Quiller Press, London 2000. 245 pages, illus. $100.00

245 Colour plates, b/w photos, ills, bibliography. The definitive history. A limited edition of 3,000 copies. Signed and Numbered. With a PURDEY book plate.

Recognizing Side by Side Shotguns, by Charles Carder, Anvil Onze Publishing, 2000. 25 pp., illus. Paper Covers. $5.95

A graphic description of the visible features of side by side breech loading shotguns.

Reloading for Shotgunners, 4th Edition, by Kurt D. Fackler and M.L. McPherson, DBI Books, a division of Krause Publications, Iola, WI, 1997. 320 pp., illus. Paper covers. $19.95

Expanded reloading tables with over 11,000 loads. Bushing charts for every major press and component maker. All new presentation on all aspects of shotshell reloading by two of the top experts in the field. (Available October 1997.)

Remington Double Shotguns, by Charles G. Semer, Denver, CO, 1997. 617 pp., illus. $60.00

This book deals with the entire production and all grades of double shotguns made by Remington during the period of their production 1873-1910.

75 Years with the Shotgun, by C.T. (Buck) Buckman, Valley Publ., Fresno, CA, 1974. 141 pp., illus. $10.00

An expert hunter and trapshooter shares experiences of a lifetime.

The Shotgun in Combat, by Tony Lesce, Desert Publications, Cornville, AZ, 1979. 148 pp., illus. Paper covers. $14.00

A history of the shotgun and its use in combat.

Shotgun Digest, 4th Edition, edited by Jack Lewis, DBI Books, a division of Krause Publications, Iola, WI, 1993. 256 pp., illus. Paper covers. $17.95

A look at what's happening with shotguns and shotgunning today.

The Shotgun Encyclopedia, by John Taylor, Safari Press, Inc., Huntington Beach, CA, 2000. 260 pp., illustrated. $34.95

A comprehensive reference work on all aspects of shotguns and shotgun shooting.

Shotgun Gunsmithing, The Gun Digest Book of, by Ralph Walker, DBI Books, a division of Krause Publications, Iola, WI, 1983. 256 pp., illus. Paper covers. $16.95

The principles and practices of repairing, individualizing and accurizing modern shotguns by one of the world's premier shotgun gunsmiths.

The Shotgun: History and Development, by Geoffrey Boothroyd, Safari Press, Huntington Beach, CA, 1995. 240 pp., illus. $35.00

The first volume in a series that traces the development of the British shotgun from the 17th century onward.

The Shotgun Handbook, by Mike George, The Croswood Press, London, England, 1999. 128 pp., illus. $35.00

For all shotgun enthusiasts, this detailed guide ranges from design and selection of a gun to adjustment, cleaning, and maintenance.

Shotgun Stuff, by Don Zutz, Shotgun Sports, Inc., Auburn, CA, 1991. 172 pp., illus. Paper covers. $19.95

This book gives shotgunners all the "stuff" they need to achieve better performance and get more enjoyment from their favorite smoothbore.

Shotgunner's Notebook: The Advice and Reflections of a Wingshooter, by Gene Hill, Countrysport Press, Traverse City, MI, 1990. 192 pp., illus. $25.00

Covers the shooting, the guns and the miscellany of the sport.

Shotgunning: The Art and the Science, by Bob Brister, Winchester Press, Piscataway, NJ, 1976. 321 pp., illus. $18.95

Hundreds of specific tips and truly novel techniques to improve the field and target shooting of every shotgunner.

Shotgunning Trends in Transition, by Don Zutz, Wolfe Publishing Co., Prescott, AZ, 1990. 314 pp., illus. $29.50

This book updates American shotgunning from post WWII to present.

Shotguns and Cartridges for Game and Clays, by Gough Thomas, edited by Nigel Brown, A & C Black, Ltd., Cambs, England, 1989. 256 pp., illus. Soft covers. $24.95

Gough Thomas' well-known and respected book for game and clay pigeon shooters in a thoroughly up-dated edition.

Shotguns and Gunsmiths: The Vintage Years, by Geoffrey Boothroyd, Safari Press, Huntington Beach, CA, 1995. 240 pp., illus. $35.00

A fascinating insight into the lives and skilled work of gunsmiths who helped develop the British shotgun during the Victorian and Edwardian eras.

Shotguns and Shooting, by Michael McIntosh, Countrysport Press, New Albany, OH, 1995. 258 pp., illus. $30.00

The art of guns and gunmaking, this book is a celebration no lover of fine doubles should miss.

Shotguns for Wingshooting, by John Barsness, DBI Books, a division of Krause Publications, Inc., Iola, WI, 1999. 208 pp., illustrated. $49.95

Detailed information on all styles of shotgun. How to select the correct ammunition for specific hunting applications.

Side by Sides of the World for Y2K, by Charles Carder, Anvil Onze Publishing, 2000. 221 pp., illus. Paper Covers. $25.95

This book lists more than 1600 names & features side by sides shotguns from all over the world, in alphabetical order. 500 + illustrations.

Sidelocks & Boxlocks, by Geoffrey Boothroyd, Sand Lake Press, Amity, OR, 1991. 271 pp., illus. $24.95

The story of the classic British shotgun.

THE ARMS LIBRARY

Spanish Best: The Fine Shotguns of Spain, by Terry Wieland, Countrysport, Inc., Traverse City, MI, 1994. 264 pp., illus. $45.00

A practical source of information for owners of Spanish shotguns and a guide for those considering buying a used shotgun.

The Sporting Clay Handbook, by Jerry Meyer, Lyons and Burford Publishers, New York, NY, 1990. 140 pp., illus. Soft covers. $17.95

Introduction to the fastest growing, and most exciting, gun game in America.

Streetsweepers, "The Complete Book of Combat Shotguns", by Duncan Long, Paladin Press, Boulder, CO,1997, soft cover, 63 photos, illus., appendices, 160 pp. $24.95

Streetsweepers is the newest, most comprehensive book out on combat shotguns, covering single- and double-barreled, slide-action, semi-auto and rotary cylinder shotguns, plus a chapter on grenade launchers you can mount on your weapon and info about shotgun models not yet on the market. Noted gun writer Duncan Long also advises on which ammo to use, accessories and combat shotgun tactics.

The Tactical Shotgun, by Gabriel Suzrez, Paladin Press, Boulder, CO, 1996. 232 pp., illus. Paper covers. $25.00

The best techniques and tactics for employing the shotgun in personal combat.

Taking More Birds, by Dan Carlisle & Dolph Adams, Lyons & Burford, New York, NY, 1993. 120 pp., illus. $19.95

A practical guide to greater success at sporting clays and wing shooting.

Tip Up Shotguns from Hopkins and Allen, by Charles Carder, Anvil Onze Publishing, 2000. 81 pp., illus. Paper Covers. $13.95

All the descriptive material and graphics used in this book have been reproduced from original Hopkins & Allen Arms Company catalogs, except the patent drawings.

Trap & Skeet Shooting, 3rd Edition, by Chris Christian, DBI Books, a division of Krause Publications, Iola, WI, 1994. 288 pp., illus. Paper covers. $17.95

A detailed look at the contemporary world of Trap, Skeet and Sporting Clays.

Trapshooting is a Game of Opposites, by Dick Bennett, Shotgun Sports, Inc., Auburn, CA, 1996. 129 pp., illus. Paper covers. $19.95

Discover everything you need to know about shooting trap like the pros.

Turkey Hunter's Digest, Revised Edition, by Dwain Bland, DBI Books, a division of Krause Publications, Iola, WI, 1994. 256 pp., illus. Paper covers. $17.95

Presents no-nonsense approach to hunting all five sub-species of the North American wild turkey.

U.S. Shotguns, All Types, reprint of TM9-285, Desert Publications, Cornville, AZ, 1987. 257 pp., illus. Paper covers. $9.95

Covers operation, assembly and disassembly of nine shotguns used by the U.S. armed forces.

U.S. Winchester Trench and Riot Guns and Other U.S. Military Combat Shotguns, by Joe Poyer, North Cape Publications, Tustin, CA, 1992. 124 pp., illus. Paper covers. $15.95

A detailed history of the use of military shotguns, and the acquisition procedures used by the U.S. Army's Ordnance Department in both World Wars.

The Winchester Model Twelve, by George Madis, David Madis, Dallas, TX, 1984. 176 pp., illus. $24.95.

A definitive work on this famous American shotgun.

The Winchester Model 42, by Ned Schwing, Krause Pub., Iola, WI, 1990. 160 pp., illus. $34.95

Behind-the-scenes story of the model 42's invention and its early development. Production totals and manufacturing dates; reference work.

Winchester Shotguns and Shotshells, by Ron Stadt, Krause Pub., Iola, WI. 288 pp., illus. $34.95.

Must-have for Winchester collectors of shotguns manufactured through 1961.

Winchester's Finest, the Model 21, by Ned Schwing, Krause Publications, Iola, WI, 1990. 360 pp., illus. $49.95

The classic beauty and the interesting history of the Model 21 Winchester shotgun.

The World's Fighting Shotguns, by Thomas F. Swearengen, T.B.N. Enterprises, Alexandria, VA, 1979. 500 pp., illus. $39.95

The complete military and police reference work from the shotgun's inception to date, with up-to-date developments.

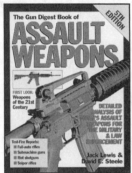